The

"Business"

of

Reforming American Schools

SUNY Series,
Restructuring and School Change

H. Dickson Corbett and Betty Lou Whitford, editors

The

"Business"

of

Reforming American Schools

Denise Gelberg

STATE UNIVERSITY OF NEW YORK PRESS

Production by Ruth Fisher
Marketing by Fran Keneston

Published by
State University of New York Press, Albany

For information, address the State University of New York Press,
State University Plaza, Albany, NY 12246

Library of Congress Cataloging-in-Publication Data

Gelberg, Denise, 1951–
    The "business" of reforming American schools / Denise Gelberg.
       p. cm.
    Includes bibliographical references (p.) and index.
    ISBN 0-7914-3505-9 (acid free). — ISBN 0-7914-3506-7 (pbk. : acid free)
    1. Educational change—United States—History. 2. Education—Aims and objectives—United States. 3. Industry and education—United States—History. I. Title.
LA212.G35   1997
370'.973—dc21   96-53673
                                                   CIP

10 9 8 7 6 5 4 3 2 1

Dedicated to the children
I have been privileged to teach

CONTENTS

LIST OF FIGURES

PREFACE

In 1988 I took a two-year leave of absence from my job as an elementary school teacher to pursue a doctorate in labor relations in education at Cornell University. As a graduate of Cornell's School of Industrial and Labor Relations many years earlier, and a teacher with fourteen years of experience in the classroom, I aimed to meld my two areas of interest—and perhaps begin a new career. I had become disillusioned with the school system in which I taught. While the children were always wonderful to work with, the school organization was a constant source of frustration. I envisioned myself ten years down the road becoming the archetypical bitter teacher, complaining about the central office, the school board, the principal, the parents, and finally, the children themselves. It seemed the time was ripe to try something new.

My studies at Cornell, which were focused on industrial relations, organization of work in modern organizations, and private sector labor law, provided me with something of an awakening. For the first time I was able to understand the organizational dynamics and legal precedents that led to a constant stream of seemingly arbitrary and often counterproductive decisions from school management. In 1990 I returned to the school system, AB.D., and calmed by a new understanding of how and why the school organization operated as it did.

The classroom and curricula that awaited me, however, were something of a puzzle. The room had no furniture, save a teacher's desk and chair. It had social studies and science texts of the usual sort—but no reading books. I was told that central office administration had decided to have elementary schools use the whole-language approach to the teaching of reading. This decision made the basal readers and workbooks obsolete because reading could be taught through literature. I was eager to try this new method—though I was annoyed when I realized that no one in the administration made sure that literature had been ordered for my class. While the furniture arrived a few days into the school term, no books were forthcoming. Had it not been for the generosity of my school's PTA and our school library, my students would not have had a single piece of literature in the class with which to embark on this adventure into "whole language."

It was not too long into the school year when my mailbox began to fill with memos on what was being called "cooperative learning." The principal enthusiastically informed the faculty that cooperative learning was a promising way to organize lessons. Children could be grouped heterogeneously. Together, they would engage in problem-solving, work on projects, and find answers to difficult questions. Those who learned more quickly would help those who had more trouble mastering particular skills. This child-to-child assistance would no longer be considered cheating. In fact, it was heartily endorsed by everyone in the district's administration.

The more I thought about cooperative learning, the more it seemed to be remarkably similar to the autonomous work teams in the Volvo plants in Sweden I had learned about at Cornell. These teams had workers of varied skills working cooperatively to produce a single car. They engaged in problem-solving together to figure out dilemmas that came up in their work. The cooperative groups I was to organize in my class seemed to be a juvenile version of these autonomous work teams that were lauded as the new wave in manufacturing.

Other changes had occurred during my leave that raised questions in my mind. The superintendent was talking to the media about site-based decision-making, whereby the district would allow teachers to make some decisions on instructional issues. The idea was attractive on its face, yet it seemed odd that he was proposing this at the same time he had instructed the district's chief negotiator to strip the teachers' collective bargaining agreement of all references to consultation on curricular decisions. The two policies were seemingly incompatible. Why would he want the contractual provision removed promising teachers the right to be involved in textbook and materials selection, if he was serious about shared decision-making?

I became intrigued about how, in the short period of my absence, the school administration's concepts of good teaching and appropriate learning situations had changed so radically. I needed to find out not only how those changes had happened but why. I wondered, too, about the etiology of the superintendent's promise of shared decision-making. Those queries were the driving force behind a research effort that culminates in this book.

ACKNOWLEDGMENTS

Although ultimately a solo effort in research and writing, a work such as this rarely comes about without support and assistance from many sources. Central to the successful completion of this project was the chairman of my graduate committee at Cornell University, James A. Gross. He spent countless hours working with me throughout my years at Cornell. His guidance, expertise, and astute reading of my doctoral dissertation, on which this book is based, was invaluable to my research and writing efforts.

A grant from the President's Council of Cornell Women helped support my research effort. A relatively new group in the early stages of its operation, the council aims to support women at Cornell in their scholarly endeavors. It is a worthy goal. I am honored to be among the first group of women helped by the council.

Many people involved in Rochester's bold experiment in school reform gave freely of themselves and their time. Their graciousness and candor were remarkable, all the more in light of the national spotlight focused on them for the last several years. Unmistakable was each person's dedication to their vision of good education.

Keeping a personal sense of balance and equilibrium while sequestered with mountains of research materials and a computer can be a daunting task. My teaching colleagues—Susan DeWinter, Lee Donner, Joan Grossman, Molly Shoemaker, and Sue Woodard—made it far easier for me to keep a healthy perspective on my research and writing. Our late Friday afternoon meetings over coffee and pastries generally turned into informal seminars. They allowed me to connect my scholarly thoughts with the reality facing teachers every day in their classrooms.

My request for a one-year, unpaid leave of absence to complete my doctoral research and dissertation was initially rejected by a top-level administrator. I was told that I had to choose whether I wanted to be a teacher or a researcher. Principal, friend, and colleague for nearly twenty years, Michael Ouckama, deserves special acknowledgment for going up against the forces of "central office" and supporting my effort to complete the research that led to this study. His efforts, coupled with vigorous advocacy from the local teachers' union, was key to turning the initial no into a yes.

My thanks go to the staff of the State University of New York Press. In particular, it was a singular pleasure to work with my editors, Priscilla Ross, Jennie Doling, and Ruth Fisher. Their words of patient wisdom helped me transform my manuscript into the book you now hold in your hands.

There are no words to express my indebtedness to my family. My parents' unwavering support of anything related to learning has given me the confidence to pursue my curiosity throughout my life. My extended family has continually played the role of cheerleading squad, encouraging me to pursue my goal of seeing this book through to publication regardless of the obstacles I might encounter. The lion's share of thanks goes to my husband, Charles Wilson, and our daughter Elsa. Ever-patient while I worked in solitude on this project, their good humored forbearance made its completion possible. In addition, my husband's computer wizardry, performed in the wee hours of the night, shaped the manuscript into the required specifications for publication.

Finally, I acknowledge the students to whom this book is dedicated. They continue to enrich my life and my work in marvelous and unexpected ways.

LIST OF ABBREVIATIONS

AASA	American Association of School Administrators
AASR	Association of Administrators and Supervisors of Rochester
AFDC	Aid for Families with Dependent Children
AFL-CIO	American Federation of Labor-Congress of Industrial Unions
AFT	American Federation of Teachers
EAI	Education Alternatives, Incorporated
GE	General Electric
GOMS	Goals, Outcomes, Measures, and Standards
NAB	National Alliance of Business
NAM	National Association of Manufacturers
NASDC	New American Schools Development Corporation
NEA	National Education Association
NLRA	National Labor Relations Act
RBEA	Rochester Business Educational Alliance
RCSD	Rochester City School District
SBP	school-based planning
SBDM	site-based decision-making
SCANS	(Department of Labor) Secretary's Commission on Achieving Necessary Skills
TQM	Total Quality Management
UAW	United Auto Workers
UFT	United Federation of Teachers

INTRODUCTION

Since the release of a report entitled *A Nation at Risk* in 1983, the media have abounded with reports of our troubled schools.[1] That report likened the ineptitude of our school system in preparing our youngsters for adult roles to national disarmament in the face of a threat from a foreign enemy. A hue and cry was heard across the nation: something had to be done to get our schools to turn out students who had skills comparable to those of children from other industrialized nations. Demands from business leaders and politicians for school reform have followed every subsequent report detailing how dismally our youngsters perform when compared to the children of our economic competitors in this new global economy.

Advocates of reform will often point to what they call a "break the mold" school as a model of what ought to become the norm in education. The media generally describe it as "a school that works," inferring, of course, that the rest of the schools do not work. More often than not, schools that are designated as "working" share three most attractive characteristics:

1. *The children are engaged in active, hands-on learning.* They work cooperatively with one another in small, heterogeneous groups, tackling problems by brainstorming in order to arrive at possible solutions. They are eager and excited about what they are studying. They are competent to describe what they are mastering and jump at the opportunity to do so. Beyond this, they fare well on both the traditional standardized tests and the new forms of portfolio assessment. Their parents remark at how their children are thriving in school.

2. *The curriculum is a model of what is called "integration across the content areas."* Rather than having a period for reading, followed by one for math and then science, social studies, and the like, subjects are studied in depth and approached in an interdisciplinary way. If the expedition of Columbus to North America is the subject to be studied, then students might read about the era, write on living conditions in the New World for the indigenous peoples, calculate the

1

provisions Columbus and his crew would have needed for the voyage, create a musical play depicting Columbus's attempt to get funding for his expedition, and build scale models of the three ships used by Columbus and his sailors. Gone are the disjointed, discontinuous, and unrelated "subjects" of study. In their place is an interconnected view of the disciplines that guides teachers and students in their study of the world and human experience.

3. *The school organization diffuses power and responsibilities among teachers, school managers, parents, and students.* Power is not concentrated in central administrative offices or in the superintendent's position. Power is shared, with most decisions about curriculum, teaching methods, and materials made at the building level by people working directly with children—and sometimes by the children themselves. In these models there are no authoritarian principals. Principals and teachers alike welcome parents into the schools as essential partners in the education of their children. Decisions are made in a collegial atmosphere where every participant in the learning endeavor has a say about how education will proceed. "Schools that work" are depicted as communities of instructors and learners, where leadership is shared at all levels of the school organization.[2] It is this type of school that operates in accordance with what has become a new orthodoxy, that is, the model of efficient education today.

The goals we have for our schools and our children, the curricula we endorse, and the relationship between the participants in the educational enterprise do not come from thin air. They are rooted in what we value as a society, the beliefs we have about the nature of childhood, the prerequisites of "the good life," the assumptions we make about gender, race, ethnicity, and economic status. The roles we have given children, teachers, parents, and school managers to play in our schools have been based upon ideas about what each of those groups ought to contribute to the educational endeavor. These ideas have been value-laden. If there is a demand today to change our way of schooling, we must wonder what underlies this urgent call for reform. Has there been a major change in our societal values? Do we really want something different from our educational system or only a better job of doing what it has always done?

I will argue in this study that today's call for reform of our nation's schools is essentially a replay of a debate on and campaign for education reform that occurred at the beginning of this century. The themes providing the impetus for both the current and the earlier debate on school reform are remarkably similar: fear of global competition, the breakdown of the family, an influx of new immigrants, rampant crime in the cities, corruption in government, and a generation of youth that seems ill-prepared to take its place as adults in society—in essence, a society nearing a state of crisis.

The participants in both the current and earlier public debates are the same: business leaders, school managers, teacher unions, government officials, and university professors. Although the personalities have changed, the perspectives these figures represent display a high degree of constancy. Their critiques of the existing system and the purpose of education are remarkably similar, too. For example, business leaders in both time periods chastise the schools as being wasteful and inefficient, for failing to prepare youngsters for the jobs that await them when they exit the schoolhouse doors. Although nearly one hundred years divide these businessmen, their arguments are nearly identical: schools must change to efficiently meet the needs of a changing economy. Business leaders in both eras find strong allies among top school executives and governmental officials in their effort to reform the schools.

It appears that, just as at the turn of the century, the chosen solution for today's perceived educational woes is that being proposed by the coalition representing business interests. That agenda for reform, however, is markedly different from that proposed by the business-minded alliance in 1900. In fact, the highly acclaimed "schools that work" are, in large measure, examples of the vision of progressive education categorically rejected by the winners of the debate on education reform at the turn of the twentieth century. How and why business today has jumped camps is illustrated in the chapters that follow.

It is a central thesis of this study that the relationship between school managers and teachers has been and continues to be a key indicator of the type of education offered children. Accordingly, an examination of teacher/manager relations will be a major theme of this book. The type and amount of participation allowed teachers by their supervisors in the design of education programs for their students is one accurate indicator of the type of pedagogical practice teachers will employ. If the goal of education is basic skills, respectful behavior, and a belief in "the American way of life," teacher participation in the design of educational programs is not necessary. Such outcomes are likely to result from mandated inputs, that is, teaching methods, materials, and curricula designed by top-level school managers and mandated for use by teachers. However, if the goal of education is to stimulate initiative, creative problem-solving, and critical thinking, the system needs teachers who themselves are capable of engaging in all these higher order intellectual operations. The system that has as its goal critical thinking students must encourage its teachers at every turn to participate in the design as well as the implementation of the educational program.

I have divided my discussion into two time periods. First, I examine the period of 1895 to 1925, the time of the first nationwide call for school reform which resulted in the centralized, bureaucratic system of schooling; a system that has shown tremendous resilience throughout this century. Chapter 1 discusses America's most commonly held beliefs, values, and assumptions at the turn of the century; ideas about the role of science, efficiency, business, professionals, education, and the individual in society. It is within the context of these values and beliefs that the debate on how education ought to proceed took place nearly one hundred years ago. Chapter 2 offers a detailed description of the design and implementation of school reform in keeping with the corporate model of organization and manufacture put forth by the coalition of businessmen, school leaders, and education professors. I refer to that design as the "pro-efficiency" model of reform throughout the study. A competing vision of school reform is discussed in chapter 3: education for individual development and democracy. This agenda was advanced by educational progressives such as John Dewey, budding teacher unions, and a small group of historians and sociologists. It was between these competing visions of education reform that the nation chose in its massive overhaul of the educational system during the first two decades of this century.

The second part of the study concentrates on the years 1961 to 1995—that is, from the first organized challenges to that established system in the 1960s to the current effort to restructure our nation's schools. Chapter 4 offers a discussion of how teachers, long disenfranchised by the system set up by the pro-efficiency reformers, organized to challenge the assumptions and practices of the established school system. Chapter 5 describes the current discussion on reforming education that began with the alarm sounded in 1983 by *A Nation at Risk*. Chapter 6 provides a detailed discussion of how the new pro-efficiency model of education proposed in the current period ironically has its origins in the agenda put forth by the educational progressives at the turn of the century. In chapter 7 I describe the ambitious effort of Rochester, New York, to reform its schools in accordance with this new pro-efficiency model.

In chapter 8 I offer my conclusions and recommendations on where to go from here to improve the lives, as well as the education, of our nation's youngsters.

I hope what follows provides the reader with a perspective to better understand both the calls for massive educational change in our country as well as the response of our schools to the demands that they remake themselves in a wholly new image.

Few of the current panaceas or proposals for
reform are new . . . and contemporary power
struggles are often new forms of past conflicts.

David Tyack, 1974

Part One

1895–1925

1

The Tenor of the Times

The schools we have today are very much the result of the decisions made by groups who held power at the turn of the century. These decisions did not go unchallenged at the time they were made, however. In fact, there were professional educators, social commentators, and some average citizens who were committed to an alternative vision of education to that promoted by a powerful coalition of businessmen, university presidents, education professors, and big city superintendents. I refer to this coalition as the pro-efficiency reformers. The former group, often alluded to in education circles as the "Deweyan educational progressives," differed dramatically from the pro-efficiency coalition in their values, assumptions, and beliefs.

Both groups saw education as an instrument for achieving a preferred future. But their differing notions about the nature of childhood, the purpose of education in society, the capabilities and rights of men and women, the threat or promise presented by immigrants and racial minorities, and the power of efficiency to cure societal ills led them to aspire to very different visions of America in the twentieth century. As a result, their recommendations for how education ought to be defined and organized in this country had little in common. Much of the popular agenda for reforming today's schools for the twenty-first century has its origins their debate.

In order to understand both the pro-efficiency and the educational progressive recommendations for school reform it is necessary to have a picture of the era in which they made their proposals. Schooling, after all, does not take place in a vacuum. A society's history and tradition as well as the economic and political systems under which it lives all contribute to the way it fashions the formal and informal education of its young.[1] In addition, the debate between the pro-efficiency coalition and the Deweyan educational progressives occurred during a period of societal crisis in America. As we shall see, the sense of crisis was to become a constant theme whenever Americans were to seriously discuss education throughout the twentieth century.

The Social Context

The period around 1900 was one characterized by powerful dislocations in society causing changes in traditional ways of living and working, challenging old ideas about the roles of family, government, and business in the social order. One cause of this upheaval was the tremendous growth in national population— a growth centered in cities ill-equipped for their sudden, geometric expansion. Chicago is a good example of this burgeoning growth. In 1885 Chicago had a population of 620,000. Five years later its population nearly doubled, with 1,200,000 people living and working within its boundaries. By 1893 there were 1,500,000 people in Chicago, testing the limits of the city's governmental apparatus to meet even their most basic needs.[2]

A great part of the surge in population was due to a massive emigration from southern and eastern Europe to the United States. Nearly all these people arrived on American shores steeped in their own rich, traditional cultures and speaking only their native tongues. Many came carrying several children in tow—children who would soon be entering the already crowded schools of American cities. Many native-born Protestant Americans were uneasy at the prospect that the immigrants, often Catholic or Jewish, might not be assimilated. The native-born white Protestants who had long been dominant in the agrarian United States saw these newcomers as a threat to their power and influence, as immigrants and first-generation Americans settled in many cities. They perceived a link between a decline in their own predominance and an increase in crime, intemperance, sin, and disorder in society. This group sought some way to inculcate their sense of morality and values into the vast numbers of foreign-born Catholics and Jews who arrived on American shores.[3]

During the years preceding the turn of the century, new, more overriding hierarchies appeared throughout society. Corporations emerged as the primary force in industrializing the nation's economy and work force. Efficiencies of scale allowed for mass production of many items previously produced by individual craftsmen.[4] The trend toward centralization of power along bureaucratic lines was not limited to the business corporations, however. The growth in urban population and the need for coordination of services fostered a series of experiments in a more systematic, centralized administration of a host of city functions led by reformers known as the "administrative progressives."[5]

The agrarian economy and way of life was becoming less and less significant as a driving force in the experience of most Americans. While 80 percent of Americans lived on farms in 1830, fewer than 25 percent did so one hundred years later.[6] Education functions once carried out by large farm families, the country church, and the rural village seemed to be neglected in the newly urbanized society. The dislocations caused by the industrial revolution—overcrowded cities, squalid living conditions, crime, drunkenness—shocked the middle class and humanitarians alike. Remedies for this degradation of life affecting a vast segment of the population were discussed with great urgency. It seemed the stability of the social order was at stake.[7]

Another source of concern for the nation was the increasing perception that America's worldwide preeminence in industry was being challenged by other nations, particularly Germany. Industrialists' concern about German competition caused them to find explanations for Germany's economic success. Interestingly, they did not find them in better German technology, vertical or horizontal integration of German firms, or better German marketing. They found the answer in the German schools. This argument was advanced by Frank Vanderlip, vice-president of the National City Bank of New York in 1905, a man who later was to become the president of the largest bank in the nation:

> In the group of great industrial nations, there has come forward in recent years one that has taken place in the very front rank among industrial competitors. That nation is Germany . . . I have had a somewhat unusual opportunity to study the underlying causes of the economic success of Germany, and I am firmly convinced that the explanation of that progress can be encompassed in a single word—schoolmaster. He is the great cornerstone of Germany's remarkable commercial and industrial success.[8]

Industrialists saw adoption of the German system of vocational education as key to America's preeminence in worldwide economic competition. President of the New York Central, W. C. Brown, stated that without it, "it is only a question of time when this country must surrender its place as a leader among the great manufacturing nations of the world."[9]

All of these forces impinging on society—industrialization, urbanization, immigration, and the resulting population surge, foreign economic competition—took place during a time when formal schooling was a relatively new phenomenon.

In the early years of the new United States, most states did not see education as part of the state's responsibility. The desirability of a well-educated working class was seldom recognized until after 1825, when social reformers endorsed education for the masses.[10]

Horace Mann, the most notable of those reformers, cited education as a way of reestablishing a sense of stability during times of turmoil.[11] In his famous Fifth Report in 1842, widely read throughout the states, Mann cited education as a means of increasing the value of labor. Although this idea was not immediately embraced by all businessmen, by the 1860s acceptance in business circles was widespread.[12] Mann's message was one that found acceptance in state legislatures across the country, as well. As a result, one of the functions the state took on during the nineteenth century was the free education of children.

By 1860 most states had established free public elementary schools.[13] By 1900 organized education had gained prestige, with the American people faithful to the notion that schooling was the remedy for every societal ill. A belief that education provided the road to safety and better times during periods of crisis was held by a wide spectrum of groups throughout the United States.[14] As old societal agencies weakened and new educational tasks appeared, larger and larger burdens were placed on the school.[15] William Graham Sumner remarked on this great faith Americans placed in formal schooling in 1906:

> Popular education and certain faiths about popular education are in the mores of our time. We regard illiteracy as an abomination. We ascribe to elementary book learning power to form character, make good citizens, keep family mores pure, elevate morals, establish individual character, civilize barbarians, and cure social vice and disease. We apply schooling as a remedy for every social phenomenon which we do not like.[16]

Thus, the American people were philosophically committed to educate the masses of children as a means of coping with the challenges they faced. The capacity of the schools, however, to fulfill this appointed task was far from certain. Just in terms of physical capacity alone, the school system was totally overwhelmed by the growth in the population of school-aged children. Existing school buildings were dilapidated. Classes of sixty children were common. The national population of high school students, less than 5 percent of total children enrolled in schools, went from 220,000 in 1890 to 519,251 in 1900. New high schools appeared at the average rate of one a day.[17] In 1800 there was no public institution providing secondary education in this country. In 1900 there were more than 6,000 free public high schools across the United States.[18]

The ward system of governance made urban schools the responsibility of neighborhood boards of education. Control of schools was decentralized and diffuse. By example, Boston had 190 independent boards of education supervising that many separate schools by the 1850s. Advocates of the arrangement argued that by enlisting the help of so many citizens, the schools stayed close to the people and fostered an interest in education. Yet, in the face of so many societal problems, the local ward board of education was cited by many critics as being unable to meet the demands being placed upon it. The flow of information throughout a city school system was erratic. Corruption—the buying and selling of teaching jobs and principalships—was common. New ideas in education—full-time, paid supervision, curriculum articulated by grades—were not being implemented by ward trustees and parents who wanted no change from the status quo. They wanted ungraded classrooms run by teachers in accordance with the wishes of the ward trustees.[19] The system of school governance was cited by these critics as being responsible for the schools' inability to remedy a host of societal ills and prepare youngsters for their future adult roles. The school system as so configured was seemingly unable to deliver the needed elixir of stability.[20] Just as today, it was this sense that the schools were failing to ensure the perpetuation of American society that provided the impetus for the debate on reforming education in the nation.

If it was a given that children ought to be educated in schools, how precisely this education would proceed, what it would comprise, how it was to be organized, who would be empowered to decide critical educational issues were far from settled questions. By 1900 two very different educational philosophies emerged. The pro-efficiency agenda was in keeping with business management trends of the day: centralization of planning and decision-making in a bureaucratic hierarchy, and the standardized treatment of youngsters via a "factoryizing" of education. The reforms proposed by the educational progressives featured a decentralized school organization and the promotion of a child-centered education based on the inherent tendencies, talents, and interests of individual students. Adherents of both educational philosophies fervently believed that their respective doctrines could meet the challenges presented by the twentieth century.

At the center of each philosophy were beliefs about which aspects of American life were to be valued, enjoyed, and encouraged, and which ought to be discouraged and perhaps extinguished. Educational philosophies were, in this sense, rooted in larger social philosophies. They were imbued with particular values, assumptions, and beliefs about the direction America ought to go during this period of change and transition. A discussion of education reform around the turn of the century, therefore, requires an understanding of the dominant values embraced by society.

Societal Values

Most discourse on the purpose of education is really about values that are not subject to empirical demonstration. The particular type of training a society chooses to provide its young is an expression of what it prizes and esteems. The public schools can be seen as an embodiment of society's ambitions and coveted goals. They represent the contact point between the older and the younger generation where values are selected and rejected. Partiality is the very essence of education. Choices about architecture, selection of teachers, courses of study, texts, equipment, teaching methods, school organization, relations between pupils and teachers, and relations between teachers and administrators—all reflect fundamental choices made about what our society ought to be and the "proper" power relationships among the members of society.[21]

Visions about the preferred future of society tend to vary, however. Different groups value things and ideas differently. The ideologies of these groups do not come from thin air; they are rooted in complex ways in the existing social structure. Ideologies held by the majority have a way of serving the dominant groups in society at a particular time. Social commentator and educational progressive Jesse Newlon, wrote in 1934 about the extraordinary power of successful businessmen in shaping public opinion: "Dominant economic groups are in a position to wield great power. The public mind is in large measure susceptible to control and direction." In many ways, our dominant values have long been those required for business and industry to thrive. Yet there have always been those who have differed in their ideas and values from those held by the majority. Education has proceeded amid the conflict among interest groups in society—both dominant and minority—and their accompanying values.

In this sense John Dewey was correct when he wrote in 1902 that the life of the school—as well as the demands for its reorganization—are integrally bound up "with the entire movement of modern life."[22] Ideas that were seriously pondered and hotly debated in America of 1900, i.e., the power and efficacy of science and efficiency to lift society from the morass of waste and corruption, the ambiguous role of the individual in an industrializing economy, the purpose of government in society, the capabilities and responsibilities of women and children in the social order—gave the school reform movement of one hundred years ago its unique character.

Efficiency: America's Secular Great Awakening[23]

The 1984 edition of *Webster's New World Dictionary* defines efficient as "producing the desired result with a minimum of effort, expense, or waste." Around 1900 the word *efficiency* had social and moral dimensions beyond the mere mechanical definition. It was during this time that efficiency became synonymous with goodness; that "right" was equated with efficient outcomes. Efficiency was used not only to denote mechanical operations—that is, the ratio between energy input and output—but also to characterize commercial, social, and personal relations. If a commercial venture was efficient, it returned a tidy profit on the money invested. If a relationship between individuals or groups was efficient, there existed social harmony. This social efficiency was usually due to legitimizing the leadership of those men seen as most expert or competent.[24] If persons were efficient they were effective, hard working, unsentimental, and virtually always male. Because efficiency was so central to what was valued, the perceived lack of it among women shut them out of important positions in society.

Work and morality—the moral obligation to work in an efficient manner— was a common societal theme in America by the middle of the nineteenth century.[25] American individualism was based on the notion that achievement and success came through efficiency, hard work, practicality, and responsibility.[26] The luminosity of the value of efficiency did not reach its peak, however, until early in the twentieth century. It was at that time that the rapid and widespread development of technological advances gave efficiency an almost magical quality. Technology made possible the performance of vast amounts of work with a minimal expenditure of human energy. It was a revolutionary idea. Remarkably, the transformation and dissemination of this idea into the realm of human and community affairs came about in short order.

The way to have efficient human affairs was to depend on professional competence and expertise. This was the unifying theme of the administrative progressives who sought to reform government. Just as the engineer could find the "one best way" to operate a particular mechanism without waste and avoiding mechanical failures, the social engineer could develop the "one best way" to administer government, design housing and living conditions, and provide for other social needs. In this sense, the judgment of one expert could be worth much more than the combined judgments of the ignorant multitude.[27] The highest degree of efficiency, in fact, was secured by centralizing authority and responsibility in one individual.[28] It was the duty of the socially efficient person to recognize this fact and cooperate once the expert decision was made on an issue of public concern.

The concept of efficiency was tied not only to the notion of specialized competence, but also to "bigness." Big railroads, big banks, big corporations had been able, in two generations, to accomplish the transformation of the country from a traditional, agrarian society to a modern industrialized nation. Large enterprises using machinery and integrated operations to capacity reaped the benefits of efficiency. The "bigness" required for efficient operation by financial and industrial concerns was also seen as a requirement for the efficient operation of many other noncommercial endeavors. Many reformers from this time—commonly referred to as the Progressive Era—proposed big government, big schools, big social service organizations to efficiently minister to the needs of the people. Small, decentralized operations were viewed as wasteful. Organizations of all types were seen to require a "critical mass" in order to attain efficiency in their operations.[29]

Large size, tied to the concept of professional expertise, could combat waste and corruption, the two most often cited evils of the time.[30] Given the problems exposed by the muckrakers of the progressive era, the idea of efficiency in the social realm held out the promise of a better tomorrow. Social efficiency suggested a moral clean-up. It implied that society was in control of its affairs; that the spread of efficient systems throughout society was not only desirable, it was possible. By 1910 an efficiency craze gripped the country. Efficiency societies, efficiency expositions, efficiency courses, and efficiency lectures were commonplace. Churches set up efficiency committees to increase membership. Feminists put forth the idea that efficient methods of doing housework would free women from subordination.

If a minority saw efficiency as a way to liberate individuals, most reformers sought to use efficiency to improve society in the aggregate through "professional social engineering."[31] Substituting guesswork with expertise, politics with competence, nepotism with professionalism, the social engineer could use his power to make society run as efficiently as a machine. Efficiency provided a reason for optimism during a time of perceived crisis. It could be used for purposes of social control. That idea was adopted by administrative progressives, lending legitimacy to their push to restructure government along rational, hierarchical, bureaucratic lines. Though the efficiency craze abated after 1915, the idea that efficiency could be used for social control remained one of its lasting effects.[32]

The high value placed on efficiency in American society throughout this century has its roots in the century's beginning. As will be shown in the chapters that follow, when alternatives to the status quo have been proposed, heightened efficiency has often been used as the primary rationale for their adoption. For example, the pro-efficiency school reformers made efficiency the centerpiece of their program. The luster of the efficiency ideal did not dim with the passage of time. In fact, at the heart of today's education reform movement can be found the argument that schools must be restructured in order for them to efficiently meet the needs of America in the twenty-first century.

Science: The Dual Promise of Efficiency and Truth

Science and the scientific method—systematized, rational knowledge gleaned from study and observation—came into its own during the years around the turn of the century. It became a driving force conditioning the development of twentieth-century American civilization. It gave us methods of investigation, knowledge, and tangible products of technological innovation.[33] It became viewed as the key to the discovery of truth and efficiency. It was essential to the notion of progress.[34] The rise of the engineering profession represented the human embodiment of this scientific ideal. Engineers applied their arcane, scientific knowledge to technology, resulting in tremendous advances in manufacturing productivity, communications, transportation, and the national infrastructure. The engineer made the benefits of scientific knowledge real and obvious for every American. The engineer's status grew by 1900 from mere "mechanic" to user of science for the commonweal. Engineering became an esteemed and influential profession.[35]

One mechanical engineer believed that by generalizing from scientific principles found in the mechanical world, human work could be done more efficiently. Frederick Taylor devised a theory of "scientific management," which he said could create a neat, understandable, coordinated world in the factory. As he got older, Taylor went beyond the factory gate and spoke of the applicability of scientific management principles "to every conceivable human activity." His system became more than a business therapy, it was also a social program. Taylor was not alone in believing that science could be the guiding principle of a better society. The social purity movement, the temperance reform movement, and the dietary reform movement all placed the value of science squarely in the middle of their policy for societal improvement.[36]

The rationality of science depended on the use of numerical data gathered during investigation and study. The use of quantitative measures became the trademark of an "objective" study, despite the fact that statistics, percentages, and graphs were often used to legitimize wholly unscientific, biased theories. In 1902 prominent educational progressive John Dewey—who based much of his reform agenda on the development of intelligence and democracy, as well as the problems of an industrializing society—rejected much of the quantitative educational research of the day because of the many conservative premises embedded within it. Merely counting things and using statistics did not produce, in his mind, "a magical guarantee of a scientific product."[37] Yet, his voice was in the minority. For most Americans, use of quantitative measures was accepted as the way to discover objective reality. This belief in the power of numbers was central to the use of science as the tool to find truth and attain efficiency at the turn of the twentieth century.

Thus, science and efficiency were two overarching themes that together changed the way Americans evaluated human behavior, national events, and institutions in their environment. Efficiency was synonymous with goodness, and science was equated with the discovery of truth. Science provided the ways and means to attain efficiency. Social organizations as personal as the family and as distant as the national government were scrutinized in the light of these ideas. If progress was to result from human endeavor, science and efficiency were the lamps lighting the path of goodness and truth leading to that better way of life. The power of this idea remains strong even today—as the twentieth century comes to a close.

The Individual in the New Social Order

Social Darwinism, the late nineteenth-century individualistic philosophy, made it abundantly clear that in the natural order of things, people were not all equal in endowments. "Inequality appears to be the divine order," wrote one prominent journalist of the era. Individuals who enjoyed power and wealth did so because they were endowed with exceptional talents that allowed them to rise to the top stratum in society. Social exclusiveness, ideas about "genealogical superiority," and ardent patriotism in the face of massive immigration found greater acceptance in society.[38] Ideas about a natural hierarchy of people and of castes based on "natural ability" were written about and discussed. Pro-efficiency reformer Charles Eliot, president of Harvard and of the National Education Association, speaking to the Harvard Teachers' Association in 1908 cited "four layers in civilized society which are indispensable, and so far as we can see, eternal": a narrow upper layer, which "consists of the managing, leading, guiding class—the intellectual discoverers, the inventors, the organizers and the managers and their chief assistants"; a layer of skilled workers who could use technology in production; a layer representing the commercial class "which is employed in buying, selling and distributing"; and finally, the "thick fundamental layer engaged in household work, agriculture, mining, quarrying, and forest work."[39]

This concept of societal castes was also expressed at this time via use of a military analogy. In 1908 Andrew Draper, first commissioner of education for the state of New York and vocal pro-efficiency reformer, proposed that the mass of society was suited for the rank of corporal. These corporals comprised the wage-earning masses. They were corporals because of their "natural inclinations." Draper felt they were important to society because they supplied the labor "for the great manufacturing and constructive industries" in a society that based its greatness, strength, and culture on industrialism. These corporals, in fact, were more important than the all too often "insipid colonels" who led "idle" lives in the arts or professions.[40] One can only surmise that as first commissioner of education for one of the most powerful states in the nation, Draper assumed himself to be among the generals of society, directing the corporals in a great and noble effort.

Draper and other members of the managing class wished to use science and efficiency to rationalize a variety of human endeavors. Seeing themselves as experts well-versed in sound scientific and management principles, they sought to direct society from above toward some vision of the good life. In so doing, they felt it necessary to have final determination of societal reform during this period of tremendous upheaval and dislocation. Expertise of the elite class was seen as preferable to participation by ordinary people in decisions affecting society. Having experts run the government for the commonweal was viewed as more efficient than the conflict-ridden, sometimes corrupt government "of and by the people."[41]

Women

Men had greater status and power than women throughout the history of the United States. As the nation increasingly turned to science, bureaucracies, and expertise to steer America in the new century, men's power became more and more established. Correspondingly, women found increased institutionalization of their traditionally low status. Although one could argue that it was highly inefficient to exclude individuals from avenues of participation in society solely on the basis of gender, scientific arguments were made to legitimize the practice and add credence to long-held stereotypical notions of women's passivity, emotional weakness, and self-sacrificing nature.

Although many women had to work outside the home in order to support themselves and their families, their right to work was only grudgingly acknowledged.

Women were seen as surplus employees to be drawn upon when needed. They were relegated to the lowest paying occupations in the economy—domestic work, mill operatives, and teaching. Obstacles to entry in occupations that earned respect, authority, and money were many. Employment discrimination was open and rampant.[42] Only one percent of lawyers were female in 1910, despite the fact that by 1900 thirty-four states permitted women to practice law. Much informal and formal prejudice existed. Women lawyers were not admitted into the American Bar Association until after World War I.[43] The American Medical Association not only refused to grant membership to women, it also barred men who held positions in medical schools in which women taught or studied. Lest the point had to be made more clear, men who served in hospitals that extended hospital privileges to female physicians could also be banned from membership in the AMA.[44] As far as being part of the elite class that could manage the new bureaucratic organizations that were becoming so prevalent at the time, it was unthinkable. Women in general were seen as having no "natural" talent for administrative tasks.[45]

Just as it is today, gender was a fundamental organizing principle in society around the turn of the twentieth century.[46] Career opportunities for women were severely circumscribed by stereotypical ideas about their gentle nature and scientific prognostications about their limited abilities. If one would attempt to guess where women were placed in the four layers of society Charles Eliot described, it seems clear that regardless of their aspirations to the contrary, they would take their place in the "thick fundamental layer engaged in household work." In a very real sense a person's gender was perhaps the greatest predictor of the position she or he could attain in society.

The Rise of a Business Culture—1850 to 1920

Historically, business has been very important to the American value system. Some historians feel that by 1815, values necessary for a business civilization became the dominant in the new nation at the expense of other value systems. Certainly by 1850, values necessary for the smooth functioning of business were widely adhered to. Ideas about obedience to authority, punctuality to the minute, the evil of wasted time or property, the virtue of personal industry were increasingly commonplace and necessary for a nation in the midst of the transformation from an agrarian to an industrialized society.[47] In the opinion of social historian Merle Curti, the commercial class replaced the clergy as the keepers of the new morality by the middle of the nineteenth century.[48]

After 1850 the United States became more and more a business-oriented democracy striving for material progress. The preeminent value of material success has been cited as one of the most important influences of business on the mainstream American culture. The importance of wealth as a measure of one's worth and the corresponding devaluation of land ownership as a means of gaining prestige were two changes in the value system after the Civil War. Merchants, publishers, lawyers, and bankers were increasingly seen as important contributors to the nation's material well-being. Cities became "mercantile centers" and helped proliferate this new value system.[49]

Concepts of democracy were also tempered by the rise in the importance of business. Although democracy was still an ideal in the political domain, it had no place in the business world. Both common and statutory law protected property rights, which encompassed not only physical assets but the activities arising from use of those assets. Ownership of a business carried with it certain dictatorial rights over the use of the property associated with that business. "Liberty" carried with it ideas about the right of the businessman to control and dispose of his property in whatever manner he felt most likely to result in profit. In this way, notions of democracy were adapted to the utilitarian desires of businessmen.[50] And democracy stopped at the door of the business enterprise.

By 1900 the new form of business organization—the corporation—was fast on its way to becoming the most powerful institution in the economy. Alfred Chandler found in his study of the ascendancy of the corporation, *The Visible Hand: The Managerial Revolution in American Business,* that this modern business enterprise replaced market mechanisms in coordinating the activities of the economy and allocating its resources. The middle and top managers who ran these corporations represented a wholly new form of businessman: people who had no direct ownership in the business who, nonetheless, had unchecked power to coordinate the internally integrated units within the corporate organization. While no managers of this type existed in 1840, by 1912 they were the dominant type of businessman in the economy. According to Chandler, "Rarely in the history of the world has an institution grown to be so important and so pervasive in so short a period of time."[51]

Technology was the driving force behind the rise of the corporation. Technological advances in materials, power sources, and machinery resulted in an unprecedented increase in the output of goods manufactured. Technology also was the key to moving these goods quickly and cheaply from the point of production to the point of distribution. This tremendous increase in output and movement of goods required a corresponding growth in markets to absorb these goods. These developments all pointed to the need for organizational change allowing greater administrative coordination.[52] This needed administrative coordination resulted in the rise of the managerial hierarchy. Chandler sees this new managerial class as the defining characteristic of the modern business enterprise. The managerial hierarchy made possible the internalizing of the activities of many business units within a single enterprise. The hierarchy allowed for coordination that resulted in greater productivity, lower costs, and higher profits than coordination by market mechanisms. Once the hierarchy had proven itself successful in carrying out its administrative function, it became a source of permanence and power. Individual managers could come and go but the hierarchy remained regardless of the individuals who filled its organizational slots.[53]

The managers who filled the corporate administrative hierarchy were salaried professionals with technical backgrounds. During the period 1870 to 1900, a period when less than 5 percent of the population attended high school, 40 percent of top corporate managers were college educated.[54] These managers were seen as "scientific men" who could deal with the need to coordinate and control vast amounts of capital and raw materials, and end waste in the form of production or distribution delays. The velocity of throughput—the number of units processed per day—was the key to economies that lowered costs and increased output per worker and per machine. Cost was the criterion on which the performance of every person in the hierarchy was evaluated.[55]

As the modern business enterprise grew, ownership became separate from management. Owners had neither the information, the time, or the expertise to play a dominant role in decision-making. By 1917 the original entrepreneurs who founded many of these corporations rarely took part in decisions about pricing, output, and the like. Stockholders in general left the running of the business to the salaried managers. Members of the corporation's board of directors held power to veto top-level decisions. They could replace senior managers with other career managers. Rarely, though, were they in the position to propose positive alternative solutions to policies developed by management—policies that often worked in the managers' self-interest rather than in the interest of the enterprise.[56]

The importance of the worker on the factory floor of the modern business enterprise lessened as that of the manager in the corporate office increased. Prior to mass production, a worker had both knowledge of and control over either part or all of the manufacture of a product. In contrast, the worker's job in mass production was simply to feed materials into machines, keep an eye on their operations, and package the final product if that was not yet done automatically. Corporations' better use of management, energy, and capital permitted greater production with fewer workers. In the manufacture of cigarettes, flour, canning, soap, and photographic negatives—industries all using continuous process machines—the role of the worker relative to these other organizational variables became far less significant to production.[57]

Frederick Taylor's ideas on scientific management further reduced the role of the worker to that of a mere executor, albeit an efficient one, of the plans designed by staff managers. Taylor saw the corporate hierarchy as being one of abilities—people would rise to their level of competence.[58] To gain maximum efficiency, therefore, power had to move up from the shop floor worker to the managerial hierarchy.[59] An individual worker had no control of his work; work that tended to be only one operation in a complicated process designed by someone higher up in the hierarchy.[60] The good worker became one who conformed to management's edicts. By the mid-1920s the institutionalization of this role for the worker had taken place. Sociologists Robert and Helen Lynd wrote in their 1929 classic, *Middletown*, that most work was "endlessly monotonous." The system they witnessed in the modern business enterprise demanded "little of a worker's personality save rapid, habitual actions and ability to submerge himself in the performance of a few routinized easily learned movements." Eighty-five percent of the workers they observed in this small mid-Western city worked under close supervision doing meaningless tasks.[61]

By 1920 the United States had become a business oriented culture where 5 percent of the corporations generated 79 percent of total corporate income.[62] American business did not just represent another interest group in a pluralistic society. It was a predominant force. Business institutions affected the rest of society in a seemingly infinite number of ways. Decisions internal to corporations had economic and social effects, which economists later termed "externalities."[63] Innovative business practices spread throughout society through interpersonal relationships, use of the print media, and the manipulation of politics. The progressive period saw the passage of laws that many businessmen wanted enacted and enforced. Finally, the goals and values of a business oriented culture established norms about how people were to behave, what they ought to strive for, and what qualities or achievements should be rewarded.[64]

Although the ascendancy of big business did not occur without skepticism and opposition from various quarters of society, by the end of World War I the middle class viewed business in a positive light. Corporate use of rationality and science to increase efficiency and eradicate waste made it seemingly the embodiment of much that was good—and certainly worth emulating—in this newly industrialized society.[65] This image of business was due, in part, to corporations' efforts at self-promotion through public relations and advertising.[66] The public mind's susceptibility to the domination by business was not only due to its public relations effort, however, but through business control of strategic avenues of influence—employment, media, and credit.[67] The effort at self-promotion by business was successful.

The businessman, by 1920, supplanted the judge, the clergyman and the professor of generations past in prestige and authority.[68] To return to Charles Eliot's image of the four layers of society, the narrow upper layer consisting of the managers and organizers was, no doubt, replete with businessmen from the managerial hierarchies of the nation's most profitable corporations.

Education—Social Control or Personal Development?

A belief commonly held by people in positions of power during the nineteenth century—the "old Americans," business and professionals—was that education could preserve the status quo because of its power to build character in American youth. When Horace Mann proposed free public education for the masses, this aspect of schooling was stressed at least as much as the intellectual discipline children might develop. According to Merle Curti, character-training was actually more important than intellectual development to the supporters of free public schools:

> We tend today to think of our American system of public schools as having been founded out of a great zeal for the welfare of the plain people. But actually this zeal was tempered by zeal for the welfare of the employers of labor, by zeal for maintaining political and social status quo.[69]

Mid-nineteenth-century education reformers such as Mann garnered the support of powerful interests by promising that schools would promote the general prosperity, eliminate social evils, and safeguard republican institutions against revolution. Schooling would have utilitarian value by teaching the children of the masses the virtues of honesty, industry, property, and respectability.[70] Schooling would insure that these children would grow into adults readily employable by the expanding industrial sector. Prominent industrialist Abbott Lawrence declared in 1846: "Let the common school system go hand in hand with the employment of your people; you may be quite certain that the adoption of these systems at once, will aid each other."[71]

The members of the lower classes in society at this time—immigrants, blacks, poor whites—also looked toward education as a tool, but as a tool for social change and personal betterment. The poor hoped that, if given the opportunity to become educated, their children would break down barriers based on class, ethnicity, and race, and join the ranks of those economically better off. In addition, they hoped that education would give them more power in the political realm.[72] Ironically, this group's hope for what education could accomplish conflicted with the hope of those who supported education to protect their vested interests. As Curti asked:

> Could the schools do both? Could they leave the wealthy with all their economic power and privileges and at the same time enable the masses to enter the upper ranks without jeopardizing the position of those already on top? Could all stand on the top of the pyramid?[73]

As subsequent chapters will show, these disparate views of the purpose of education would persist throughout the twentieth century, coming to the forefront of public debate during periods of proposed educational change.

Conclusion

The sense of crisis bearing down on America at the turn of the century was the impetus behind demands for radical change in the way education was carried out. American society had to choose between alternative visions of education reform; visions that were rooted in particular ideas about how things ought to be. Ideas about education were influenced by beliefs about the efficiency of business methods, the power of science to reveal the truth, and the worth of the individual in society.

The business corporation embodied much of what was considered valuable at the turn of the century. Using science and technology, professionally trained managers could plan and coordinate the efforts of thousands of people in order to bring mass produced goods to market quickly and cheaply. Borrowing from the principles of corporate management, the administrative progressives began a reorganization of government that would take decisions out of the hand of local citizens and politicos and into the hands of expert managers. Professionals of all types gained power and status by virtue of their ability to use science in the service of their clients. Together, business, professionals, and the administrative progressives offered America the promise of a better life through efficiency and expertise.

The educational progressives looked upon many of these trends with alarm. Concern for the individual in the work place and the polity gave them reason to worry that what was seen as progress by many was actually a danger to the individual citizen's well-being. The pro-efficiency reform coalition, however, was made up of men who reaped the benefits of the new trends: businessmen, professors, and schoolmen who hoped to accomplish in education what the administrative progressives were accomplishing in government. Accordingly, their program for education reform embodied the principles of efficiency, science, and expert leadership.

A sense of crisis, a dependence on education to provide stability, a love of efficiency, and an admiration for business methods characterized this period. As we shall see, these were to become common themes in every period of education reform throughout the twentieth century.

2

The Pro-Efficiency Reforms Transplant Business Methods to the Schoolhouse

Every manufacturing establishment that turns out a standard product or series of products of any kind maintains a force of efficiency experts to study methods of procedure and to measure and test the output of its works . . . Our schools are, in a sense, factories in which the raw products (children) are to be shaped and fashioned into products to meet the various demands of life. The specifications for manufacturing come from the demands of twentieth-century civilization, and it is the business of the school to build its pupils according to the specifications laid down. This demands good tools, specialized machinery, continuous measurement of production to see if it is according to specifications, the elimination of waste in manufacture, and a large variety in the output.[1]

This quotation comes from what became the most influential treatise on school management during the first decades of the twentieth century, Ellwood Cubberley's *Public School Administration.* Cubberley's allusion to business management practice, and his view of manufacturing and education as analogous ventures producing products demanded by society, went to the heart of the pro-efficiency plan for reforming the nation's schools for the twentieth century.

Many scholars of the history of education have concluded that business was indeed the most dominant force in the shaping of the education system during this era.[2] Princeton historian Thomas Cochran, a scholar of the effect of business on American culture, concluded that by 1910 business was highly valued and seen as a model for schools to follow.[3] Margaret Haley, an educational progressive and critic of the influence of business on schools at the turn of the century, wrote in her memoirs: "To such an extent had our industrial ideal, which is essentially monarchical and military, vitiated the public mind of that period that it had been easy to carry over this industrial ideal into the administration of the schools."[4] Conformity to authority, low costs, wealth accumulation, and efficiency through science were the driving values in business.[5] Schools were particularly vulnerable to the power and ideology of business during a time when they were under attack for failing to cope with the many societal problems of the day. The solution to many of these problems was, in the minds the pro-efficiency reformers, the transfer of modern business methods of organization, management, and production to the schools of the nation. The key to this application of business principles to the schools was the emergence of a class of educational administrators who, like the administrative progressives, were eager to apply successful business doctrines and practices to public endeavors.

The pro-efficiency coalition was made up of men who held positions of power and authority in American society: businessmen, presidents of prestigious universities, and superintendents of urban school districts. University professors specializing in the new field of educational administration joined with these men to create a useful consensus of "experts" on the reorganization of American schools. Stanford historian David Tyack referred to this coalition as an "interlocking directorate"—a group of men who operated at the upper layer Eliot's "four layers in civilized society." Tyack concluded that "several key groups within Eliot's thin 'upper layer' joined together in the campaign to centralize control of schools on the corporate model and to make urban education socially efficient."[6] What follows is a description of how this coalition advanced its agenda for school reform, as well as the specifics of that agenda. The genesis of much of what constitutes education as we know it today can be traced to this coalition's ambitious plan for educational reform nearly one hundred years ago.

The Coalition's Strategy to Shape School Reform

These reformers aimed to reorganize education. But before this could be done, the basic question of who would control the schools had to be settled. The pro-efficiency reformers knew that in order to have a professionally controlled bureaucracy—a central tenet of sound business management—they would need to change existing governance laws completely, taking power away from politically controlled local ward boards of education. They campaigned actively, and on many fronts, in favor of a socially efficient system of schooling based on business models and run by professionally trained school managers.[7]

There were three components to their campaign to implement the pro-efficiency model. The first element was to identify and define the problem with the existing education system, and propose an alternative to that system. The second critical hurdle was to publicize both the problem and the solution as defined by the pro-efficiency coalition in order to sway public opinion in favor of its position. The final element of the strategy was to lobby state legislators to embrace and mandate the pro-efficiency model of school reform.

The school survey became a favorite technique used by the pro-efficiency reformers to implement the first element in their campaign.[8] School surveys, often conducted by professors of educational administration playing the role of efficiency expert, asked and answered two questions. First, What return was the community getting from its investment in the schools? Second, How could the investment be made to yield greater returns? Often laymen in organizations such as the chamber of commerce would bring in these efficiency experts to point out faults in the schools and then propose the corporate model of reform. Other times the members of a board of education would hire efficiency experts to survey their district's operations.[9] The use of surveys was strongly supported by pro-efficiency university professors and superintendents, as well as the United States Bureau of Education, the Rockefeller General Education Board, and the Russell Sage Foundation.[10] Private philanthropy, in fact, initiated and funded most early surveys of urban school systems. Financial aspects of school operations were prominent in most survey reports, which were filled with business and industrial terminology.[11] Suggestions for school reform were always in keeping with the pro-efficiency agenda.

Once the problems of waste and inefficiency were identified by the efficiency experts by means of the school survey, pro-efficiency reformers realized the second strategic goal by turning to the media to publicize the findings articulated in the survey report. One great advantage these reformers had was their access to—and frequently control of—the mass media and the magazines read by opinion leaders. Giving the example of the effort to implement the pro-efficiency model in New York City, historian David Tyack wrote,

> In the battle to destroy the ward school boards in New York . . . the reformers enjoyed nearly total control of news and editorials in the major newspapers of that city as well as an inside track to such periodicals as *Harper's Weekly, The Outlook,* and *The Critic.* Thereby they could define the nature of the problem in such a way that their remedies seemed self-evident and opposition to reform selfish and misguided.[12]

University presidents of institutions such as the University of Chicago, Columbia, and Harvard, created a consensus of experts on the need to reorganize the schools along pro-efficiency lines. These men were privy to the intimate circle of the business elite. Joining with business and professional men—and occasionally their reform-minded wives—they carried out the third element of their campaign by lobbying state legislatures to pass laws that would abolish ward control of schools, replacing it with a centralized school governance model.[13] This group of pro-efficiency reformers was joined by the state education associations, typically dominated by men in the new profession of educational administration. These associations proved to be the most persistent of lobbyists. They worked closely with colleagues in the education schools of universities and the state departments of education to encourage legislatures to alter much of the legal framework governing public schools.[14]

The Specifics of the Pro-Efficiency Agenda for Reform

Changes in Governance and Organizational Structure

In 1898 the president of the University of Chicago, William Harper, issued a report on the reform of schools that would be influential for the next thirty years.[15] The University of Chicago was a relatively new institution of higher learning, founded through the philanthropy of John D. Rockefeller. Harper was an advocate of the corporate form of governance, which had already worked so effectively in industry. His own university modeled its governance structure on the corporation: president, board of directors, and full-time administrative staff.[16] His report recommended a similar governance structure for the public schools. The board of education would approve policy and hire a trained, expert manager—the superintendent—to run the system. The school superintendent would have full control of the organization, much like a corporate president controlled a business. The report's recommendations were presented to the Illinois legislature in 1901 in the form of the Harper bill, a piece of legislation that had strong support from the business lobby.[17]

Central to the consolidation of the power of the superintendent was the reformulation of the mission and composition of the local school board. Unlike the local elected ward school board, which made vital decisions about the staff, curricula, and materials used in the neighborhood school, the centralized school board's role was to be advisory, with all professional functions left to the school superintendent and his assistants. Just as the corporate board of directors had

little power to influence the day-to-day management of a firm, because ⟨
nical expertise needed to administer so complicated an enterprise, the sc\
would defer to its hand-picked educational executive, the school superinte\
his staff of experts. Prominent pro-efficiency reformer and Stanford University professor of educational administration, Ellwood Cubberley, said it was in the:

> Interests of efficient administration for the board to leave all executive
> functions to carefully chosen executive officers, who act as its representa-
> tives. In this regard the evolution of city school control has kept in touch
> with the best principles of corporation management and control.[18]

All local ward trustees in a given municipality would be replaced by one small,
powerful central board of education composed of businessmen and other men of
affairs.[19] Cubberley hailed the concept of the small board composed of business
and professional men, because it would do less debating than was common
under the ward system and get more work done. In fact, he felt the typical board
meeting would be about one hour long, with no speeches or oratory on how
school business ought to be conducted. He wrote there would be no more need
for debate "than there would be in the conduct of a national bank."[20]

School managers sought to attain legitimacy by sharing in the auras surround-
ing two powerful figures of the day: the businessman and the professional.
Separate and distinct from teachers and teaching, school managers got their
authority not from experience with children, but from their university credentials, which attested to the fact that they had mastered the principles of business
management. The school manager was an "education executive." He could
measure inputs and outputs in school systems as a tool of management, rationalize school structures and curricula to fit new industrial and social conditions,
and rid schools of politics and corruption through the science of administration.[21]
Cubberley wrote that the noble men embarking on the path of school management were doing "pioneering work," blazing "a trail for others to follow."[22]

Thus, this school reform proposal envisioned the school system as a "quasi
public corporation."[23] Governance of schools by the people—working-class,
ethnic, uneducated and educated alike—was to be substituted with the discretion
of professional school administrators and a small group of businessmen and
professionals on school boards.[24] In this way the goal of educational efficiency
would never be held captive to the political needs of local elected ward trustees
beholden to their constituents.[25] School systems could become large, bureaucratic organizations with decision-making power concentrated at the top of an
administrative pyramid.

The similarities between the organizational chart of the typical corporation and the ideal school system proposed by Ellwood Cubberley were far from coincidental (see figures 2.1 and 2.2). The business corporation and the "quasi public corporation" of the school would both operate under the belief that those at the top had the right and the duty to control decisions that would intimately affect those at the base of the organizational pyramid.

Despite this "top-down" model of decision-making, the underlying premise of the proposed legal system of centralized school governance was the notion that the people—albeit quite indirectly—would control education, either through their elected state legislators or the locally elected school boards. This idea provided a sense of legitimacy that would allow school boards and their appointed administrators to exercise vast discretion in deciding educational matters. Like the managers of industrial concerns, school managers accepted as their own the legal theory of management rights—that is, the authority of management sprang from their obligation to serve the interests of the stockholders.[26] In the case of the school manager, the stockholders were, in a theoretical sense, the members of the public. In fact, public school managers often aimed to please their most influential stockholders—the business community.[27]

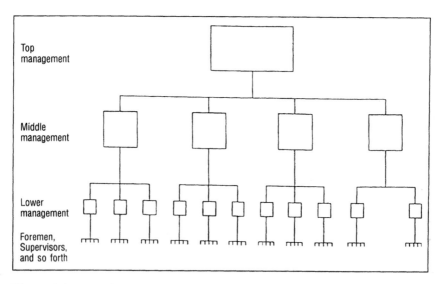

Figure 2.1 The hierarchical structure of the modern business enterprise at the turn of the century. Source: *The Visible Hand: The Managerial Revolution in American Business* by Alfred D. Chandler, Jr. ©1977 by Alfred D. Chandler, Jr. Reprinted by permission of Harvard University Press.

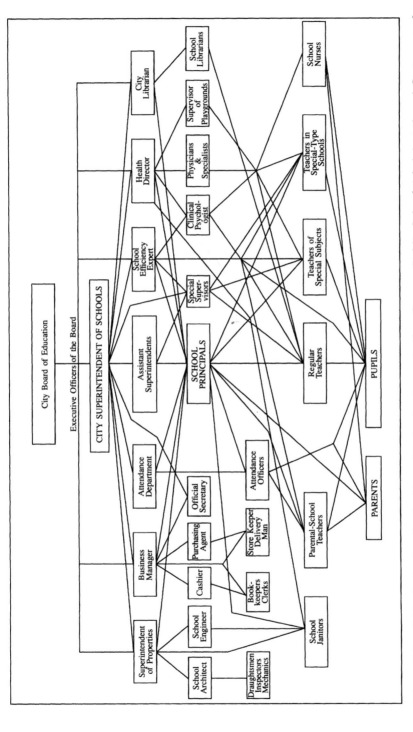

Figure 2.2 Cubberley's plan for the hierarchical school organization. Source: *Public School Administration: A Statement of the Fundamental Principles Underlying the Organization and Administration of Public Administration.* (Boston: Houghton-Mifflin, 1916.)

These public school managers shared with their comrades in industry the belief that they alone, as a class, were competent to make vital decisions that went to the core of their organization's mission, be it profit-making or education.[28] Then superintendent of schools, Andrew Draper, voiced this belief as he made the argument for taking power away from local ward trustees and teachers in Cleveland: "The leaders of the intellectual life of the city will have to evolve a plan; and the masses will have to be educated to its support."[29]

The concept of having both the legal as well as the moral right to exercise power over the educational enterprise, much as the private businessman had complete control over his firm, was wholly accepted by school administrators. This sense of rightful power emanated from many of the managers of the day.

After ten years of centralized governance, a New York City teacher commented in regard to her difficult working conditions, "I could have borne it better, but from the Superintendent down every man made me feel he was the sole owner and proprietor of the city schools and that I had intruded on his private business."[30] The school managers' power—legitimized by professional ethos, the business ideology of the day, and eventually by statute—gave teachers, parents, and students in education few legitimate outlets for participation in decisions about how education was to proceed.

Scientific Management of the School Organization

Organizational reform suggested by men like Cubberley, Harper, and Draper, was the first step in making schools function more like successful businesses. But organization was not enough. Once ensconced in power, the professional school administrator had to use management principles tested and proven in business— the principles of scientific management—in order to reform school operation. The hallmark of scientific management was to end improvisation by people throughout the organization and replace that improvisation with rules developed by management. These rules were based on the "science" of the job to be done.[31]

Key to this system of management was conformity by people at all levels of the organizational pyramid to the central authority at the top. It was the job of the experts to divide tasks into simple parts, and then coordinate the efforts of large numbers of people according to the top managers' master plan.[32] It was the job of those below these managers to obey. In fact, the first rule of efficiency was that once an order was given, everyone involved would follow it instantly and without question. The goal of professional managers was to make sure that the order would "go of itself through the works" and not be stopped by anyone deciding to second-guess the man at the top.[33] William Bagley, a pro-efficiency reformer and University of Illinois professor of education, wrote in 1907 that the need for "unquestioned obedience" was "the first rule of efficient service." The school situation was "entirely analogous to that in any other organization or system—the army, the navy, governmental, great business enterprises or small business enterprises, for that matter."[34]

The idea of functional specialization was also borrowed from the business model of scientific management by these education reformers. Cubberley remarked in his book, *The History of Education*, that functional specialization in the factory had obviated the need for one worker to be able to create an entire product. Using the example of the manufacture of a coat, Cubberley showed how thirty-nine different workers, each doing the same task over and over again, could together produce coats rationally "in a thoroughly organized clothing factory." (see figure 2.3)

FIG. 233. THE DESTRUCTION OF THE TRADES IN MODERN INDUSTRY

Under the old conditions of apprenticeship a boy learned all the processes and became a tailor. To-day, in a thoroughly organized clothing factory, thirty-nine different persons perform different specialized operations in the manufacture of a coat.

Figure 2.3 Cubberley's example of the functional specialization used in the manufacture of a coat.[35] Source: *The History of Education: Educational Practice and Progress Considered as a Phase of the Development and Spread of Western Civilization.* (Boston: Houghton-Mifflin, 1920.)

Expert management coordinated the efforts of all thirty-nine of these workers, as well as those of all the other employees in the plant. Generalizing from the factory example, Cubberley recommended functional specialization in the schools, with specialists in varying aspects of the school operation taking responsibility for one isolated aspect of the enterprise. The efforts of all these specialists were coordinated by the superintendent. The classroom teacher no longer had control over the totality of a child's educational program. There were teachers of special subjects like music and art, as well as supervisors monitoring their work. A host of different supervisors watched over the performance of school janitors, nurses, clerks, regular classroom teachers, and teachers in schools for the "defectives, delinquents, and children for some reason in need of special attention and care."[36] Using data gleaned from the newly rationalized department of school records, the superintendent coordinated the work of all these many departments resulting in less waste and heightened efficiency. The superintendent was the final judge of the appropriateness of means to ends in the entire system.[37] In this way, schools made use of the principles of scientific management to turn out an array of educational products to meet the needs of society, the most important of which was a labor force ready to fill jobs in industry.[38]

The ultimate expression of scientific management in education was the development in 1908 of the "platoon school" by Gary, Indiana, school superintendent William Wirt. Wirt was an advocate of adding art, music, and industrial education to the academic program. He wanted to show those in favor of low taxes that it could be done without incurring great cost. Wirt's innovation was to departmentalize grammar schools, having children as young as six years of age move from room to room to get instruction from teachers of special subjects. When one group was in homeroom getting the "three R's," another group was engaged in music, shop, gym, or playground activities. When the bell rang, children would shifted to another class. The plan kept costs low by anticipating full utilization of the entire school facility at all times.[39] This idea appealed to the pro-efficiency reformers. The "Gary Plan," as Wirt's idea was called, was lauded as using "the lamp of science" to help schoolmen modify their methods along the lines of business, industry, and the professions in order to efficiently deliver educational services to the largest number of children.[40] Proper implementation of the platoon school concept could showcase the expert abilities of the new "professional school manager" in his application of advanced business principles to the school setting.

Key to the platoon school's departmentalized program was the sorting of youngsters into tracks that yielded the best return on the investment in education. Charles Spain, deputy superintendent of the Detroit school system and a strong advocate of the platoon school, wrote: "The largest factor in an individual's progress seems to be his capacity to respond to the instruction which he receives."[41] Therefore, the way to educate youngsters of varying abilities was to once again rely on the business principles of division of labor and functional specialization. Special teachers instructed groups of students of apparently similar ability in subjects deemed suitable for them.

As we have seen, the pro-efficiency reformers openly subscribed to a castelike view of society. They used scientific testing to determine who would benefit most from either academic or manual education. Using data gathered from psychological tests, children judged best-suited for manual labor received a heavy dose of shop and household arts.[42] This differentiated curriculum also steered those children judged academically able—by virtue of high test scores—into more rigorous academic courses. This was labeled "individualized" instruction by advocates of the platoon school.[43] It also fit hand in glove with the pro-efficiency reformer's often articulated patrician view of human potential.

Schools Deliver Readymade Knowledge

These education reformers advanced the idea that there was a science of education on which all curriculum and teaching methods could be based. Once industry made clear what educational products it desired, this science would allow school managers to devise the one best way of teaching the skills and curricula necessary to produce the desired ends. Professor Franklin Bobbitt of the University of Chicago, and one of the most influential men in the field of educational administration at the time, championed the transfer of scientific management to education. Bobbitt attributed the vast increase in productivity in industry to management's takeover of decision-making on the precise methods to be used in manufacturing.

Applying this same idea to education, Bobbitt made the case for supervisors studying the various methods teachers were using, measuring the results, selecting the best one, and putting it into effect throughout an entire school system. To illustrate this idea, he gave the example of finding the one best way to teach neat penmanship:

> Suppose among schools that give sixty minutes per week to drill in penmanship, it is found that one group of schools distributes the time into thirty minute periods twice a week; another group of schools has twenty minute periods three times a week; another group distributes the time into

twelve minute periods of drill five times a week; a fourth group distributes the time into six minute periods ten time a week, or a short period twice each day. Now suppose each of these groups of schools to be measured in the first week of the school year by the Thorndike or Ayres writing scale as to quality, and tested by the stop watch as to speed. If they are then measured again at the end of the year in the same way, it is possible to determine which of the modes of distributing the sixty minutes of time for teaching the writing is superior.[44]

The Thorndike referred to by Bobbitt was statistician Edward Thorndike, a reformer who had an unbounded faith in the ability of quantified methods to result in the discovery of educational truth. He believed everything could be measured and that the resulting measure would give objective data upon which decisions should be based.[45] Thorndike wrote in 1918:

> Whatever exists at all exists in some amount. . . . Education is concerned with changes in human beings; a change is a difference between two conditions; each of these conditions is known to us only by the products produced by it. . . . To measure any of these products means to define its amount in some way so that competent persons . . . will know how large it is, with some precision, and that this knowledge may be recorded and used. This is the Credo of those who, in the last decade, have been busy trying to extend and improve measurements of educational products.[46]

Armed with data measuring changes in these educational products—standardized tests measuring skills and academic intelligence—management could develop and mandate a curriculum and methodology for all teachers and students to follow.

Although they promised to use science to find the one best way to educate youngsters, the majority of school managers were not equipped through their training to actually provide answers to the basic questions presented by the educative process.[47] The new field of graduate study in educational administration focused on the mechanics of running a school system—accounting, finance, building maintenance. It gave future school managers scant knowledge of pedagogical practices or theories of curriculum development. Thus, when these managers were placed in the role of planners of the educational process, they could only rely on the mechanistic concept of transmission of a predetermined set of facts, skills, and habits from teachers to children.

This concept of education fit perfectly with the kind of work in which most of the children would later be engaged as adults—fortuitously assigned tasks, chiefly at the behest of other people, and devoid of intrinsic meaning.[48] The reformers' application of business principles and practices to the process of education, thus, represented a fine match between what industry needed and what school managers were equipped to deliver.

Vocational Training for Future Employment

By the 1890s it was clear that business supported the idea of having schools shape youngsters into future employees. Jane Addams, noted social reformer of the period, said in 1897:

> The business man has, of course, not said to himself: "I will have the public school train office boys and clerks for me, so that I may have them cheap," but he has thought, and sometimes said, "Teach the children to write legibly, and to figure accurately and quickly; to acquire habits of punctuality and order; to be prompt to obey, and not question why; and you will fit them to make their way in the world as I have made mine.[49]

Certainly, schools taught children the basics of literacy and numeracy, attuned them to the idea of obedience to authority, and accustomed them to extrinsic incentives for achievement.[50] But by the early 1900s businessmen wanted more; they wanted schools to do the very type of vocational training to which Addams referred. Businessmen's need for mechanics was growing. The National Association of Manufacturers (NAM) headed a campaign to promote vocational education as a means of using the schools to create young adults equipped with the technical and mechanical skills industry needed.[51] The NAM made it clear to educators through addresses at National Education Association (NEA) annual conventions and its interaction with local school superintendents that "industrial education" was necessary for economic prosperity in the face of competition from countries like Germany. Economic competitors had advanced systems of vocational education. Pro-efficiency reformers such as Andrew Draper and Ellwood Cubberley rallied to industry's cry for education in the manual arts to insure the nation's economic health, championing the cause of vocational education in the schools.

Cubberley justified this advocacy of industrial education by disavowing the traditional American ideal of economic mobility. He wrote that schools should "give up the exceedingly democratic idea that all are equal, and that our society is devoid of classes." Schools should adapt to the existing social structure:

> Increasing specialization . . . has divided the people into dozens of more
> or less clearly defined classes, and the increasing centralization of trade
> and industry has concentrated business in the hands of a relatively small
> number. . . . No longer can a man save up a thousand dollars and start in
> business for himself with much chance of success. The employee tends to
> remain an employee; the wage earner tends to remain a wage
> earner . . . success is higher up the ladder now than it was a generation ago,
> while the crowd about the bottom increases every year.[52]

It made sense, therefore, to prepare the majority of students for subordinate roles
in the economy. Vocational education met this need for educating Eliot's "thick
fundamental level" of civilized society.

The highly influential old guard of the NEA, and the business philanthropists
and lobbyists of the pro-efficiency coalition, worked to promote acceptability of
the idea of schools training children in the manual arts so they might enter the
work force with the skills required by industry.[53] Business gave large sums of
money to establish vocational schools. J. P. Morgan alone contributed $500,000
to endow the New York trade schools. By the early twentieth century most such
commercial and vocational schools established by business philanthropy had
been absorbed into the public school systems.[54] In 1909 the NAM could report
that "industrial education has taken a firm and lasting hold upon the people of
this country."[55]

New York school superintendent William Maxwell resented greatly this ca-
pitulation by educators to the NAM's and other business groups' demands. In a
1913 article he wrote:

> The educational world is now seething for the introduction of industrial or
> trade teaching in the public schools. That agitation, as every one knows,
> originated with the manufacturers. They had practically abandoned the
> apprenticeship system of training workmen. No longer training their own
> mechanics, they have found it difficult to obtain a sufficient supply of
> skillful artisans, unless they import them from Europe at great expense.
> Out of this dilemma the exit was obvious—persuade the State to assume
> the burden. . . . And, as a first step to secure their ends, they and their
> agents in unmeasured terms denounced the public schools as behind the
> age, as inefficient, as lacking in public spirit. . . . The arrogance of the
> manufacturers was two-fold—first, in condemning the schools for not
> doing what thinking men had never before considered it the duty of the
> schools to do and what the traditions of thousands of years laid it upon the

manufacturers to do; and, second, in demanding that the State . . . should then proceed to pay the bills for training their workmen.[56]

Yet Maxwell represented a minority view among fellow urban superintendents and education professors. Most of these educational leaders agreed that schools had to be changed to accommodate the needs of an industrialized America.[57]

Relations between Managers and Workers: The Business Model

As we have seen, the business model of labor relations in the era of scientific efficiency assumed expert leadership from managers and obedience from the workers in the organizations. Responding to the educational progressives who felt the teacher had to be free to devise instruction appropriate to individual students, William Bagley characterized such a plan as leaving the "teacher and pupil to work out each his own salvation in the chaos of confusion and disorder." Much better in terms of the goal of education—that is, getting "the largest dividend upon material investment of time, energy and money"—was the teacher's use of management-prescribed group routines until the children all behaved uniformly, having incorporated the desired habits into their behavior. Deviation from management's plan was an offense of the worst kind, and one that could not be tolerated in a system that valued economy above all else:[58]

> *Unquestioned obedience* is the first rule of efficient service. The classroom teacher owes this to his superiors, and whenever he cannot yield such obedience, his resignation is the only alternative. . . . Certain requirements are made in the way of results. Pupils must be taught certain facts, drilled into certain habits, in each grade. The superintendent demands these results of his principals, the principals pass on the demand to the classroom teachers, the classroom teachers exact the required work from the pupils.[59]

Anticipating outcomes-based education by some eighty years, Bagley called for the teacher to be held responsible by her supervisors for meeting these predetermined student outcomes—skills and habits. Her performance would be rated on the degree of success she had in imposing these outcomes on her students. While Bagley suggested that the teacher might be granted some discretion in devising techniques to attain those outcomes, "rigid results" would still have to be attained. Bagley admitted that from the outside this organization might look like "an autocracy," but assured his readers that when viewed from the inside, "it is almost a democracy."[60]

The reformers recommended a type of teacher training that would emphasize the means of realizing the ends devised by management. Although Bagley said it would be ideal for teachers to understand the ends as well as the means of education, as even "the humblest subordinate" could have an influence on children, he felt it was unrealistic to expect teachers to grasp the large ideas that professional school managers were to make their stock and trade.[61] Therefore, he devoted the bulk of his influential book for prospective teachers, *Classroom Management: Its Principles and Technique*, to the "plan of treatment" that teachers should use on their charges. Recommending rigid techniques for every aspect of classroom practice—passing in the halls, fire drills, passing to the blackboard, distributing "wraps," the orderly arrangement of books and materials, going to the bathroom, and the tidiness of the room—Bagley insisted, "anything that approaches rigidity and exactness, even remotely, is vastly to be preferred over the 'hit or miss' manner of dealing with troublesome questions."[62] Teacher training, thus, was to become an exercise of committing routines to memory. Questioning whether those procedures or methods were either necessary or beneficial had no place in the education of future teachers.[63]

As in industry, pro-efficiency reformers rejected the idea that those at the bottom of the hierarchy would see any need to join together in an association to represent their interests. Despite this, once centralization became a reality, teachers in many cities banned together in what were to become the first teacher unions. These teachers sought to organize for equal pay, pensions, and tenure. They were routinely viewed by pro-efficiency reformers as either hysterical or a threat to the dominance of professional school managers. Ellwood Cubberley decried unionization and the demand by unionized teachers that they have a say in decision-making on educational issues. He saw unions as dangerous because

> Not fully understanding administrative difficulties and the administrative point of view, [they] may unintentionally but nevertheless seriously interfere with the proper and effective working of school administrative officers. Our teachers mean well, but they often lack knowledge on administrative questions and the special problems of their work.[64]

Adopting Frederick Taylor's argument that unions were an obstacle to scientific management, school managers asserted that teacher unions would interfere with the management's prerogatives to run the organization efficiently. They made this their battle cry in their effort to ward off teacher unionization. It was, in fact, a battle cry that would be heard for many years to come.

The pro-efficiency coalition successfully lobbied state legislatures to institutionalize its recommended superior/subordinate relationship between school managers and teachers. Perhaps the most important legal development for the future of teaching as a profession was the acceptance by legislatures and courts of the pro-efficiency coalition's position that teachers ought to be dismissed for failure to obey a school manager or school board. Even in states that required just cause for dismissal, a teacher's lack of loyalty and obedience to her supervisor or the school board was consistently deemed "insubordination" and grounds for dismissal. Teachers owed the board and its chief executive officer loyalty because of their legal authority. If their actions prevented teachers from serving the best interests of their pupils, if their policies contradicted the professional judgment of the teacher, there was little recourse except resignation. Submission to this legally recognized higher authority was a condition of continued employment.[65]

The supervisor's legal and de facto power to dictate the means, methods, and content of instruction was to become nearly monolithic. Marian Dogherty, a teacher at the turn of the century, wrote in her 1943 memoir that "it was with that first class that I became aware that a teacher was subservient to a higher authority. I became increasingly aware of this subservience to an ever growing number of authorities with each succeeding year, until there is danger today of becoming aware of little else."[66] As the Lynds noted in their second study of Middletown in the 1930s, the school managers' quest for ever-more efficient techniques dismayed the city's teachers as they watched "the administrative horse gallop off with the educational cart."[67] By the onset of the Depression, the dominance of business-minded school managers over educators with any competing vision of education was complete.

The Gender Dimension

A powerful way for the pro-efficiency reformers to deal with teachers' efforts to organize as a countervailing force to school management was to focus on the gender of the teachers forming those unions. An example of this strategy can be seen in the exchange between Margaret Haley and the U.S. commissioner of education, William Harris. Haley, founder of the Chicago Teachers Federation, broke with the NEA protocol forbidding women or teachers to address the audience during the 1901 annual national convention. Speaking extemporaneously before the gathering, Haley linked low teacher salaries and Chicago's failure to collect tax revenue from powerful corporations. When she finished, the president of the NEA, William Harris, ambled to his feet, pointed his finger at Haley and said:

> Pay no attention to what that teacher down there has said. I take it that she is a grade teacher, just out of her classroom at the end of the school year, worn out, tired out, and hysterical. I have repeatedly said that these meetings held at this time of the year are a mistake. If there are more hysterical outbursts after this, I shall insist that these meetings be held at some other time of the year.[68]

School managers could add sexual stereotypes to the arsenal of weapons businessmen of the era used to weaken unions that challenged their prerogatives to manage their enterprises unfettered.

Certainly, the fact that the vast majority of teachers were women made it easier for the pro-efficiency reformers to minimize the significance of any attempt to have a say in how schools should operate. The reformers' proposed authoritarian relationship between school managers and school teachers was nothing short of a reiteration of the prevailing stereotypes of women in society: docile, subservient, inefficient, incapable of managing anyone but another woman or a child. By proposing that women follow the orders of men, and that women would actually prefer following orders than thinking for themselves, the pro-efficiency reformers were in the mainstream of popular thought. Just as the idea of strong, independent, innovative women was anathema to most of American society, the notion that teachers could be either independent or innovative was never entertained by these education reformers. And, as in the case of Margaret Haley, any teacher who dared to challenge the pro-efficiency coalition or its agenda for reform could be branded as nothing more than a "hysterical" woman.

Despite the greater proportion of women in the teaching ranks, they were to be vastly underrepresented in educational governance positions as the pro-efficiency reforms began to take hold.[69] It became obvious that a by-product of the bureaucratization of the schools was the gender structuring of job opportunities in a way that discriminated against women. As administration grew in status as well as compensation, women found themselves increasingly shut out of principalships. Under the ward system of governance, a majority of principals were often "principal teachers" who split their time between the classroom and office duties.[70] Typically, these positions were filled by veteran female teachers. Administration in the new centralized hierarchy ceased to be either part-time or the province of veteran teachers, however. It became a series of specialties, its offices filled by full-time, specially trained persons who had little contact with the classroom. The superintendents, supervisors, and principals who governed school systems, inspected and evaluated the lower ranks were most often male. In 1920, 92 percent of all secondary school principals were male. In 1922, more than 99 percent of school superintendencies were held by men, with only thirty-one women superintendents in the entire nation.[71] The teachers these male school managers inspected, evaluated, and reported on were, by and large, women.[72]

Responsibilities within the school system were segregated by gender in accordance with a few rules of thumb. Men were most likely to be found in managerial positions that conferred the greatest power, pay, and prestige. Men were given positions where they had to supervise other men. If women were given administrative jobs, those jobs entailed supervising other women or children. Jobs involving interface between the school system and the public were filled by men because of their higher status in the community. The few women who were given administrative positions were more likely to have jobs that looked inward toward the school organization.[73] This gender structuring of jobs resulted in a growth in the income gap between men and women employed in school systems, with the salaries of female educators falling greatly behind those of males working in public education.[74]

The result of the gender division within the school system was, in historian David Tyack's words, a "pedagogical harem." School managers had many women dependent on them for their employment and working conditions.[75] In fact, the employment of women as teachers correlated highly with the pace of bureaucratization. In 1880, before centralization had begun, women represented 57 percent of all teachers. In 1914, as school systems around the country began to implement the pro-efficiency reforms, 80 percent of teachers were female.[76] As we have seen, the vast influx of women into teaching resulted in no proportional increase in women holding positions of managerial authority.[77]

Educational progressive George Counts noted in the 1930s that the visible subordination of teachers to their supervisors was educational to the students who witnessed this subservience. It reinforced for them the power and seeming propriety of the status quo in regard to gender roles.[78] Further, it made the male role—administrator—the norm of success and professionalism in education, while relegating the female role—teaching—to that of underling.[79] For the millions of youngsters who spent their childhood witnessing the subordination of female teachers by male school managers, these lessons may have been retained longer and with greater intensity than those of the academic variety.

Parents and the Community at Large

Once the pro-efficiency reforms were institutionalized through legislation, teachers were not the only participants in the educational endeavor who had to submit to the will of the school board and its administrative staff. Parents were the big losers in this realignment of power relations represented by the change in educational governance legislation. Parents could not decide what school their child would attend, at what age the child would begin school, what subjects the child would study once in school, what texts the child would read, how long the child should continue education, or under what circumstances they might withdraw their child from school. The child was legally becoming as much a creature of the state as of the parents.

The centralized, professional administration, which was legally empowered by the 1920s, represented a reallocation of power away from both the parents and the community at large. Yet, while teachers protested centralized decision-making as autocratic, the public at large acquiesced to the pro-efficiency agenda in the hope that it would take corruption and waste out of education and bring some of the successes of industry into the realm of education. The antidemocratic nature of the centralization of decision-making in the hands of school managers was accepted by many as the price that had to be paid for increased efficiency in the operation in schools. While administrators made the system their own, the public found the system complex, and hard to influence.[80] A community had to take it on faith that the governance system set up by lawmakers indeed represented the public interest as promised by the legal theory underlying school governance laws.

Conclusion

Business in this period was in a position of prestige and influence. Businessmen's beliefs, values, and opinions were widely admired and accepted. Business philosophy became a key characteristic of American society, prompting Calvin Coolidge to say "The business of America is business." When problems in society were articulated by the muckrakers of this era, administrative progressives pointed to business principles of rationality and efficiency to allow government to address them. When the schools were roundly criticized—often by business itself—for failing to cope with the societal dislocations caused by immigration and industrialization, it is little wonder that the new profession of school administration looked to business philosophy, practices, and principles to address this failure to adapt to changing circumstances.

Yet business played a direct role in the attempt to redesign the nation's educational systems as well. Businessmen joined forces with educators such as Draper, Bobbitt, and Cubberley to create the pro-efficiency coalition in an effort to shape the nations' public school systems in the image of the business corporation.[81] Organizations such as the NAM publicized the need for reform. Businessmen's campaign for utilitarian, vocational education through the press and the NEA created a desire for a new role for education—and a responsibility not previously borne by the school—namely, trade apprenticeships. Corporations used philanthropy to further this aim and to encourage the adoption of its agenda for reform. Businessmen took seats on boards of education to insure their role in policy formulation, including taxation rates and selection of a superintendent. Lobbying for legislative changes that led to the adoption of a corporate governance model as well as a mandate for vocational education was one more means by which business succeeded in having education molded in its own image in order to serve its interests. All of these strategies were to be relied on many years later when business once again was to see the need for massive redesign of America's educational system. Addressing the uneven power equation of labor and business in regard to participation in the process of education, economist Roger Babson said in 1914:

> However successful organized labor has been in many ways, it has never succeeded in directing the education of its children. Capital still prepares the school books and practically controls the school systems.[82]

This control was aimed at producing stability during unsettled times as well as an army of "corporals" ready to take orders in American industry.

While the power of business was enormous, the allure of science and efficiency great, and the legitimacy of the professional school manager on the rise, the reform of the schools in accordance with the tenets of the pro-efficiency agenda did not go unchallenged. As we shall see in the next chapter, reformers with a very different set of values and experiences were simultaneously championing an entirely different concept of school reform: education for individual development and democracy. Although the educational progressives' chances for prevailing at the time were slim, their proposals are important, not only because they put the pro-efficiency reforms in bold relief. They also form the heart of much of today's agenda to restructure the nation's schools.

3

An Alternative Reform Agenda— Education for Individual Development and Democracy

Two ideals are struggling for supremacy in American life today: one the industrial ideal, culminating through the supremacy of commercialism, which subordinates the worker to the product and the machine; the other, the ideal of democracy, the ideal of the educators, which places humanity above all machines, and demands that all activity shall be the expression of life. If this ideal of the educators cannot be carried over into the industrial field, then the ideal of industrialism will be carried over into the school. Those two ideals can no more continue to exist in American life than our nation could have continued half slave and half free. If the school cannot bring joy to the work of the world, the joy must go out of its own life, and work in the school as in the factory will become drudgery.[1]

This quotation, taken from Haley's 1904 address to the annual NEA convention, captures the spirit of the educational progressives. Haley and other progressives—most notably John Dewey—agreed with the pro-efficiency reformers on one point: the fight to control the course of school reform was crucial to the future of the nation. Haley framed the debate between the pro-efficiency and the progressive agendas for reform in terms of a war between two antithetical visions of what the country could become. It is no accident that Margaret Haley entitled her autobiography *Battleground*. She saw herself as a soldier in "the long war for academic freedom . . . social and economic justice."

49

Educational progressives were as fervent in their opposition to the pro-efficiency coalition's corporate model of school organization and governance as the pro-efficiency reformers were in their campaign for its adoption. The progressives' vision for education challenged the assumptions, practices, and conclusions inherent in the proposal put forth by such men as Ellwood Cubberley and Franklin Bobbitt.[2] It is in this articulation of dissent that the roots of the current education reform agenda can be found. Contemporary calls for teacher professionalism, decentralized school governance, and child-focused education all derive from the prescription for reform devised by the educational progressives.

Historian Barbara Berman has commented, "the most outstanding feature of the pro-efficiency group is their virtual lack of training or interest in teaching or teacher education."[3] In contrast, many of the educational progressives had significant teaching experience in the public schools or in the normal schools that trained teachers. A number of these dissenters were women, a gender not represented in the pro-efficiency coalition. Leaders of the first teachers' unions were among the most vocal members of the educational progressives.

Another group represented in the voice of dissent was academicians—philosophers, sociologists, and historians—who felt strongly about the power of education to safeguard the nation's participatory form of government during a time when powerful commercial and administrative interest groups threatened the very possibility of a democratic state. These educators and democrats shared the idea that positive change in education could only be accomplished from inside the classroom. In this respect, they differed absolutely with the pro-efficiency group, which sought to change education by establishing external or environmental controls through organizational techniques.[4]

The Progressives' Contrasting Vision of Education

Although these reformers saw education as playing a crucial societal role, they felt the only way for society to reap its benefits was for education to focus on the needs, talents, and interests of individual children. Believing that all education had to take its lead from the laws of human development elucidated by the new discipline of child psychology, the educational progressives scorned the attempt to apply the mechanistic model of production to the education of individual human beings.[5] The idea that any organizational model could take precedence over the needs of developing children was spurned by a leader of the educational progressives, Ella Flagg Young:

The laws governing the development of the soul are not subject to conditions arising in a crudely developed social organization. The laws may be ignored, and the organization may continue, but at a sacrifice beyond estimation.[6]

John Dewey argued that rather than concentrate reform efforts on administrative reorganization and readymade curriculum, "the center of gravity" of the entire education effort should be transferred to the child:

It is a change, a revolution, not unlike that introduced by Copernicus when the astronomical center shifted from the earth to the sun. In this case the child becomes the sun about which the appliances of education revolve; he is the center about which they are organized.[7]

Using the example of the ideal home where the intelligent parent recognizes what is best for each of the children in the family and is able to supply what each child needs, Dewey proposed a type of education that took its lead from the individual child.

Dewey opposed the pro-efficiency coalition's concept of education because it sought to ignore the complex and idiosyncratic ways that children develop, as well as the fluid and ever-changing fund of knowledge. He mocked their mechanistic notion of education: "There is a certain amount—a fixed quantity—of ready made results and accomplishments to be acquired by all children alike in a given time." He felt the pro-efficiency reformers had decided upon some desirable amount of knowledge, divided that into six or twelve years of school life, and then ordered that children every year master "just the proportionate fraction of the total," finishing the whole by the end of their schooling. The mechanistic model would go further, he scoffed, mandating how much ground was to be covered by children and teachers during any given hour or day, so that "everything comes out with perfect evenness at the end."[8]

The pro-efficiency model, Dewey asserted, was an absurd approach to education. Beyond the fact that knowledge was viewed as a static, lifeless mass of facts and skills, this view of education promoted a passivity in teachers and children alike in its attempt to impose uniform curricula and methods on their work in the classroom. Rather than try to teach a fixed set of knowledge, Dewey believed education should aim at preparing children to think for themselves, even if that preparation led to their revising or rejecting what adults accepted as truth. A key conviction underlying the progressive agenda was that children had to be guided into becoming critical thinkers who could judge hitherto accepted institutions and customs in light of the ever-changing social landscape.[9]

A fundamental reason for the educational progressives' opposition to the pro-efficiency reforms was their basic disagreement with its underlying values, beliefs, and assumptions. Competition, social and economic castes, and obedience to hierarchical authority—so valued by the pro-efficiency reformers—were vigorously opposed by these progressives. Perhaps the most fundamental difference in their value systems was the educational progressives' belief in the inborn worth and uniqueness of the individual and the role education could play in the development of the individual's potentialities. The progressives believed that education could help individuals develop their inborn power of self-determination.[10] A respect for the basic goodness and originality of each person was central to their entire educational philosophy:

> Every soul may not have sufficient individual energy to command recognition as being talented, but there are inherent in each those tendencies which, with their infinitesimal variations in grouping, make a being different from others—a being peculiarly itself. If these varied tendencies, elements of strength, be developed in accord with the mental life-process, then will each human being know the joy of living in accord with its better, its true, nature.[11]

Compare those thoughts, expressed by Young in 1900, to those of leading pro-efficiency reformer William Bagley:

> One . . . can see in the mechanical routine of the classroom the educative forces that are slowly transforming the child from a little savage into a creature of law and order, fit for the life of civilized society.[12]

The progressives did not share the pro-efficiency reformers' ideas on the "savage" nature of young humans beings. The essential dignity of the ordinary person was a basic tenet of their philosophy. In fact, they felt that independent, original thought was within the reach of all people, not only the "thin top layer of society." Every individual—including individual children—had the right to freedom of thought and action. For children, that freedom had to be cultivated in skillful and appropriate ways, but its recognition was the a priori assumption underlying all their theory and practice.[13]

According to the progressives, the fundamental equality of each person engaged in the educational endeavor, be it the child, teacher, principal, or district administrator, had to be recognized in order for each individual to develop fully. Writing about the ethics governing the relations between individuals, Ella Flagg Young wrote that people had to be seen as more than cogs in the proverbial wheel if human potentiality was to be realized. Young asserted that subserviency and fear were the lowest motivators of human action. On the other hand, freely selected ideals chosen for their contribution to the attainment of a better life were the highest motivators of conduct. Ideals in this sense were not ethereal wisps disassociated from life's practicalities. In Young's mind, they were behind every act of will and gave color and tone to the individual's entire mental life. Clearly, the question of harmonizing the ideals and action of all the individual members of an organization was not one that could be answered by administrative fiat.[14]

Young and the other educational progressives put great stock in cooperation—rather than competition—as the guiding principle of human relations. Dewey declared that the type of schooling recommended by the pro-efficiency reformers could only engender competition between youngsters:

> The mere absorbing of facts and truths is so exclusively individual an affair that it tends very naturally to pass into selfishness. There is no obvious social motive for the acquirement of mere learning. . . . Indeed, almost the only measure for success is a competitive one, in the bad sense of that term—a comparison of results in the recitation or in the examination to see which child has succeeded in getting ahead of others in storing up, accumulating, the maximum information. So thoroughly is this the prevailing atmosphere that for one child to help another in his task has become a school crime.[15]

Young went so far as to assert that the level of power in an educational system was determined by the degree in which the principle of cooperation was made incarnate in developing and realizing the aim of the school. The purpose of the school was twofold: helping each soul develop its inborn power of self-determination and preparing individuals for active cooperation and participation in the greater community. These aims were not in opposition, but rather were "two phases of the same unity."[16]

These reformers believed that all persons had the natural right to free expression in their work. The idea that someone who submitted to the drudgery of perfecting a dull routine was deemed "faithful" or "conscientious" was repugnant to Young.[17] Dewey decried the fact that so many people of the era were employed as "mere appendages" to the machines they operated. He found appalling the idea that workers had no opportunity to develop their imaginations and insights as to the social and scientific values found in their work.[18] Jane Addams, social reformer and ally of the educational progressives, made reference to the same example of functional specialization in the work place used by

Ellwood Cubberley in her 1909 book, *The Spirit of Youth and the City Streets*. Her assessment of the process could not have been more different from Cubberley's, however:

> It takes thirty nine people to make a coat in a modern tailoring establish-
> ment, yet those same thirty nine people might produce a coat in a spirit of
> "team work" which would make the entire process as much more exhila-
> rating that the work of the solitary tailor, as playing in a baseball team gives
> more pleasure to a boy than afforded by a solitary game of hand ball on the
> side of a barn.[19]

A brand of cooperation that would enhance each individual's power of initiative, develop the full human potential, and keep all people intellectually alive and open to change was exalted by the educational progressives as a value that should pervade all endeavors, be they in the work place, in the school or in society at large.[20]

Finally, the progressives were committed to a type of education that would lead to the realization of a truly democratic society. The basic principle of democracy was that every individual be counted and treated as a person.[21] In this sense, the educational progressives' philosophy of education fit hand in glove with the requirements of democratic government. As Young said, the goals of individual development and societal good could be accomplished simultaneously. Before she left her position as the superintendent of Chicago schools in 1915, she presented this vision to her staff:

> Some day the system will be such that the child and the teacher will go to
> school with elastic joy. At home in the evening, the child will talk about
> the things done during the day and will talk with pride. I want to make the
> school the great instrument of democracy.[22]

Inherent in her statement was the idea that the school experience had within it a theory of government. Young consistently rejected the notion that an undemo-cratic school system could prepare students for citizenship and participation in democracy.[23] William Kilpatrick, a professor of educational philosophy at Co-lumbia, agreed with Young's vision of the linkage between the school and de-mocracy. Schools that relegated teachers to positions as subordinates and children to roles as automatons could only teach children to be obedient and subservient to some distant autocrat. If children were to become participants in a democratic society, they had to live democracy on a daily basis in their school life. Relying on the relatively new science of learning theory, Kilpatrick insisted that to learn democracy, children had to experience democracy firsthand.[24]

Dewey, too, fervently believed that the processes of schooling had to be congruent with the character of a democratic society. He spent his life speaking and writing about his vision of school as a miniature community that would help children develop social power and insight so that they might take their places as citizens in a cooperative and democratic society.[25] He wrote that our nation had:

> To make each one of our schools an embryonic community life, active with types of occupations that reflect the life of the larger society and permeated throughout with the spirit of art, history, and science. When the school introduces and trains each child of society into membership within such a little community, saturating him with the spirit of service, and providing him with the instruments of effective self direction, we shall have the deepest and best guaranty of a larger society which is worthy, lovely, and harmonious.[26]

An image of schools more different from that conceived by Franklin Bobbitt or Andrew Draper would be hard to evoke.

A Prescription for Child-Centered Education

Unlike the business model of education reform, which emphasized teachers' production and efficiency over their human and intellectual interaction with students, the educational progressives put the quality of the teacher-child contact at the center of their agenda.[27] A constant theme of the progressives' critique of the pro-efficiency school reform agenda was that it failed to recognize the teacher as the primary educator in the school system. Ella Flagg Young found it ironic that pro-efficiency reformers treated teachers as subordinates when they represented "the only part that functions for the true end of the school."[28] All education began and ended with the child and the teacher. Official bureaucracy was dilatory at best, and antithetical at worst to this crucial interaction.[29] Whatever support the teacher needed for successful pedagogy would determine the type of school structure that would arise. This was an example of Dewey's proposed change in the center of gravity of education.

Inherent in this vision of education was a respect for the power of the teacher to devise the best means of meeting the needs of individual children. This was a critical difference from the pro-efficiency reformer's version of the teacher as operative. The educational progressives saw teachers as creators—as well as executors—of curricula. They valued the teacher's experience as well the credentials earned through formal academic training.[30] Young decided early in her career that the teacher played the crucial role of creating a favorable learning environment. A lifelong advocate of quality teacher preparation, Young recognized that every class was conducted in a manner commensurate with the teacher's intelligence, training, and sympathy.[31]

Innovators in educational practice like Friedrich Froebel, originator of the German kindergarten, and Colonel Francis Parker, head of the schools in Quincy, Massachusetts, agreed that the root of all educative activity could be found in the instinctive, impulsive attitudes of the child, not in the presentation of external material. Children's games, play, and imitation were the foundation on which teaching could take place.[32] Parker's Quincy Method interrelated the several subjects of the curriculum in order to enhance their meaning for the child. It emphasized sharing and self-expression among children.[33] The fixed course of study—for example, math taught in isolation from science or social studies—was rejected in favor of a child-centered, interdisciplinary type of education.[34]

The ideal of a partnership between the teacher and the child, formed to help that child develop inherent talents as well as the ability to be a critical thinker and a problem solver, was the idea that energized the educational progressives' reform agenda.[35] The teacher needed a significant knowledge base in order to integrate basic skills into the life experience of the child. Beyond that, the teacher needed respect for the child's natural curiosity, for it was that curiosity that was the basis for all learning. Dewey gave the example of how a child's desire to make a box could be used by the teacher to present the child with a real life situation that was certain to teach valuable lessons; lessons that would stand the child in good stead throughout life:

> Take the example of the little child who wants to make a box. If he stops short with the imagination or wish, he certainly will not get discipline. But when he attempts to realize his impulse, it is a question of making his idea definite, making it into a plan, of taking the right kind of wood, measuring the parts needed, giving them the necessary proportions, etc. There is involved the preparation of materials, the sawing, planing, the sandpapering, making all the edges and corners to fit. Knowledge of tools and processes is inevitable. If the child realizes his instinct and makes the box, there is plenty of opportunity to gain discipline and perseverance, to exercise effort in overcoming obstacles, and to attain as well a great deal of information.[36]

Although Dewey supported the idea of children working in what was referred to as the "manual arts," he differed completely from the pro-efficiency supporters of vocational education. The purpose of children working in carpentry or cooking was not to prepare them for routine employment, but to help them acquire insight into natural materials and processes, "points of departure whence children shall be led out into a realization of the historic development of man." Dewey believed that children who might very well spend their adult lives engaged in the manual trades ought to have a sense of insight into the social and scientific values embedded in their work. Dewey referred to Plato's definition of a slave as one who in his actions did not express his own ideas, but those of another man. The type of education proposed by Dewey would enable working men and women to see within their "daily work all there is in it of large and human significance."[37]

Dewey felt that if teachers were to follow the lead of the child's natural curiosity, they could not be harnessed to the administrative directives proposed by the pro-efficiency reformers. Indeed, the educational progressives felt that the public school teacher needed as much autonomy and freedom as the college or university professor.[38] Young declared that freedom was inherent in genuine teaching. Every teacher had to possess freedom in order to carry out the responsibility of fashioning lessons and experiences suited to the needs and desires of individual children; experiences that would teach them not only the three R's but develop their initiative in thought and action.[39]

In order for teachers to cultivate critical thinking in the child, they themselves had to be free to question all things. The teacher needed to be a model of vigorous, public-spirited thinking, challenging commonly held ideas and assumptions. The example presented by the teacher would, as the child's maturity allowed, help the child develop the ability to question existing institutions and practices in the community and the nation. Armed with that sensibility, the child would be equipped to later take his or her place as a citizen in a democratic society.[40]

The Professionalization of Teaching

In the business model of education presented by the pro-efficiency reformers, the teacher was likened to a mechanic executing the same predetermined process over and over again on the raw material that came down the assembly line. In contrast, the educational progressives saw the teacher's job as characterized by a great degree of indeterminacy. While the ultimate goals were the same for all children—the development of their innate aptitudes, critical thinking, and social cooperation—how those lofty aims would be realized in concrete terms would vary from child to child. This indefiniteness required the teacher to use judgment and discretion, developed over years of study and experience, to best serve the interests of students. That description of teaching put it squarely within the definition of what turn of the century society deemed "professional" work.

Samuel Haber, scholar of the early development of the professions in America, has written that the characteristic markers of a profession were the following: advanced education, work with an "elevated" purpose, licensing legislation, a secure income, an association of practitioners which could restrict entry, and a sense of duty that could act as a check on the desire for income maximization.[41] The professions, in general, swelled in both type and number from 1880 to 1900 as science and the attack on egalitarianism presented by Social Darwinism gave greater status to those who did esoteric work.[42] Although they took exception to the elitism inherent in Social Darwinism, the educational progressives sought to add teaching to the position of authority and honor already enjoyed by medicine, the professorate, and other learned occupations.

The educational progressives rationalized their call for the professionalization of teaching by characterizing teachers "as a company of scholars engaged in the education of youth."[43] Teachers needed to have a deep understanding of both the subject matter to be taught and the means of relating this knowledge to the minds of those to be instructed; to be aware of the common experiences of childhood that could be utilized to lead children toward the understandings presented by this knowledge.[44] The art of melding these two areas of expertise, combined with the managerial ability required to run a class where children moved about doing varied tasks simultaneously while the teacher worked with an individual child or small group of children, all pointed to the elevation of the occupation of teaching to the professional level.[45]

Ella Flagg Young championed the idea of professional teaching founded on broad scholarship and good judgment. Teaching was an art. No "cookbook" formula devised by school managers and education professors could substitute for superior teaching.[46] Progressive author and professor George Counts also placed his faith in education on the shoulders of the teacher. He warned, however:

> If the person presiding over the classroom is meanly gifted, if he is inadequately or inappropriately prepared for his post, if he lacks a clear and sufficient conception of his responsibility, and if he is surrounded by unsuitable working conditions, there is no hope.[47]

Counts emphasized that the selection, the training, and the working conditions of teachers were the key factors to the realization of the teacher as a professional. He called for men and women of "intelligence, spirit, capacity for leadership, and devotion to the popular welfare" to be drawn into the schools. Without these qualities, teachers would merely be, "obedient to their superiors, meticulous with respect to small matters," and wholly unsuited to the job of devising child-centered, socially conscious education. Teacher training would need to include both a broad, liberal education, and an opportunity for future teachers to consider the interplay between profound questions of national social policy and educational policy. Only then could teachers become the educational statesmen and women for which Counts crusaded.[48]

Counts also spoke of the need to improve the working conditions of teachers in order to attract and retain persons of the highest caliber to the teaching profession. "That teachers should have adequate compensation, reasonably secure tenure, and a high degree of freedom from annoyance at the hands of educational laymen is axiomatic. . . . Without security and freedom professional competence is impossible."[49] The educational progressives supported early teachers' unions that had as their primary goal the attainment of professional working conditions. Margaret Haley went so far as to proclaim an identity of interests between teachers and children. "The same things that are a burden to the teacher are a burden also to the child. The same things which restrict her powers restrict his powers also."[50] John Dewey joined the American Federation of Teachers (AFT) at its inception in 1916, and carried "card number one" of the teachers' organization throughout his long life.

The School Organization: A Community of Equals

Ella Flagg Young came up with a unique and innovative solution to the problem of coordinating the efforts of the members of the ever-larger organizations taking the country by a storm. Young was no pie in the sky theorist. Singular among women educators, she ascended the hierarchy of positions in education, becoming the most powerful woman educator of her time. During her lifelong career in education, she was a teacher, principal, assistant superintendent, professor of education at the University of Chicago, head of the Chicago Normal School, superintendent of the Chicago school system, and president of the NEA.[51] Despite the similarity of her credentials to those of the pro-efficiency reformers, she differed completely from their belief that the best way to accomplish the goal of organizational coordination was to create a hierarchy of power, with those below forever following orders of those above.

Young's solution to the problem of organizational coordination was to have all persons commit to a common ideal and then have "every member, from the least responsible to the executive at the top," harness their intellect and emotion in an effort to make that ideal a reality. Coordination would come through what we would call now employee participation in decision-making—that is, every member of the organization contributing to the development of creative means of realizing some valued end.[52] In a very real sense, the origins of the current movement to empower teachers, to include them in problem-solving and decision-making, can be traced to the organizational theory articulated by Young and embraced by the educational progressives at the turn of the century.

The proper role of administrators in this plan was to safeguard the flexibility necessary for education to proceed; flexibility in grading, class organization, teaching methods and materials, school architecture, and furniture all essential to this educational philosophy.[53] Administrators needed to continually confer with teachers in order to reduce the dangers of the more insipid, mechanistic aspects of schooling.[54] Together, administrators and teachers were to engage in a dialogue addressing not only the means and methods of the educational process, but also the ideals and goals for which the entire organization was to strive.[55] The educational progressives envisioned school managers and school teachers forming an alliance of fellow professionals.

Viewing teachers as "the intellectual equals—indeed, the superiors—of many executives and supervisors," Jesse Newlon insisted that administrators share the responsibility for decision-making with the professional teaching staff:

> The question is not whether decisions, vital decisions, as to policy are to be followed after they are made but, first, whether all the professional workers in the schools, each according to his abilities, are to have a part in the making of these larger decisions; and second, whether decisions are to be subject to constant review by those members of the professional staff who are concerned with carrying them out.[56]

A school superintendent in Denver, Newlon rejected the idea that expert school managers ought to make all important decisions without the obligation of consulting with the teaching staff. This model, he proclaimed, "must be consigned to oblivion."[57]

Young's concept of school governance appeared on its face to be an alternative extreme in its ideas about power sharing. To secure the requisite freedom of thought in schools there needed to be "organizations for the consideration of questions of legislation." Young said that these organizations, which she called "school councils," would ban any "voice of authority." Both teachers and principals would be represented on these councils. John Dewey, a colleague of Young's at the University of Chicago, embraced her idea for co-determination of educational questions. Not only was this participation essential for the child oriented education he proposed, it was imperative in a democratic society:

> If there is a single public school system in the United States where there is official and constitutional provision made for submitting questions of methods, of discipline and teaching, and the questions of the curriculum, textbooks, and so forth, to the discussion and decision of those actually engaged in the work of teaching, that fact has escaped my notice. Indeed, the opposite situation is so common that it seems, as a rule, to be absolutely taken for granted as the normal and final condition of affairs . . . until the public school system is organized in such a way that every teacher has some regular and representative way in which he or she can register judgment upon matters of educational importance, with the assurance that this judgment will somehow affect the school system, the assertion that the present system is not, from the internal standpoint, democratic seems to be justified. . . . What does democracy mean save that the individual is to have a share in determining the conditions and the aims of his own work; and that upon the whole, through the free and mutual harmonizing of different individuals, the work of the world is better done than when planned, arranged, and directed by a few, no matter how wise or of how good intent that few? How can we justify our belief in the democratic principle elsewhere, and then go back entirely upon it when we come to education?[58]

Educational progressives felt that through school councils, curriculum would grow from the inside out rather than being given to teachers and children as a foregone conclusion. Jesse Newlon, a school principal at the time, wrote in 1916 that teachers working together for two or three years—investigating, debating, and finally adopting a set of curricula—would "teach better and with more understanding and sympathy than they could ever otherwise teach."[59] Newlon was steadfast in his advocacy of professional teachers participating in school governance. Writing nearly twenty years later, having experienced shared governance in the Denver school system, Newlon said:

> Unity of purpose will come from continuous group study of the problems of education, from staff meetings for which teachers share fully in mapping out the programs. Through their own associations, teachers will contribute to the formulation of policies.[60]

The progressives were committed to councils as the means by which schools could develop a philosophy of unity and a curriculum that would make theory and practice a seamless whole.[61] The result of these councils would be to make possible child-centered education as well as further the goal of using education as a force for democracy and social reconstruction. As Young described it, "the intellectual power, as well as the spontaneity of feeling," in every member of the organization would be joined in the commitment of the common ideal of educating youngsters.[62]

Conclusions: The Effects of Progressivism on Education

The educational progressive design for reform—child focused education emphasizing a "hands-on", interdisciplinary engagement of children—required a unique assignment of roles and responsibilities for school teachers and managers. In order for individualization of education to proceed, teachers needed to be free to create the appropriate program for their students. Managers were seen as supporting the critical interaction between teachers and children. Together, teachers and managers would join with parents and children to fashion goals for the school community that all participants could support. By working as partners and constantly reviewing their progress toward meeting those goals, the education provided children would continually improve.

The educational progressives were supported primarily by academicians who saw their program as being consistent with democratic values. Columbia and the University of Chicago set up laboratory schools to implement their ideas. A number of small private schools were established in accordance with progressive principles. A handful of public systems attempted to implement their ideas. Yet support among governmental officials and business leaders for this program of individualized schooling for youngsters from all strata of society was virtually nil. Given the prevailing values of the day, as well as the forces backing the pro-efficiency agenda, it is no surprise that the educational progressives' call for reform became, as historian Raymond Callahan put it, a "cry in the wilderness." As will be shown in chapter 6, it would take the passage of more than seventy years and radical changes in international markets before the proposal for organizing education in this nation developed by Dewey, Haley, Young, Parker, and Newlon would be taken seriously by those who had the power to try to force its implementation in the nation's schools.

During the first two decades of the twentieth century, those with the power to shape education reform threw their weight behind the pro-efficiency agenda.

They succeeded in transforming much of the legal framework governing public schools, and molding schools in accordance with their vision of good education. The state constitutions establishing governance structures for school systems gave schools their direction and permanence as institutions. State statutes and administrative law determined the content of curricula and the relations between those involved in the educational endeavor.[63] By 1925 the pro-efficiency reforms took root across the nation. Andrew Draper's ideal of coordination between the educational and industrial systems of the nation was realized with this widespread implementation of vocational education.[64] Efficiency in education, which had begun as a means of reconciling traditional values to the demands of a new society, was transformed into the purpose of education.[65] Schooling became utilitarian and, according to the Lynds, "instrumental to the day-by-day urgencies of living." For many children education became training in specific skills that they would later use in the factory, the office, or the home. It was no accident that vocational instructors were often more highly paid than teachers of academic subjects.[66]

The education delivered by the newly centralized school systems found favor with those who stood to gain from its implementation. Courses in civics stressed values that businessmen championed: respect for property, law, contracts, and private enterprise.[67] Employers got the brand of education they wanted; a brand of education where utility and morality were stressed. In the 1920s many parents too, favored a utilitarian education that would prepare their children for a place in what appeared to be an increasingly affluent American society.[68] The Anglo-Americans who worried about the assimilation of the many immigrants who came to the United States during the first decades of this century were relieved by civics courses that aimed at Americanizing the children from immigrant families—courses that stressed "discipline" and "self-control" over expression of feelings and ideas, group cooperation over individual gratification.[69] As the Lynds found in Middletown, the point of civics courses was to make sure every child saw him or herself not as an individual, but as part of the larger group.[70]

Most teachers coped as best they could in meeting the often conflicting demands of the school organization and the needs of individual children. Early teacher unions that sought to act as a countervailing force to centralized administrative control were quashed in the 1920s by employer resistance and adverse court rulings. Although individual teachers had little recourse when faced with mandates from school managers, some teachers tried to implement pieces of the educational progressives' agenda for education. Despite the organizational obstacles they faced, this minority of teachers created a classroom climate that encouraged student expression. Stanford professor Larry Cuban referred to this phenomenon as the development of "hybrids" of teaching practice—hybrids which grafted progressive pedagogy onto the mandated form and content of teaching. Confronting conflicting expectations from their supervisors and progressive pedagogical leaders, these teachers worked out their fundamental dilemma by creating hybrids adapted to the conditions they faced.[71]

The contradictions these teachers tried to reconcile mirrored larger ones in the culture at large. They had their roots in conflicting values that coexisted in society. As Cuban delineated them:

> Individual concerns versus collective needs of the group; the values surrounding play and leisure time in an achievement-based society that often looks first to the bottom line of the profit-loss statement; the tension between seeking efficiency, getting more bang out of each dollar, and creative self-development. These conflicting values have grown up side by side in our culture and exist uneasily in both public and private institutions.[72]

The hybrids teachers developed were awkward compromises aimed at handling these conflicting social values. Over the thirty years following the centralization of schools, some of these practices eventually were granted official sanction by school managers.

By the 1950s classrooms, particularly at the elementary level, were characterized by a somewhat more informal atmosphere than those typically found in 1920. Yet as John Dewey viewed these changes near the end of his life, he noted how little had truly changed from so many years earlier:

> The most widespread and marked success of the progressive movement has been in bringing about a significant change in the life conditions in the classroom. There is a greater awareness of the needs of the growing human being, and the personal relations between teachers and students have been humanized and democratized. But the success in these respects is as yet limited; it is largely atmospheric; it hasn't yet really penetrated and permeated the foundations of the educational institution. The older gross manifestations of the method, of education by fear and repression—physical, social, and intellectual—which was the established norm for the educational system before the progressive movement began have, generally speaking, been eliminated. . . . The fundamental authoritarianism of the old education persists in various forms.
>
> There is a great deal of talk about education being a cooperative enterprise in which the teachers and students participate democratically, but there is far more talk about it than the doing of it.[73]

The hardy resistance of the "fundamental authoritarianism" Dewey observed was dependent upon a stability of all the conditions he wrote about some fifty years earlier: the mechanics of school organization, the grouping of children in classes, the arrangement of grades, the machinery by which the course of study was made out and laid down, the method by which it was carried into effect, the system of selecting teachers and of assigning them to their work, of paying and promoting them. His conclusions of 1902 were equally applicable in 1952:

> We forget that it is precisely such things as these that control the whole system . . . the reality of education is found in the personal and face-to-face contact of teacher and child. The conditions that underlie and regulate this contact dominate the educational situation.[74]

The power of the school organization to determine the type of education offered youngsters is apparent by the resounding success of the pro-efficiency reforms. The goal of the reforms was "efficient" education of the masses, with a heavy stress on drill, routine, and an unquestioning obedience to orders given by a higher authority. Sorting youngsters into tracks that would lead them to future roles in the industrial work force became an institutionalized function of the schools. Although the educational progressives continued to protest against the idea of using the schools as a tool of social efficiency, their criticism had little effect on the classroom experience of the children and teachers of this country. As time would pass, disagreement about the goals of education would continue, but the organization set up to meet the goal of social efficiency would remain fundamentally unchanged.

Part Two

Challenges to the Pro-Efficiency
Model of Education
1961–1995

4

The 1960s and the Challenge to the Schools

> The power elites consisted, then, in setting the agenda for the schools, and the superintendent's professional freedom existed within those boundaries. . . . But what was often not noticed in the 1950's, with its urge for business-as-usual, was what was not on the agenda. This "other face of power" was becoming apparent, however, to the leaders of new protest movements, who were stymied in community after community when they tried to force local elites to face up to the inequities protestors sought to correct. To bring about real social change they would have to build new coalitions, use new methods, and reach to higher levels of government for leverage.[1]

The apparent calm of the 1950s belied the beginnings of protest movements mounted by African-Americans, advocates of the poor, teachers, and women; movements that would challenge the symbiotic relationship between businessmen, professionals, and school managers. These men, who served each others' interests, shared a common set of understandings and values. They created schools that reflected the inequalities in their communities and the nation. The challengers to the lay elite and school administrators questioned the type and quality of education offered to American youngsters, the power relations between school managers, teachers, and parents, and the bureaucratic school organization that had been created by members of the pro-efficiency reform movement some fifty years earlier. Groups that had been denied equal rights and dignity no longer regarded their status as fixed in the order of things as they mounted their challenge to the status quo.[2]

This chapter will focus on one of the many attempts to change the status quo in education during the 1960s. It will give an account of the challenge mounted by organized teachers in their effort to improve their working conditions and alter their role in the bureaucratic, centralized school organization. In the story of what has been called the "teachers' rebellion" lies the genesis of the teacher unionism that flourished in the sixties, the model of teacher professionalism proposed by these unions, and school boards' and managers' responses to this call for reform.

The Social Context

Just as at the turn of the century, the 1960s were marked by a sense of crisis for many Americans. The demand made by African-Americans for legal recognition of their right to participate fully in every aspect of life—most particularly in schooling and employment—questioned the nation's ability to make good on its democratic ideal of equality for all citizens. The urban riots of the mid-1960s demonstrated the explosive potential of a class of people systematically denied access to the best of what society had to offer. Society needed to respond in some way to the demand for equal rights put forth by Americans of color. The passage of the Civil Rights Act of 1964 and the judicially mandated racial integration of traditionally segregated public schools marked the beginning of lawmakers' and adjudicators' commitment to a policy of equal opportunity for the nation's minority populations.[3]

Many women in the sixties challenged the sexual stereotypes that served to shut them out of positions of power and authority, and reduced their earnings to only 55 percent of those of men.[4] The highly respected and compensated professions remained nearly all male bastions of power and authority into the 1960s.[5] 1964 marked a turning point in the history of working women. Title VII of the Civil Rights Act forbade discrimination in the hiring and promotion of personnel in large sectors of the economy—not only on the basis of color—but also on the basis of gender. The passage of that legislation encouraged women to aspire to occupations and professions from which they had been customarily barred. The attitudes that governed interpersonal relationships in our culture and sanctioned only a few working relationships between men and women were attacked by a growing feminist movement.

The 1960s brought a rebellion of many middle-class young people against a culture that prized business productivity, materialism, competition, efficiency, and conformity to rules and routines over other, competing values—for example, self-realization, free expression, and cooperation. A half-century of growing tolerance of and even admiration for large-scale, complex corporations and bureaucracies came to a halt as a large segment of American youth questioned many long-held attitudes and assumptions about the corporate culture. Business support of American military involvement in Vietnam fueled the fire of this youthful protest against what had been respected and valued for much of the century. As historian Louis Galambos put it, "In music, dress, and political action, young Americans fought a highly organized, impersonal system that seemed to control their future without regard for their feelings, goals or even their lives."[6]

On the political front, Americans felt threatened by a communist regime in the Soviet Union that had beaten the United States into space with the Sputnik mission in the fall of 1957. Four years later the Soviets were first to launch a human being into earth orbit. The Soviets' successful space program gave Americans reason to question their international supremacy in science and technology. The reaction to the apparent superiority of the Russian system was strong—and often resulted in Americans taking a critical look at the nation's schools.[7] In March 1958 *Life* magazine began a series of articles entitled "The Crisis in Education." The article warned, "The geniuses of the next decade are even now being allowed to slip back into mediocrity. . . . We must recapture an honest respect for learning and for learned people."[8] This mediocrity probably referred to the fact that academic subjects in the public high school curricula— mathematics, sciences, foreign languages—comprised only 20 percent of the course offerings. This represented a marked drop from the 1910 figure of 80 percent, which characterized high schools before the full implementation of the pro-efficiency reforms—reforms that stressed utilitarian and vocational education. Only 55 percent of high school students were enrolled in math classes, compared with the 1910 enrollment of 90 percent. A similar decrease in physical science enrollments existed. In place of the old academic subjects were some two hundred new subjects ranging from hairdressing to drivers' education.[9]

Andrew Draper's call for education of the masses in the manual arts had become a reality. The only difficulty appeared to be that the needs of business and the nation had changed. Had the United States lived in a world of static technology and international relations, Draper's concept of education would not have been called into question. The fact was, however, that despite the changing times, the schools remain fixed in a model of education developed nearly fifty years earlier to suit the needs of a newly industrialized society.

The *Life* article criticizing the nation's educational system was not an aberration, but an early sign of a new education reform movement. Analogous to the sense of crisis that marked the period around the turn of the century, many in society felt that the cure for the many problems facing society was a revamping of the nation's schools. Neither liberal reformers nor conservative critics had much praise for the educational establishment. Liberals condemned the schools for failing to develop the talent and potential of every child and for perpetuating the evils of racism, sexism, and class stratification.[10] Business disparaged the schools for failing to produce a crop of graduates that would make America the undisputed leader in the world. An article entitled "The Low Productivity of the Education Industry" appeared in *Fortune* nearly a year after Sputnik. The author wrote, "For the schools, no less than the automobile industry, have an inescapable production problem." The author argued that the schools were failing to "optimize the number of students and to minimize the input of man-hours and capital."[11]

In fact, business had already begun to criticize the schools before the launch of Sputnik. The president of the Los Angeles chapter of the chamber of commerce complained in a 1956 article in *U.S. News and World Report* that students "are getting fewer and fewer courses that train them to think clearly. . . . Our public education system has a responsibility to anticipate the needs for *its product*—trained students—in the quantities required and with the skills necessary . . . the job has not been well done"(emphasis added).[12] In many ways, the debate of so many years earlier was revived between those who saw education as a process of realizing individual human potential and those who viewed education as a mechanistic production function—an essential element in the nation's economic supremacy.

As in the earlier debate, both sides shared the conviction that education was key to securing a vision of a preferred future for the nation as it faced an uncertain and tumultuous present. It was within this context that the greatest challenge to the existing distribution of power within the schools was mounted by newly militant teachers seeking professional status and influence over the form and content of education.

A Picture of the State of Education in the Sixties

Ellwood Cubberley would have been pleased to see the system of education that existed in over 34,000 local districts across the nation in 1962.[13] Despite ostensible local control of education, school governance, the relations between the adults in the educational system, and the resulting education offered to children were remarkably similar across the nation.[14] School boards were filled with white Protestant business and professional men; men Cubberley believed would understand the principles of rational, efficient management. School board members in the 1960s were most often proprietors of stores, bank officials, professionals, or managers. Only 8 percent of board members were workingmen. In keeping with Cubberley's vision, boards rarely had more than one woman member.[15] Again, in accordance with Cubberley's design, board members served without any monetary compensation. They were generally elected by between five and ten percent of the eligible voters in a community, suggesting that rather than being representatives of a majority or a consensus of the community they were, in fact, independent centers of power.

School board members had difficulty finding the time to deal with complex issues—for example, equal educational opportunity, local real estate taxes, bond issues. These issues required so many hours of study to address fully that unpaid, part-time board members most often chose to take the advice of their hired executive officer, the school superintendent.[16] David Tyack and Elisabeth Hansot concluded in their study of school leaders of this period that "There is little evidence that busy school board members had the time or inclination to try to influence the everyday decisions required in running a school system." Claiming impartial expertise, and controlling the flow of information to school board members, a superintendent often had little trouble winning approval of his policies and practices.[17] Occasionally boards rubber-stamped the recommendations of a superintendent under his threats of resignation should his policies not be approved.

Superintendents, for their part, often saw school boards as interference to overcome rather than the legally empowered school policymakers whose lead he was to follow. Yet the superintendent needed to be careful to avoid clashes with the powerful forces in the community.[18] He had to respect what one scholar of school governance referred to as "the zone of consent" within which he could act with impunity.[19] This prevented him from recommending any changes in the school program or organization's operation that would meet with strong resistance from a community's power elite.[20]

Because the managerial bureaucracy was empowered to run all facets of the school organization, who school boards chose to fill management positions had important implications for how schools would operate. The choice of the superintendent was perhaps a board's most significant decision. In that decision the typically male, white, Protestant, Republican business and professional men selected male candidates to fill the superintendent's slot, just as boards had earlier in the century. In 1922 more than 99 percent of superintendents were male. That proportion endured more than fifty years later.[21] Being male was not an advantage only for candidates for the superintendency. The ratio of male to females staffing all the layers of the managerial bureaucracy continued to increase following the pro-efficiency reforms.[22]

Perpetuating gender discrimination in hiring was only one way boards reinforced the status quo. A study done by James Coleman in the 1960s on the educational opportunities afforded poor and minority youngsters found that lay citizens serving on school boards had three interests that together led in the direction of a system of differentiated education for children from different backgrounds. School board members sought: 1) an excellent education for their own children, 2) to keep property taxes low, and 3) to preserve the existing social order. Coleman found a "greater educational effort expended on children from better backgrounds." This preferential treatment came about by "close linkages of the school administrators and staff with the structure of power in the community," which "helped create greater opportunity for children from 'better' families." Academic and vocational tracks tended to segregate social groups in larger schools. Despite the possibility of advancement for especially talented youngsters, schools tended to perpetuate the inequalities found in society. Coleman found that the children of the poor and depressed minority groups tended to fall further behind in academic achievement in each successive year of schooling. The most striking example of this was found in the racially segregated schools of the south. White, middle-class psychologists and educators pointed to the children's "cultural deficit" as the cause of their poor performance in school, rather than a failure of the educational system to meet the needs of children who lived in poverty.[23]

In accordance with the school governance laws designed by the pro-efficiency reformers in the early part of the century, "the people" controlled education through their elected representatives in the legislature and on the local school board, and funded education through their state and local taxes. The alignment of this legal theory with the reality of who controlled schools was meager at best. Day to day control of public education, in fact, was in the hands of the members of the professional school management. While in smaller and rural districts the local elite could exert influence on management's decisions, this was not true in larger, urban districts. Political scientist Marilyn Gittell found that the power of the bureaucratic school management was directly proportional to the size of the school district, with urban districts being totally controlled by the professional, tenured managers occupying positions in the school hierarchy. Gittell wrote in 1967, "Large city school systems have taken on the shape of massive corporate enterprises, increasingly distant from the public." She concluded that the school organization was a "closed system" dominated by the bureaucratic elite; a system that shut out the public, parents, and teachers. It was a system, she declared, that was able to withstand efforts by those outside the bureaucracy to change the status quo.[24]

While school superintendents had to work within the limits set for them by the powerful members of the community, they attempted to minimize pressures emanating from *within* the schools by designing rules and regulations by which their school organizations were to function.[25] Control was the guiding principle and to gain that control superintendents tended to think in terms of models presented by both the military and the corporation—that is, the central office had to have authority over every decision in the organization.[26] They were encouraged to use these models by their graduate training, the business sector, and by school board members who themselves were often businessmen. They also received support for using an industrial model of management from academicians who promoted the idea that universal management principles could be applied in the business setting and the school situation alike.[27] The key to running a tight ship was to have teachers obey the mandates generated by the school management, just as William Bagley had suggested in 1907. That requirement for obedience from teachers existed and remained unchallenged until the 1960s.

The nature of the teaching profession itself remained remarkably unchanged in the forty years following the effectuation of the pro-efficiency reforms. Teaching continued to be a feminized occupation in the decade of the sixties, with 68.6 percent of teachers being female (1961). Teachers continued to attain a far higher level of education than did the average citizen. By the end of the decade a large minority of teachers held graduate degrees.[28] Study after study found that despite the increased educational attainment of teachers—often associated with professional status in other occupations—the bureaucratic organization established by the pro-efficiency reformers provided no position of influence for teachers in the power structure of the school. They were shut out of educational policymaking, which occurred within the confines of the managerial bureaucracy.[29] Despite the fact that most teachers felt they were professionals who ought to have ultimate authority over major educational decisions, much as Margaret Haley had argued in 1904, their discretion was limited to their presentation of mandated materials and their relationship with their students.[30]

Identical to the situation at the turn of the century, teachers had no say over their terms and conditions of employment. School managers unilaterally decided how much teachers earned, where and what they taught, how long their day was, and how heavy a workload they carried. A former superintendent for Philadelphia schools wrote in the 1960s that school employers had a sense of proprietorship over the conditions of employment for teachers.[31] In many districts teachers were compelled to punch time clocks, monitor lunchrooms, and spend considerable time on paperwork required by their supervisors.[32] The beginning salary for teachers in 1965 was $4,928, compared to an average beginning salary for new college graduates of $6,792. The maximum teacher's salary in New York City in that same year was $11,950, while the school superintendent in New York earned $40,000. A 1965 study found that 29 percent of teachers needed a second job to make ends meet. Many people entered teaching for a while, but did not stay on to make it a lifetime career. In fact, only 20 percent of beginning teachers remained on the job after five years.[33]

Teachers who stayed on in highly bureaucratized schools had to deal with conflict between their self-perception as professionals and the requirements of working in a rule-driven hierarchical organization. The professional desire to stress loyalty to clients' needs and interests frequently clashed with the requirement to be an obedient employee, committed to following orders devised by supervisors in the school hierarchy.[34] Wharton School of Business professor George Taylor wrote that the "traditional wisdom" allowed that "teachers should follow instruction from above in their teaching even though their professional calling requires a high degree of intelligence and a questioning mind."[35] As we have seen, this conflict was rarely if ever discussed by pro-efficiency reformers so many years earlier because of their strong belief that the superior judgment of the school management would result in decisions beneficial to all concerned. Cubberley was certain that independent teacher judgment was often misguided, if well intentioned, and thus proposed that it be limited to only the most minor details of the school operation.[36] In short, the role conflict experienced by teachers in the 1960s was never recognized by the early twentieth-century pro-efficiency reformers because the professional element of teachers' work was systematically denied by their prescription for reform.

The result of this role conflict was that teachers often had to make a choice in regard to whom to serve—their students or their supervisors. Teacher union leader Albert Shanker rhetorically asked the following questions in a 1967 article:

> If a teacher stood up at a faculty meeting and refused to carry out a proposal of the administration that his professional knowledge and experience showed to be in error, would this display of professional integrity be approved? Would he be rewarded or would he then find it advisable to seek another position?[37]

A 1965 study of over 800 teachers in Oregon found that teachers' great fear of sanctions from within their school organizations made most teachers refrain from doing what Shanker proposed—namely, challenge administrative directives. Teachers not only failed to challenge direct orders they felt to be educationally misguided, they censored themselves in their classroom presentation of material in order to steer clear of administrative wrath. While many critics of the schools felt teachers avoided controversy because of fear of groups such as the John Birch Society, the author of the study, political scientist Harmon Zeigler, concluded that, "teachers are more threatened by the conservatism of the educational establishment than by the conservatism of the community." The zone of consent school managers worked within was a narrow one on issues that challenged the status quo in politics or the economy. Superintendents and other school managers who had to interface with the community made it known to faculty that the successful teacher was a cautious teacher who did not provoke debate, upset routines, or make trouble.[38]

Besides limiting discussion to noncontroversial topics, how did teachers in the sixties run their classrooms? The regimentation of tasks in accordance with the principles of scientific management existed, but not to the degree hoped for by Franklin Bobbitt.[39] Although the "human relations" movement in management provided teachers with occasional proforma consultations with school managers, decisions about teaching materials, methods, class placement, course offerings, and purchasing remained with administrators who worked above teachers in the school hierarchy. The goal of securing uniformity in both means and ends throughout every classroom and school within a district remained. While some teachers attempted to individualize the means by which children learned, they were held accountable for outcomes determined by school managers far removed from children and classrooms.[40] This, coupled with ever-growing class sizes due to the postwar baby boom and mandated use of prescribed texts made individualizing education a near impossibility for teachers.[41] Larry Cuban studied teaching methods from the early part of the century to the 1960s and found a remarkable continuity. He quoted Gloria Channon, a teacher in a New York City school, in her description of the kind of education offered elementary school age children in the sixties:

> Children sit at their desks for hours. Notebooks and textbooks become the main focus of their activity. Lessons are formally organized into spelling, penmanship, reading, composition, and math. Silence and good behavior are at a premium.[42]

The regulations imposed on teachers and children by the central office of the school administration help to explain the perpetuation of a classroom atmosphere and "organizational climate" established so many years earlier. The following rules were distributed to teachers in the *Staff Bulletin* published in 1968 by 110 Livingston Street, the headquarters of the New York City school bureaucracy:

- During recitation lessons, pupils should raise hands to indicate desire to make a contribution, they should be encouraged to speak in full sentences.

- Pupils must ask permission to go to the bathroom.

- Gum chewing is forbidden anywhere in the school building. The teacher MUST set the example.

- Pupils should empty their desks regularly under the routine supervision of the teacher and everything other than approved books and materials should be discarded on the spot or taken home at 3:00.[43]

It is doubtless that William Bagley, a proponent of routinizing even the most mundane procedure in schools, would have endorsed these regulations. Such rules were indicative of the robustness of the model of school management that emphasized control, uniformity, and standardization of operating procedure. Regulations such as this, combined with the continuation of departmentalization of instruction, tracking by ability as measured by standardized tests, single age grouping, and textbook-driven instruction established so many years earlier, insured constancy in the kind of education children were offered up to the 1960s. Little of substance changed in the daily life of the teacher or student in the American classroom from 1920 to 1960. To quote Philip Jackson, a critic of American schools, educational change "could be more easily traced by a butterfly than by a bullet."[44]

Teachers Challenge the Status Quo

Teachers do not want the power to be heard and then turned down; they have long been listened to and consulted. But no matter how hard teachers have argued and demonstrated and reasoned, there has always been a point at which the principal could say, "No." If they appealed to the superintendent and the school board, the power to affirm or reject has again been in the administration. Now teachers are demanding for themselves the equivalent power of saying, "No." This power intends to ensure decision-making in consort, by working things out together. The adjustment this requires of administrators is not easily made.[45]

On April 12, 1962, half of the New York City teaching force struck the public school system, picketing schools across the city while some five thousand teachers rallied at city hall. The strike had national significance. In the words of Marjorie Murphy, historian of teacher unions, "Hundreds of thousands of other teachers and public employees in other parts of the country looked to the New York strike as an important precedent." Charles Cogan, leader of the strike, called April 12th a "turning point" in the history of education in New York. By the mid-1960s a National Education Association (NEA) official observed that public school teachers worked in "a state of ferment bordering on rebellion." The sixties represented a departure from docility and conformity for teachers as they attempted to implement revolutionary changes in their role and their responsibilities in the educational endeavor.[46]

With the exception of teacher strikes for higher pay during the years immediately following World War II, concerted activity on the part of classroom teachers was virtually nil from the post–World War I era to the 1960s. The teacher militancy of the sixties was motivated by grievances that were rooted in the pro-efficiency reforms instituted in the early part of the century.[47] From a historical perspective it appeared that teachers once again had taken up the battle for teachers' professional rights led so many years before by early teacher unionists Margaret Haley and John Dewey.

Teacher Grievances

The grievances listed by the New York teachers in 1962 were representative of teachers' grievances in school districts across the nation. Most of the grievances arose from the ability of the centralized, bureaucratic administration to wield power with impunity. Rebellion against the centralization of power in the hands of school management characterized both the early union movement and the revived movement of the sixties.[48] The ability of a principal or supervisor to punish an outspoken teacher by assigning that teacher a difficult class or burdensome schedule was an often heard complaint of teachers in the sixties. According to Albert Shanker, leader of the New York City teachers' union, United Federation of Teachers (UFT), objective measures for assignment and promotion were needed to counteract the abuse of power by school managers.

> At the present time, in the majority of cases there is a system composed of politics, patronage, and petty types of terror. Most teachers feel that if they are outspoken in a faculty conference, they will be much more likely to be assigned to a difficult class the next year.[49]

For their part, school managers defended their prerogatives in assigning teachers, claiming they were most competent to make appropriate assignments. Teachers questioned this assertion of expertise in the sixties, citing a lack of hard evidence that could prove the superiority of managerial discretion over an objective method of assigning teachers to classes or schools, for example, seniority.[50]

Teachers also complained of poor working conditions that did not square with their concept of professionalism. Shanker said, "A trained teacher should not be required to patrol cafeterias or to place children on buses." The right to a duty free lunch period became part of a campaign known as "the right to eat." Growing class sizes due to the baby boom added to the workload of teachers significantly. Margaret Haley had cited smaller class size as an example of the identity of teachers' and children's interests. Teachers in the sixties picked up the argument, making the case that teacher welfare was inextricably tied to the welfare of students. "Teachers want what children need" became a rallying call.

Teachers also rejected the belief that in order to be dedicated to the students' welfare they had to ignore their own. The desire to upgrade their salaries to a level commensurate with their education was part of an effort to permanently bury the idea that teachers were self-sacrificing missionaries content to work for any wage and under any condition thought appropriate by school boards and managers.[51]

New York City teachers brought 150 grievances to the attention of the public during their 1962 strike. As militancy spread to other cities, many teachers told their own stories of arbitrary, biased, insensitive, or abusive treatment on the part of school managers—the "sanctions" political scientist Zeigler found that teachers feared.[52] Teachers across the country pointed to centralized, bureaucratic authority as the cause of many of the problems they perceived in education. Teachers argued they were unjustifiably shut out of decision-making on issues central to their work.[53] A team of sociologists studying teachers in the early 1970s concluded that "decisional deprivation" was strongly linked to the rise in teacher militancy—that is, participation in fewer decisions than desired on hiring, selection of teaching materials and methods, resource allocation, faculty assignments, establishing discipline policies, and resolving learning problems of individual students.[54] Disillusioned with proforma consultation procedures by which teachers' recommendations were often ignored, teachers decided that meaningful participation in decision-making could happen only if they united and used their collective strength to create a force that school management could not ignore.[55]

Why the Sixties?

A confluence of factors led to this rebellion by teachers against a system of authority to which they had acquiesced for more than forty years. A teacher shortage gave teachers a greater sense of security as they mounted their challenge to school boards and managers. Due to the National Defense Education Act passed after the launch of Sputnik, there was considerably more federal money available to schools for improvements in teachers' salaries. Both the civil rights movement and the dawning feminist movement offered models to teachers who sought a reallocation of power and resources within the educational system. Within the ranks of teachers arose capable and charismatic union leaders who introduced teachers to the prospect of changing the relationship between teachers and school managers, and organized them into a force to be reckoned with.[56]

Some contemporary analysts offered another explanation of the rise in teachers' militancy. Borrowing from economist John Kenneth Galbraith's theory of countervailing power in economics—those subject to a monopoly's power try eventually to equalize that power—they asserted that teachers were uniting in order to create a countervailing power to school managers. Managers had used their monopoly of power to prevent an equivalent power relationship and mutual power accommodation between themselves and school teachers since the early 1900s. The teachers' militancy, they proposed, was an effort to end that monopoly and equalize power. Once power was redistributed, teachers would have a significant voice in all major educational decisions within their legitimate concern.[57]

All the above conditions contributed to the teachers' stirrings for change. Yet their revolt against the status quo would not have taken shape as it did had the nation not perceived a challenge to its well-being coming from both international enemies and internal dissenters. The threats to the nation's preeminence and stability led Americans to turn once again to education as a weapon in its arsenal against those threats. Questions arose about the efficacy of long-held practices in education—both pedagogical and organizational. Proposals for "open education" and alternative schools made by those who subscribed to Dewey's brand of pedagogy were taken seriously by a surprising number of Americans. Many constituencies questioned the form of school governance set up by the pro-efficiency reforms, as well. Proposals for community control of schools, state control of the schools, and metropolitan school districts were but three of the many alternatives suggested and given consideration.[58]

As in the first part of this century, education was seen as an instrument for providing stability and perpetuating the social order. Among leaders in business and government, its major purpose continued to be providing industry with employees who were appropriately skilled. The major difference between the sixties and the first part of the century, however, was how "appropriate" was defined. Business and government now wanted the system to produce more highly skilled workers, particularly technicians and engineers who could put America indisputably ahead of the Soviet Union. In terms of Charles Eliot's vision of a four caste society, the question of the day was how to fill the "narrow upper layer" of inventors and managers, and the second layer of skilled technicians with graduates who could meet and surpass the Soviets.

The perceived crisis in education and the call for improved teacher performance resulting in better student outcomes provided teachers with an opening for the airing of their own complaints about the system, as well as their recommendations for change. Since bureaucratic management had apparently led to such poor results, teachers asserted, there was reason to believe that teacher empowerment could result in better educational outcomes for children.[59] Teachers declared that if they were to be held responsible for better student performance, they ought to be given the power to make decisions about the form and content of the educational program. Teacher leader Albert Shanker put it this way:

> When children leave school, not reading and not writing and not counting and not getting jobs, more and more local groups are turning on the teachers in the schools and on the supervisors and on the training institutions—the universities who turn out these teachers—and saying it's your fault. And the more that pressure comes—(and I might say it's not unhealthy; I think parents whose children are leaving schools and not making it have a perfect right to come forward and say what's the matter and who's doing something wrong and why isn't something different being done)—the more the responsibility is placed with us and the blame is placed with us the more we have to demand the right to make decisions which can change the failure for which we are being blamed.[60]

Shanker declared that the flip side of accountability for educational outcomes was the authority to share in the governance of schools. Improvement in the system would not occur, he asserted, without it.[61]

The Goal: Professionalization of Teaching

From the time of the pro-efficiency reforms until the 1960s, school boards and managers called teachers "professionals" in order to keep them cooperative, servile, and antiunion. According to Marjorie Murphy, "The ideology of professionalism in education grew into a powerful anti-union slogan that effectively paralyzed and then slowed the unionization of teachers."[62] As Albert Shanker wrote in 1967 in regard to the word "professionalism":

The word itself is becoming more and more a dirty word for teachers. It is a word that the administrator uses to criticize anything to which he objects. He says, "You are not being professional." He implies, "Be good; be obedient; do not rock the boat." The concept of professionalism that is practiced in most of our school systems is more appropriate to a military establishment. George Orwell has shown that the meaning of a word can be turned into its opposite. That is what has been done to "professionalism."[63]

According to Shanker and other teacher leaders of the sixties, professionalism implied a system in which people with expertise were free to exercise decision-making power in that area of special competence. 1960s advocates of professionalism in teaching often used the example of medicine—at that time the best example of professional autonomy in the design and execution of professional work.[64] Before the rise of health maintenance organizations and the cost-cutting revolution in medicine, the medical model was the paragon of expert independence:

The physician has an interest in professional autonomy, in his medical supplies and equipment, in the quality of nursing and other supporting activities, and in his overall conditions of professional practice. It is erroneous to think that non-professionals are uninterested in such matters, but there is a widespread acceptance of the professional's legitimate involvement in them.[65]

The philosophy of professionalism made it clear that practitioners had a deep and abiding interest in, as well as legitimate authority over, all matters that bore upon the standards of their practice. Given the fact that they worked in a publicly funded enterprise, teachers translated that philosophy to mean that they ought to share decision-making with school boards and managers on everything from pupil-teacher ratio to the addition of a school librarian. Any condition that affected their ability to render professional service to children was within the purview of what they perceived to be a legitimate professional concern.[66]

It was clear to teachers that other professions had gained the power and authority to control their occupational practice by practitioners uniting together in associations. As Myron Lieberman wrote in his 1956 book on the professionalization of teaching, established professions demonstrated that "occupational groups don't achieve professional status until the members of the groups concerned participate *en masse* in the movement to achieve professional status."[67] In order for teachers to share power with school boards and school managers, they too would have to organize and make their case for a realignment of power relationships within the schools.

The American Federation of Teachers (AFT), established nearly fifty years earlier, rose from years of quietude to demand professional working conditions for teachers. The National Education Association (NEA), long a bastion for administrators of the pro-efficiency bent, shed its administrator domination in the sixties. It became an association comprised solely of teachers working—often in competition with the AFT—to upgrade teachers' status within the schools.[68]

The AFT was first to level a scathing attack on the efficacy of the existing bureaucratic system of running schools. The NEA, comprised of both teachers and school managers until the late sixties, put forth a more muted critique of the bureaucratic form of school organization.[69] The AFT, however, was joined in its assault of the status quo by some scholars of effective organizational practices, political scientists, and writers sympathetic to its crusade. The pro-efficiency reformers' concept of the expert neutral school manager was attacked as fallacious. Superintendents, they argued, were subject to powerful pressures from multiple interests, and intent on pursuing their own career goals and self-interests—that is, hardly the captains of education depicted by pro-efficiency reformers like Ellwood Cubberley.[70] The pro-efficiency assumption that the superintendent and those below him in the bureaucracy would make wiser decisions than the lay populace or teachers was clearly erroneous, they pointed out, given the state of education in the 1960s.

The ethic of blind obedience to bureaucratic authority was cited by AFT leaders and teacher supporters as the most troublesome aspect of the hierarchical form of organization because it prevented teachers from using their judgment to meet the needs of their students. As George Taylor wrote:

> There is a need for change in a system which, to a marked degree, measures teacher performance in terms of obedience, respect for authority, and adherence to bureaucratic rules and regulations as much or more than in terms of intellectual achievement and a desire to experiment.[71]

The reality that teachers were systematically shut out of decision-making was often cited as the fatal flaw in the system, and one that teacher professionalization would remedy.

The fact that teachers were typically female and managers tended to be male added another dimension to the fight for professional self-determination among teachers. Studies of occupations that failed to attain professional status despite the advanced education and expertise of their practitioners found that gender was one important determinant of this "semiprofessional" status. Sociologist Amitai Etzioni found occupations that were predominantly female—teaching, nursing, social work—were generally denied professional autonomy.[72] While Myron Lieberman cited the predominance of women as a deterrent to professionalization of teaching in 1956, the feminist movement of the sixties, as well as the Civil Rights Act of 1964, made questionable the assumption that gender would be a deterrent to professionalization in the 1960s.[73]

Teachers and their advocates offered an alternative model to the bureaucratic relationship between school managers and teachers that characterized the status quo. Managers would be transformed from controllers and directors of the school organization to supporters of the professional services delivered by teachers. Again, the medical model was used to show how dual lines of authority—administrative and professional—might work in education. On the one hand, school managers might maintain the right to make certain administrative decisions—for instance, scheduling, transportation, ordering from vendors. Decisions on instructional and professional issues, however, would be made by teachers. An advocate wrote:

> Teachers are now demanding "revolutionary" things—the right to decide for themselves how students should be grouped for instruction; the right to decide how to work most effectively with colleagues (in teams, self-contained, etc.); the right to be represented, not by one member but by a majority of members at local school district committees in charge of developing courses of study; the right to evaluate colleagues and to determine which of their colleagues gain tenure; the right to select department chairmen and supervisors; the right to accredit and approve courses of study for colleges and universities that prepare teachers.[74]

In 1968 president of the NEA, Elizabeth Koontz, expressed the idea that nothing short of legal recognition of teachers' right to professional self-governance would do if teaching was to become a profession.[75]

Implicit in this call for greater decision-making power was the assumption that teachers had the expertise to make better decisions than either school boards or school managers. Teachers could offer little evidence to support this belief, since they had never been allowed to exercise their presumed expertise. Instead of empirical evidence they relied on the theoretical argument that, as professionals trained and experienced in the specifics of the learning process, they could more knowledgeably make those decisions that most directly affected the classroom.[76] Picking up on the argument made by Jesse Newlon so many years before, teachers believed that they—better than any other group— could make informed decisions that would prove beneficial to their students.[77] The public was asked to support the position taken by Albert Shanker that the "increase in teacher power will mean that teachers are going to be deeply involved in solving some of the major school problems."[78] What was to be taken on faith was the assumption that education would improve because of it.

Despite the lack of confirming evidence to support their position, teachers and their organizations took its veracity as a given. The only problem they saw was how to make the realignment of power relations between school boards, managers, and teachers a reality. Advocates of professionalization of teaching stated without apology that teachers would have to become militant in order to force a change in power relations. As Myron Lieberman explained, "power is not usually *given* to a group. It is *taken* by it. More precisely, the public does not actively give power to a group; rather, it acquiesces to a taking of power by the group."[79] The idea of a militant teaching force was contrary to society's stereotype of the mild-mannered, self-abnegating teacher. In order to change the public image of teachers and win public approval for their grab for power, teachers tried hard to make the point that an empowered teaching force was in the public interest—not only because education would improve as a result— but because of the example professional teachers could set for their students. Advocates of teacher empowerment picked up on an argument made by George Counts in the 1930s. Students learned more about the social order by observing their teachers' subservience to authority than they did from civics texts. Albert Shanker carried the argument forward by asserting that the teachers' effort to professionalize their occupation, to win power within the school organization, and to obtain working conditions that enabled them to do their best work with children, would teach children a lesson more important than specific facts or skills:

> When the children have left the teachers and schools behind them, they will remember more what the teacher has taught by his actions than what words have come out of his mouth. I think that the ultimate goal toward which teachers must direct their new power is to have children come out of their schools having learned that their teachers are men and women of knowledge who are not afraid, who have a personal dignity, and who deserve their respect. They may not remember the derivation of Pythagorean theorems and the names of the capitals of all the states, but the chances are that they will remember whether they had a teacher that stood on his feet or that crawled on his knees.[80]

Thirty years later, when teacher unions are generally viewed solely as advocates for their members' narrow economic interests, it is important to note that at the time of their rebellion, central to their agenda was an effort to win for teachers a place at the educational decision-making table; professionals sitting as equals with school managers and board members.

NEA and AFT: Two Approaches to Professionalizing Teaching

The NEA and the AFT proposed different means of realizing the goal of teacher empowerment. Until the mid-1960s, the NEA fancied itself an independent professional association in league with the American Bar Association and the American Medical Association. While it supported professional status for teachers, it rejected any assumptions or tactics that smacked of unionism in its efforts to upgrade teaching to a profession.[81] The AFT, on the other hand, made no bones about being a labor union long affiliated with the AFL-CIO. In the 1960s the NEA proposed that teachers and school boards engage in "professional negotiations" through which teachers could co-determine educational policy decisions. It was a model that stressed the unity of all professionals involved in education.[82] The AFT decided to rely on collective bargaining, legally sanctioned for the private sector since the 1930s, as the means by which teachers could substantively change the role and responsibilities of teachers in the school organization.[83]

As one critic of the NEA pointed out in the 1930s, if teachers had been included in the National Labor Relations Act, the NEA would have been in serious trouble as a company union.[84] The NEA had always had public school teachers as members, yet the leadership of the association had often been in the hands of teachers' employers—school managers. When teachers became vocal about their grievances in the sixties, the school managers within the NEA were originally supportive of the concept of letting teachers participate in decision-making. In 1963 the American Association of School Administrators (AASA), an administrative division of the NEA, supported professional negotiations on matters as diverse as curriculum, salaries, and recruitment of teachers.[85] The managerial group proposed that the superintendent of schools be a neutral third party in negotiations between the board and the teachers. "He should review each proposal in light of its effect upon students and work closely with both the board and the staff representatives in an attempt to reach agreement in the best interests of the educational program."[86]

The NEA attempted to walk a tight rope, balancing the vested interests of their members from school management and the demands for change coming from their teacher members. The NEA leadership accepted the AASAs proposed role for the superintendent—that is, the neutral advocate of what was best for education, hoping to satisfy both constituencies.[87] Key to the early concept of professional negotiations as understood by the administrative quarter of the NEA, however, was the idea that school managers' power would not be diminished. They saw themselves as managers for the school board and instructional leaders to the staff.[88] They expected to remain as such. The NEA's dual support for both managers and teachers was to become its critical weakness as the decade of the sixties progressed.

The NEA saw collective bargaining as an ideological construct that was inconsistent with teachers' demand for increased professionalism. Marjorie Murphy writes, "it was anathema to the association to engage in collective bargaining because the term itself was embedded in unionism."[89] The application of labor laws and precedents to education was rejected absolutely by the NEA. In regard to the scope of negotiations, the NEA again differed from the industrial model of collective bargaining by apparently eschewing the doctrine of managerial prerogatives so central to the determination of those issues that an employer would have to engage in bargaining:

> The broad scope of negotiations which are contemplated under professional negotiation procedures bears no relationship to the industrial relations delineation between management prerogatives and negotiable matters. The philosophy inherent in professional negotiation is that teachers, in common with other professional practitioners, have a deep and transcendent interest in all matters which may bear upon the standards of their practice. Any other position [is] in direct conflict with the spirit and purpose of the process.[90]

In keeping with its rejection of the industrial model, NEA repudiated the use of strikes in conjunction with negotiations. If negotiations were to be discussions between professionals and equals, "moving together toward some goal not predetermined," there would be no place for coercive tactics in the process.[91] Professional negotiations were not to be an adversarial process— but rather "a partnership . . . in which the classroom teacher, the administrator, and the board— join together in an effort to improve the teaching climate in the community."[92]

The AFT presented a challenge to the preeminence of the NEA as the organization representing teachers in the 1960s. Although the NEA membership greatly outstripped that of the AFT in 1961, the AFT put itself in the forefront of the battle for teacher empowerment. It aggressively sought to represent teachers at the bargaining table and capitalized on the adversarial elements in the relationship between school teachers and their supervisors by excluding school managers from membership.[93] The AFT sought to use the industrial model of collective bargaining, replete with the right to strike, but enhancing it by broadening the scope of negotiations to include issues that went to the core of educational policymaking. According to Charles Cogen, president of the AFT, the difference between the NEA and the AFT was clear. "The NEA approach is a grudging attempt to adapt to a new idea without disturbing the status quo. The AFT is frankly seeking to establish a new status for teachers by means of a bargaining process."[94] The strategy proved attractive to teachers. By 1965 the AFT membership was more than three times that of the NEA.

The AFT operated with certain basic premises. Collective bargaining would establish a democratic relationship between school managers and teachers. At the heart of the process was the recognition that teacher organizations had the right to negotiate with school boards not only on salary and benefits, but on professional matters as well. With the coming of collective bargaining, unilateral decisions on such issues as class size, teaching load, transfers, and building safety would come to an end.[95] AFT leader, David Selden, responded when asked to draw the line between what was negotiable and what was not in this manner: "There is no line. Anything the two parties can agree on is negotiable." Demands that teachers be allowed to elect their own principals, decide curriculum, select texts, determine the school calendar, and recruit, assign and discipline their colleagues were all part of the AFT agenda in the early 1960s.[96]

Although the NEA and the AFT disagreed on how to reach the goal of teacher professionalization, they did agree on the need for collective action to improve the status and power of teachers in the education endeavor. Both associations' agendas were in agreement with Myron Lieberman's assertion:

> A group which is too weak to protect its immediate welfare interests will usually be too weak to protect the public interest as well. Teachers need power to protect academic freedom, to eradicate racial segregation in education, to secure more and better instructional materials, and to do many other things that have little or no relationship to teacher welfare. If teachers are weak, they cannot protect the public interest in education. This is why the weakness of teachers as an organized group is one of the most important problems in American education today.[97]

Once organized, the argument went, teachers could become a pressure group for change and improvement within the educational system. Both the NEA and the AFT agreed on the need to lobby state legislatures to carve out and legitimize a new role for teachers in education.[98]

At the time it was uncertain whether the NEAs and the AFTs efforts, either alone or combined, would lead to the attainment of professionalism in teaching. Certainly, upgrading teaching to a profession would require serious adjustments in the balance of power among school teachers, their managers, and school boards. Teachers were attempting to enter into what had long been regarded the realm of management. Whether school boards and administrators would move aside voluntarily—or could be pushed aside forcibly by militant teachers—was unknown. Sociologist Etzioni predicted in the sixties that teachers would never be granted professional status.[99] The events of the decade indicated that things would likely change for school teachers and school managers, but in ways that were hard to predict at the time.[100]

Schools Follow the Business Model Once Again

In many ways the NEA model of professional negotiations was an ideal of co-determination by equals, similar to the type of school governance proposed in 1900 by Ella Flagg Young. Yet the model did not take into account the inertia represented by the hierarchical, bureaucratic organizational structures found in education. It ignored the realities of the status quo in terms of power distribution among groups both within the schools and in society. It underestimated the tenacity with which those who were empowered by the status quo—school managers and boards—would cling to their prerogatives. While NEA members from school management initially endorsed a broad scope of negotiations, they did so with the understanding that decisions would ultimately rest with the board and its hired managers—that is, negotiations would, in effect, grant teachers the right to be consulted. The following is a statement from the AASA in 1963:

> We believe that the right to discuss pros and cons and to participate in developing a program does not imply the right to make decisions. Although consensus should always be patiently sought and will often prevail between staff and the school board, the board must retain its responsibility and legal right to make decisions.[101]

School managers originally supported teacher involvement in decision-making in the hope that it would lead to greater organizational efficiency. Yet once it was clear that teachers wanted genuine power sharing—and that they did not share their supervisors' publicly stated vision of the school organization as "family"— school managers opposed teachers' efforts with vehemence.[102] The fact that the demand for equal power was coming from a group that was predominately female made teachers' concerted activity all the more vexing for male managers who had often seen themselves as paternalistic protectors of the weaker sex.[103]

Eventually the NEA was forced to recognize the inherent contradictions in its support of both school managers and school teachers by the remarkable success of the AFT after 1961. The NEA model, which eschewed the strike threat as too "blue-collar," lacked sufficient power to overcome the resistance of management to teachers' demands for a genuine change in their status. The AFT, on the other hand, made significant gains through a series of strikes that crippled school districts in cities all across the nation. It was becoming clear that the AFT strategy represented a better fit to school systems than the NEA had initially been willing to acknowledge. As the sixties proceeded, the NEA backed away from its original approach to gaining professional status for teachers and adopted one nearly indistinguishable from that of the AFT—including the exclusion of school managers from membership.[104]

Both the NEA and the AFT had two immediate goals—improved teacher welfare and increased teacher decision-making power. They hoped attainment of both would lead to the ultimate goal of teacher professionalization.[105] Because the teachers' goal of professional autonomy presented a fundamental challenge to managerial control, it soon became the mission of school managers to make certain that the hoped for increase in decision-making authority for teachers would not become a reality. Industry offered school boards and managers a model for coping with the teacher rebellion that would safeguard their managerial prerogatives. Industry had dealt with labor conflict for decades. In the 1930s industrial unions challenged the whole concept of the employer's property rights by staging sit-ins in automobile factories. Yet by the 1960s such open rebellion by industrial unions was rare.

Much of corporate America practiced a system of labor relations that had efficiency of the firm and labor peace as its dual goals; both goals to be accomplished while managerial prerogatives were preserved. That was a model of labor relations that school management could accept as it faced its open confrontation with teachers. Precisely because the centralized school systems of the nation had originally been modeled on the business corporation, it turned out to be a model that was remarkably adaptable to the school setting.

The Role Played by Management Rights

Howell Harris, a scholar of the ideology of management rights, has said, "The main function of managerial ideology was (and is) to justify the continued possession of power and autonomy by the business elite in a pluralistic and democratic society."[106] That ideology—which supports the position that only management can determine the corporation's objectives, design plans for executing those objectives, and coordinate the efforts of all involved in the enterprise—was codified into law around the turn of the century by state statutes governing incorporation. Managers were empowered because they were to act as stewards for the absentee owners of the business—the stockholders.[107] Harris explains how this stewardship lent legitimacy to management's position of power:

> Management is the "steward" or "trustee" of the various groups with an interest in the firm; it devotes itself to "service" them, and gains legitimacy thereby. Management claims that it is in the best position to reconcile and satisfy the numerous and conflicting demands made of it . . . There is no need for unions, the state, or others to impose specific, enforceable obligations upon it.[108]

School boards and managers had long ago adopted this ideology of management rights, adapting it to the public setting in which they operated—that is, they represented the populace rather than the stockholders. The school governance laws passed as part of the pro-efficiency reforms codified this ideology into law. In seeking to fulfill its duty to further the public good, the school board could not share its power with any group other than managers hired to administer board policy. This legal concept of the school board as representative of the governmental sovereign was used by boards in the 1960s to defend the position that sharing decision-making power with teachers would be an illegal delegation of their authority.[109]

Both boards and administrators contended that the final decisions on educational policies had to remain with the policymakers who were accountable to the electorate.[110] The fact that only a small fraction of the electorate participated in school board elections, or that school managers were not popularly elected to their positions of power and authority, were realities rarely mentioned by those who held up the sovereignty doctrine as a bar to sharing decision-making with teachers. Also never discussed was the fact that many school managers below the superintendent held tenured positions within the school bureaucracy and were rarely removed from their positions regardless of their effectiveness. For the army of bureaucrats who determined the day-to-day operation of the schools, accountability for their performance was not an issue.[111]

School superintendents and boards viewed teacher militancy as an illegitimate attempt "to take over the operation of the school system." They criticized the AFT for not following "its sister unions in private industry in respecting managerial prerogatives." Managers vowed to stiffen their resistance "to creeping emasculation of the right of the administration to initiate educational policies for which the state holds them accountable."[112] Bernard Donovan, New York City school superintendent during the late sixties, feared that teacher unions aimed to strip school managers of power and "make them clerks in the organization."[113] As a former superintendent and professor of educational administration put it, "No good superintendent can handle a district where nothing is left to manage, where it's all been given to the teacher unions."[114]

The fear that unions aimed to strip management of power, tie its hands in decision-making, and generally emasculate those in management positions, was one that school managers shared with industrial managers. The following is a comment made by a corporate manager in 1946:

Restriction on management freedom is a big issue. This isn't breast beating. We've got heavy responsibilities for making quick, accurate, and effective decisions. Sometimes there are considerations that we can't divulge or *that wouldn't be understood* if we did. We're held responsible for the success of them but the Union isn't. It takes complicated maneuvering to run a business and all of the parts have to be kept working together. You have to have a good deal of free play in the rope for that . . . It's the cumulative effect of one area of freedom after another being reduced and the promise of still more that gives us real concern.[115] [emphasis added]

School managers' fears mirrored those of this industrial manager who decried the encroachment of the union on what he perceived to be his right to manage. Both school and industrial managers believed that the workers were unable to grasp the complex issues that a manager had to cope with on a daily basis. This manager's comments are reminiscent of Ellwood Cubberley's belief that teachers were unable to work through difficult problems, although school managers could do this with ease. This inherent elitism was another facet of the managerial ideology that both industrial and school managers subscribed to—and which had its roots in Social Darwinism. Clarence Randall, vice-president of Inland Steel, put it this way:

In industry as in government or anywhere else, there are two classes of people; there are those decide and those who carry out. You cannot organize human society on any other basis than that . . . In private enterprise, management is the decider.[116]

Employees were part of the class that needed to be directed; who owed respect and deference to the members of the ruling class—their employers. The members of the managerial class assumed they were best qualified by training and ability to exercise power over workers. According to Harris, managers viewed unions who challenged this idea as "a source of confusion, divided loyalties, friction, and restriction on management, which after all best knew and served the real interests of its employees."[117]

While business managers had a deep-seated preference for operating without the interference unions represented, they wanted to make employees and society feel their managerial prerogatives were morally just, not merely a result of management's power. After World War II they successfully convinced the public that unfettered union power represented a threat to the American way of life, efficiency, and "free enterprise."[118] School boards made the same argument in the 1960s. Harold Webb, the executive director of the National School Boards Association, wrote that teacher unions' demands for shared decision-making represented a threat to the bedrock "upon which we have built our way of life,"—the locally elected lay school board. The existing system of school governance was "adequate to meet the challenges of the times." Teachers should continue to channel their concerns through the superintendent; boards should, of course, consider input from all groups. Ultimate power, however, must rest with the superintendent and the board, as only they could represent the best interests of children. Webb asserted that teachers unions and collective bargaining, on the other hand, did not "meet the best interests of the children and do not serve the welfare of the community." They were organizations set up to advance the interests of teachers at the expense of youngsters.[119] As in industry, school management used a moral argument to shore up support for the existing distribution of power. The media tended to support school management, citing the growing power of teacher unions as a threat to school governance, and striking teachers as models of lawlessness that children might follow.[120]

The Business Method of Managing Employee Conflict: Collective Bargaining

The New Deal labor policy assumed conflict between labor and management was basic and permanent due to the structure of the employment relationship and the separation between roles and interests of managers and employees. To minimize this conflict and attain labor peace, public policy endorsed collective bargaining for workers in industry in the 1930s.[121] The introduction of collective bargaining into an enterprise put an end to management's unfettered freedom to deal with its employees wholly as it wished.[122] Critical labor theorists such as Karl Klare have pointed out, however, that the collective bargaining law, the National Labor Relations Act (NLRA), wholly accepts and reinforces both the basic management rights ideology and the organizational hierarchy that allow for employer control of the work place. While labor law acknowledges that workers should be protected from certain unilateral management dictates via collective action, it also formalizes dispute resolution to reinforce management control over enterprise goals and direction of the work process.

Wholly ignored by the NLRA is the point, espoused by labor leaders like Walter Reuther, that the workers' interest in the welfare of the firm is as great as that of the stockholders. The law is only marginally concerned with worker participation in significant industrial decisions. Klare wrote in regard to the law, "Its real preoccupations are with efficient management of the enterprise, with establishing a governance process that . . . maintains 'uninterrupted production.' " The inevitability of the managerial hierarchy or its role in efficiency is never questioned by the law.[123] It was this model of handling employee conflict that was to be chosen by many state legislatures to handle the challenge to school management mounted by teachers in the 1960s.

The model of collective bargaining that developed in the private sector over the decades following the enactment of the NLRA fit well with the principles of scientific management—management planned the production process down to the most minute detail and employees implemented those plans. In return for acceptance of a union role in setting wages, hours, and working conditions, management would retain the power to develop it plans for running the firm without interference from or participation by employees. Job control unionism—that is, employees' rights, pay, and obligations are tied to highly articulated and delineated jobs—fit hand in glove with scientific management.[124] Even unions such as the United Auto Workers (UAW), which had attempted to win a say in production and pricing decisions after World War II, reluctantly backed away from that position in return for major advances in wages and fringe benefits.[125]

The private sector model of collective bargaining, therefore, assumed that management alone should determine the best interests of the enterprise. Decisions about plant size, product line, and the location and continuation of the enterprise were among the decisions reserved for management. Management also had the right to impose work orders that had to be, except in very rare cases, obeyed by employees.[126] To insure that managerial prerogatives remained untouched, the scope of issues that management was required to bargain over was restricted by the federal courts in the decades following the enactment of the NLRA. James Atleson, scholar of American labor law, has written that the legal determination of whether or not an issue was a mandatory subject of bargaining was value-laden. Court decisions restricting the scope of bargaining often cited the employer's need to have "freedom to manage" and make decisions unencumbered.

The assumption courts often made was that exclusive managerial control over decisions such as capital investment and liquidation of assets was in the public interest. Adjudicators rejected the union position that it was in its members' interest to work as partners with management to help ensure the long-term financial health of their firm. The other assumption courts made was that employees and their representatives were unable to make financial and operational considerations intelligently. In other words, courts adopted the management rights ideology in its totality.[127] The result of the elimination of these issues from the collective bargaining process and their relegation to management's exclusive prerogative effectively negated the mutuality of decision-making in industrial life.[128]

Industrial democracy, long a goal of many employees and union leaders, was not furthered by the institutionalization of collective bargaining in the private sector. Atleson has written that collective bargaining "has little relationship to the modern conception of industrial democracy for it accepts as a basic premise the authoritarian and bureaucratic nature of the enterprise." Workers continued to be confined to their duty to obey work rules and their superiors' commands. The law of the shop floor—"management acts, workers grieve"—recognized management's right to make entrepreneurial decisions and shop floor actions. Management retained the right to direct, reward and punish its subordinates.[129] In Atleson's view, collective bargaining did little to disturb the status quo of power distribution in industry:

> Although I do not mean to disparage the accomplishments and value of collective bargaining as a device for limiting otherwise arbitrary or at least exclusive exercise of managerial power, the institution does not seem to have altered basic legal assumptions about the workers' place in the employment relationship.[130]

It was this model of collective bargaining that was to be transferred to the nation's schools.

The Collective Bargaining Model Applied to Education

In 1967 the New York state legislature adopted the recommendations of George Taylor and Archibald Cox in the passage of legislation that permitted collective bargaining by public sector employees. Neither Taylor or Cox had particular expertise in public education. Taylor was a business school professor; Cox an expert in private sector labor law.[131] The legislation they crafted, commonly known as the Taylor Law, lumped teachers together with all other non-managerial public employees. The stated purpose of the law was:

> To promote harmonious and cooperative relationships between government and its employees and to protect the public by assuring, at all times, the orderly and uninterrupted operations and functions of government.[132]

The Taylor Law was modeled on the NLRA. It gave public employee unions the right to bargain over wages, hours, and terms and conditions of employment. It outlined illegal employer and union practices, much as the NLRA delineated unfair labor practices for management and labor in the private sector. It set up an administrative tribunal to interpret the law as disputes arose. It differed from the NLRA by outlawing strikes by employees of government agencies. Heavy penalties were levied on union members and union leaders who engaged in an illegal strike. In lieu of the strike weapon, the Taylor Law provided for mechanisms that might help the parties to resolve impasses at the bargaining table—mediation and fact-finding. The Taylor Law served as a model for labor legislation in the many states that were to grant public employees bargaining rights in subsequent years.[133]

The industrial model of collective bargaining, which was transferred with only minor modifications to the education setting, focused exclusively on the labor aspect of teaching.[134] Just as "wages, hours and terms and conditions of employment" had been interpreted in the private sector to allow unions to pursue the goal of improved employee welfare, public sector labor law legitimized teacher unions' goal of improving teacher welfare—but no more. Public sector bargaining laws did little to address the goal of teacher involvement in policymaking—a goal that was a prerequisite for the attainment of teacher professionalism. While a few states passed separate legislation for teacher bargaining, which offered teachers the right to be consulted on policy issues, these same laws generally included either specific or general management rights clauses stating that policy determination was the exclusive right of management.[135]

As representatives of school management and school teachers began to meet at the bargaining table, it became apparent that—as in industry—management was more willing to give its employees money than it was to share decision-making power. School superintendent Charles Young's speech to a meeting of the Pennsylvania School Boards Association in 1967 illustrates this position:

> It is well that we do not deceive ourselves about the issues being raised by teachers. They are not what they appear to be on the surface. The real issues

are not wages, hours, and conditions of employment. Very few boards or administrators will deny the need for vast improvements in all of these areas. The bedrock issues are concerned with bi-lateral policy determination between boards and teacher organizations. They are concerned with the dilution of the delegated authority of the administrative staff.[136]

A study of contracts settled through 1974 found that bread and butter demands were, in fact, less frequently contested by management during bargaining than were demands focusing on the mission and the content of work performed by teachers. Although the bread and butter demands were more fiscally expensive, they were not the basic challenge to managerial authority that the teachers' professional goals represented.[137] As labor relations scholar Ida Klaus summed it up, management approached the teacher demand for joint decision-making on policy issues as a problem of "containment."[138] John Metzler, a management consultant with expertise in industrial labor relations, advised school managers to be sure to negotiate only over issues that were directly tied to teachers' employment relationship, and to deal with their professional issues some other way:

> The essential role of management in negotiations, therefore, is to make every effort to separate these relationships, to negotiate upon the problems of the employment relationship and to devise a means by which the demands of the teachers in the professional relationship are satisfied.[139]

The model of collective bargaining favored by school management was one that was adopted by adjudicators as they fleshed out the meaning of the bargaining statutes. Unions were empowered to represent the welfare interests of their members, but teachers continued to be legally and functionally divorced from responsibility for the effectiveness of the school organization. The collective agreements reached at the bargaining table rarely addressed themselves to the many fundamental problems facing schools at the time. Collective bargaining was prevented from "contaminating" the policymaking function of management through the application of the legal principle of the illegal delegation of authority by courts and administrative agencies.[140] As the New Jersey supreme court ruled, policy should be proscribed from collective negotiations because "only school boards have a primary responsibility to the public at large, as they have been delegated the responsibility of ensuring that all children receive a thorough and efficient education."[141]

Albert Shanker vented his frustration at the use of this argument to shut teachers out of educational policymaking:

We're told that everything that doesn't cost money is educational policy. Class size—well, you teachers can't be sitting here negotiating class size, because class size isn't really a benefit to teachers, it's a benefit for students and since you haven't unionized students yet, you can't talk about that. More effective schools, well that's an interesting idea but it is a question of how you put schools together—and that is not for employees to say. Your job is to negotiate for working conditions, and so forth. So public employees, whether at the public school level . . . or in the universities, are generally faced with a wall . . . non-money issues can't be discussed because these are matters of policy in which governmental officials have to make decisions, not employee organizations.[142]

The early battle over the scope of bargaining in education was a battle over the degree to which policymaking authority was to be shared between teachers and school boards and managers.[143] For management, a narrow scope of mandatory subjects of bargaining was key to the preservation of its managerial prerogatives. For teacher unions, a broad scope was essential to dealing with professional issues through the mechanism of collective bargaining. Some experts in labor relations supported the concept of a broader scope of bargaining in education than in the private sector because teachers did not have the right to strike.[144] Judge Harry Edwards, a law professor in 1973, advocated for a broad scope of bargaining for all public employees because of the power of collective bargaining to solve problems. He wrote, "The collective bargaining process is in part a therapeutic process, and it should permit the parties to address fully all problems which affect the bargaining relationship."[145]

Most legislators and adjudicators disagreed with Edwards, however. They subscribed to the legal principle of managerial prerogatives for school management. They supported management's position that policy determinations were legitimately and solely within its domain. They then attempted to divide teachers' "employment issues" from their "professional issues," which often impinged on educational policy. This categorization was difficult to make because working conditions and educational policy were frequently intertwined.[146] Joseph Shedd and Samuel Bacharach, scholars of labor relations in education, criticized the presumption that a differentiation could be made between working conditions for teachers and educational policy:

If curriculum or student grouping policies are inconsistent or poorly thought out, if needed time and other resources to plan and carry out one's responsibilities are not available, if opportunities to expand one's subject knowledge and pedagogic skills are not continuously available, or if students enter one's own classroom without the knowledge and skills they need to master the material to be covered, teachers' work lives are rendered more difficult as a consequence . . . the notion that a distinction either can or should be drawn between "educational policies" and "working conditions" is a patent fiction.[147]

Despite the difficulty in drawing such a distinction, adjudicators labeled issues either "working conditions" or "policy issues" in the decades following passage of collective bargaining legislation in order to decide whether the school employer was required to bargain over them with the teachers' union.[148] Few courts took into account teachers' claims of special, professional status in the educational process, relying strongly on industrial precedents to determine the legal scope of bargaining.[149] Adjudicators' rulings generally supported school management's position on limiting the scope of bargaining in order to draw a line of demarcation between the teachers' labor contract and educational policy. While teachers could bargain over the "impact" of management's policy decisions on their working conditions—another practice imported from industrial relations—they were unable to bargain over the policy decisions themselves.[150]

School managers were successful, then, in preserving their managerial rights. Yet, industrial management experts like Metzler encouraged them "to devise means by which the demands of the teachers in the professional relationship are satisfied."[151] This had to be done without relinquishing any real decision-making power to teachers. The solution school management found acceptable was the establishment of "joint study committees" where teachers and managers could discuss policy issues outside the bargaining relationship. By 1970, 59 percent of districts in New York state had set up such committees. This method of institutionalizing teacher consultation soon was used in districts across the country. Sometimes provisions for these committees were put into the collective bargaining contract.[152]

A national study of organized teachers' status published in 1979 found that the joint study committees were often lacking both in effectiveness and visibility. In no case did teachers have the final say on either curriculum design or selection of teaching materials through participation in such committees. Their efficacy was dependent upon whether or not the school administrator involved had a "participative" leadership style.[153] In other words, school managers' power to decide educational issues was undiminished.

The Effects of Collective Bargaining in Education:

The fact is, professional negotiations probably hold a greater potential for
the improvement of education than any series of events or activities which
have occurred in the last fifty years.[154]

Collective bargaining in education was held up by many of its supporters as
a means for initiating a systematic change in the type and quality of education
offered students in this country. Yet because professional issues could not be
dealt with via the model of collective bargaining that was adopted, its effect on
the educational system was far less potent than either its advocates or detractors
expected it to be. A study of Connecticut schools conducted more than a decade
after collective bargaining for teachers was legalized found that bargaining had
no significant effect on either school governance or educational policy. The
study found few contract provisions that determined such matters as the content
of the curriculum, the methods of instruction, or the choice of textbooks and
teaching materials.[155]

While there were some 105 teacher strikes during 1967 and even more during
1968, strike activity dropped off significantly in the 1970s. By 1970, twenty-
three states had passed legislation for collective bargaining in education, nearly
all twenty-three imposing severe penalties on striking teachers. Bargaining resulted in teachers gaining a 27.8 percent increase in real wages from 1961 to
1971. Even with this increase, though, the average salary for beginning teachers
lagged 26 percent behind those of other college graduates. Teachers' position
relative to other professions did not move up either in status or compensation as
a result of collective bargaining. Their position within the school organization
remained unchanged, as well.[156]

Collective bargaining had little effect on the hierarchical bureaucracy that
characterized school organizations since the first decades of the century. As
one analyst phrased it, "The old regimes may be shaken, but they have not
been toppled."[157] Collective bargaining, in fact, became part of the centralized
bureaucracy, making schools more bureaucratic rather than less so, with bargaining occurring at the central level and resulting in more rules, regulations,
and routines than had existed prior to bargaining.[158] The "job control" brand
of unionism imported from industry resulted in contracts that divided tasks
among specialists and specified many details of teachers' work.[159] The structure of authority relationships remained hierarchical, with no wholesale restructuring of the traditional control patterns affecting school policy or its
implementation. Although unfettered freedom of action for management was

restricted somewhat on personnel issues, superintendents retained much of their earlier initiative in policymaking.[160] The bilateralism hoped for by teachers and feared by school managers never materialized. If anything, collective bargaining resulted in bringing school boards and managers closer together in order for them to present a unified opposition to organized teachers.[161]

The teacher union came to play a narrow, economic role within the school bureaucracy. It secured for teachers guaranteed preparation time, breaks, a mandated length of workday, and rules outlining evaluation procedures.[162] The proposal to mimic the dual lines of authority found in medicine—administrative and professional—never developed in education. The goal of shared decisionmaking on professional issues remained unrealized twenty years after teachers were granted the right to bargain.[163] Organized teachers gave up this goal in the 1970s in return for a living wage and fair treatment from their supervisors.[164]

One effect of bargaining was to clarify the relations between school managers and teachers by reemphasizing the roles and responsibilities that each had been given when centralization was implemented at the beginning of the century.[165] The concept of the teacher as a worker was clearly articulated by collective agreements that specified the working conditions under which teachers labored.[166] Though after the 1960s it was clear that teachers had the potential to be militantly disobedient, the contract reiterated what education law had stated many decades earlier: teachers had to obey their supervisors or face discipline or discharge for being insubordinate. Teachers were still subject to the dictates of their managers on what to teach, the sequence in which to teach it, the students they were to teach, the materials they could use, and the principal to whom they were to report.[167] Teachers were first and foremost employees, aspirations for professionalism not withstanding.

In 1966 George Taylor hoped that collective bargaining would improve the chances of developing an educational program adapted to the needs of a changing world. Expressing the belief that a weak educational system imperiled the national safety, he suggested that a realignment in the relations between boards, superintendents, and teachers could address some of the problems inherent in the schools. He saw an opportunity for improvement in education by giving teachers the collective bargaining rights enjoyed by private sector employees:

> Inspired teaching and professional dedication is not compatible with government by mimeograph or with moonlighting as a way of life for teachers. The constructive contributions which teachers can make, on the basis of actual classroom experience, have not been adequately mobilized in the formulation of educational programs.[168]

It is ironic that Taylor chose to utilize the private sector model of labor relations in the hopes of tapping into teachers' expertise in the formulation of policy. Collective bargaining was of little consequence for the effectiveness of schools precisely because it did not provide a method by which teachers' expertise on educational issues could be mobilized. Issues centering on the effectiveness of a school system remained completely within the realm of management prerogatives. Collective bargaining could not help teachers contribute to making schools more effective or productive places for children to learn. In fact, it left the central core of instruction untouched. One elderly Pittsburgh teacher summed it up this way: "They end up giving teachers more money and sending them back to the schoolroom, but that's not the answer. There's a lot more questions . . . that are bothering the teachers."[169] The goals of shared decision-making and professionalism, which motivated teachers in their insurgency against the status quo in the sixties, would have to wait for another day.

Why the Transfer of an Industrial Model Occurred

In the tumult of 1965—with teacher strikes and demands for power sharing—no one was sure what school manager-teacher relations would look like in 1975. It was possible that a wholly new set of roles and responsibilities could have been assigned to school teachers, managers, and boards; roles that were uniquely designed for the education setting. Yet policymakers decided to handle the crisis in a way that used industry as the exemplar, resulting in a near identity between school manager-teacher relations and business manager-employee relations. Why did policy makers follow industry's lead once again?

1) Schools and corporations had similar governance models, bureaucratic forms of organization, power distributions within their organizations, and an "input-output" production function.

While some analysts of labor relations in education feel the industrial model was a bad fit for education, its transfer to the schools occurred so easily because it was actually well suited to education as it was so organized—in accordance with the pro-efficiency reformers' design.[170] Schools were still charged with the function of producing an array of educational products—that is, graduates that could take their places in the work force. Recall that political scientist Gittell found strong similarities between the bureaucratic school organization and corporations. Their organizational charts were remarkably alike, just has Ellwood Cubberley had proposed so many years earlier.[171] School managers acted much like their cohorts in industry and subscribed to the same ideology of management rights.

The structures, procedures, and processes that characterized the industrial model of collective bargaining complemented and even supported the top-down managerial ideology that existed in schools in the 1960s. In addition, school boards were as enamored of business methods and principles in the 1960s as they were in 1910.[172] It is not surprising that school management was willing to follow their cohorts in business and tolerate the industrial model of collective bargaining, which assumed the inviolability of their management prerogatives.

2) *The ideal of public control of the public schools made the teachers' demand for co-determination on educational issues seem undemocratic.*

The theory of school governance—whereby the school board safeguarded the interests of the community, and the school management worked as the board's steward—was invoked in an effective way by teacher union opponents. Far less effective was the teacher unions' exploitation of the dissonance between the theory of democratically controlled schools and the reality of the bureaucratically run education system. Basic governance laws, therefore, remained intact— the public, via the school board, could continue to delegate decision-making to school managers, but not to other school employees.

3) *Teachers lacked the strength to "take power."*

Lieberman said that no one would voluntarily share power with teachers; that they would have to force those who had power to move over and make room for them at the table. Although organized teachers had the brawn to force policymakers to respond in some way to their discontent, in the end they could not overcome management's power to shape that response in a manner that would leave its power and authority intact. The legislated strike prohibition and the accompanying penalty for its violation—often loss of two days pay for each day on strike—was severe enough to generally inhibit teachers from using the strike weapon in their effort to win gains in decision-making authority.

4) *The backlash to the turmoil of the sixties.*

The teacher unions made the argument that teachers who stood up for their rights set noble examples for their students. Many Americans, particularly Americans who were in positions of power and who benefited from the status quo, found this argument unpersuasive and possibly dangerous during the sixties. With race riots occurring in many cities and frequent, massive demonstrations by opponents of the Vietnam war, it seemed that the country had perhaps more than its share of people willing to back up their beliefs with action. If anything, many conservative Americans were looking for more obedience—not less—in this time of turmoil. Ironically, the sense of crisis in education gave teachers the opportunity to voice their complaints through collective action, but their concerted activity heightened the public's sense that education was in disarray.

Ultimately the public's desire for peace and order made it lose patience with the teachers' demands for change. While it was true the schools needed to improve, they could not improve while crippled for weeks at a time by striking teachers. If America was to meet the Soviet challenge, at the very least schools needed to be in session. To put it in the vernacular, the public sentiment toward teachers became, "Stop crabbin' and do your job."

5) Those who were empowered to design and shape the new relationship between school teachers and managers came from the industrial sector.

The bargaining laws for the public sector were crafted by persons whose expertise lay in business management and private sector labor relations. In the years following the enactment of those laws, most of the people who were charged with the responsibility of administering those laws, and those who acted as neutrals in bargaining disputes, came from the private sector. Many of these administrators, adjudicators, and neutrals were quick to analogize from their industrial experience in education.[173] They used precedents they were familiar with, whether or not they made sense in the context of education.[174] The private sector case of *Fibreboard Corporation v. the National Labor Relations Board* was often cited by adjudicators as they ruled to limit the scope of bargaining in education.[175] One analyst of teacher bargaining concluded that some courts seemed hostile to the whole idea of giving teachers the right to bargain at all.[176]

6) The United States emerged from the sixties with the status quo jarred, but not overturned.

Ultimately, what the teachers had been demanding—shared decision-making power and professional status—were not things society was willing to grant them. The acceptance of managerial rights in the work place was widespread not only among the movers and shakers in both government and business, but among many citizens living and working in the lower and middle rungs of society. Business and business values began to regain their formerly high status as the convulsions of the sixties subsided and business as usual became the norm once again in the decade of the seventies.[177]

And though the Civil Rights Act made discrimination against women illegal, long-held beliefs and myths about the proper roles for men and women were hard to debunk. More than twenty years after the passage of the legislation outlawing discrimination on the basis of gender, career chances for men and women in society—and in education—remained unequal.[178] A successful American space program did legions to dissipate the criticism of the nation's schools. What it boiled down to was the fact that the relationship between school teachers and their managers reflected the values and ideologies that were dominant in the greater society, no less in 1975 than in 1905. Once again, the relationship between the players in education was constrained by what society prized in the world of business, what it would tolerate in the way of independent action from employees and women, and what it expected from the educational system.

For teachers the industrial model of collective bargaining left many issues central to their reform agenda unresolved. According to historian Marjorie Murphy, organized teachers mounted a formidable offensive in the battle to change the status quo of power distribution in schools, but lost despite their ambitious plans and collective action:

> Union leaders came on the scene and fought what they called "the good fight." They often gained a small foothold in the economic world, but in every encounter they lost ground on the political front until they finally had very little political ground to stand on at all. Teachers' unions, which are public employee unions, are narrow economic organizations because historically that is all our conservative society has allowed.[179]

Conclusion

The teacher rebellion in the 1960s represented a reiteration of the criticisms of the bureaucratic, hierarchical form of school organization first voiced by teachers like Margaret Haley many decades before. The complaints were the same: low pay, difficult working conditions, lack of professional influence over what shape education was to take, abusive supervisors. The reawakening of teacher unionism forced these issues into the open and compelled society to respond to the teachers' critique of the schools. As with the sense of crisis at the turn of the century, society turned to business models to find the means to deal with the upheaval caused by teacher militancy in the sixties. Rather than reopen discussion on the more fundamental and troubling question of who was to be empowered to decide issues central to the school's mission, society sought to deal only with the question of how to maintain the uninterrupted operation of the schools. As in business, the maintenance of efficiency through labor peace became the goal of "labor relations" in education. Society refused to address the argument made by organized teachers that an overhaul in the system of governance set up so many years before might result in greater efficiency and better educational outcomes. It focused on the somewhat easier question to deal with: how to get teachers to stay in their classrooms.

Acknowledging the need for material gains for teachers was the one way to assuage teachers. Making it perfectly clear that society was unwilling to offer teachers any power in educational decision-making, that it was content with what had been—and wanted more of the same for the foreseeable future—was the other way society forced teachers to accept the status quo. Just as Americans ultimately turned away from the many proposals made in the sixties for alternative education—proposals reminiscent of the educational progressives' prescription for child-centered education made so many years earlier—it turned down the teachers' proposal for power-sharing in schools.[180]

By the 1970s, the teacher shortage had turned into a teacher glut, America had put the first man on the moon, college students were more concerned about their careers than injustice, and teacher militancy had become something about which only historians could write. The teacher rebellion against the turn of the century bureaucratic governance model had been quashed. Etzioni's prediction that teachers would not be recognized as professionals turned out to be right on the money. In the quiet of the 1970s teachers could take some comfort, though, in society's acknowledgment that they had as much right to bargain over their wages, hours, and working conditions as the employee working on the shop floor of a General Motors plant.

5

A Renewed Sense of Crisis
and a New Management Model
Spur Education Reform, 1983–1995

Our Nation is at risk. Our once unchallenged preeminence in commerce, industry, science, and technological innovation is being overtaken by competitors throughout the world. . . . We report to the American people that while we can take justifiable pride in what our schools and colleges have historically accomplished and contributed to the United States and the well-being of its people, the educational foundations of our society are presently being eroded by a rising tide of mediocrity that threatens our very future as a Nation and a people.[1]

The 1983 release of the report *A Nation at Risk* is often referred to as the starting point of the current major initiative to reform our nation's schools. The report was important for many reasons, not the least of which is that it linked superior economic performance by countries like Japan and Germany to a failure in the American educational system. In so doing it echoed the sentiments of early industrialists such Frank Vanderlip who warned in 1905 that Germany would soon overtake the United States economically because its fine educational system surpassed our own.

A Nation at Risk warned in 1983 that "If an unfriendly foreign power had attempted to impose on America the mediocre educational performance that exists today, we might well have viewed it as an act of war."[2] Those words started business, political, and educational leaders on an intensive search for ways to improve the academic performance of American youngsters just as early industrialists' concerns provided the motivation for the pro-efficiency reforms.

This chapter will illustrate the power of business to focus the discussion of school reform on problems that concern business and remedies that serve business interests. Just as in the early part of the century, the primary purpose of the educational system has been defined as making youngsters ready to take their places in the work force. In seeking to fulfill that purpose, schools are being encouraged anew to adopt a business management ideology—this time an ideology suited to the postindustrial age.

Societal Crisis Once Again Provides the Context for Reform

The sense of crisis engendered by *A Nation at Risk* has been heightened by disturbing societal phenomena, many of which were present during the 1960s—for example, substance abuse, rising crime, and racial division. A worsening of these problems has led to a sense of cultural decline reminiscent of the end of the nineteenth century, when urbanization, industrialization, and massive immigration led many WASP Americans to wonder whether the nation could withstand the many pressures being placed upon it.

In the contemporary period, many Americans lay blame for many societal problems on the loss of traditional or "family" values. William Bennett, secretary of education in the Reagan administration, refers to the index of leading cultural indicators—a creation of the conservative Heritage Foundation—to illustrate "how precipitously American life has declined in the past thirty years." He cites a 560 percent increase in violent crime, a 419 percent increase in "illegitimate" births, a tripling of the percentage of children living in single parent homes, a 200 percent increase in teen suicide, and an almost 80 point drop in Scholastic Aptitude Scores. Bennett blames much of this "social regression" on "the enfeebled state of our social institutions and their failure to carry out their critical and time-honored tasks." As in past periods of perceived crisis, education is singled out as both a contributor to societal problems as well as an instrument for their eradication. Bennett suggests that in order to reverse this American cultural decline, our educational system must "recover a sense of the fundamental purpose of education, which is to engage in the architecture of souls."[3]

Whether or not one agrees with Bennett's commentary on the data, the statistics on the condition of childhood indicate that children are growing up without many of the familial and societal supports that existed previously. In 1994 the U.S. Census Bureau reported that only 50 percent of children lived with both of their parents; 1.8 million children lived with neither parent.[4] This reality, coupled with the rise in two-earner families, have led to many children growing up without enough nurturing and guidance from caring adults. Television has become a prime conduit of information and cultural beliefs for children, with many hours of each day being spent in front of a television. Lack of positive interaction between attentive adults and children is linked in the minds of many Americans with children failing to embrace long-held values—self-control, conformity to the cultural majority's way of life, and acceptance of authority. Our schools, which continue to be based on the old pro-efficiency model, are places that require children to exhibit behaviors that reflect these very values. Children who cannot subordinate their individual wants to those of the group or the teacher, and children who cannot control their impulses in compliance with rules and routines, are children who have a difficult time in the environment that characterizes most schools. Teachers report that a large proportion of their students, particularly those coming from poor and minority families, are unable to function successfully in the classroom. The teachers cite a lack of parental support, physical and sexual abuse, neglect, poverty, and parents' substance abuse as the primary reasons for their students' inability to thrive in the school setting.[5]

The rise in violence in everyday life is often taken as another indicator of social distress. Violence has become a constant threat for many poor children living in American cities. The development of bulletproof vests for youngsters to enable them to walk to school in relative safety epitomizes the severity of the problems facing many inner-city children living in poverty.[6] Yet despite the media depiction of violence as a problem unique to urban America, it is not restricted to streets of the inner cities. As Bennett points out, nationally violent crime is up more than 500 percent in the last thirty years. Schools are not immune to this phenomenon. Violence against teachers and students *within* school buildings is cited as a problem by teachers in all fifty states. Nationally, 5,000 secondary school teachers are physically attacked by their students or the students' parents every month. Safety has become a new and critical concern in education.[7] Kenneth Geiger, former president of the NEA, has called for a national investment of $500 million to make schools safe havens for children and their teachers.

In 1968 the Kerner Commission, established by President Lyndon Johnson in the aftermath of inner-city riots, warned that the United States was in danger of becoming two unequal societies, one black and one white. The racial inequities and economic disparities that fueled those riots were not eliminated by the social programs instituted by President Lyndon Johnson's Great Society. On the contrary, the situation is now more complex due to increased Hispanic and Asian immigration and growing income disparities in the nation.[8] For a generation after World War II income disparity lessened. However, income inequality increased 22.4

percent from 1968 to 1994. While the top 20 percent of families earned 42.8 percent of all income in 1968, they took home 49.1 percent of all income earned in 1994.[9] Correspondingly, the middle class and poor's share of earned income dropped during the same period. In addition, the percentage of families considered middle-class dropped from 71.2 percent in 1969 to 63.3 percent in 1989. The percentage of families living in poverty increased from 17.9 percent to 22.1 percent during the same period.[10]

All these figures translate to more children living in poverty now than in any time since 1965—nearly one in four. Our childhood poverty rate is more than double that of any other major industrialized nation. Contrary to popular stereotypes depicting childhood poverty as an urban, minority, welfare phenomenon, these children most often come from white, working-class families living outside major metropolitan areas.[11]

The problems associated with poverty in our culture make the school experience a difficult one for many poor children. Not only do they enter kindergarten "behind" on measures of school readiness, the disparity in their skills and those of children from middle-class homes grows as schooling progresses, despite the "compensatory education" instituted by federal legislation during President Johnson's war on poverty. As the gap widens, children are sorted in accordance with the tracking mechanisms first instituted by the pro-efficiency reformers so many years ago; mechanisms in keeping with concepts of societal castes and Social Darwinism. The tracking begins in elementary school, with poor and minority children disproportionately labeled "learning disabled," "speech impaired," suffering from "attention deficit disorder" (ADD), or in need of remedial services.[12] A 1990 study on science and math education reported that tracking mechanisms continue to segregate students by both race and income in secondary schools. Jeannie Oakes, the study's author and a professor at the University of California, wrote:

> To the extent that placement in classes at different ability levels affects students' opportunities to learn—and the evidence from our study suggests that the effects are quite profound—minority students disproportionately suffer whatever disadvantages accrue to students in low track classes.[13]

In the 1980s high school completion rates varied by race, with 59.8 percent of black, 47.5 percent of Hispanic, and 75.5 percent of white students graduating in 1985. Children labeled as having a handicapping condition such as a learning disability had a high school graduation rate of 41.5 percent. One year after leaving high school only 29.2 percent of these youngsters were employed, earning an average of $4.35 an hour.[14] The racial and economic divisions in our society are replicated in the school setting, with long-term negative consequences for children from poor and minority families.

Just as the nation has had only limited success in eradicating racial division, gender discrimination continues to be pervasive thirty years after the passage of Title VII of the 1964 Civil Rights Act. In 1994 the median weekly earnings of female managerial and professional employees were 71 percent of those of their male counterparts.[15] Despite a continual increase in educational attainment and work experience by women, they face what has come to be known as a "glass ceiling," which prevents them from rising to positions of power and authority throughout both the private and the public sector. Women hold only about 7 percent of top management jobs across the United States. No longer able to have openly prejudicial policies, employers continue to keep women out of top positions by assigning them to staff positions that are not considered training grounds for top management, such as public relations, communications, and human resources. Even when promoted to equal rank, they are given less responsibility, authority, and compensation than men.[16]

The professions, a nearly all-male elite for much of the century, were forced to accept women into their ranks with the passage of Title IX of the Civil Rights Act in 1972, which outlawed discrimination in educational institutions. Thus, while only 307 women were granted law degrees in 1964, 14,421 J.D. or LL.B. degrees were conferred to women in 1985, representing 39 percent of all law school degrees.[17] Yet, the glass ceiling operates in the very legal system that is charged with outlawing gender discrimination. Despite the fact that women have entered the legal profession in large numbers since the mid-1970s, twenty years later only 14 percent of federal judges are women, and they are most often found at the magistrate, rather than the district or circuit court level.[18]

Women in school systems experience the same type of glass ceiling their sisters bump up against in other areas of employment. Gender stratification, which accompanied the institutionalization of the centralized school bureaucracy, still exists in education today. Women continue to predominate in numbers, but not in authority, in our schools. Despite "affirmative action" and "fair hiring practices" mandated by law, the educational hierarchy is basically unaltered. Women are at the base of the hierarchy in classroom positions, and men fill the ranks of the managerial pyramid.[19] New York state is illustrative of this gender stratification. In 1989 women earned 57 percent of all graduate degrees in educational administration and 60 percent of all school administrator certificates. These numbers represent what could be expected from a state teaching pool that is 60 percent female. Yet in 1991, 8.5 percent of school superintendents, 37 percent of elementary principals, and a scant 1.8 percent of junior and senior high school principals were women. In total, there were fewer women in positions of school management in New York state in 1991 than there were in the early part of the century, before female elementary school principals were replaced by men.[20] The picture in New York is in keeping with that of the rest of the nation.[21]

The economic implications of gender stratification in schools continue to be negative for women. In 1992, while the average salary for school superintendents nationally was $83,342, and the average salary for high school principals hovered around $70,000, teachers' average salary was $32,808. Even the least authoritative position in school management, the assistant principal, had an average salary some $13,000 higher than that of the average teacher.[22] It is clear that in order to move ahead financially, a teacher must leave the classroom and enter the ranks of school management. As is apparent from the New York statistics, despite obtaining the required graduate training and licensing, women are not often being appointed to the managerial positions that offer the greatest remuneration.

The entire education system is laden with institutional arrangements and practices that lead to women earning less than men throughout their working lives and into their retirement. Pay differentials occur in education even within the same job classification. Secondary school principals—usually male—earn more than elementary school principals, many of whom are women. Women high school teachers nationwide earn an average of $2,300–3,300 less than their male counterparts, holding experience and training constant.[23] In addition, pensions for teachers are often set up to penalize women for interrupting their employment for reasons of child rearing, forcing them to lose the years of credit accumulated before the birth of their children.[24] Ironically, women coaches have lost out by Title IX's requirement that boys' and girls' teams be funded equally. Before the enactment of the law, coaching of girls' teams was often an unpaid or low paid position held by women. As a result of the requirement for equal pay, many men have moved into coaching girl teams, taking over a field that had been almost entirely female.[25]

The education system, then, reflects the gender bias that is widespread in the greater society. Researchers who have studied the effect of gender bias on girls have concluded that they often receive lesser educational experiences and opportunities than those offered to boys. A 1992 study sponsored by the American Association of University Women found that from kindergarten on, girls are treated differently from boys by their teachers; treatment which praises them for being "good" rather than for being curious, challenging, or persistent. These behaviors are either tolerated or sometimes praised when exhibited by boys.

Videotapes associated with the study show that even when a teacher knows the purpose of the taping—to see how evenly she treats boys and girls—she gives boys far more attention than girls. She permits boys to call out answers, while insisting that girls sit quietly and raise their hands to ask permission to speak.[26]

Differential treatment for female students extends beyond being required to raise their hands to speak. Revelations about sexual harassment of female high school students by their male teachers followed the case of *Franklin v. Gwinnett County School District*, 112 S.Ct. 1028 (1991). The case, which went to the Supreme Court, brought attention to a problem that is nationwide in scope. The court ruled that schools must hold the same standards of any work place.[27] Far from being exempt from the prevailing problems associated with gender in our society, our schools contribute to the perpetuation of those problems into the next generation.

Today's Schools Continue the Pro-Efficiency Model

The scope of today's school enterprise would astound even Ellwood Cubberley. By 1987, 4,311,941 adults were employed in schools across the country. Of that total number, only 52.9 percent were classroom teachers, with the remaining 47.1 percent made up of central office and building administrators, aides, counselors, clerical workers, and support staff. By 1993 classroom teachers represented only 52.2 percent of total staff.[28] Today's principals rarely come to their jobs directly from the classroom. Serving for a number of years in other administrative posts has become more the norm than the exception for new principals.[29] Big schools, highly recommended by the pro-efficiency reformers, remain in favor, with the average school size approaching 500 students.[30] The consolidation movement, which began during the pro-efficiency reforms, continues despite current research that indicates that a bigger facility does not necessarily translate into a better education for children. States persist in offering financial incentives to small districts in order to encourage them to merge.[31] While there were some 34,000 districts across the country in 1962, that number was reduced to less than 15,000 districts by 1992.[32]

The status of teachers in the school organization remains what it has been throughout the century—the base of the bureaucratic pyramid. Teachers are not recognized as professionals either within the school organization or in society at large.[33] Despite the early salary gains following enactment of state collective bargaining laws, teachers' salaries dropped in real terms after 1972, not hitting the 1972 level again until 1986.[34] The average starting salary for beginning teachers continues to be substantially lower than salaries for college graduates in any other field.[35] Ten percent of teachers hold down a second job to supplement their income.[36] Research show that despite their relatively low salaries, teachers collectively spend millions of dollars to supply their classrooms with needed materials.[37] As in the 1960s, the retention rate of new teachers, particularly among those who have other employment opportunities, remains low.[38]

Parents continue to be shut out of participation in decisions that affect their children. In accordance with the pro-efficiency model, professional school managers continue to make all substantive decisions about children's class placement and educational program. The schools do not have substantial and systematic outreach programs designed to inform families about school practices.[39] Parents have no right to share in the development of school policies or curriculum. The decision-making power on these issues continues to rest with the school board.[40] Attendance at school board meetings remains extremely low, with a tiny fraction of the electorate attending even one meeting in any given year.[41] Turnout at annual school board elections still rarely tops 10 percent of registered voters.

The type of education afforded youngsters by the system remains precisely what the pro-efficiency reformers hoped it would be: a system that sorts youngsters into vocational and academic tracks, equipping children with the skills needed for an industrialized society. Daily life in school remains unexciting, with most students merely "putting in their time" rather than enjoying their school experience.

Those who look upon school as a means of earning the necessary credentials to move ahead in the future tend to submit to the school regime; those who see no connection between school and entry into a good job or college, often do not. Typically, it is students from this latter group who engage in disruptive behavior. Their behavior can lead to suspension from school. Many times they are the students who become school drop-outs at sixteen.[42]

Statistics on school outcomes do not support *A Nation at Risk*'s assertion that there is a decline is the actual performance of the educational system. There is, in fact, evidence that the schools are doing as well—or even better than—they have ever done. High school graduation rates have increased from 29 percent in 1929 to a historic high of 74.1 percent in 1989. The 1970 drop out rate of 17 percent decreased to 11.2 percent by 1994.[43] Proficiency in reading has not significantly changed over the last twenty years, with achievement continuing to be strongly linked to parental educational attainment and number of hours spent watching television each day.[44] The proportion of students who end their study of math before algebra—15 percent—is down considerably from the pre-Sputnik era, when 45 percent of high school students took no math courses at all.[45]

Economic realities may be changing, but the schools we have today fulfill the promise of the pro-efficiency model better than they ever have.

Despite the alarm sounded by *A Nation at Risk* the average American feels the neighborhood school is meeting his or her expectations. All parents expect schools to teach the "three R's"—basic reading, writing, and numerical skills. Middle-class parents expect their schools to provide their children with the necessary credentials for entrance to good colleges. When polled, most parents say that they are satisfied with their children's academic performance.[46]

Acquisition of basic skills has remained the number one purpose of schooling throughout the century.[47] Consensus, however, is lost once schools aim to go beyond basic skills. Brown University professor Theodore Sizer puts it this way:

> Some Americans do not see the schools as engines both of information and intellectual liberation. Indeed, they find the latter—especially when so described—to be intolerable. The schools, they insist, are to teach young people what is true, what is right, and what is wrong. Anything beyond that is anathema.[48]

The alternative education movement in the 1960s, which attempted to implement many of the early educational progressives' recommendations, was defeated by a societal push for minimal competencies and slogans such as "back to basics."[49] There is much evidence that, despite the oft-heard cries about the decline in the quality of education, most Americans today have the type of schooling they want.[50]

The Catalyst for Radical Change: Fear of Economic Decline

> Giving our students the best education in the world is a moral imperative, and, especially, an economic necessity.[51]

When *A Nation at Risk* was published in 1983, political officials at both the state and national level were urged by business leaders to neutralize the threat posed by the "rising tide of mediocrity" emanating from our schools. Political officials' first attempt to rid the nation of this mediocrity was very much in keeping with the pro-efficiency model—to impose more top-down controls on individual schools and school districts. More stringent rules and mandates, accounting procedures, and compliance monitoring were among the strategies state legislators and education departments used to tighten up school operations in the hope that more directives and controls would lead to better student and teacher performance.[52] In 1988 the Carnegie Foundation for the Advancement of Teaching conducted a study of the effects of this first wave of reform. Ernest Boyer, the head of the Carnegie Foundation, concluded that this top-down approach to reform was irrelevant to the "human enterprise" of education.[53] Many commentators concurred with Boyer's assessment, pointing out that this approach led to little if any change in what had become standard classroom practice throughout much of the century.

The top-down reforms implemented following *A Nation at Risk* had the curious effect of making many people question whether the pro-efficiency model had reached the limits of its usefulness.[54] Adding more mandates for schools and teachers to follow—and more bureaucrats to monitor their compliance—seemed to result in very modest gains in student achievement at best, and a waste of tax dollars at worst. American students continued to rank low in international comparisons of student achievement as measured by standardized test scores. It appeared to do nothing to give America the "competitive edge" in global competition called for by *A Nation at Risk*. Reminiscent of the two earlier periods of this study, business leaders and policy pundits warned that unless something was done to change the way we educate our youth we would be unable to compete with Japan, Germany, or future economic competitors. Robert Reich, secretary of labor in the first Clinton administration, wrote in 1989:

> In the new global economy, nearly everyone has access to big break-throughs and to the machines and money to turn them into standardized products at about the same time, and on roughly the same terms. The only factor of production that is relatively immobile internationally, and on which the future standard of living of the nation uniquely depends, is *us*—our competence, our insights, our capacity to work productively together.[55]

Since the first wave of reform, policy pundits have cautioned that unless a major restructuring in education occurs, citizens can anticipate a marked drop in the American standard of living in the very near future. Marc Tucker, head of the National Center on Education and the Economy, has pointed out that Korean employees work twelve hour days and make $3,000 a year in Korea's electronics industry. These workers are better educated than many American workers, but their earnings are a fraction of the earnings of their American counterparts. Tucker warns that the days are numbered for minimally educated, middle-class members of America's work force. As a nation we have two choices: we can either lower pay rates to match those of foreign workers, or maintain pay rates by increasing employee productivity via a vast increase in employees' skills. Since the former is an unacceptable alternative, he argues, we must turn to the education system to make sure the employees of the future will have new skills and competencies necessary to maintain our standard of living.[56]

The upgrading of skills of the American work force, thus, is viewed as central to the perpetuation of American preeminence in the world economy and the American way of life. Representatives from the business community and some economists argue that a failure to invest in future American workers will result in sluggish productivity growth, joblessness, and declining real income.[57] This message has been sent far and wide, in media as diverse at the *Wall Street Journal, Psychology Today,* and *McCall's Magazine.*[58] The argument is always the same. Blue-collar jobs will rapidly decline in what is now termed "the post-industrial era."

Peter Drucker, management guru, has written:

> Knowledge will become our true capital base and premier wealth-producing resource . . . we are on our way to becoming a society in which the passport to virtually all good jobs, high salaries and social prestige will be . . . the equivalent of a college diploma.[59]

Drucker and a host of other management experts and labor economists assert that unless we are willing to accept a future where the vast majority of our citizens are relegated to jobs in the service sector paying poverty wages, we must rethink our way of educating our youth to prepare them to use their minds in the "knowledge work" of the postindustrial era.[60]

The argument then focuses on the point that the skills and behaviors schools have taught most children—children tracked below the top track—throughout the twentieth century are not sufficient for the type of work that will be waiting for them when they reach adulthood. *A Nation Prepared,* a 1986 follow up to *A Nation at Risk,* asserted that we need not wait for the twenty-first century for this phenomenon to occur. Employers today are complaining that graduates of the school system are unable to do the "increasingly complex work required of them."[61] They are not being prepared to interact with the technology of the information age.[62] The general population seems to share the notion that the educational system does not ready children for employment. A Roper poll conducted in 1990 found that 58 percent of Americans felt that schools did a poor or fair job of preparing students for work.[63] A nationwide study of math achievement by students lends some credence to this belief: only 5 percent of high school seniors demonstrate the skills needed for high-technology work. Lamar Alexander, secretary of education in the Bush administration, commented upon release of the report, "If our aim is to be first in the world in math by the year 2000, we had better fire up our engines, because we have an enormous challenge ahead of us."[64] In order to meet that challenge, instructional methods first used in the days of Ellwood Cubberley—textbook-driven, lecture-style pedagogy—must be given up. In its place should be something entirely new; something that would equip children for employment in a high-technology, knowledge-based economy.[65]

The call for reform in teaching methods and educational experiences has been unlike most calls of reform since the 1920s in a critical way: systematic change is being demanded by people who have the power to place their agenda for reform in the vanguard of proposals for educational change. Both business and political leaders are demanding a break with education as we have known it throughout the century. Joseph Alibrandi, chief executive officer of the Los Angeles–based Whittaker Corporation, spoke for most of the business community when he said, "The public schools don't work worth a damn. Band-Aids won't work anymore. We need a total restructuring."[66] This desire from the business sector for radical change in schooling has not occurred since the time when it worked as part of the "interlocking directorate" to reconstruct public education at the dawn of the twentieth century. As with that earlier partnership, the stated goal of these reformers is to reshape education so that it can provide the nation with workers who will outdistance the international competition.

There is a growing sense that many of the institutions that came into being during the progressive era at the urging of business and the administrative progressives—for example, bureaucratic government—are now nothing more than "wreckage of our industrial era." In order to move ahead, that wreckage must be cleared away.[67] The pro-efficiency model of schooling is portrayed as being part of the wreckage of the industrial age, neither efficient nor effective in meeting the needs of America in the twenty-first century.

The Influence of Business on the Current Reform Effort

School people usually resent any implication that their services are comparable to those of workers in industry. But the fact remains that supervision in schools has been patterned after supervision in industry. In recent years industry has made great changes in its methods of supervision, while schools generally have been following methods that have been abandoned by industry as unsatisfactory.[68]

School reform efforts in 1900 and 1960 were highly influenced by corporate organizational structures, management principles, and production processes. Schools today are no less vulnerable to the influence of the newest version of sound business management. A new management model aimed at changing how American firms do business underlies virtually all discussion on reforming our educational system.

The New Management Model

Total Quality as a management strategy is infiltrating almost every facet of business. As a result, fresh horizons in training and development, education, reward and recognition, and employee empowerment are opening up. New value systems are being forged, continuous quality improvement is close at hand, and "zero defects" is no longer a nebulous concept.[69]

Scientific management, once embraced by managers in both the private and public sectors, has been pronounced dead by management experts. The management principles developed by Frederick Taylor in the early part of this century lived and flourished in many segments of society for decades. Even after scientific management was no longer seen as the sure-fire way to maximize efficiency, its underlying assumptions about human motivation and hierarchical control lingered on in business and government.

Yet today those assumptions about how management can best achieve high productivity are rejected out of hand. A new model of efficient management has taken its place, contradicting nearly all of what Frederick Taylor espoused. This new model, which most often goes under the name of Total Quality Management (TQM), assumes that in order for firms to stay one step ahead of the competition, they must look for new ways to be both efficient and effective. Efficiency continues to be defined as the relationship between inputs and outputs. Effectiveness, a new term often used in the TQM model, refers to meeting the customer's expectations and getting the job done right. Total quality refers to reducing production errors to nil, and meeting—or even exceeding—the customer's expectations in a world of quickly changing customer needs.[70]

The way companies are supposed to attain this level of "total quality" is by maximizing the talents of every person working within the organization. Authoritarian management styles are out; participative management styles are in.[71] Teamwork and employee empowerment are seen as increasing communication across functions and departments, reducing adversarial relations between management and labor, and producing ever-higher quality goods and services for customers. Continuous improvement is the catchword of the day. Through analysis of data, teams of workers and managers are to strive together to pinpoint problems and ceaselessly outstrip their prior performance.[72]

In TQM there is both the internal and the external customer who must be pleased. Traditionally, the only customer who mattered was the one who purchased the final product or service produced by the organization. Under TQM the internal customer is that person or unit who receives the output of a given manager, employee, or department. Theoretically, the internal customer's needs and expectations must be met if quality products and services are to be delivered to external customers. The example given is of the fire-bucket brigade—each member on the line must deliver the bucket without water spillage to the next person if the brigade is to succeed in putting out the fire.[73]

New roles for management and labor are supposed to emerge from this model. Whereas the traditional model focused on efficiency alone—that is, reducing costs of inputs to outputs, and often let workers bear the brunt of new efficiency techniques—the new model postulates a win-win situation for both workers and managers:

> In a quality situation everyone wins—the satisfied customer, the company with increased business, the workers whose jobs are not threatened. In all likelihood, the workers have had important and creative input into the product or service. This is the norm in total quality companies, where employees are empowered to participate in decisions affecting their work. When quality is everyone's business, a participative work culture emerges.[74]

The new ideology of *cooperation* as the means for making American companies more competitive has been adopted by both management experts and government agencies such as the department of labor. By making use of the knowledge that employees at every level of the organization possess, management will be able to insure that the best decisions will be made on all issues. This will result in better quality products, reduction in both costs and production time, and higher corporate profits. In theory, employees derive both greater job satisfaction and job security from a system that asks for and utilizes their expertise.[75]

Continuous improvement requires continuous training. The TQM model presupposes that employees will receive training, retraining, and skill upgrading. In this sense, the total quality firm is a teaching and learning organization. Workers must be trained to function in teams. Managers must be trained to change from directors to "coaches" or "facilitators." Everyone has to be educated in more refined processes of data analysis. Rewards and recognition for solving tough problems through use of newly acquired skills are to be built into the organization's incentive and compensation structure.[76]

Perhaps the greatest fundamental change from Taylor's model to the new management paradigm is the underlying assumption that employees *want* to do their best. Taylor assumed that workers' natural inclination was to do as little as possible. He wrote that in the case of the average workman:

> Instead of using every effort to turn out the largest possible amount of work, in a majority of cases this man deliberately plans to do as little as he safely can—to turn out far less work than he is well able to do—in many instances to do not more than one-third to one-half of a proper day's work.[77]

According to Taylor, it was management's job to structure every facet of the workers' tasks so they could not give less than their maximum effort. In the TQM model, managers are supposed to trust that workers want to give their best effort. Managers are to give them the leeway and support to do it. When workers do not perform well, managers should look first to the organization to see what hindrances to good performance exist. David Harding, a manager with Jaguar cars, summed up the change from old to the new management model this way:

> A company needs to move from the traditional view of managers giving directions to the notion of managers as leaders who spend a significant amount of time listening to people. . . . People want to do their best. Managers don't have to motivate, cajole, kick and coerce people. We must, instead, define management's job as finding and eliminating the road blocks that prevent people from doing their best. This demands a major change in management attitude, style and perception.[78]

This idea has been summed up as the 85–15 principle—85 percent of poor worker performance is due to failures in the system, 15 percent is due to worker ineptitude or lack of motivation.

Another principle of the new management model is that outstanding performance by an individual is most unlikely if that person is treated as a subordinate. This point is reminiscent of Ella Flagg Young's ideas on human motivation and creativity. Just as Young argued, management can command ordinary performance from obedient workers treated as subordinates, but extraordinary performance cannot be dictated from above. Today's experts in human motivation argue that creativity and superior achievement arise from a personal drive and commitment to an organizational goal or vision.[79] Thus, employee participation and teamwork between management and labor serves not only to improve decision-making in the organization, but to insure that employees will be committed to achieving the firms's goals. This commitment, in turn, leads to higher employee productivity.

The requirements of the total quality model—focus on internal and external customers, continuous improvement, data analysis done by everyone in the firm, and employee involvement in decision-making—requires a flattening of the bureaucratic managerial hierarchy first established in corporations around the turn of the century. Decentralization of operations is key to implementing the TQM process. It has been done in some of the largest and most visible American corporations with much media fanfare.[80] The negative aspect of this downsizing has been the firing of many thousands of middle managers who were employed in corporate hierarchies. General Electric chief executive Jack Welch was given the moniker "Neutron Jack" as he laid off tens of thousands of employees, many of whom came from the ranks of GE management. The result of this reduction in hierarchy has been to push decisions down to the lowest possible level of the organization, empowering employees to make those decisions. Welch elaborated on why this was the right course to take. GE needs to:

> Engage every mind in this place. They've got to feel good about being here. They've got to feel their contributions are respected . . . we just happen to think (this) is the right way to do it. Breaking down boundaries, taking away hierarchy. The idea is to liberate people.[81]

Welch added that he has taken GE down this path of apparent work place democracy for one reason: "To be competitive. To win."[82]

Decentralizing operations is supposed to result in faster and better communication between the customer and the firm, resulting in higher sales and greater customer satisfaction. Products and services are assumed to be better suited to individual clients, which again ought to result in higher sales and repeat customers. The new organizational structure theoretically should foster a greater versatility on the part of each unit, making it, once again, better able to meet customer needs. William Grabe, an IBM vice-president, writes that for corporations to succeed in the current era, they must start behaving like small businesses, "stop speaking their own language and learn to speak the language of their customers."[83]

The New Management Model, Widely Adopted

Most executives of large companies have embraced this management model during this era of corporate restructuring. In a survey of some of the nation's largest firms, the Conference Board found that while only 16 percent had instituted TQM prior to 1983, 60 percent had done so since 1986.[84] Top-level support for the TQM process is associated with good progress toward its implementation. When top management—CEOs and senior vice-presidents—supports its adoption, employees at lower levels of the organization are more likely to accept the new model. However, even in companies where top management strongly supports TQM, lower level managers are far less enthusiastic about it.[85] Lower level managers who have not been able to adapt to a "participative" style have been let go. According to Larry Schein of the Conference Board, "The shift toward participative management has been difficult for some managers who were socialized in an authoritarian culture. Unable to adapt, these people become both cultural and economic casualties."[86] Among managers who accept the TQM process, that acceptance is heavily colored with resignation—that is, middle and front line managers feel that TQM results in a net loss of power for them.[87]

As in the progressive era, government is seeking to reorganize its operations in keeping with the latest principles of business management. Government has long been urged to imitate business in order to become more efficient. In the current period that means dropping the bureaucratic model—seen as very "businesslike" in the early part of the century—and adopting the new management model that focuses on empowerment, delegation of decision-making to employees, a customer orientation, teamwork, and management through "leadership."[88] David Osborne and Ted Gaebler, authors of the 1992 best seller, *Reinventing Government*, give many examples of a "radically different way of doing business in the public sector."[89] Their treatise basically accepts the premises of the TQM model. It illustrates how adoption of the TQM process has resulted in maximal productivity and effectiveness in agencies as diverse as hospitals, jails, municipal government, schools, and housing services.

A heavy emphasis on the customer is key to Osborne and Gaebler's argument—"customer-driven systems force service providers to be accountable to their customers."[90] Competition, they argue, can revitalize public institutions that have abused the monopoly on public services they have enjoyed throughout the century. Following the lead of risk-taking business entrepreneurs, public sector agencies must adapt to the marketplace, or else stagnate and die as people who can afford private alternatives—be they in mail delivery or education—abandon the public sector offerings.[91] Adapting services to the needs of the customer, relinquishing the "one size fits all" mentality typical of most bureaucracies, and emphasizing results rather than rules and regulations are some of the ways Osborne and Gaebler claim that government can mimic the best in business practices.

Schools are Urged to Adopt the
New Management Model

Osborne and Gaebler count themselves among the many in business, government, and academia who are urging schools to redesign themselves in accordance with the new definition of sound business organization and management. Management experts cite many parallels between industry and schools that make the adoption of the new management model logical: both have large organizations, unions are entrenched in both large corporations and schools, managers in both enterprises are accustomed to unilateral decision-making, and, perhaps most important, both schools and industry are under great pressure to change their operations.[92] Given these similarities, schools are advised to use industry's recent attempt at restructuring as the template for reform.

David Kearns, former CEO of Xerox and deputy secretary of education in the Bush administration, is one of the most vocal advocates of the use of the TQM process in the schools.[93] Kearns credits TQM with making Xerox profitable in the face of stiff Japanese competition in the photocopying industry. He suggests that schools will become more productive places:

> When they take seriously the idea that the customer is all important. They must tailor their offerings to the needs of the customer, and they must believe that in a fundamental sense, the student is always the customer.[94]

In the trash bin must go the uniform treatment given youngsters. It must be replaced with a custom-tailored education for every child. Kearns attacks traditional school management as an impediment to improved productivity, just as traditional business management hampered industry in its competition with the Japanese:

> Lockstep myopic management is still the norm in American education today, just as it was in American business while the Japanese were relentlessly taking over market share after market share in industry after industry.[95]

Kearns insists that just as business management was forced to change to stay competitive, school managers must drop the scientific management model in order to develop the world-class schools needed to develop a world-class workforce. Kearns admits his interest in schools is both selfless and selfish. He cares about education, "because profits depend on it. Without it, our society will founder, and our businesses will, as well."[96]

Kearns outlines several principles gleaned from industry that he asserts will lead to the world-class educational system upon which our economy depends. He suggests that management should become a service center for teachers rather than a command post from which directives flow. Parents and students should have the ability to choose a particular school to meet individual needs. Under a choice plan, schools would become individual profit-and-loss centers, with those schools attracting the greatest number of customers being the most profitable. With decentralized decision-making, schools would have the needed flexibility to keep their customers. Teachers could make decisions about hiring and firing of colleagues, curricula, and materials. Performance measurements of student achievement would indicate the school's organizational effectiveness and efficiency. The public could then hold teachers and principals accountable for student successes and failures.[97]

Kearns's advice is echoed by legions of writers, policy pundits, and academicians. Schools should adopt new business management practices in order to create the workers we will need in the coming century. Entrepreneurial schools, strategic planning, cost-cutting measures, "just in time" inventory control, employee profit-sharing plans are but some of the many ideas that schools are encouraged to implement during this period of criticism and calls for reform.[98] Phillip Schlechty, head of the Center for Leadership in School Reform, provided a translation of the new business management model for educators in his book *Schools for the 21st Century*.[99] His thesis is as follows: "school leaders, like business leaders, must come to understand that if America's schools are to meet the needs of the 21st century, then—like America's corporate structure—they must be reinvented."[100]

The goal of this reinvention is to make schools more productive so that business may become more productive:

> In a very real sense, those who are leading the restructuring of schools and those who are leading the restructuring of America's enterprises are in the same business . . . the success of school leaders at restructuring schools will determine the long-term success of American business.[101]

School must be restructured so that children are customers of "knowledge work," teachers are leaders and inventors, curriculum is seen as the raw material of the education process, the principal is the "leader of leaders," the superintendent is the CEO, and the school is the new corporate entity.[102] School managers will "orchestrate," "coach," and "encourage." Superintendents will "express visions and assess results."[103] Schlechty is candid about the motivation behind his recommendation for shared decision-making. He sees it as a way to get better results out of schools through the implementation of a "quality" approach.[104] Quality in education is defined by Schlechty as students "learning things that are valued by the constituencies whose support must be maintained." Business ultimately is one very important external customer that schools must aim to please. Teachers and administrators are urged to "get a handle on . . . a quality indicator" and use it to measure student

ASSISTANT SUPERINTENDENT FOR
CURRICULUM AND
INSTRUCTION
F.J. Turner School District
Beloit, Wisconsin

The F. J. School District has an exceptional opportunity for a qualified Assistant Superintendent to provide executive direction and leadership for the District's Instructional Services.

Nationally recognized for its pioneering efforts in continuous quality improvement, the district is seeking a strong and collaborative leader whose training and experience in curriculum development, implementation, assessment, and improvement will augment current team efforts. Knowledge of TQM and computer systems required.

F. J. Turner is a district of 1,200 students and 79 professional staff located on the Wisconsin-Illinois border. A regionally competitive compensation package is available.

The deadline for application is **March 18, 1994.**

For information contact:

**Dr. Charles A. Melvin, Superintendent
Beloit-Turner Schools
1231 Inman Parkway
Beloit, Wis. 53511**

Figure 5.1. Advertisement for assistant superintendent requiring knowledge of TQM. Source: *Education Week,* March 2, 1994. Reprinted with permission of the School District of Beloit Turner.

outcomes. A results-oriented school culture must permeate the school. Poor performance must be analyzed in light of TQM's 85–15 principle, with the assumption that the bulk of performance problems stem from school system failures rather than personal failings.[105]

The business model of successful management is potent. As Raymond Callahan demonstrated in regard to the scientific management model, schools have been exceptionally vulnerable to the power and influence of business management principles.[106] That vulnerability continues into the present. One need only scan the pages of any popular education publication to see how TQM is weaving its way into the everyday discourse on educational issues. Knowledge of TQM is becoming a required qualification for applicants to positions in school management: (see figure 5.1.)

Advertisements by business consultants on how to implement TQM in the classroom, the school, or the district appear in nearly every issue of publications such as *Education Week*. (see figures 5.2 to 5.4)[107]

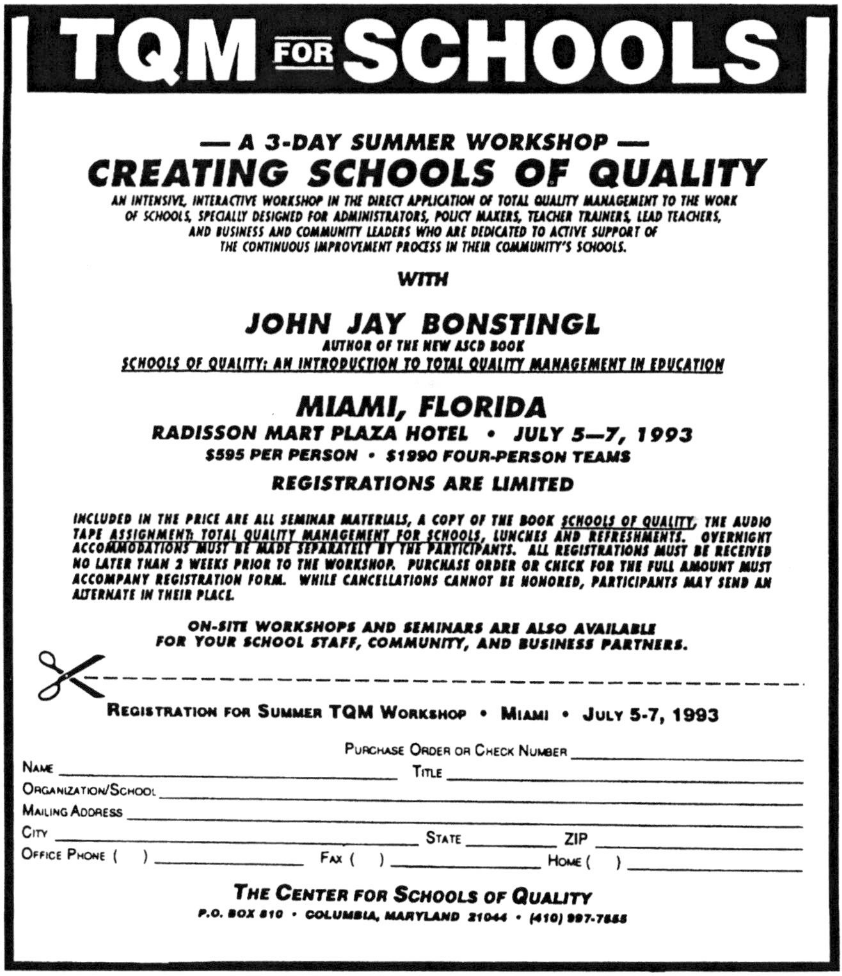

Figure 5.2. Advertisement for a workshop that teaches application of TQM in the schools. Source: *Education Week,* May 17, 1993. Reprinted with permission of Jay Bostingl.

Figure 5.3. Advertisement for a video, "Leading Schools to Quality," through the aplication of TQM. Source: *Education Week,* February 16, 1994. Reprinted with permission of National Educational Service.

Books with such titles as *The Quality School*, the *Quality School Teacher*, and *Total Quality Management for Schools* are proliferating.[108] The National Alliance of Business sponsored the book *Using Quality to Redesign School Systems.* (see figure 5.4.)

Figure 5.4. Advertisement for the book, *Using Quality to Redesign School Systems,* sponsored by the National Alliance of Businesses. Source: *Education Week,* March 2, 1994. Reprinted with permission of Jossey-Bass Publishers.

Cities as small as Tupelo, Mississippi, and Johnson City, New York, are implementing the TQM process in their schools.[109] Associate executive director of the American Association of School Administrators (AASA), Lewis Rhodes, says TQM is "surfacing all over the place."[110] TQM is fast becoming the new rage in school management.

Business Plays a Direct Role in School Reformation

Education once again seems to be following the lead of business in its most recent effort to remake itself in a new image. How did this come to pass? This mimicking of industrial managerial practice is due not only to the general influence of business success in our free enterprise society. Business has immersed itself in the education sector in order to recast the school organization in the new image of the efficient organization.

Business Defines the Problem and the Solution

Given the host of issues facing educators at the close of the twentieth century—school children compromised prenatally by cocaine, increased childhood poverty, difficulty in attracting and retaining the best young people in teaching, to name a just few—it is not immediately apparent why the nation's attention has been heavily focused on education's contribution to the skill level of the American work force. This has occurred because, as a nation, we continue to accept the premise that the primary purpose of education is to ready children for the world of work. In the current period, business has analyzed the economic utility of the K–12 public education system—a production facility for future employees and college students—and found it to be wanting.[111] Blaming employee skill deficiency for slow growth in productivity rates, business has taken an offensive stance on the issue of why some American companies are not as productive as their foreign competitors.[112] The National Association of Manufacturers, the National Alliance of Business, and the Business Roundtable are among the business associations that have pointed the finger of blame at what they see as schools' inability to turn out large quantities of highly skilled graduates—graduates who are able to think, reason, and solve complex problems. Thus, the problem in education is not, for example, that schools are suffering from the same serious afflictions that exist in the broader society. Rather, it is that children do not exit school ready to take "hi-tech" jobs.

Just as in the first decades of this century, the solution devised by business fits neatly with its definition of the problem in the schools. In the current era, the problem is defined as schools not meeting the needs of its major "external customer." Business has devised a solution to that problem. In 1989 the Business Roundtable, a group made up of the chief executive officers of 218 of the nation's largest corporations, developed a nine-point program for educational change. The program called for high expectations for all students, outcome-based education, strong and complex assessments of student progress, rewards and penalties for schools, greater school-based decision-making, an emphasis on staff development, the establishment of prekindergarten programs, provision of adequate social and health services, and greater use of technology in the schools. The Business Roundtable crafted this agenda with the idea that it would become a template with which to craft comprehensive legislation on school reform. In 1995 it revised this template to include parental choice and heightened safety and discipline in the schools, while dropping its call for adequate social and health services for children.[113] Just as business encouraged surveys of school systems in the first decades of this century in order to identify their "inefficiencies," the Roundtable is conducting an analysis of every state in the nation to identify gaps between what each state has done and what it still must do to conform to the group's reform program. In addition, the Roundtable has embarked on an effort to sway the opinion of civic, business, and education groups on the issue of how schools ought to be changed.[114]

While the Business Roundtable has a strategy for school reform that is national in scope, business leaders in states and cities have also developed plans for school change. In 1990 a group named the Arizona Business Leadership for Education issued a call for statewide reforms very much in keeping with the Business Roundtable's goals. The group demanded radical change in school practices in order to reverse what it deemed to be a downward slide in educational quality.[115]

In 1991 a coalition of corporate executives, education leaders, and community activists formed LEARN, the Los Angeles Educational Alliance for Restructuring Now. LEARN was co-founded by Richard Riordan, millionaire businessman, and the current conservative Republican mayor of Los Angeles. Under the leadership of Robert Wycoff, LEARN's chairman, and president and CEO of the Atlantic Richfield Corporation, the coalition developed a reform plan for the city's schools, which was unanimously approved by the Los Angeles board of education. The plan is similar to the agenda developed by the Business Roundtable: decentralizing of the school bureaucracy, holding staffs accountable for student outcomes, conducting staff development, and making social services and medical care more available for needy children and their families. LEARN spent more than a half-million dollars on a publicity campaign over nine days to get their message out to the people of Los Angeles.[116]

Business has initiated a wide range of school-business partnerships over the last ten years. Since *A Nation at Risk*, business seems to have decided that the best way to influence schools is to work directly with them.[117] For their part, reform-minded school leaders have agreed to these partnerships because business makes a powerful ally in getting the investment necessary to change the way schools operate. Phillip Schlechty recommends that schools accept the help business offers in getting reform ideas off the ground:

> In my own experience, I have found that business leaders . . . can be powerful allies in the school restructuring effort. Among other things, such leaders, once they are fully enlisted in the school reform movements, can help serious reformers convince impatient newspaper editors and politicians who want instant results with little investment of time or dollars that the kind of reform that is needed takes time and requires considerable investment.[118]

Schlechty argues that when a CEO from a company like Xerox points out the difficulties inherent in reform, "politicians and editors tend to listen."[119] Another reason educational leaders are willing to form partnerships with business is that business has the money to mount lobbying and publicity campaigns to get the message of reform across to legislatures, the schools, and the public.[120] Even school leaders who support the status quo are hard put to resist overtures from business. They are vulnerable to the significant pressures business can exert. Just as business can sway public and media opinion in favor of school reform, it can turn that opinion against a school leader who refuses to cooperate in a school-business reform agenda. As in the early part of this century, the strong alliance between school leaders and business is based on the hope that each will be able to serve the other's interests.

The National Alliance of Business (NAB) has made promotion of school-business partnerships high on its agenda. Once concerned primarily with vocational education, the NAB has broadened the focus of its efforts. It created a board designed to turn local school-business partnerships into long-lasting coalitions aimed at school restructuring.[121] The NAB sponsored a project with the Harvard Business School whereby twenty-one business students worked in local school-business partnerships. The NAB published a report stemming from the work of these business students entitled, *Education: The Next Battleground for Corporate Survival.*[122]

School-business partnerships have become pervasive. By 1991, 50 percent of the districts in the nation had established some form of partnership with area businesses.[123] One type of partnership involves corporations allowing public school systems to start satellite schools on corporate property. The purpose of this "on-site" school is to decrease employee absenteeism and turnover, while helping the company recruit good employees. Schools report decreased transportation and construction costs as a result of these corporate satellite schools.[124] Another form of partnership provides for corporate executives to act as mentors for administrators, teachers, or students.[125] Businesses also send employees to work as members of the newly formed school decision-making teams so that schools will know what business requires of its employees in the work place.[126] Corporate executives have been sent to schools to act as "principal for a day" so that they may better understand what demands are made on school managers.[127]

Businesses have promoted the concept of the "school-to-work link" to remedy what has been decried as the worst school-to-work transition in the industrialized world by a wide spectrum of critics of the schools.[128] School-to-work programs are supposed to make learning more engaging for high school students by connecting the school to the work site. The basic element of school-to-work programs is the opportunity for students to learn work place skills during or after the school day. The manner in which this idea is carried out can vary. Businesses in California support "Career Academies"—schools within schools that aim to mesh academic and vocational instruction around a career theme. The business community provides mentors, on-the-job training, and summer and after-school work experience. Business helps to shape the curriculum of these academies through advisory committees.[129] Worklink, created by the Educational Testing Service, and piloted in Tampa, Florida, matches high school students to jobs in the private sector. The program aims to provide a mechanism for employers to hire well-qualified entry level workers while giving students a reason to work harder in school.[130] Other school-to-work programs are proliferating across the country, striving to make the path from school to work clearer for students to see and easier for them to set upon. In 1994 some of the nation's leading corporate executives formed the National Employment Research Council to promote business involvement in school-to-work programs. According to council member and Ford Motor CEO, Alex Trotman, the group of corporate leaders has the "greater objective of raising the competitiveness of the United States in an increasingly global marketplace."[131]

Business has also acted as a philanthropist for projects that replicate modern business management principles or further the education reform agenda favored by associations like the Business Roundtable. The business community has sponsored competitions for "break the mold" schools or examples of "bottom-up" reform.[132] Business has funded research on improving "educational productivity."[133] Corporations have provided financial support for new "charter schools," which operate independently from existing school district regulations.[134] IBM has given Pennsylvania State University one million dollars to launch a program called "Links with Suppliers" that will assess the necessary competencies of high school seniors headed for engineering or technical colleges.[135] Corporations such as Xerox, Kodak, Proctor and Gamble, and Nynex have provided funding for training teachers and administrators in the team approach to solving problems, a key facet of the TQM process.[136]

Perhaps the most notable among educational philanthropy is that of Walter Annenberg, billionaire former head of the Annenberg communications empire. Annenberg announced a half-billion dollar gift to education in January 1994. $50,000,000 of the bequest went to the New American Schools Development Corporation (NASDC), an organization headed by David Kearns, to fund development of "break the mold schools." Kearns and Brown University's Theodore Sizer advised Annenberg as he deliberated on the distribution of the bulk of his endowment. Annenberg ultimately chose to fund reform efforts in major urban school systems—with the proviso that the funds not flow through traditional bureaucratic mechanisms. His endowment promises more than $380,000,000 to reform projects in New York City, Chicago, Los Angeles, and Detroit schools.[137]

Beyond forming partnerships with schools and funding school reform research and projects, a portion of the business sector has supported the "for-profit" takeover of education. Chris Whittle, a Tennessee businessman, originally set his sights on developing a chain of for-profit private schools that would incorporate the business agenda for school reform. Among those who joined Whittle in his effort—referred to as the Edison Project—were several leading researchers in education. The announcement of the addition of Benno Schmidt, former president of Yale University, sent ripples of controversy through education circles. The Edison Project soon changed its focus from creating new for-profit schools to taking over the management of existing public schools as a for-profit venture. Whittle hired the superintendent of Detroit schools, Deborah McGriff, to help sign up districts for Edison's services. The Edison Project was awarded contracts to run three charter schools in Massachusetts, and existing schools within the public districts of Mount Clemons, Michigan, Wichita, Kansas, and Sherman, Texas. The business community has been a strong supporter of the Edison Project wherever it has won contracts to privately manage the public schools.[138]

Whittle did not originate the idea of "for-profit" management of schools. Education Alternatives, Incorporated (EAI) predated the Edison Project. Through the 1994–95 school year EAI provided private management for public schools in Baltimore, Maryland, Dade County, Florida, Duluth, Minnesota, and Pinckney,

Michigan. EAI promises to use modern management strategies that will improve the quality of instruction while lowering the costs of a district's operations. Despite lawsuits from disgruntled stockholders and stiff opposition from the AFT, EAI has been considered a viable option by a number of boards. Also jumping on the privatization bandwagon is the Disney Corporation, which entered into an agreement with a Florida school district to build and help run a "state of the art" public school.[139] As with the Edison Project, the business community has embraced the idea of contracting out to EAI and other firms, characterizing it as allowing school boards to "steer, not row" by hiring others to provide expert managerial services.[140]

Business is playing an active role on many fronts of the education reform movement, but it realizes that the changes it wants will not happen without support from the public. To end the satisfaction most people feel about their own neighborhood schools, business has launched a massive public relations campaign to get the public behind its reform agenda. The Business Roundtable spearheaded the development of a major five-year public service advertising campaign devoted to making the public see the need for radical changes in their local schools. The "Keep the Promise" campaign was begun in 1992. It involves television and newspaper advertisements evoking the theme that the nation has promised every child a future, and that schools must change if that promise is to be met. The ad agency in charge of the campaign, Young and Rubicam, has aimed to humanize the issue by running spots on Baby Jessica, the child who fell down a well in Texas some years ago. The voice over goes as follows:

> No country comes to the aid of a child the way we do. Imagine if the same effort that went into saving that little child in Texas went into keeping the promise that every child in America gets the best education.[141]

It is noteworthy that the ad focuses entirely on the benefits education can confer on the child, making no mention whatever of what educational change can do for the economy.

Finally, business executives have gotten directly involved in education since 1983 by taking positions that give them the power to analyze the problems in education and devise solutions that correspond to their analysis. Lewis Branscomb, vice-president and chief scientist of the IBM Corporation chaired the task force that wrote *A Nation Prepared*. David Kearns, former CEO of the Xerox Corporation was appointed the deputy secretary of education under Lamar Alexander in the Bush administration. He then became chairman of the New American Schools Development Corporation(NASDC). John Anderson, a former IBM executive, was appointed the president of NASDC in December of 1993.[142] Norman Deets and John Foley, executives with Xerox, joined the National Center on Education and the Economy, an influential think tank on education reform issues. Christopher Cross, former executive director of the Business Roundtable's education initiative, sat on the Maryland state board of education.[143] Louis Gerstner, IBM's CEO, headed the "Education Summit" of forty-three governors and a like number of business leaders in the spring of 1996. By having business-men in positions of authority and influence in agencies and forums that shape the education reform agenda, business has yet one more means of determining the direction we take in school change.

How Government Has Reacted

In the debate about school reform, government has joined forces with business, embracing the idea that schools should follow the example set by new business management practices. Both the federal and state governments accept the premise that restructured schools are necessary for America to compete in the global economy. Teacher involvement in decentralized decision-making and team problem-solving are but some of the recommendations states have made to local school districts.[144] Many of these recommendations have been made at the urging of business coalitions such as the Business Roundtable, which have lobbied governmental bodies for changes in schools.[145]

State-level business group support is strongly related to whether a governor, legislature, or state education department encourages local school districts to decentralize decision-making. States that do encourage this type of decentralization often provide financial incentives to districts that provide training for personnel in consensus decision-making, and develop pilot curriculum projects.[146] Many states have set up "quality" awards for education similar to the Malcolm Baldrige National Quality Award, which recognizes successful implementation of the TQM process in the private sector. The U.S. Commerce Department, which administers the Baldrige Award, has developed a Baldrige-type award for education to recognize schools that incorporate "quality principles" in their operation.[147]

The federal government has embraced the new ideal of the adequately skilled employee developed by business, as well as the idea that schools should change in order to produce such workers. The secretary of labor in the Bush administration, Anne McLaughlin, formed the Secretary's Commission on Achieving Necessary Skills (SCANS) to define the skills needed for employment, and to develop a dissemination strategy to transmit those defined skills to the nation's schools and homes. SCANS reported that "more than half our young people leave school without the knowledge or foundation required to find and hold a good job." The commission agreed with Peter Drucker, concluding that "good jobs will increasingly depend on people who can put knowledge to work."[148]

SCANS recommended five competencies that every youngster ought to have upon entering the work force to insure good job performance. Among these competencies are: knowing how to participate as a member of a team, understanding complex interrelationships, working with a variety of technologies, and using resources effectively. These competencies are "applicable from the shop floor to the executive suite." They are based on what SCANS refers to as the "three-part foundation":

1. Basic skills—reading, writing, math, listening, speaking.
2. Thinking skills—decision-making, problem solving, reasoning.
3. Personal qualities—responsibility, honesty, sociability.[149]

SCANS ends its report with the idea that just defining this foundation and the needed competencies for future workers will not suffice: "Schools must teach them." It suggests that all Americans "become revolutionaries in the cause of education." The goal of the revolution is to "create an entire people trained to think and equipped with the know-how to make their knowledge productive."[150]

The Clinton administration is carrying forward the goals of the SCANS Report. President Clinton signed the School-to-Work Opportunities Act in May 1994, which funds school-to-work programs aimed at developing necessary skills for employment. As he signed the bill he called it a "whole new approach to work and learning."[151] Clinton believes education is a foundation for economic growth and productivity. Accordingly, his administration is committed to altering how education proceeds so that American workers are the best equipped in the world. He refers to this commitment as the "human capital" element of his economic growth strategy.[152]

Conclusion

Once again, as in the first decades of this century and during the 1960s, changes in education are being driven by a perceived crisis in American society; a crisis resulting from the internal threat of an unraveling social fabric and an external threat of competition from other nations. Education is again seen as both a causal factor in the crisis and a means for its alleviation. *How* exactly education can defuse this crisis situation has been strongly influenced by new management models, especially the Total Quality process. Through its influence and power, business has dominated the education debate, directing attention away from long-standing domestic problems like racial, economic, and gender disparities and toward international economic competitiveness. By focusing the debate on outcomes, many of the daily problems facing teachers, students, and their parents are being shunted to the periphery of the discussion. Half the relatively new teachers believe that many children come to school with so many personal problems that for them school success is virtually impossible.[153] Concern for the underlying social problems that strongly correlate to poor school outcomes for children is not at the core of the agenda crafted by business and governmental officials. As the twentieth century comes to a close, America is once again focusing its attention on a reform agenda designed primarily to create a new generation of educational products for employers—with near total disregard for the personal difficulties children face—by revamping schools in accordance with popular business management principles.

The similarities between the role played by business in the present period of education reform and that which business played at the beginning of this century are striking: criticism is leveled at the schools for failing to prepare children for their roles as future employees, business sponsors surveys aimed at revealing the failings in the existing system, publicity and the media are utilized to make the public see the need for educational change. In both reform efforts, business philanthropy gives support to examples of the preferred model of education, business leaders play an influential role in educational organizations sponsoring reform, and form alliances between themselves and school officials. An orchestrated lobbying effort to persuade legislatures to reform the schools in accordance with business goals characterizes both reform efforts, as well. In both the earlier and the current period, education becomes the business of business, because it is identified as being central to American firms staying competitive in the global economy.

Nearly one hundred years ago business urged the schools to adopt the new bureaucratic corporate structure and to employ the principles of scientific management in the education process in order to attain heightened efficiency. Today's prescription for educational change disassembles that bureaucracy and implements the principles of TQM. Although the *hows* of school reform are different, the *why* that drives reform in both periods remains the same: efficiency in the preparation of youngsters for entrance to the world of work. In the next chapter, I will discuss the details of how the new pro-efficiency coalition aims to meet this long-standing goal given the changing definition of the "good employee" in the final years of the twentieth century.

6

The New Model for Efficient Education

The fin de siècle attempt to reorganize and redefine schooling aims to throw out many of the organizational structures, personnel roles, and instructional methodologies instituted by the early pro-efficiency reformers. In a twist of irony, many structures, roles, and methodologies now being proposed have their roots in the agenda put forth so many years ago by the educational progressives: John Dewey, Ella Flagg Young, and Jesse Newlon. More ironic still is the fact that it is in the name of economic survival, efficiency, and productivity that these reforms are now being proposed.

Today's education reformers share with the early educational progressives three major premises: 1) schools need to be decentralized operations, 2) teachers must function as professionals, and 3) education has be tailored to meet the needs of individual children. What most contemporary reformers do not share with the educational progressives, however, is their vision of education as a means of personal intellectual liberation, and, secondarily, a vehicle for reconstructing American society in keeping with democratic principles. While nearly all of the components of the current educational reform agenda originate with the educational progressives, the motivation behind the two reform efforts could not be more different.

Decentralize and "One Thousand Flowers Will Bloom"[1]

Ella Flagg Young was perhaps the first advocate of school councils composed of teachers and principals; councils that could act with authority on educational

141

issues. Young instituted these councils in Chicago in the last decade of the nineteenth century. Today, advocates of reform consistently point to "site-based decision-making" (SBDM) as key to reforming our educational system. Rejected out of hand by the early pro-efficiency reformers at the turn of the century, school councils are now seen as an antidote to the school hierarchy and bureaucracy instituted by those reformers—now considered to be the antithesis of efficiency in management.

What Is Wrong With the Top-Down Model

It is paradoxical that the hierarchical form of organization touted by men like Ellwood Cubberley as the paragon of efficiency is now seen as the major roadblock to productive schools. One could ask how a form of educational organization that was seen as efficient for the good part of a century could now be seen as ineffective. The answer comes from an examination of how education is now being defined and by whom. When *education* was interpreted as teaching children the rudiments of the three Rs, obedience, punctuality, and neatness—that is, the skills necessary for employment in mass production industries—the managerial bureaucracy was highly efficient at producing those desired outcomes.

Since 1983, however, the business-education-government coalition—the *new pro-efficiency reform alliance*—has redefined the components of an adequate education.[2] It is no longer enough to teach students what their parents and grandparents were taught when they were children. Now children's critical thinking and problem solving skills must be developed; their creativity is to be encouraged. Further, it is no longer acceptable, either economically or politically, to write off the majority of our youngsters as being unable to master "higher level thinking skills." All children are to be educated in accordance with this new definition of education. To meet this new goal, the current organizational structure must be disassembled.[3]

Linda McNeil has persuasively argued that the purpose of our schools as they are currently organized is control: top-level managers control middle-level managers, middle-level managers control teachers, teachers control students, and all the adults tightly control the content of the curricula offered children. Control, after all, was the pro-efficiency reformers' hope for the centralized bureaucracy—decisions made by professional school managers at the top of the hierarchy would be implemented uniformly throughout the school organization. The problem with control, however, is that it contradicts what learning is all about.[4] Genuine learning—that which results in a deepening and broadening of understanding—involves asking questions and seeking answers. The search is often messy, nonlinear, riddled with "mistakes," before the learner arrives at a satisfactory explanation, solution, or answer. Learners go about the task of learning in a variety of ways. Uniformity is the exception rather than the rule when children learn about their world and gain competencies. While a school organization that has control as its number one purpose may be "a smooth running operation," it can never be an organization devoted to authentic teaching and learning.

In the new concept of efficient school operations, engagement—not control—of students is the goal. Efficient schools must, therefore, be places where students are genuinely engaged. Serious learning takes involvement, intensity, loyalty to the task. Such hard work can be done by no one but the learner.[5] The new definition of efficiency in schools also assumes innovation to be continual, as teachers devise programs, projects, and problems to engage individual students. Research shows that innovation requires collegiality among teachers and school managers as they together plan offerings that meet the diverse needs of all the children.[6] The efficient school, therefore, must break down barriers between school teachers and their managers, letting them collaborate in the development of strategies that will help children attain ever-higher skill levels.

Theodore Sizer, professor of education at Brown University and head of the Coalition of Essential Schools, has written about this new concept of efficiency in terms of secondary education:[7]

> If truly "scientific" managers were today given the task of freshly designing ways and means for adolescents to become educated, they would doubtless create mechanisms very different from those we have inherited. . . . If effectiveness, productivity, and the avoidance of waste are important ends, an analysis of our practices would start at the base of the existing hierarchy, at the triangle of the student, teacher, and the subject they confront together. The primary question would be, How can adolescents be assisted in learning most efficiently?[8]

Sizer says because students differ, efficiency requires adaptability, which in turn requires that teachers have a large measure of autonomy. Further, since the energy and morale of teachers are crucial influences on the success of students, efficiency demands than teachers be freed from distracting and demeaning duties and given control over their work. Finally, efficient schools require teachers to know their students well. In such schools fewer—not more—students per teacher leads to greater efficiency of operation.[9]

Why Site-Based Decision-Making (SBDM) is Efficient

What leaders in American business are learning, and what educational leaders must learn as well, is that treating employees as important contributors to the enterprise, valuing their contributions, and involving them in the decision-making structure so that they can contribute increases not only productivity but employee satisfaction as well.[10]

Unlike the educational progressives who viewed decentralized decision-making as key to realizing their goal of democracy in the schoolhouse, the new pro-efficiency agenda points to better productivity in education as the primary purpose of decentralization. The decentralized model of decision-making is supposed to result in better outcomes because of the ability of those closest to students to tailor a program to their specific needs and learning styles. In theory, decentralization of decision-making authority in schools will operate just as employee involvement in decision-making operates in those industries that need the flexibility to compete in ever-changing product markets. Ultimate goals continue to be considered the prerogatives of upper management. However, once a goal is decided upon by senior management, the best way of reaching that goal is decided upon by people who formerly were at the base of the bureaucratic hierarchy. In a school district the superintendent and school board might set a goal of grade-level reading ability for all students. While every school in the district would be responsible for reaching that goal, how each school might teach reading would be left to the discretion of the school council. Its decision-making authority would be maintained as long as it was able to reach the pre-ordained goal. This model assumes that along with decision-making authority comes accountability for results.

Just as TQM has some basic assumptions very different from those of the scientific management model, the assumptions underlying the plan for school-based decision-making differ greatly from those of early pro-efficiency reformers. First, power is not viewed as a zero-sum game. According to Gary Philips, executive director of the National School Improvement Project, "Power is like kindness. You give some and it grows."[11] The combined wisdom of all participants empowered to make decisions will result in a synergy that outstrips the wisdom of a small cadre of managers at the top of the managerial pyramid.[12] This idea mirrors the sentiments of Ella Flagg Young when she wrote in 1900:

The level of power in the educational system is determined by the degree in which the principle of cooperation is made incarnate in developing and realizing the aim of the school.[13]

Another assumption of the decentralization model is summed up by Philips as, "One destination, many roads." While Franklin Bobbitt was certain there was a "one best way" to teach everything from penmanship to math, the new model believes there is no such thing as "the one best way." As Sizer puts it, "each school must be shaped by its own people and must respect the community it serves."[14] Sizer's idea is very much in keeping with the type of education espoused by educational progressives.[15] John Dewey favored decentralized decision-making on curricular issues almost one hundred years ago:

> The fact that (the course of study) is fixed by board of education, superintendent, supervisor, by a power outside the teacher in the class room who alone can make that course of study a living reality, is a fact too obvious to be concealed.[16]

By beginning with the particular inclinations of a child or a community rather than those of some authority standing outside the critical teacher-child interaction, educators at the school level will be more successful in teaching youngsters. As John Dewey put it, "the child becomes the center of gravity about which the appliances of education revolve; he is the center about which they are organized."[17]

Studies done in the 1980s on what came be known as "effective schools"— schools that got good results with poor, inner-city children—indicated that these assumptions about the "efficiency" of decentralized decision-making could be supported empirically. According to research conducted by University of Illinois professor Susan Rosenholtz, effective schools encourage teachers to adapt schoolwide instructional programs to the needs of their individual students. Collective decision-making makes possible the deliberate evaluation, discussion, and modifications necessary to develop the highest quality instructional program. Rosenholtz's research showed, too, that these collective deliberations lead to heightened teacher clarity about particular instructional goals and pedagogical methods. In effective schools the principal and the staff are in agreement both about the goals for students and the means to reach those goals. Principals often disregard district directives in order to allow teachers to use the methods and materials they find to be most efficacious. Finally, just as has been postulated by TQM, participants in decision-making have a sense of ownership of the school's instructional goals and a stake in the future of the collective enterprise. In other words, pushing decisions down to the school level and empowering teachers to make decisions on instructional issues can result in better school performance than top-down bureaucratic decision-making.[18]

Giving teachers the power to work collectively to devise instructional programs and select appropriate materials is also linked to the goal of having children develop the abilities to think critically, to problem-solve and be cooperative team players. As George Counts said sixty years ago, and Albert Shanker reiterated some thirty years later, teachers who are forced into roles of subservience are not likely to develop critical thinking in their students. In 1986 *A Nation Prepared* concurred: "Teachers must think for themselves if they are to help others think for themselves, be able to act independently and collaborate with others, and render critical judgment."[19] With the changing definition of education comes the change in the role teachers are to play in the endeavor. Now that education is supposed to go beyond routine skills and prepare students for solving complex problems, teachers should be freed from the requirement of obedience to managerial directives on curriculum issues. They must be allowed to exercise discretion in devising instructional strategies that work for children with varying interests, needs, and talents.

Finally, much has been written on why the school—rather than the school district—must be the center of educational change. Writing in this vein has been done predominantly by those in the reform movement who accept the social philosophy of the educational progressives—not only their agenda for organizing education. These reformers point out that once education is defined as including inquiry and reflection, it is clear that teachers must be free to reflect upon their work with children and upon ways in which they might do their work better. Teachers in this model are not consumers of educational research, but researchers themselves, seeking ever-more productive means of helping their students develop as thinkers and problem solvers. Teachers in a school building are, thus, their own change agents and active, critical consumers of their own and others' knowledge in the context of their own practice. As Kenneth Sirotnik, professor at the University of Washington, summed it up, "Schools are not only places for teaching critical thinking; they are also places for thinking critically about teaching."[20]

Decentralization and Management's Role in the School

There is some confusion over what role school managers will play in the decentralized school system. It is clear that pushing decisions down to the school level ought to reduce the need for supervisors and directors who, in the hierarchical model, made certain that orders from the top were being implemented. Most proponents of SBDM recognize that there will be some cuts of managerial positions. Yet it is not clear what the duties and responsibilities will be for those managers who remain in the system. Also not apparent is the degree of power they are to share with—or give up to—their former subordinates. Depending on the predilections of the education reformer addressing the issue—and the reasons behind his or her call for reform—the role for management varies.

Theodore Sizer is a reformer who hopes to implement Dewey's ideals of pedagogy and democracy through empowerment of individual schools. Although he shares many ideas on the specifics of restructuring education with the new pro-efficiency reformers, he parts company with them in regard to their definition of purpose of education. He writes that the state has no right to insist that children exit the school system "employable."[21] Sizer also disagrees with the new pro-efficiency movement in regard to the role management ought to play in a restructured school system. He recommends a massive allocation of power away from school managers and toward teachers, students, and parents. Sizer does not agree with Philips's idea that when managers give power to others, everyone gains. He asserts there will be winners and losers in school restructuring and managers will be on the losing side.

> If more authority is to be given to the schools to chart their own courses, those agencies previously assigned to direct these schools must be eliminated. Keeping them around—"revising their mission"—is an evasion. If new missions derive from new powers, let them do so *de novo*. But asking previous "power centers" to give up power, and the habits that accrue with it, and to figure out something else to do is futile. They will not give up power.[22]

Sizer feels that there must be a total delegation of authority so that schools may be able to develop their own character and program. This total delegation would allow for a vast reduction in the number of central office managers. The lines between teachers and principals would blur. The principal would once again become, as in the days before the early pro-efficiency reforms, a principal teacher.[23]

Sizer represents a minority opinion, however. While the new pro-efficiency reformers share Sizer's advocacy of SBDM, they do not share all of his reasons for supporting it—that is, it is both moral and democratic. As Phillip Schlechty puts it, this is not about "truth, beauty, and justice."[24] Rather, SBDM is an instrument top management can use to get the highest degree of efficiency and effectiveness out of the organization. These new pro-efficiency reformers do not often emphasize their belief that management retains the power to determine the strategic plan, the goals, and the vision for the school organization. What they do emphasize is management's duty to solicit input from all the "stakeholders" before it arrives at decisions that affect the future of the school organization. The fact is, for these reformers, management still is the locus of power.[25]

Schlechty describes what he sees as a suitable merging of central direction and teacher involvement in decision-making:

> The system has taken a great deal of time involving teachers in the creation of policies and programs and even more in training and informing those who were not directly involved in formulating policies, procedures, curriculum guides, and so on. Moreover, it is commonplace for the principal to take the lead in conducting training and work sessions at the building level where frank discussion of the meaning and intent of central directives is carried out. Most important, mechanisms are established whereby individual teachers and school faculties have—and feel they have—an impact on subsequent thinking about policies and procedures. . . . This type of system is based on human values and human commitments, not on rigid control structures and impersonal management arrangements.[26]

The superintendent, according to Schlechty, should continue in the role of CEO—an industrial comparison first made so many years ago by Ellwood Cubberley.[27] The difference is that in the current era, a CEO not acknowledging the benefits to the organization of seeking input from the rank and file is becoming rare.

Schlechty's conception of the role to be played by managers in SBDM is echoed by advocates of school restructuring. While power is to rest with management, how management exercises that power is to change. Managers will continue in their role of leaders, in both the school and the district. As leaders, they will operate as "brokers of improvement," giving teachers resources and information necessary for them to work more effectively and make better decisions.[28] Peter Drucker says the manager—in both industry and schools—will act as an orchestra conductor who cannot tell a French horn player how to play but who can focus the musician's "abilities on enhancing the orchestra's communal performance."[29] Of course, the conductor continues to select the music the musicians are to play. Marc Tucker, head of the National Center on Education and the Economy, speaks for many experts in school reform when he says that top management should choose the goals of the district, communicate them clearly to all members of the organization, and evaluate how well individual schools meet those goals.[30] In keeping with the TQM concept of managers as facilitators, central office administration will become a service center offering resources and technical assistance to schools.[31]

Perhaps most controversial in the SBDM model are the new responsibilities associated with the principalship. The principal is often seen as the nexus of restructuring efforts, accepting additional autonomy and accountability on behalf of the school staff and passing it through to the teachers and the larger community. There is consensus on the notion that the principal will change from a middle manager for the district to either a facilitator or leader for his or her own school. There is some tension, however, between the expectation that the principal will take responsibility for the school's outcomes—the leader's role— while having teachers empowered to make the decisions which lead to those outcomes.[32] Even in theory, the principal's role in SBDM is not clearly worked out. As I will discuss later, this has been the cause of apprehension among school principals.

An interesting twist in the discussion of the new way school managers are to manage is the idea that managers should become less "macho" and more feminine. The following speaks legions about the stereotypes associated with gender in schools—and, for that matter—in society:

> We need to shift our thinking about what it means to be a strong superintendent. We need to develop some gentler, more feminine images of leadership to accompany our tough, masculine images of leadership ... superintendents need to pay more attention to the unheroic dimensions of leadership if they are to promote local autonomy and professionalism. Superintendents must not only have a personal vision, but they must also work with others to develop a shared vision and to find the common ground; they must not only have answers, but also ask the right questions ... they must not only wield power but also depend on others and develop caring relationships; they must not only exercise leadership, but also nurture the development of leadership throughout the school district.[33]

The "feminine" version of management stresses collaboration, empowerment of others, inclusiveness, and caring, while the "masculine" version of management emphasizes competition, dominance, achievement, and success.[34] Assuming for a moment that these gender-bound styles of management are accurate, one wonders how this feminization of managerial practice will occur given the preponderance of men in the ranks of school management.

Decentralization Leads to New Roles and Responsibilities for Teachers

Under SBDM, teachers are to assume control over decisions that were historically the province of others, especially school managers. Teachers look favorably upon this proposed involvement in what has traditionally been deemed "administrative" issues.[35] This new role for teachers resurrects Jesse Newlon's idea that teachers have to be given control over their work if education is to denote more than rote learning and obedience to authority. Among the new responsibilities for teachers often mentioned is collective decision-making on schoolwide issues such as hiring colleagues, developing curricula, allocating school budget monies, and developing self-evaluation tools. Individually teachers are to accept greater responsibility for mentoring new teachers on staff, providing professional development for their colleagues, and evaluating peers. Collectively and individually, under SBDM teachers are to become responsible for issues that go beyond the confines of their own classroom.[36] This heightened level of responsibility makes possible the professionalization of teaching, a goal shared by the educational progressives and the teacher unions of the 1960s. Later in this chapter I will discuss in some depth the design for developing the teaching profession.

Decentralization Opens the Schoolhouse Door to Parents

Ella Flagg Young advocated for the inclusion of parents in school affairs because, practically speaking, it was essential to educating the child. As is true of all facets of her educational philosophy, however, parental involvement in the life of the school was also an ethical issue. Parents and teachers together had the moral obligation to work together to create a unity of experience for the young in order to give children the greatest opportunity to grow and develop.[37] Most new pro-efficiency reformers recommend that parents be included on site-based councils. Few among them go beyond Young's practical rationale to support their recommendation, however. They point out that children do not generally do well in school without the support and involvement of their parents. Some reformers use the metaphor of a partnership to invoke a proposed new relationship between professional educators and parents—that is, in order to get the best student outcomes, educators must become partners with parents. There is also some recognition that to be successful, schools cannot concentrate solely on the child, but must address the needs of the parent, for the two generations are interdependent.[38]

TQM provides another metaphor to describe the new role for parents in the SBDM model: parent as customer. The school must discover the needs and expectations of its parent-customers if they are to keep them happy. Some reformers recommend including parents on school councils in order to solicit these customers' ideas about educational programs, discipline, and the like. Other reformers disagree, stating that business does not include the customer in its internal decision-making process.

Whether parents as customers are included on councils or not, inextricably tied to this idea is the parental right of school choice—that is, parents can move their children to a school that meets their expectations for quality education. Under "choice"—and unlike the early pro-efficiency model—parents, not school managers, decide what schools their children attend, and what programs work for their children. Ellwood Cubberley's assumption that the professional school manager always knows better than the parent is put to rest along with other tenets of the old pro-efficiency agenda.

The Role of Teacher Unions in the SBDM Model

Most experts on decentralizing operations in both the private and the public sectors see unions as a useful tool for organizational change.[39] Despite this expert support for some degree of bilateralism, school management has typically acted unilaterally in its efforts to implement the SBDM model. Although over 70 percent of the nation's districts have collective bargaining agreements with their teachers, few have attempted to decentralize operations via a bilateral agreement between school management and the teachers' union.[40] A unilateral management initiative sometimes occurs at the urging of the state education department or local business coalitions. It results in unions usually having little say on issues as central to SBDM as selection of teacher representatives to school councils, and determination of matters to be decided by those school councils.[41]

Some big cities, however, have received a lot of media coverage for their use of collective bargaining as a tool for designing the SBDM model for their districts. New York City, Dade County, Florida, Los Angeles, Cincinnati, and Rochester, New York, are some of the highly publicized examples of districts that have used collective bargaining to design and implement decentralized decision-making.[42] A progress report on perhaps the most notable of these experiments—the Rochester city school district—will be the focus of the next chapter.

Since the vast majority of districts continue to use the industrial model of bargaining adopted in most states during the 1960s and 1970s, there is much discussion about how collective bargaining might evolve to address the empowerment of teachers in decision-making. Some experts in the field of labor relations in education have suggested that the industrial model may be replaced by one specifically adapted to education in order to accomplish this goal.[43] In this new incarnation, collective bargaining would be used to address issues of educational policy—previously considered to be in the domain of "managerial prerogatives" and, therefore, not subject to mandatory bargaining. The confrontational stance that frequently characterizes current school management–teacher union relations might be tempered by an attitude of collaboration and trust. But, as some commentators have pointed out, the contentious nature of bargaining might remain; only the items traded would be different.[44] As *A Nation Prepared* recommended:

> The focus of bargaining can and should be changed. Unions, boards, and school administrators need to work out a new accommodation based on exchanging professional level salaries and a professional environment on the one hand, for the acceptance of professional standards of excellence and the willingness to be held fully accountable for the results of one's work, on the other.[45]

In this new model of bargaining in education, teachers would no longer exchange obedience to management for wages and benefits; they would swap accountability for results for professional salaries and working conditions.

Teacher Professionalism: A Key Ingredient to the Reform Recipe

The new pro-efficiency reformers are abandoning the early pro-efficiency notion of the teacher as operative, transmitting knowledge and facts handed down by higher authorities. They are espousing a concept of teaching first delineated by the educational progressives: engaging students via a variety of experiences in order to promote deep understanding and the discovery that knowledge is constructed and contested.[46] Theodore Sizer describes the secret of teachers who are successful in this latter type of teaching—a rarity in today's American high school:

> What makes them especially so is their judgment, their ability to find the appropriate recipe for engaging the attention and ultimately the minds and energies of their particular students. Adaptability is at the core of their

judgment. Their work suggests no Pill for Good Pedagogical Judgment that can be packaged and distributed by school authorities.[47]

Reformers argue that for this concept of teaching to become the norm rather than the rare occurrence, teaching must be accorded professional status. Heavy monitoring and control of teachers must be replaced by professionals exercising their judgment and discretion to meet the varied needs of their students.

The late Ernest Boyer, who headed the Carnegie Foundation for the Advancement of Teaching, said:

> It is time to recognize that whatever is wrong with America's public schools cannot be fixed without the help of those already in the classroom. To talk about recruiting better students into teaching without examining the circumstances that discourage teachers is simply a diversion. . . . In the end, the quality of American education can be no greater than the dignity we assign to teaching.[48]

Boyer's sentiments reflect a basic tenet of the educational progressives' agenda. Businessmen and government officials who want to have graduates ready to become "competitive employees" agree. They have become convinced that reform efforts must focus on teachers and teaching. *A Nation Prepared* summarized the argument this way:

> In this new pursuit of excellence, however, Americans have not yet fully recognized two essential truths: first, that success depends on achieving far more demanding educational standards than we have ever attempted to reach before, and second, that the key to success lies in creating a profession equal to the task—a profession of well-educated teachers prepared to assume new powers and responsibilities to redesign schools for the future.[49]

In this new model of education, the teacher—not the school manager—becomes central to hoped for outcomes from the educational system.

Sixty years ago educational progressive George Counts wrote that for teaching to become a profession it would require improved university training, vastly improved working conditions, and the recruitment of gifted people into the occupation.[50] His prescription for professionalism is nearly identical to that currently being promoted by the new pro-efficiency coalition. The contemporary call for teacher professionalism can be broken down into three components: 1) redesigned teacher education for new teachers, 2) better salaries and working conditions for all teachers, and 3) professional improvement for teachers already in the classroom. Together, these three proposals aim to reconstruct teaching to bring it in line with occupations traditionally granted professional status by society.

A Revamping of Teacher Education

Traditional teacher education continues to follow the model designed by the early pro-efficiency reformers many years ago. Since teachers were not supposed to create curricula, their education has been heavily focused on teaching methods. Few elementary teachers major in something other than "education" in college. Most secondary teachers also typically major in education, albeit with some course concentration in a particular discipline. In 1985, education majors had the lowest SAT scores of any college major.[51] This fact has led many reformers to argue that on average, the education major draws the least able students. Teacher colleges, formerly called "normal schools" in the days of William Bagley, have been criticized as being "certification mills where the minimally qualified instruct the barely literate in a parody of learning."[52]

A Nation Prepared outlined the type of skills professional teachers ought to be prepared to demonstrate upon entering the classroom. It is doubtful that traditional teacher education programs will be successful in training new teachers in these skills:

> Teachers should have a good grasp of the ways in which all kinds of physical and social systems work; a feeling for what data are and the uses to which they can be put, an ability to help students see patterns of meaning where others see only confusion; an ability to foster genuine creativity in students; and the ability to work with other people in work groups that decide for themselves how to get the job done. They must be able to learn all the time, as the knowledge required to do their work twists and turns with new challenges and the progress of science and technology. Teachers will not come to school knowing all they have to know, but knowing how to figure out what they need to know, where to get it, and how to help others make meaning out of it.[53]

This description of the teacher harkens back to Dewey's very demanding image of the teacher as a person with a broad knowledge base as well as an understanding of how to guide youngsters through their very individual, idiosyncratic paths of intellectual growth. Dewey recommended that teachers have the benefit of both the traditional university education and pedagogical training. Today's reformers often recommend something quite similar—future teachers should have an academic major as well as early induction experiences in the life of the classroom.[54] They believe that mastery of content and the complex social relations of the classroom will be achieved through a combination of rigorous academic learning and clinical practice.[55]

Upgraded Working Conditions

Raising salaries to a level competitive with other professions would go a long way in attracting some of the "best and the brightest" into teaching. The problem is that even Albert Shanker, long-time president of the American Federation of Teachers, agrees that a raise large enough to do that is not likely in the near future.[56] In fact, in times of fiscal crisis teacher salaries are often singled out by school boards and citizens as the reason for a school system's financial predicament, despite the fact that teachers' salaries generally account for less than half of the total school budget. Since an influx of money to fund markedly higher salaries is improbable, Shanker and others have suggested that a significant improvement in the working conditions in which teachers must practice would represent another powerful incentive in the recruitment of good candidates into teaching.

Many reformers have agreed that managerial dictates are one of the biggest deterrents to enticing bright young people into teaching. In the opinion of the New York State Industrial Cooperation Council, the inability of teachers to assume control over their work leads to attracting and keeping only "incompetents, because the best minds will not submit to conditions which no self-respecting intelligence likes to put up with."[57] A study of high school sophomores found that by the tenth grade, students view their teachers' working conditions as unattractive. They are clearly aware that teachers must follow state curriculum edicts and administrative directives. One student who was interviewed for the study called teaching "boring work" due to the need for teachers to follow these mandates step by step. The student added, "I would rather . . . be able to reach students my own way. I wouldn't teach in the public schools because they limit you too much and you have to be careful about what you say."[58]

Shanker agrees that unless working conditions in education change, students like this perceptive fifteen-year old will rarely entertain the possibility of becoming a teacher:

> We can't expect to recruit top-notch candidates to go into our classrooms unless we offer them the challenge and opportunity to exercise their creativity and judgment, the chance to control their working lives, the stimulation of frequent exchanges with their peers and a sense of being part of an intellectual community.[59]

SBDM and teacher professionalism go hand in hand. Yet reformers warn, it is not enough to say that decisions on curriculum, materials, scheduling, and resource allocation will be made by teachers at the building level. Provision must be made to give teachers the time needed to engage in "reflective practice." They must be freed from using their time in hall and cafeteria duty, in copying assignments on the Xerox machine, in providing playground supervision.[60] Training in collaborative decision-making needs to be provided. Resources must be made available to enable school councils to engage in their own research and to develop their own projects and programs. Teachers require the basic trappings of today's professional workplace—a desk, a phone, a computer, a quiet place to work. Reformers caution that without these working conditions, SBDM and teacher professionalism will remain grand designs rarely executed in reality.[61]

Continuous Professional Improvement for All Teachers

An assumption of the TQM process is that members of decision-making teams will continually improve and update their skills through ongoing training and education. In keeping with this basic principle of TQM—as well as the goal of teacher professionalism—is professional development for the nation's 2.4 million teachers. The vast majority of these teachers are products of the state teacher colleges now being so roundly criticized. Further, they have spent their careers in organizations that have demanded obedience in following curriculum guides from state education departments or textbook companies. Most of these teachers are ill-equipped to play the central role carved out for them in the radical overhaul in the educational process now being recommended by reformers. Unless these experienced teachers are introduced to new pedagogical techniques, the future of school reform is doubtful. Thus, opportunities for professional growth are being recommended by every advocate of serious reform.

Central to this idea of professional growth is ending the isolation of individual teachers working separately in their own classrooms. In place of the idea of individual practitioners—each striving to implement the mandated curriculum—is the concept of the collegial group of school or district professionals working to create a program uniquely suited to their students. Susan Loucks-Horsley, a senior associate at the Regional Laboratory for Educational Improvement, describes the ideal collegial teacher group as a learning community "where adults are always asking questions, seeking answers, and investigating."[62] To accommodate this idea of teacher as learner, teachers must be encouraged to participate in school improvement efforts, group and individual research projects, curriculum creation, and assessment development. The goal is to have teachers working together as colleagues, effectively adapting school programs to students through a transformation of their teaching.[63]

Essential to this theory of professional development is the use of teachers as experts. Since the time of Edward Thorndike, the father of quantitative educational research, teachers have been told what works and what does not work by outside experts who have used "scientific" methods. Educational research has been used by managers as a rationale for their directives to teachers. Throughout the century, scientific researchers have discounted the knowledge teachers acquire through experience as being "subjective," "folklore," and "value-laden." The premise has been that only science can discover "empirical, objective, and value-free" truth. In the new model of the professional teacher, however, the "science" of educational inquiry is merged with the "folklore" of educational practice. The dogmatic split between research and practice is replaced by teachers and researchers working side by side in continual inquiry on educational issues.[64]

As with all facets of the current reform initiative, the purpose of continual professional improvement is to change the traditional pedagogical practices used in schools throughout this century. By having teachers work together to grapple with questions of how skills valued by society can best be taught, and how student progress toward mastery of those skills can best be assessed, reformers are hopeful that teachers will devise alternatives to what has been standard practice for most of this century. In a real sense, the point of professional improvement is to make teachers into learners again. As in the TQM model found in industry, teachers are called on to continuously improve their performance by collectively evaluating their experiences with students and analyzing quantitative and qualitative measures of student achievement. In both education and industry, the point of this collaborative effort is a transformation in "business as usual"—a transformation that is aimed at dramatically improving the effectiveness of the organization, be it school or business.

Unions' Role in Promoting Teacher Professionalism

Teacher professionalism was a goal of early unionists such as Margaret Haley. It remained a goal throughout the tumultuous 1960s, when a reinvigorated AFT and a transformed NEA gained the right of collective bargaining for teachers. The current reform agenda has given unions some reason to believe that powerful elements in society are serious about professionalizing teaching. The AFT and the NEA have tread the waters of this reform current with different strokes, swapping places as the "leader in reform" over the last decade. All this as they simultaneously worked to protect the more mundane interests of their members.

In the mid-1980s the AFT made SBDM a bargaining goal in many urban school districts represented by its locals. The strategy was successful in a number of larger cities. The incorporation of SBDM in the teachers' contract opened the door to other innovations that bolster the concept of teaching as a profession. Toledo instituted a system of peer review whereby teachers acted as mentors for and evaluators of their colleagues.[65] Hammond, Indiana, entered into an unprecedented twelve year "living contract" that aimed to provide educators more flexibility in responding to schools' needs.[66] In 1989 teachers and school managers in Dade County, Florida, joined together to invite proposals for designing and operating forty-nine new schools in what became known as the district's Saturn School Project, a take-off on the General Motors' division based on labor-management teamwork.[67] A 1989 study by the RAND Corporation found that progress in school reform was linked to a strong teachers' union local and progressive union leadership.[68] AFT initiatives during the late 1980s were aimed at demonstrating that unionism and professionalism were not contradictory terms.

Although the NEA did not embrace SBDM as quickly or as enthusiastically as did the AFT, by 1991 NEA endorsed SBDM as a bargaining goal so long as provision was made for voluntary participation by schools.[69] The NEA chose, however, to focus its efforts to professionalize teaching by developing innovative pedagogical reforms. The NEA Mastery in Learning Project aspires to couple academic research on learning with teachers' collective experiences in order to have schools and districts devise more effective teaching strategies. NEA also supports "learning laboratories," which assists local affiliates that choose to engage in broad plans to restructure their schools in collaboration with school boards, businesses, and community leaders.[70] NEA created a research center to promote experimentation by teachers and schools in hopes of positioning itself to the forefront of school reform.[71]

As the story of the AFT reform experiment in Rochester unfolds in the next chapter, it will become clear that the union's strong support for school reform has had a price. Among those who keep track of the unions' rivalry as well as their efforts to support reform, it appears the AFT has lost its early lead in spearheading reform. As of this writing, the costs connected with the AFT big city reform experiments, coupled with the NEA sustained effort to promote pedagogical innovation, put the NEA slightly ahead of the AFT in efforts to represent and develop the professional element of teaching.

Out with the Factory Model, In with Dewey's Concept of Child-Centered Education

Young people grow intellectually, physically, and socially at different rates, often with mysterious spurts and stops along the way. Both doting parents and cool-eyed researchers know that. Some kids excel in language and flounder in mathematics; the hotshot in one area is not necessarily great in another. Further, not all kids pay attention at school at any given moment, for benign or deplorable reasons. So, by their high school years the youngsters' potential and actual school performance often diverge: "ninth grade" is an administratively useful concept, but one that tells a teacher far less about a student's intellectual and emotional development than the grouping would suggest.[72]

The old pro-efficiency model of education glorified the notion that dissimilar children—raw materials—could be molded into an array of standardized educational products by use of uniform curriculum and routines. William Bagley wrote in 1907 that habit building was the essence of education. The law of habit building was the following: "Focalization of consciousness upon the process to be automatized, plus attentive repetition of this process, permitting no exceptions until automatism results."[73]

Education was to be an impersonal matter; school a place where routines dominated the efforts of children and teachers. While the extreme rigidity proposed by Bagley relaxed somewhat over the years, schools have continued to be impersonal, bureaucratized places, with children's individual differences rarely addressed by uniform curriculum, grading by age, or assignment to teachers by "objective" criteria.[74]

This model of education is now being rejected out of hand because it is no longer considered to be well-suited to American economic needs. The tracking and sorting mechanisms that direct the majority of youngsters into courses that do not demand serious work or intellectual rigor are now seen as dysfunctional in an economy that hopes to win the day by having the great majority of workers engage in "knowledge work." Dewey spoke passionately about having children be the center of gravity for the educational endeavor. Reformers today agree, believing that the only efficient and effective way to create a generation of people who can think critically is to insure that serious learning is done by all children. Theodore Sizer put it this way:

If the school is to justify its existence . . . it has to push all kids to do such "serious work." . . . This does not mean that there is One Best Curriculum.

Nor does it mean that everyone will learn at the same rate or in the same way. Nor does it mean that everyone will strive steadily all the time. It means that the same meaningful standard is set for all, that the kids know it, and that the school will help them achieve it, whatever the cost and however long it takes.[75]

Traditionally, school authorities have mandated inputs—number of minutes a week of math, what constitutes a course in basic geometry, the textbook to be used. The new concept of education focuses instead on outcomes—all children will reach predetermined levels of achievement in areas deemed essential by important participants in the education reform discussion.[76] The inputs necessary for different children to reach those levels will vary. Some children may demonstrate accomplishment in all skills by sixteen; others not until twenty-two. Whatever it takes—and however long it takes—every child is to reach a level of competency in areas judged essential by society.

The performance standards often recommended in any discussion on outcomes-based education bear a close identity to a report by the Department of Labor's Secretary's Commission on Achieving Necessary Skills (SCANS). Facility with basic skills, realistic problem-solving, teamwork, ability to analyze data, tolerance of diversity are but some of the oft-stated abilities graduates of a child-centered, outcomes-based program are to demonstrate.[77] While agreement by a broad cross section of society on these outcomes has not yet been reached—and may, in fact, be very difficult to achieve—leaders in education, business, and government are vigorously supporting outcomes similar to those chosen by SCANS.[78]

A new orthodoxy about how schools are to go about achieving the commonly stated outcomes is quickly forming. The student is to be seen as a worker actively engaged in rigorous, demanding, and interesting work. The curriculum is to be integrated across the disciplines, with depth of understanding taking priority over the number of subjects covered. "Less is more" is the motto of this new model for education.[79] Original sources are to replace textbooks, with literature taking a preeminent role in the teaching of reading. Higher order thinking skills and learning how to learn are to take the place of rote drill and memorization. Basic skills will be taught within the context of projects, hands-on activities and real-life experiences out in the community. The teacher will act as an expert coach, guiding individual students toward the predetermined outcomes in unique and varied ways.[80]

To demonstrate commitment to the idea that all children can master higher order thinking skills—and to teach children the skills necessary to work in teams in the work place—tracking is to be replaced by what has come to be known as "cooperative learning."[81] In the model of cooperative learning, children of varying academic abilities work together in small groups to design and complete projects, or solve complex, real-life problems. In keeping with Dewey's criticism of competition among students, advocates say that cooperative learning encourages students to spend less time worrying about class rank and more time on their work.[82] They also say that by expecting more of students who would traditionally be consigned to the lowest tracks, students will meet those expectations given the support of the cooperative team and the teacher-facilitator.[83]

This child-centered approach to education also assumes that the traditional use of time and space in schools will be significantly changed. Use of space will be flexible so that students can work alone, in small groups, with a mentor, or with an entire class.[84] The ideal school will look nothing like of the "egg crate" design so typical of American schools today. In addition, students will not have to switch classes as the bell rings every forty minutes to mark the end of one "subject" and the beginning of another. They will take fewer classes of longer length each day, allowing time for in-depth study, reflection, and project development.[85]

The metaphor of school as *factory* is replaced by school as *community* under the new model of efficient education; a metaphor that has its origins in John Dewey's vision of education. In a community, the citizens know one another, convene town meetings to hash out communal problems, and work together for the common good. Communities that are cohesive tend to be small rather than large. Successful communities often engage in boosterism to build spirit among the members. They incorporate values in everything they undertake. Communities have parents as well as children, and businessmen as well as teachers. They are inclusive of all generations and diverse points of view. Trust and respect between diverse community members is the grease that reduces friction as they live and work together. Reformers today suggest that those elements of the successful community be replicated in schools, and that the "school as community" metaphor be the driving vision behind all reform efforts.[86]

Finally, in the new model for efficient education, standardized tests take a back seat to what is being called "authentic assessment." Scientifically designed, norm-referenced tests were first used by the early pro-efficiency reformers to sort youngsters into what were seen as appropriate tracks—only the top 5 percent of students could score in the 95th percentile or above.[87] They were never meant to test depth of learning or the ability to use school knowledge in real situations. Given the new push for all students to become critical thinkers and problem solvers, the norm-referenced test is now seen as being of limited usefulness by the new pro-efficiency reformers. A recent study by the National

Science Foundation supports their position. It concludes that these tests result in children knowing less than they might have if the tests were never given. *Newsweek* reported the study's findings this way:

> Standardized tests were supposed to hold teachers' feet to the fire—make them work hard to fill little minds with the concepts, principles and facts of science and math. The minds do get filled—for about as long as the test lasts.[88]

The study found that students who memorize math formulas for exams are unable to recall and use them six months later. Information is retained only if it is connected to other concepts and facts. The learning of isolated information that is encouraged by standardized tests is, by necessity, only temporary learning.

In lieu of testing for student progress by having them fill in bubbles with a number two pencil, reformers say students' competencies should be tested by having them engaged in challenging tasks. These "authentic" assessments will be designed to test for deeper understanding in and across subjects, and to encourage student reflection on performance.[89] At the heart of many recommendations for this type of assessment is the portfolio of student work. For example, a student's math portfolio might contain a wide range of materials that demonstrate the student's ability to learn and understand math beyond a rudimentary level—for example, a solution to an assigned problem, a problem made up by the student, a paper done for another subject that includes math, or entries from a journal. Portfolios could contain nonwritten materials such as video or audiotapes. A student's self-assessment might also be part of the materials contained in the portfolio.[90]

The call for child-centered education is reminiscent both of the recommendations of the early educational progressives and those of advocates for alternative education in the 1960s and early 1970s. The often short-lived experiments in alternative education of two decades ago bear a striking resemblance to the type of school proposed by the new pro-efficiency reformers.

Amos Houghton, a teacher in an alternative school in Arlington, Virginia, in the 1970s, commented on the differences between it and the traditional school:

> Teaching here is infinitely more challenging than in the traditional school. I'm putting in more hours. I've never read so much in my life. But the ultimate reward is the depth in which you get to know the student personally in a school of 200 instead of 1600. Oh, I've had some adjusting to do. This is not a neat and tidy school. But . . . this is not as important as a relaxed atmosphere. . . . We don't have rules like hall

passes that must be signed by a teacher for a student to leave the room. We've dropped the authoritative aspect in the teacher-student relationship and we find that kids are not tensed up, don't feel persecuted and are more amenable to our ideas.[91]

Houghton's school was designed by a group of students and teachers. Both teachers and students came to the school by choice. The leader of the school was a head teacher. "Town meetings"—open to students and teachers alike—were held to celebrate successes, discuss problems, and vote on solutions. Students designed elective courses with teachers. Teachers developed internships for students in the Arlington and Washington, D.C., area. A lottery and waiting list had to be established to deal with the number of parents hoping to have their children enrolled in the school. Experiments like this school are now being held up as exemplars for all in education to follow.[92]

The recommendations for school reform—decentralization, teacher professionalism, and child-centered education—aim to move what has been seen as "alternative" education into the mainstream. Child-centered education fits hand in glove with SBDM. The new model of efficient education holds schools responsible for outcomes, but frees educators from regulations about how to achieve them—much as the TQM system allows shop floor workers to devise their own means of realizing top management's goals for the firm. Further, since child-centered education demands much more of teachers than has been the case historically, an upgrading of their status befits their new responsibilities. Teacher professionalism, SBDM, and outcomes-based education are the three interlocking elements that together form the conceptual triad of efficient and effective education today.

Reactions of School Management to the New Reform Agenda:

It is . . . clear that support from (the superintendent) and other administrators is crucial in implementing the planks of restructuring. A number of analysts, for example, have noted the capacity of principals to significantly hamper district efforts to decentralize governance and management of schools. . . . Others have described principals' ability to squelch restructuring initiatives bubbling up from the teaching core. . . . Finally, there is evidence that support of the local school board is needed if transformational changes are to flourish in school districts.[93]

Despite all the talk about restructuring education, the legal foundation under-lying our system of school governance has remained unchanged since the imple-mentation of the early pro-efficiency reforms. School boards and school managers today continue to have all legal decision-making power in local districts.[94] In addition, there have been no changes in labor law that would recognize the proposed professional status of teachers in the school organization.[95] Given the distribution of power in our school systems, no departure from "business as usual" will occur unless those legally empowered to make decisions about the allocation of tangible and intangible resources choose to adopt the recommen-dations of the new reform model. How school boards and managers react to calls for radical change will determine when—or whether—decentralization, teacher professionalism, and outcomes-based, child-focused education will become the reality of school life.

The new pro-efficiency reformers spare no criticism for school boards, super-intendents, and other school managers who operate in accordance with the tenets of scientific management. School boards are reproached for trying to micromanage their districts rather than focusing on broad educational policy-making. The low voter turnout in board elections, the tendency of board members to represent individual constituencies rather than the needs of the larger community, a board's ability to tolerate mismanagement on the part of school managers, and failure to coordinate activities with other branches of local government are but some of the complaints leveled at the local school board system of governance. The biggest problem with school boards, according to critics, is their complacency about the quality of their educational policies.[96]

Bureaucratic school management has taken many direct hits from reformers who cite it as the primary weakness of the public school system. The bureau-cracy is chastised for being fundamentally concerned with perpetuating itself and its members' perquisites. It is charged with obfuscating the real concerns in education by its pervasive use of doublespeak and educational jargon. Admin-istrators are accused of failing to either reward excellence or punish incompe-tence at all levels of the school system. The managerial bureaucracy is charged with wasting huge sums of public money and even perpetrating a form of "child abuse" on the nation's young.[97]

Superintendents, in particular, have come in for heavy criticism from those proposing school change.[98] Nathan Glazer, a professor of education and social structure at Harvard, has written:

> The key to what is needed is the recognition that organizations of the size
> of the big-city school district, with their huge central staffs and "chief

executive officers," are simply not necessary when the task is one of running schools at the elementary and secondary level. Worse than not being needed, they only make trouble.[99]

Glazer points out that the Catholic archdiocese of New York educates 115,000 children with only thirty-five employees at its headquarters. The New York City district has some 900,000 enrolled, with 6,000 employees working for central administration. Glazer charges that the only positive thing that superintendents are able to do is hold the media and various interest groups at bay. They are rarely, if ever, the source of fresh ideas in education. He concludes that "the big-city superintendency is broken, it can't be fixed, and the question now is, how do we get out from under it, and its attendant bureaucracy?"[100]

School boards and superintendents have responded to the torrents of criticism, in part, by taking aim at one another. Superintendents decry board members as "power hungry" and "intrusive."[101] The National School Boards Association cites managerial bureaucrats as champions of inertia and enemies of school improvement.[102] Far from being the kind of ideal relationship outlined by Ellwood Cubberley so many years ago, board-superintendent relations have deteriorated to an all-time low. For advocates of radical school reform, this is yet another indication that the early pro-efficiency model of school organization has reached the limits of its usefulness.

It is understandable that most boards and superintendents feel threatened by calls for decentralization of school governance and professionalization of teaching. Despite reassurances from most reform theorists that power will grow as it is shared, many board members and school managers see the reallocation of power to schools as a net loss for them. A top official at the National School Boards Association calls restructuring "the R word"; a union ploy to takeover management of schools and thus to take power away from boards.[103] Boards have felt that reports such as *A Nation Prepared* have been slanted in favor of teachers; teachers being the enemy, the adversary represented by labor.[104] School managers, too, are alarmed at the prospect of a "union juggernaut" that will severely limit their ability to operate unilaterally. Scott Thomson, former executive director of the National Association of Secondary School Principals, has said, "Where we part company with the two teachers' unions is that they are interpreting empowerment and restructuring as a committee of teachers in effect managing the school."[105]

The fear that teacher unions aim to take over the schools is identical to that expressed by school managers during the 1960s. Albert Shanker remarked at this identity in a 1990 article entitled, "Why Managers Are Scared":

What goes around, comes around. This spring as I was debating the former
school superintendent of one of our largest cities on the question of how
much power teachers . . . should have in running schools, I suddenly felt
as though I had stumbled into a time warp. I was back in the 1960's, in the
midst of one of those debates about whether teachers . . . had the right to
engage in collective bargaining and, if they did, what this would do to the
balance of power.[106]

Managers today are making some—but not all—of the same arguments they
made in the 1960s. One point that is reminiscent of the 1960s is that good
managers always have and will continue to listen to the concerns of their subordinates. Another is that if management is to remain accountable to the public
it must have the power to make ultimate decisions about how the school is to
be run. Eli Brent, president of the Associated Administrators of Los Angeles, has
said that if teachers are to make decisions, "we don't want parents coming to us
complaining."[107]

The arguments are not, however, all identical to those made in the 1960s.
Although management wants to safeguard its traditional prerogatives, the new
ideology represented by such management systems as TQM requires an adjustment of management's explanation of its *raison d'être*. As in industry, any top-
level school manager who hopes to stay employed must—at the very least—pay
lip service to the virtues of broad-based participation in decision-making by
people at all levels of the school organization. Accordingly, collaboration with
teachers and parents must be lauded by school managers. The synergy of joint
efforts must be touted.

However, as Lewis Rhodes points out, all decision-making requires "process
standards." Quality management can provide such standards and the "supportive
infrastructure" that can coordinate the myriad of decision-making interactions,
allowing schools to strive for "world class standards."[108] And, when it is time to
make final decisions, school managers believe that they need to remain empowered to do so.[109] This belief remains rooted in a fundamental elitism about who
becomes a school manager, and who remains in the classroom. According to
Joanne Yatvin, a former teacher and principal, and currently a superintendent,
most school managers and boards ascribe to the same basic elitism on which the
entire old pro-efficiency agenda was premised.

Convinced that they are the only intelligent, competent, and caring people
around, they fear those barbarians in the classroom, teachers and children,
who, if allowed would dissipate all our public treasure of time and money
hacking away at rough stone wheels as our nation sank into chaos.[110]

Even managers who openly embrace the idea of teacher participation in decision-making insist on reserving for themselves the right to set goals for the school organization.[111] Charles Vidal, a principal lauded for exemplifying the new management style, sees himself as the leader of the school community. He decides the destination for his school, but allows teachers to help him find the best way there:

> We discuss problems. I don't give (teachers) any solutions. I know where I want to go as an administrator, but my teams can give me a road map. I don't veto anything. And the reason is that they usually come up with better solutions than I do.[112]

Inherent in Vidal's statement is the idea that he has the right, as a manager, to set the direction for the school and find the best means of implementing his vision. The fact that he chooses to include teachers in the search for those means does not diminish his right to do so alone or veto the teachers' proposals if he so desires. Vidal exemplifies the new pro-efficiency ideal of the "participatory" leader who decides to share his decision-making authority with teachers because it leads to better outcomes.

School boards have responded to the calls for reform in a way that would preserve their power as well. As in the 1960s, they have made the argument that they are the best example of democracy at work—a group of elected lay officials controlling a fundamental public service.[113] In order to respond to the new management model so popular in business, however, the National School Boards Association formally endorsed both labor-management cooperation and collaborative partnerships of "teachers, administrators, parents, taxpayers, and students" so that all may "feel they have a stake in the outcome of educational efforts." While the National School Boards Association feels all the stakeholders should collaborate on educational decision-making, it is clear on the point that "final decisions must be consistent with applicable laws, regulations and board policies."[114] In other words, members of an individual school council can make any decision they like—as long as the decision complies with what the board has already decided and does not infringe on the board's legal prerogatives.

In the relatively few districts that have embarked on a reform effort, school boards and managers are careful to preserve their traditional rights and powers. Fearing loss of control, school boards either gingerly dole out some authority to individual schools or patronize the community with "consultation."[115] They also veto decisions made by local school councils on issues as central to the reform agenda as what assessment instruments are to be used to measure student progress.[116] School managers frustrate reform initiatives by demanding schools wade through bureaucratic red tape, delaying payment of grant funding, and holding schools to district requirements for things as mundane as where or when a meeting is to be held.[117] In other words, just by operating as they always have, school managers are able to prevent substantive change from occurring.[118] In a related strategy, school managers and boards can maintain the status quo by "massaging" reform ideas to fit existing conditions, resulting in no material change in school practices.[119]

Even when managerial positions are cut by school boards or superintendents aiming to please constituents who want the school hierarchy to be flattened, the number of school managers tends to remain the same. Washington, D.C.,'s experience is illustrative of this phenomenon. Despite a 1989 school board decision to cut 800 nonschool-based personnel, the Washington school bureaucracy actually grew between 1989 and 1991. Central office managers assigned to school buildings refused to participate in the effort to trim the size of Washington's centralized school bureaucracy. While continuing to draw salaries, they all went on sick leave rather than vacate central office headquarters. Legal counsel for a parents' advocacy group said that for central office managers returning to a school "is like going back to the steel mill or the coal mines." She added, "to leave central office to become a principal is considered a humiliation and a denigration."[120]

School managers have gone on the offensive in the larger society in order to boost their tarnished image. The Principal's Public Relations Network produced a series of public service announcements for television on the importance of school administrators. The spots aired across the country in the spring of 1993. They highlighted the essential role played by principals and assistant principals in setting high expectations for students and in inspiring students to achieve. This television campaign joined a series of radio spots that were previously airing nationally for two years.[121] It followed one waged in the print media. The American Federation of School Administrators ran a series of paid advertisements in *Education Week* during 1990 to discredit the idea that empowering teachers through SBDM would result in better learning situations for youngsters. Citing research on the importance of strong principals in effective schools, the president of the federation, Ted Elsberg, characterized the effort to implement SBDM as "a battle for control of the schools . . . being waged by self-interested groups and the kids are the losers."[122] Elsberg continued on this theme in subsequent ads stressing that the whole point of teacher empowerment was "to remove the authority of the building administrator." He added that there was no evidence to suggest that giving teachers the authority currently inherent in the building manager would result in any improvement in educational outcomes.[123]

As in industry, middle and front-line managers appear to be most resistant to implementation of the pieces of the reform agenda that take away their unilateral decision-making authority. In perhaps the most extreme move to protect their jobs and their traditional prerogatives, principals in some districts have gone to court to stop implementation of reform initiatives. They have not prevailed in a single case.[124] While top management has maintained its legitimacy in the eyes of the business-education-government reform coalition, the members of the managerial bureaucracy have very few supporters. The professional school bureaucrat—once lauded as being essential to efficiency in education—is a victim of the new vision of efficient school operation.

Conclusions

One wonders how John Dewey, Jesse Newlon, or Ella Flagg Young would react to the education reforms being suggested by today's coalition of business, education, and government leaders. So much of this new pro-efficiency reform agenda harkens back to their philosophy of progressive education. The decentralized form of school governance was recommended and implemented by Ella Flagg Young in Chicago nearly one hundred years ago. The professionalism of teachers was championed by Jesse Newlon and the Denver school system he headed in the 1920s. The philosophy of child-centered education has its origins in John Dewey's writings and the University of Chicago Laboratory School he headed at the turn of the century.

It is interesting that the educational progressives suggested that their agenda for education was less wasteful and more efficient than that being proposed by men like Ellwood Cubberley and Franklin Bobbitt. John Dewey often spoke of the "uninvested capital"—human talent—that was rarely mobilized in the factory model of education that focused on "pouring in" facts rather than "drawing out" the innate abilities and interests of students.[125] It is this uninvested capital that today's reformers insist can no longer be ignored. Ella Flagg Young wrote that school managers who handed goals to teachers could never hope to have a highly efficient teaching corps. To Young efficiency was dependent on the teaching corps being unified by a goal cooperatively developed by the teachers, principals, and superintendents.[126] Her ideas sound remarkably modern, totally in keeping with the current reformers' belief that efficiency is served when all the "stakeholders" share common goals and commitments.

Jesse Newlon firmly believed in the nineteenth-century adage, "as is the teacher, so is the school." He felt that the progress of education was almost completely in the hands of the classroom teachers of the country. Given that belief, he advocated for superintendents to "release leadership" to teachers so that they might share in the task of developing educational policies and programs, and attain a truly professional status.[127] The efficient school superintendent was one who was freed from tiresome supervision of teachers and one who could concentrate on the ultimate purposes of education. For Newlon, efficiency meant "the employment of social methods for the accomplishment of broad social purposes." Democracy was, perhaps, the greatest purpose that education could serve in Newlon's mind. Democratic administration of schools—not close supervision of teachers—alone could efficiently serve that purpose.[128]

And here is where the agendas of the educational progressives and the new pro-efficiency reformers part company. With the exception of educators such as Theodore Sizer, most reformers today are motivated by a far less expansive view of efficiency than that which drove Jesse Newlon. Democracy in the schoolhouse is not the point of the current reform agenda; the point is higher levels of achievement for more students so that America's place as a world economic leader can be maintained. The educational progressives began with the premise that every child had the inborn right to be offered the opportunity to develop as a unique individual. They were driven by a sense of morality and a respect for the rights of all individuals involved in education. The organizational structures, roles, and educational methods they recommended followed naturally from their belief that education is fundamentally a moral undertaking. The progressives had a deep commitment to their agenda as a means for insuring an active, thoughtful citizenry in the American democracy. The majority of the new pro-efficiency reformers have a much narrower vision of the purpose of education—and it is one they share with men like Andrew Draper, William Bagley, and Ellwood Cubberley of the early pro-efficiency movement: preparing youngsters for their future roles in the work force while maintaining the status quo in the distribution of power and wealth in society. As such, they will promote and support the progressive agenda only so long as it is viewed as being instrumental to the realization of those goals.

Even with the support of the new business-education-government coalition, it is far from certain that the road map for education reform provided by the educational progressives can be implemented. Perhaps the biggest obstacle to genuine school reform is the social pathologies that affect children's lives, yet remain unaddressed by the new pro-efficiency agenda. In addition, the contemporary reform coalition proposes to dismantle a system of education that has become deeply entrenched in American life. The seeming permanency of the bureaucratic form of school organization, and the tenacity of all parties who have vested interests in the system, represent barriers to reform. In addition, many Americans seem married to a very simple concept of education—basic competency in the three Rs and obedience to authority—behaviors the current system of education is organized to deliver. It is not clear how the necessary funding or political support will be garnered to provide professional working conditions for more than two million teachers nationwide. While the "school as community" is an appealing concept to most Americans, making that ideal a reality will require a revolution in the attitudes of many students, parents, teachers, and administrators.

However, if there is anything to be learned from the school reform movement that took place at the beginning of this century, it is that when leaders in business, education, and government join together, they represent a formidable force for educational change. Although it did not happen in a day, a week, or a year, the early pro-efficiency reformers were able to radically alter the American system of education in one generation despite significant opposition from local political bosses, organized teachers, farmers, immigrants, and small rural communities.

The reformers today who are trying to implement so much of the progressive agenda may yet prevail, despite the stubborn resistance to change from those both within and outside school organizations. One-hundred year-old ideas have been injected with a new vitality by business's call for workers who can do more than just obey orders. A new management ideology believes participation by all members of the enterprise leads to heightened efficiency and economic viability in an increasingly competitive global marketplace. Additionally, the motivational value of fear—fear of economic decline, fear of withdrawal of public support for public schools—cannot be underestimated in terms of mobilizing both citizen and educator support for the new vision of efficient education. But change, if it is to happen, will not occur quickly, easily, or without conflict. Rochester, New York, a leader in the new pro-efficiency reform movement, illustrates how much controversy can be excited by the effort to alter "business as usual" in education. We turn now to this ambitious venture in school reform.

7

Rochester, New York, a Laboratory for the New Pro-Efficiency Reforms

Rochester, long home to such corporate giants as Eastman Kodak, Xerox Corporation, and Bausch and Lomb, became famous for something other than housing the headquarters of these Fortune 500 companies in the fall of 1987. Newspapers across the country gave coverage to an agreement between the Rochester city school district and the Rochester Teachers Association that promised salaries as high as $70,000 for public school teachers. While word of high teacher salaries spread, less public attention was focused on the parties' agreement to attempt to restructure every facet of the school system in accordance with the tenets of the new pro-efficiency agenda. However, among both advocates and foes of that agenda, as well as scholars and commentators on the state of education in America, the agreement catapulted Rochester into the center of the discussion on school reform.

The story of Rochester's foray into school restructuring is important for many reasons. It provides an example of the precipitating factors behind the reform movement, the coalition of business, education, and government leaders that together define both the problem and the solution in education today, and the difficulties inherent in any attempt to dismantle the educational system established at the turn of the twentieth century. As such, I have chosen to use the Rochester experience to illustrate these dimensions of the movement to radically alter schooling in America today.

A Sense of Crisis Leads to a Reform Initiative

Since the first use of quantitative measures of educational achievement at the beginning of the century, there has been a strong link between children's socio-economic status and their success in the school setting. Although never exempt from the general rule that poor children have a difficult time prospering in school, until the mid-1980s the linkage between poverty and school performance did not present a major problem for the Rochester city school district (RCSD). In 1970 there were about 6,000 Rochester families that fell below the poverty line. By 1980 that number had grown to some 8,000 families. The 1980s, however, brought a geometric growth in poverty in the city, along with a concomitant departure of middle-class families to the suburbs. By 1990 some 52,000 poor families lived within the city limits.[1]

In Rochester approximately 70 percent of the children live in families that fall below the poverty line.[2] Recent statistics cite Rochester as being thirteenth nationally in childhood poverty. Poverty is associated with many serious problems for children—substandard housing, medical care, and nutrition. In Rochester, poor children's problems begin before they are born. In 1990, 50 percent of the babies born to teen mothers in St. Mary's Hospital tested positive for cocaine.[3] Nearly half of the children born in Rochester are born to teenagers or unmarried women. Well over half of the children entering kindergarten are assessed as being one or more years behind national norms for math and reading readiness.[4] Young adolescents coming from poor families in Rochester are in deep academic trouble. Forty-five percent of 7th to 9th graders fail a core academic subject. When legally able to leave school at sixteen years of age, 30 percent choose to do so without completing their high school education.[5]

School failure is also tied to race. Black students fail in Rochester's schools three times as often as do white students.[6] Data on school suspensions indicate that black male students are more likely to be suspended than any other group.[7] Suspensions are often imposed after violence has occurred between students or after physical attacks on staff members.[8] Despite the fact that 70 percent of the district's students are African-American or Latino, after 11th grade, high schools serve primarily white students, minority students being far more likely than white students to drop out of school.[9]

The status quo in Rochester in the mid-1980s was not unlike that of many urban districts around the country. The managerial bureaucracy was unwieldy, with one administrator for every six teachers. Nearly every manager at the central office level was an "insider," having come up through the ranks of the RCSD managerial hierarchy. Of the 2,500 teachers, 97 percent were rated as being above average or superior by their supervisors, a proportion in keeping with national figures.[10] Relations between the teachers and the district had been adversarial, with an illegal teachers' strike crippling the district in 1980. The education offered students was in keeping with the early pro-efficiency model established many decades before, adapted only to make room for the "compensatory" and "special" education programs added after the 1960s. Teachers found that the numbers of students being labeled as needing these programs was growing, making their jobs more difficult and frustrating.

Nancy Sundberg, a special education teacher since 1973, tracked her former students to see how they fared after leaving her. She found that none had graduated from high school, or were "well employed." Over half of her former students were caught up in the legal system. Some of them were parents, "but not doing well with their parenting." By the mid-1980s she came to the conclusion that what typified the status quo in education was intolerable. She set about on a personal journey to devise other ways of educating youngsters.[11]

Sundberg's sense that the district was in crisis was shared by the top leadership in the community and in the RCSD. In 1986 the Urban League of Rochester issued a report called *A Call to Action*. The report declared that there were deeply rooted, systemwide problems within the RCSD. At about the same time as the Urban League was critiquing the district, newly appointed superintendent Peter McWalters directed an assessment of the problems associated with student performance in Rochester. This assessment zeroed in on four systemwide problems that needed to be addressed: high rates of student failure in core academic subjects, the system's inability to respond to the varying readiness of children entering the schools, disproportionately high rates of suspension and special education placements among minority students, and the large proportion of students who did not complete high school.[12] This report, along with *A Call to Action,* is often cited as initiating the search for ways to change schooling in Rochester.

As Adam Urbanski, president of the Rochester Teachers Association (RTA), expressed it, the "status quo" was just a euphemism for "the mess we're in."[13] He was of the opinion that change was "urgently necessary, risk essential." Superintendent McWalters, a man with an atypical career path to the superintendency, said he found the correlation between socio-economic status and school failure personally "offensive."[14] He was in favor of drastic solutions for what he saw as drastic problems in the district.[15] A shared sense of crisis, along with a growing personal friendship, allowed these representatives of management and labor to abandon traditional adversarial stances and work together to devise means of addressing the district's problems.[16]

McWalters and Urbanski were joined by the dean of the University of Rochester's graduate school of education and a leading member of the business community in the attempt to devise a model for educational change. In 1987 they decided to seek out the advice of the Carnegie Forum on Education and the Economy in Washington, D.C., the sponsor of the report, *A Nation Prepared:*

Teachers for the 21st Century.[17] The four were persuaded by the point of view expressed in the forum's report—that is, America's ability to compete in world markets was dependent upon schools producing graduates with advanced thinking skills—and that the key to producing those students was the creation of a teaching profession equal to the task.[18] The forum's argument led these representatives from the educational and business communities to attempt to reinvent Rochester schools in hopes of meeting the needs of a changing school population, while simultaneously addressing the economic imperatives faced by the members of the business community. The point was not to buttress the schools that existed—but to replace them with something totally new.[19]

McWalters' vision of school reform was very much in keeping with the recommendations of the new pro-efficiency reformers. Joanne Scully, hired from outside the RCSD by McWalters to be Director of School Improvement in 1988, recalls this vision:

> Peter's priorities were real, real clear. I have them memorized. They were decentralization, hiring the best and the brightest, busting the bureaucracy, and professional development (for teachers).[20]

McWalters' ultimate goal was to improve student performance in an equitable way so that the newly popular phrase, "all kids can learn," would become a reality in Rochester.[21] In keeping with the new value managers place on employee involvement in decision-making, he believed strongly that he could not reach that goal without the involvement of teachers:

> I don't believe I can get there without my teachers fully engaged in solving the problems with me. And you don't get that unless you pay them, and you expect them to do it, and your union starts talking about student performance as one of the reasons for its existence.[22]

McWalters felt, too, that since the paramount aim of school reform was to change classroom practice, changes centering on teaching and learning would have to be carried out by classroom teachers. McWalters decided that the most productive route to school reform was through the people who would be charged with implementing it—the district's teachers.[23] In the words of Thomas Gillett, vice-president of the teachers union, McWalters lived a belief that to change the system "he had to do it *with* teachers, not *to* teachers."[24]

The Rochester teachers union is a local of the American Federation of Teachers (AFT). Urbanski has been a vice-president of the AFT for many years. Early on in the current reform movement, the AFT embraced the concept of shared decision-making, yet only a few of its locals had gotten it into their contracts by 1987. There was pressure placed on Urbanski to get shared decision-making in his district. If he could negotiate this into the contract, it would represent a victory for the AFT in its attempt to use collective bargaining as a vehicle for school reform.[25] For Albert Shanker, AFT president, Rochester represented an opportunity to realize his long-held ideal of employing collective bargaining as a means of professionalizing the occupation of teaching.[26]

McWalters had support from the school board for his idea of working through the teachers union to implement change. Catherine Spoto, a longtime member of the RCSD board and past president, explains the board's rationale:

> Part of the reason why we chose to do this was because (and many of my board's colleagues statewide and nationwide . . . thought we were crazy to do this) we were very clear in saying, "Look, if you have a strong teachers union you're not going to change schools without them. You need to work with your union." And you can't, as some people would like to, differentiate between teachers and the union. You need to work . . . in partnership with your union. I still believe that. I believe that is essential.[27]

The board was willing to depart from the traditional bargaining agenda and open up negotiations on issues that legally and customarily fell within the realm of educational policy in order to bring teachers on board in the effort to improve student achievement.

The resulting three-year contract agreed upon by the district and the RTA in 1987 was an ambitious attempt to implement the whole of the new pro-efficiency agenda for reform in one fell swoop. The driving idea behind the agreement was the goal of making teaching into a profession in the manner recommended by *A Nation Prepared*. One sentence in the contract bound the parties to an effort to develop site-based decision-making—referred to as "school-based planning."[28] The aim of this decentralization of decision-making was, in the words of the Carnegie Forum's Marc Tucker, to transform a system that was "overwhelmingly bureaucratic and hostile to fresh ideas" into one that would welcome them.[29] Although no details about either the composition or responsibilities of the school-based planning teams were included in the agreement, both Urbanski and McWalters said they expected teachers to play a strong role on the school councils, and thus to have a new voice in school decision-making.[30]

In order to make a commitment to professionalizing teaching, the contract created a career path for teachers—the Career in Teaching program. New teachers would enter the system at the intern level. After completing their internship, teachers would stay at the "resident" level until they became permanently certified and tenured, at which point they would reach the "professional" level. While most teachers would remain at this third level, the position of "lead teacher" was established for those deemed qualified for assuming leadership roles in the district.[31] Salaries for teachers at this fourth level could reach the highly publicized $70,000 figure at the end of the three-year agreement.[32] The point of the career path was to enable teachers to earn high salaries without leaving the classroom for jobs in school management. A concomitant factor was the desire to lessen the wage differential between those who held managerial positions and those who worked directly with children.

Catherine Spoto describes the board's view of this career path for teachers: "Part of what the contract was to address was that very issue, that people could indeed move ahead (financially) and stay with kids and be a teacher."[33] The details of the roles and responsibilities for each of these categories within the teaching staff were to be worked out at a later date by union and management representatives.[34] However, Urbanski was often quoted as saying that lead teachers "will have the Clint Eastwood attitude toward teaching." He declared that because they were the best, "they ought to get the toughest assignments, on the assumption that if they can't do it, it can't be done."[35]

Just as *A Nation Prepared* suggested, the teacher union and district exchanged professional level salaries and a promise of professional working conditions on the one hand, for a willingness to be held fully accountable for the results of their work, on the other.[36] Both Urbanski and McWalters repeated time and again that the point of these reforms was to improve student outcomes. Restating an idea first articulated by Margaret Haley, Urbanski said with confidence that "the interests of the teachers and the interests of the kids are one and the same." He added that "it would be unreasonable to permit access for teachers to decision-making without building in accountability factors." Urbanski went so far as to say, "if you do not see appreciable outcomes in student performance, then I would not argue for a substantial increase" in subsequent salary settlements.[37] McWalters called accountability the catchword—that is, teachers who were included in substantive decision-making could be held accountable for student performance.[38] Faithful to the new pro-efficiency model of school reform, the point of restructuring the roles and responsibilities for adults in the education endeavor was to improve "the bottom line,"—that is, student achievement. Yet, as with other facets of the 1987 agreement, no specifics were included in regard to what criteria would be used to evaluate student performance.[39]

The contract had several provisions that represented a departure from traditional bargaining in education and an embrace of the new pro-efficiency education reforms. To demonstrate a commitment to improving communication between teachers and parents—a key feature of the new reform agenda—the RTA agreed to establish a Home Based Guidance Program whereby every middle and high school teacher would maintain a direct line of communication between the home and the school for twenty students. In an effort to demonstrate a departure from the industrial model of teacher unionism, the RTA agreed to give up the requirement that seniority determine teachers' transfer rights. Under the new plan, school-based councils would choose the most suitable candidate for transfer into a building.[40] This "give-back" also showed a commitment by the RTA to the idea that every school would develop a unique character under school-based planning. Different teachers—regardless of their seniority—would work best in these different settings. The parties agreed to develop a system for peer remediation of teachers whose performance was deficient. This represented a break with traditional positions held by both the union and management. The union admitted there were more than a handful of teachers who were performing poorly, and management relinquished its role as sole overseer of the teaching function.

The schools that Urbanski and McWalters envisioned as resulting from the 1987 contract were consistent with the oft-heard recommendations from the new pro-efficiency reformers. Since students would have to think for a living, schools in the restructured Rochester system would teach them to engage in critical thinking. All students would be held to high academic standards, regardless of race or economic status.[41] Schools would become centers of inquiry where both teachers and students were continually learning.[42] Teachers would be free to replace traditional classroom practice with a more child-centered approach that could take account of the different needs and talents of individual children. Parents would be welcomed partners in the education of their children, and schools would become integrated into the community at large.[43]

The principles of TQM can also be found woven within the fibers of Rochester's reform strategy. The idea of a trust built on the interdependence of labor and management was central to the Urbanski/McWalter alliance. School-based planning emanates from the belief that the productivity of schools is critically dependent on the degree to which teachers understand and share the school's mission and participate in the development of programs that shape their work.[44] Though not a part of the collective bargaining agreement, school choice at the high school level was instituted shortly after the contract went into effect. Under choice, RCSD parents were seen as customers who could leave schools that were unable to meet their expectations. The underlying assumption of this plan was that competition for customers would make schools less complacent and more adaptive in their offerings.[45] Talk of changing the organizational culture of the RCSD, of creating an attitude of continual striving for improvement, and of supporting facilitative management followed quickly on the heels of the landmark agreement.[46] Finally, the basic idea that the school system—not the people working in it—was the cause of poor student outcomes relies on the 85–15 principle—85 percent of the RCSD's problems were due to the system. The incorporation of these ideas into Rochester's reform strategy was due not only to the currency of these ideas in industrial management circles and in society, but also to a concerted effort by Rochester's business community to influence the course of the district's change effort.

The reforms came about because of the district's inability to get good results with children coming from poor and minority families. It was premised on the notion that, as Joanne Scully puts it, "from the ashes rises the phoenix," With poor children and decrepit buildings, the district would do better by radically changing its way of operating. McWalters believed change could happen throughout the system—not only in hothouses of innovation headquartered in separate buildings—if only the right organizational conditions could be created.[47]

The Rochester experiment in change promised the parents, the taxpayers, and the business community better results. Yet the details of the plan for organizational change were sketchy. A promise was made by the RCSD and the RTA that the hammering out of details would be done by all the constituencies involved in the RCSD community—the members of RCSD's three other unions, parents, business leaders, and community members.[48] While the top leadership in the district—a group that shared many of the same beliefs—had drawn the broad outlines of the change plan, constituencies that were less in harmony had the job of making the plan workable.

As many in Rochester came to describe it, the start of the school improvement effort was somewhat like building an airplane while it was taxiing down the runway.[49] The risks for those who agreed to initiate the restructuring effort—the board, the superintendent, and the leadership of the RTA—were great. The community and the nation were eagerly awaiting tangible signs that what came to be known as "the Rochester experiment" was working. While Urbanski, McWalters and Shanker cautioned that the community had to make a long-term commitment to change, that education was complicated, and that patience was essential, the media and the citizenry readied themselves for evidence that those high salaries for public school teachers were resulting in better outcomes for children.

Business, an Active Partner in Reform

It is not surprising that the Rochester business community was in on the ground floor of the school reform effort. Historically, Xerox and Kodak have always played an active role in a wide range of community affairs in the greater Rochester area.[50] Beyond that history of involvement, however, business got interested in school reform in Rochester for the same reasons that business has taken a leading role in the national debate on educational change. Catherine Spoto, RCSD board president, says local business understands "this is a high stakes game in terms of the whole economic imperative."[51] Thomas Gillett, RTA vice-president, is of the opinion that business joined with schools to improve education for children because they want employees they can use. He says that they realize that if they do not do something about how children are leaving the school system, "they're not going to be able to operate in this economy." Gillett adds that in Rochester business is going beyond rhetoric and promoting educational reform in tangible ways.[52]

As has been the case nationally, business in Rochester has played a critical role in defining both the issues facing public education and ways of addressing those issues. As the Rochester Business Educational Alliance (RBEA) puts it, "our children are the primary feeder stream for our colleges and our places of employment."[53] David Kearns, former Xerox CEO, expresses the belief that the difficulty with schools is their "ossified management structures," which prevent them from delivering a high quality product to these external customers.[54] The vision business has brought to the Rochester school reform endeavor is one of a high performance organization similar to that which can be found in any highly competitive industry in America today. The way for schools to become "quality" organizations is for them to adopt the principles of TQM that earned Xerox the Malcolm Baldrige Quality Award in 1989.

The Rochester business community is operating under the assumption that principles of management are universal—an assumption that has been made by business leaders across the nation throughout this century. Norman Deets, one of Xerox's executives who began working with the RCSD in 1989, adhered to this belief:

> When I first got here, somebody asked me what I know about education. I don't know anything about education, but I know about how to make decisions, how to restructure management, and how to put together a quality product.[55]

Deets and his colleague, John Foley, believe that TQM has much to offer schools. It is an enabling strategy whereby schools will be able to raise performance standards for children and improve accountability for teachers and school managers. Underlying their work with the school system is the assumption that by implementing participative management, employee involvement in decision-making, "continuous improvement," and the principle of meeting the customers' needs, schools can—like Xerox did—transform themselves into high performance organizations turning out high quality products.

The breakdown in the analogy is that while businesses that do not meet their customers' expectations risk going out of business, schools do not.[56] Thus, one of the first jobs business executives involved in school reform have set for themselves is making the staff of the public schools see a reason for abandoning long-standing managerial and pedagogical practices. The growing popularity of the privatization movement—in the form of the school vouchers or firms such as EAI—provides such a rationale for reform. Either public education changes its way of doing business and delivers better outcomes, or privatization will become a reality—public schools will go out of business.

The Carnegie Forum on Education and the Economy played a central role in the development of the Rochester reform strategy. Within a few months of the ratification of the contract between the RTA and the RCSD, the forum's executive director, Marc Tucker, left to launch a think tank in Rochester called the National Center on Education and the Economy.[57] The Center was wooed to Rochester by the city's business and education leaders, as well as by a promise of financial support by New York governor Mario Cuomo. Cuomo's director of policy management for the state, Henrik Dullea, said at the time of the move that the center's agenda "fits perfectly" with Cuomo's education and economic development programs. Adam Urbanski welcomed the center's arrival in Rochester, calling it "an ideal marriage between a national policy-development institute and a local laboratory." He added that, "all these theories and highfalutin' ideas don't mean anything unless it can be demonstrated that they can be translated into local, practical realities."[58]

The National Center made the RCSD experiment a top priority. Tucker immediately chaired a local coalition of school and business leaders focused on education reform.[59] Tucker also worked with the district leaders to develop a strategic plan for the RCSD, a central tenet of the TQM management philosophy.[60] Norman Deets and John Foley were "loaned" full-time by Xerox to the National Center, to work with the Rochester district on instituting the "total quality" approach.[61] Together with other staff from the National Center, they trained at least two members from each of the original school-based planning teams in group decision-making processes.[62]

Members of the business community helped to develop the desired student outcomes, which are to be the guiding light for the school district. Soon after the National Center arrived in Rochester, Kodak and Gannett funded a Louis Harris poll of the community to identify the goals it holds for students.[63] The RBEA ran a project to develop the specific goals and outcomes for the Rochester area schools. That venture, the Monroe County Educational Outcomes/Standards Project, aims to "prepare today's young people for a successful life in the twenty-first century." The outcomes the project decided upon are to be "the foundation for systemic change in school curriculum and instruction."

The ultimate, hoped-for result of the project's work is to "provide a competitive work force for the Greater Rochester Area."[64] The project assumes that the school is the supplier for employers like Eastman Kodak who seek "the competitive employee." Examples of the type of knowledge, skills, and attitudes recommended for the competitive employee match the prerequisites for engaging in TQM. Exiting high school students should be able to assess situations by:

- applying knowledge of cause and effect relationships,
- anticipating the future while working in the present and drawing upon the past,
- thinking and working from whole to part (divergent) and part to whole (convergent),
- gathering, analyzing, interpreting, and integrating information,
- identifying customers,
- formulating relevant questions,
- visualizing alternatives and outcomes.

High school graduates should be able to plan their work by:

- setting goals with measurable outcomes,
- making decisions using factual information and logical reasoning,
- organizing and prioritizing information,
- identifying and allocating resources appropriately.[65]

The project lists other attributes of the competitive employee: ability to adapt, to share information and data quickly, to understand science and math, to take pride in work accomplished, to commit to the organization, to develop a cross-cultural perspective. If one recalls the type of skills the early pro-efficiency reformers hoped students would master—neatness, punctuality, submission to authority, following directions, the three Rs—it is clear that the demands the new pro-efficiency reformers are making on the schools are radically different from and much more rigorous than those made by their predecessors. The Rochester district has adopted many of these demanding recommendations in its "Goals, Outcomes, Measures and Standards" (GOMS) program.[66]

In order for schools to meet the expectations of the area employers—external customers—the National Center made the adoption of the TQM process throughout all levels of the RCSD a high priority. Foley and Deets worked with Joanne Scully, director of school improvement, to create a school improvement model based on TQM that school-based planning teams could utilize. Scully recalls, "What we did was a translation of TQM to school language. . . . I was the bilingual translator."[67] The resulting guidelines suggest that teams:

1. use school performance information to improve student success,

2. set objectives consistent with identified needs and RCSD goals,

3. plan activities to accomplish objectives,

4. monitor progress of the plan, and

5. report the plan as well as the results of the plan to the school community.[68]

According to John Foley, this process lets teachers state the problem, devise solutions to the problem, and implement change. He gives the example of a problem: "All children are different." Theoretically, teachers can devise teaching strategies to get all children to meet the district standards regardless of their differences, implement their teaching strategies, then reassess to see how close they have come to meeting those standards. By continually monitoring progress and refining teaching strategies, the TQM principle of continual improvement will come to life in the education setting.[69]

In accordance with the TQM model, Foley and Deets recommended new roles for the personnel in the RCSD. Both men worked in central office headquarters, and ran meetings in accordance with TQM principles, so that these top managers might learn by modeling how their responsibilities would be altered by TQM. Foley and Deets suggested that TQM be demonstrated by RCSD's top managers on a daily basis—that they model for their subordinates how one operates under TQM.[70] The two consultants advised them to solve problems after an analysis of data and information rather than what Foley and Deets call the "ready, fire, aim syndrome."[71] Deets and Foley urged principals to be "facilitative," making sure the school environment was conducive to doing a good job. Principals should take care of the 85 percent of the 85/15 principle so that teachers and students can do their best work. They advised managers to allow teachers—the people at the bottom of the organization who have important information—to problem-solve, if not actually make, decisions.[72] Participative management, should not, they declared, be a threat to managerial prerogatives because managers get more done when everyone pulls in the same direction. Foley dropped the term "employee empowerment" and started using "employee involvement" so that managers might feel less threatened by the idea of including subordinates in problem-solving. According to John Foley, the four-day training that he and Deets provided was generally well-received by the participants.[73]

Besides getting intimately involved in creating the district's desired student outcomes and helping to train personnel in the TQM process, business in Rochester has made a commitment to getting the reform agenda implemented by becoming directly involved with schools and students. Daniel Wegman of the Wegmans supermarket chain heads a student mentoring program that provides jobs, tutoring, and scholarships for RCSD students. The Kodak 21st Century Learning Challenge represents a multimillion dollar commitment to getting the reform agenda implemented in a variety of ways. The Kodak program provides training for school teams in TQM.[74] It provides released time for Kodak employees so that they can serve as parent members of school teams.[75] Under the 21st Century Learning Challenge, Kodak employees can adopt a school to help develop math and science lessons with teachers. The Learning Challenge enlisted 1,500 volunteers for mentoring RCSD students in need of adult help and guidance. It provides career education for high school students as well as teacher-worker exchanges.[76] Catherine Spoto feels that the hundreds of Kodak employees who work in the schools are among the strongest supporters of the school district's effort to reform itself.[77]

Rochester area businesses provide other types of support for the school system. They are strong advocates for the district's early childhood education program. Jack Hostutler, president of the Industrial Management Council, backs it for the following reasons:

> Early childhood education may well be the best investment a community can make in its future. It is sound educationally, economically and socially. The payoff can be significant in both productive and satisfying lives for young people and in a well-prepared work force able to maintain a competitive edge. Early education of children must be a top priority if we expect to properly prepare them for the future.[78]

This statement fairly sums up the motivation behind all business involvement in the Rochester reform experiment. Spending time and money on the schools is seen as both a morally good and economically sound investment of time and money in the members of the upcoming generation.

Why the RCSD Welcomes Business Involvement

Leaders of the Rochester school community—the school board, superintendent, and union leadership—see business interest and support as a big plus to the reform effort, even as they acknowledge the fact that business support is fueled by its own enlightened self-interest. Peter McWalters saw utility in the corporate model for the management of the schools, although he warned there were some limitations to its adaptability to the education setting.[79] RTA vice-president, Tom Gillett, feels that companies like Wegmans are genuinely trying to improve things for children through their mentoring and tutoring programs.[80] Catherine Spoto welcomes the support of business because corporations like Kodak and Xerox have struggled to change themselves. They—better than other constituencies in the community—understand how hard it is to change. She points out, "They know it's not by the snap of your fingers that you change an institution." They also understand the "vast difference between the private and the public sector" in regard to the media searchlight that focuses on every misstep made as change is attempted. When the rest of the community attacks the district, the business community's support remains solid. Spoto feels comfortable with the partnership her district has made with the business community because the goal of the tradition liberal arts education and business needs have finally converged. As she puts it, "this isn't about training . . . the mission of education (now) is for people who can think creatively, solve problems, work cooperatively, deal with complex issues, (and) be able to cope with ambiguity." She feels the partnership with business is focused on "remaking our schools . . . on real educational issues." It is substantial and serious.[81]

The Response of School Managers
to the Reform Experiment

The model of school reform proposed in Rochester assumed a sharing of managerial power with teachers and parents. While much lip service was paid to the idea that "power grows as it is shared," it was also possible that power would change hands from central office managers to building principals and the constituencies of individual schools—representatives from each of the three unions and parents. Superintendent McWalters, an atypical superintendent in that the bulk of his experience in education was garnered in the role of teacher, saw the bureaucratic school organization as an enemy of change. He had no qualms about stating publicly that school managers ought to respond to teachers' needs, not dictate to them.[82] He communicated freely with the leadership of the RTA, often leaving his managerial colleagues in central office out of the communications loop.[83] Given McWalters' apparent partiality for the teachers' point of view, the managers in the school system felt that there would be little power-sharing and lots of power loss for them under the 1987 contract agreement, which promised decentralized decision-making and teacher professionalism.

As has been the case nationally, school managers in Rochester regarded the possible emergence of teacher professionalism as a threat to their managerial prerogatives. The much publicized partnership between Urbanski and McWalters, along with the 1987 contract to which they agreed, made the administrators in the district feel like second-class citizens, according to Joanne Scully. Even though representatives from their ranks had the opportunity to flesh out the plan drawn in broad strokes in the contract, bitterness remained:

> There was a lot of resentment on the part of the principals that this thing was being done at all. We didn't prepare those principals. We didn't do anything for them, and when we emerged with the model (of school-based planning), even though they knew they'd had a chance to get it the way they wanted it, which they did, they still resented the fact that the only real negotiations in that room were between two folks.[84]

Catherine Spoto corroborates Scully's assessment of school managers' feelings about the reform process.

> People who belonged to other bargaining units, like the administrators, felt shut out of the reform process even though in that contract—in the agreement to agree—you had people from the various constituency groups coming together to say, "This is how school-based planning will work" . . . essentially, the fact that you used the teachers' contract to move the reform agenda created an environment where other people felt "axed out."[85]

In the opinion of Thomas Gillett, the entire idea of including teachers in decision-making was rejected by central office administrators, as well as by many principals:

> Their view is why do we need this for? We know how to run the system. That's why we're here. That's why they appointed us as assistant superintendents, directors or whatever.[86]

According to Gillett, even school principals who accepted the concept of including teachers in decision-making as a means of improving school performance,
disliked the genesis of the idea in RCSD:

> Some principals are smart enough to know . . . that the way they're running
> schools now, if they are using the traditional model, isn't the best way . . .
> if you want to get the most out of a staff you can't do things the way the
> district wants you to do things. It will not lead to "maximum productivity,"
> to use the (TQM) model. A lot of principals have liked different aspects of
> the reform agenda. By the same token, they have disliked the fact that it's
> perceived as a teacher union/superintendent partnership.[87]

The administrators' union responded to the 1987 contract by attempting to
block implementation of key features of the "Career in Teaching" program—that
is, peer mentoring for new teachers and peer remediation for tenured teachers
performing poorly, by instituting a lawsuit. The suit argued that the program
violated state law and encroached on the administrators' duties.[88] Richard Stear,
president of the Association of Administrators and Supervisors of Rochester
(AASR), said his union feared that mentor teachers who were released from the
classroom for the programs would take on "quasi-administrative positions." He
added, "Administrators are licensed and certified to evaluate. If an administrator
loses that function, you lose the job."[89]

Adam Urbanski called AASR's suit a blatant attempt to block school change
in an effort to preserve what had traditionally been managerial "turf."[90] The
administrators union did not prevail in court in its effort to protect what it saw
as uniquely managerial functions.

The professional relationship between Richard Stear and Peter McWalters
could best be described as strained. Stear had little respect for McWalters because of his failure to take the traditional route to the superintendency. Stear
commented that McWalters:

> Didn't go through the experiential track and that was in my mind a very
> strong detriment to his grounding in practicality, to his lack of understand-
> ing of administrative role and function, and that exacerbated part of the
> problem in the "agreement to agree" contract.[91]

Stear is of the opinion that McWalters and Urbanski were "philosophically in
tune" because McWalters was "a teacher in administrator's clothing." While he
credits McWalters with being good at "philosophy, the grand scheme, the broad

stroke," he faults him for having little sense about how to make his philosophy operational.[92] His low regard for McWalters was not changed by McWalters' continual bypassing of AASR in district communications. Principal Charles Moscato recalls how administrators were cut out of important decisions as a result.

> There was virtually no communication between central administration and the AASR union and (information) went directly to the teachers. So a lot of things were happening that administrators should have been involved in but (weren't).[93]

Richard Stear became an articulate opponent of the reform effort almost from its outset. He challenged the whole idea of using collective bargaining for educational change.[94] He often called the RTA/RCSD agreement a two- rather than a three-legged stool that could not possibly stand. The bilateralism between the teachers and the superintendent was the rub for administrators, Stear admits. He calls the 1987 agreement "aristocratic" rather than "democratic" because every constituency was not included.[95] Stear argued from the start that leaving administrators out of the many changes sweeping through the district was a major weakness of the reform plan. While the initiators of the restructuring plan begged for patience from the community, from the beginning Stear challenged the idea that the reforms would lead to changes in school culture or improvements in student performance.[96]

From the outset of the reform initiative, Adam Urbanski has been a vocal proponent of the idea that school managers typically act in an autocratic fashion, hampering teachers from doing their best work. Stear calls the depiction of school managers as dictatorial and paternalistic "mythology." Stear says Urbanski is fueling:

> One of the mythologies of modern education. I'm sure that like the bad cop or the bad teacher, we can all find a bad principal or a bad administrator who functioned in that kind of dictatorial, paternalistic . . . factory model method. I'm sure you can find examples of that. But it seems to me that if you have an effective school . . . you're going to find administrators working precisely in the way that they're described as typically not working. I would suspect that more often than not, that is the model—and that the exception is this kind of dinosaur mentality.[97]

He argues that good school managers have always been facilitative, have tried to beat the system, and have rejected the status quo. Despite AASR's loss in the courts, Stear continues to defend the idea that certain functions are uniquely managerial—for example, teacher evaluation. While the system needs to be changed, he rejects "the thesis that you have to shoot everybody, or even certain somebodies, to have a revolution."[98]

The role principals are to play in restructured schools is one that has been either poorly defined or defined in contradictory ways by supporters of school change in Rochester. Principals state confusion over what their new role is to be, beyond being "facilitative."[99] Some teachers in Rochester feel that principals ought to be the person in each building who makes sure orders are placed, supplies exist, and the buses come on time.

Nancy Sundberg, a teacher recognized within the RCSD for her innovative approach to education, articulates this idea of the school manager:

> In my ideal school there is one manager in place of a principal, and everybody else is in a teaching position. . . . It's possible that a manager could do all the business stuff, all the logistics—and help with the clerical staff, the cafeteria, the buses, the ordering. . . . There is absolutely no doubt in my mind that this manager could be some of the very fine secretaries I've seen around here.[100]

It is this very idea that makes school managers in Rochester bristle. Principal Charles Moscato rejects the suggestion that school managers become low-level functionaries in the system.

> I would never go along with the perception that some people have that we should become plant managers, that we would be responsible for making sure the place is clean, that it's safe, and that there's enough t.p. . . . I still consider myself the educational leader in the building. We (principals) still set the tone. We don't always have the resources or the time to do it first hand, but at least we can give the direction.[101]

Fear that principals might be relegated to such "plant manager" positions has caused the AASR president Stear to reject out of hand the notion that administrators be anything short of instructional leaders.[102]

The failure of the lawsuit left intact the perceived threat to managerial functions inherent in the 1987 reforms. Administrators, particularly those at the central office level, had to find other ways to prevent the implementation of reforms that might compromise their prominence or power in the school organization. Under the new model, central office was to support buildings in their efforts to reinvent themselves. The simplest way for central office to fend off change was to fail to cooperate with individual school planning teams or principals who required a transfer of power, money, or discretion.[103] By early 1992 it was clear that central office administration had not reshaped itself to become the support service proposed by the reforms. Business as usual continued on. Catherine Spoto commented that one goal of the reform was to:

> Decentralize and to restructure central office in ways to provide better services and support to schools, and to evaluate the performance of the people in central office based upon how well those goals were met. That has not been done.[104]

Another way to hamstring the reform effort was to refuse to cooperate with the RTA/RCSD program for peer remediation for tenured teachers who performed poorly. As the idea was fleshed out by a panel made up of equal numbers of teachers and school managers, no teacher would go into "intervention" as they called it, without referral by the building principal or supervisor. After two years, only twenty-eight teachers out of the district's 2,500 had been recommended for intervention. Urbanski charged that administrators refused to cooperate with a program they saw as a usurpation of their duties. Stear countered that few people were referred, because only a few were so dysfunctional as to require such help. Yet even the RTA took exception to the idea that so few teachers were having serious difficulties in performing their professional responsibilities.[105]

Still another way for central office administrators to fail to promote the proposed organizational change was to virtually ignore the training in TQM offered by Norman Deets and John Foley of the National Center. The strategic plan devised by Marc Tucker along with McWalters, Urbanski, and top RCSD managers was to build a highly efficient, nonbureaucratic school organization. TQM was the process by which this organization was to be built. Yet the administrators privately refused to accept the premises or the practices inherent in the TQM model, despite public commitments to implementing TQM.[106] According to Joanne Scully, there was a discrepancy between what central office administrators said they were doing and what they were really doing in relation to TQM. This discrepancy proved to be frustrating for Deets and Foley.[107]

In 1991 Peter McWalters was offered the job of state commissioner of education for Rhode Island. McWalters' acceptance of the position forced the school board to find a replacement for the man who led the district down the path of restructuring. Whom the board chose speaks legions about the power of Rochester's school managers and the resilience of the traditional management model. No national search was conducted to find a replacement for McWalters. Twelve days after McWalters announced his resignation, the board promoted Manuel Rivera, a central office administrator, to the superintendent's post. In the classroom for only four years, he moved into school management while still in his twenties. He practiced a management style more in keeping with the early pro-efficiency reforms than the new. He had the full support of AASR. Richard Stear felt Rivera understood the key role school managers must play in education.[108] A year into his tenure as superintendent, Charles Moscato praised Rivera for including administrators in decisions that affect the district:

> I think we have a superintendent that recognizes the value of and the need for administration in its changed format, which has yet to be fully developed. He is now looking for us to provide leadership. He wants us to be very much involved.[109]

Rivera returned the administrators' support in kind. When New York state comptroller Edward Regan cited the RCSD for being first in the state in estimated excessive administrative costs, Superintendent Rivera defended the size of the school bureaucracy. Charging Regan with faulty methods of data analysis, Rivera said that the large sum RCSD spent on administrative costs was necessary due to the large numbers of special education and "English as a second language" students. Rivera said of Regan's report, "There are undergraduate students I know at Harvard who can do a better job of analyzing this data."[110]

One year into his tenure, those persons who supported the 1987 reforms were not impressed with Rivera's performance. Thomas Gillett characterized Rivera as a top-down style manager who surrounded himself with a small circle of advisors who were not known for their expertise.[111] Joanne Scully, hired by McWalters to lead the district into site-based decision-making, described Rivera as more of an old-style school manager who believes there is a "one size fits all" solution to complex problems. While she concurred with Rivera that there were schools that were "sick," she disagreed that they were all sick in the same way, or that they needed the same medicine. Although she allowed that Rivera had better managerial skills than McWalters, she felt that individual schools were the last place that Rivera focused his attention.[112] Finally, business leaders who very much want the district to change its way of operating became impatient with Rivera's inability to implement changes they recommended—for example, cuts in central office management. Arthur Aspengren, president of the Industrial Management Council, graded Rivera a "D" after one year in the role of superintendent.[113]

The characteristic of McWalters that irked Rochester school managers as well as some community members was his partnership with Adam Urbanski. Manuel Rivera made certain that Urbanski was the last person he was seen consulting with on district problems. As the local newspaper put it:

> First, there was the "Adam-Peter show" when Rochester teachers union leader Adam Urbanski and former superintendent of schools Superintendent Peter McWalters worked in tandem. There is no "Adam-Manny" show. More than a year in his position, Superintendent Rivera has made no move to have to share the podium when he announces new efforts.[114]

Beyond the lack of a personal rapport with the RTA president, Rivera returned to hardball managerial tactics in dealing with the district's teachers. During protracted contract negotiations in the 1992–93 school year, Rivera unilaterally changed the terms of the existing contract by requiring teachers who were absent for one day to bring a doctor's note to their supervisor upon their return to work. Calling it "a bureaucratic temper tantrum," RTA's Gillett filed a charge of "illegal practice" with the state's Public Employee Relations Board.[115] Latent for six years under the McWalters' regime, the model of adversarial relations between school managers and teachers reemerged. After nineteen months of negotiations, Rivera and Urbanski signed a four-year contract in December 1993 that provided financial incentives for high performing schools, expanded the peer mentoring program, and gave teachers meeting "professional standards"annual raises of 3.5 percent.[116]

In the midst of a budget crisis and school safety controversy in the spring of 1994, Manuel Rivera submitted his letter of resignation to the school board. He planned to join Christopher Whittle's venture in for-profit management of schools, the Edison Project. Rivera expressed his excitement at the prospect of not having to deal "with all the barriers that one can sometimes be confronted with in a public school system." Rivera's responsibilities at the Edison Project are to focus on the implementation of Edison's partnerships with public school systems. Clearly frustrated by his two and a half years at the helm of RCSD, Manuel Rivera sees privatization of school management as the preferred route of school operation. He commented, "I would love to see that happen in Rochester and perhaps in some other cities in the state of New York."[117]

The Fate of the Reforms through Spring 1994

School-Based Planning (SBP)

Two things are key to understanding the fate of SBP in Rochester. The first is that it was closely tied to the promise of better outcomes for students by leaders of the reform movement. The effect of SBP on the students' education and achievement will be discussed at length later in the chapter. The second point central to comprehending how SBP has fared is that, as Joanne Scully puts it, "Only one sentence in the contract launched all this mischief."[118] That open-ended sentence in the 1987 contract committed the parties to the development of an SBP model. The vagueness of that sentence allowed different constituencies—and even people within the same constituency—to have different visions of the changes SBP would bring to the district in terms of roles for adults and innovations in teaching methods. It created a situation ripe for conflict.

Initially, the big question inherent in SBP was whose power was going to be shared. Was it the board's power, or top management's traditional prerogatives, or principals' authority, or the RTA's control over working conditions that was going to be allocated to the SBP teams in each building? The board was not sure about what prerogatives it was willing to share, so it was purposefully vague.[119] The board emphasized, however, that SBP was a *school* governance model, rather than one for *district* governance.[120] Teachers were euphoric at the idea that they might control the affairs of their schools.[121] Principals were fearful that SBP was the beginning of the end of their limited control over what happened in their buildings.

Joanne Scully tells the story of the principal who called her as SBP was first getting started. She recalls him saying:

> I can't believe what this thing called SBP has done to my school. It has made monsters out of teachers that I have always been able to work with. . . . They came in on Monday . . . absolutely miserable and off the wall saying they're going to put me in my place and now all these decisions are going to have to be shared.[122]

Scully worked hard with principals to make them realize that, according to her understanding of the SBP model, district power was not being shared—only building power. And that, as she pointed out, was not very great.[123] It is not apparent whether that afforded any comfort to principals who feared SBP would cause them to lose their power base, which was precisely and exclusively at the building level.

Despite the lack of a clear statement of new roles and responsibilities for the board, school managers, and teachers, Rochester launched SBP in an ambitious way, mandating that every school develop an SBP team with representatives from every bargaining unit, as well as parents. As mentioned earlier, initial training was provided by the National Center for two members from every team. However, the ongoing training and support research has found is necessary for team success was not provided by the district.[124] Without this degree of support, many teams failed to function as anticipated by McWalters, Urbanski, Tucker, and the school board.

Catherine Spoto explains what happened:

> One of the key things around SBP is that . . . it's a governance model . . . and . . . people got caught up in power struggles. There was a fundamental lack of clarity about what the fundamental mission of a team was. Some teams got caught up in micro-managing the school.[125]

Joanne Scully, director of SBP in the district from the time of its inception, is of the opinion that the arrival of SBP accentuates whatever exists before in a given school. Good schools have gotten better under SBP; bad schools have gotten worse:

> School-based planning . . . makes (one of) two things happen: It's like pouring gasoline on a problem. If it was a little problem before, it will accelerate it. If things were going well in a school, things will go better.[126]

There are some examples of the hoped for educational innovation arising from the collaboration of team members. One elementary school has chosen to reallocate the personnel within the building so that every teacher is now a classroom teacher, rather than having some teachers function as "specialists" and others function as classroom teachers.[127] Another school chose to implement a holistic curriculum, providing training for the faculty in holistic instructional methodologies.[128] The fair hearing of ideas available under SBP seems to increase the likelihood that those ideas will be given a chance for implementation. Nancy Sundberg gives the example of her middle school team passing favorably on a Technology Immersion Cluster within Douglass Middle School. Without SBP, the originators of the plan would have had to find a principal willing to house the pilot project. With SBP, teachers with innovative ideas are given an open forum to air their proposals to colleagues and parents, as well as to administrators.[129]

The positive experiences with SBP have been outnumbered by the negative ones, however, probably for the reason Scully gives—it accentuates whatever preceded its implementation. RCSD was and is a district with many problems, not the least of which are underlying differences in constituencies' assumptions about what "ought to be" in terms of power allocation for adults or educational goals and standards for children. Often, SBP teams have broken up into warring factions; the parent constituency, the teachers, the administrators—all pulling in different directions and making sure their turf or interests are protected. In Nancy Sundberg's opinion, the biggest disappointment of SBP has been the "bickering" between these factions.[130] Joanne Scully has been called on to act as referee for teams that have been at each other's throats, occasionally literally as well as figuratively.[131]

Parents complain bitterly that teachers on SBP teams try to exclude them by using educational jargon. They do not feel that teachers treat them with respect because they are often poor and not as educated as the teachers. They argue that they are made to feel as though they are stepping on the professional territory of teachers when they attempt to develop solutions to educational problems. They also complain that teachers look upon them with blame for their children's school problems. Hans DeBruyn, RCSD parent negotiator, has said that "we are not the problem; we are part of the solution." Yet it appears that teachers have yet to accept parents on SBP teams as coequal partners.[132]

Principals in SBP are in the awkward position of getting direction from central office and of being responsible for moving the district's reform agenda along, while being only one constituency—management—among several on the SBP team. Under the guidelines drawn up for SBP after the 1987 contract, the principal is to chair the school team.[133] Yet decisions must be made by consensus—all constituencies must agree to a proposal. The principal is held accountable for moving the district's agenda along, yet under the SBP guidelines, has no authority to do so.[134] This contradiction has caused many principals to decide to take charge of the teams' work.

After her initial euphoria at the prospect of SBP veteran teacher, Mary Toole, now says she feels betrayed by SBP. In her school the principal has taken over many of the functions that she hoped would belong to the team, including the decision about how often the team should meet. She says that if teachers do not agree to the principal's proposals, he retaliates against them for their lack of support.[135] Although she feels the team has been empowered to make some decisions, the limited scope of their decision-making power has become a source of personal disappointment.

The ambiguity of the principal's role is key to understanding the problems Rochester has had in implementing SBP. Principals are now hired by SBP teams. Instead of being interviewed by central office administrators, candidates must go before teams and present their philosophy and ideas. This was seen as central to creating a compatible school community with all participants working toward the same vision in the same way. However, the idea has been compromised by the fact that principals are still part of "district management" as well as part of the school community. Charles Moscato explains how being hired by the school team—but being answerable to central office—has affected how principals approach both job interviews and their work, once hired:

(SBP) presents a whole new set of behaviors for someone interviewing for a position because all of us have gone through it and all of us have been rejected by several committees before we have finally found one. It's changed. I remember when you used to go in, you were interviewed by administrators who were trying to find an administrator for a building. You had to come in and be kind of a hard-nose. "This is what I'm going to do. . . . " They were looking for that kind of thing. You cannot do that when you sit before a panel of teachers and secretaries and custodians . . . and parents. So you have to kind of find the middle road where you're going to have to establish a relationship with that committee real quickly. Once you get the position, then you can go ahead and do the kind of things that need to be done. If you sat in an interview and said, "Well, yes, I do collect plan books once a month," you're dead. . . . So you don't say those kinds of things. But yet, when I came in here that's what I did. I started collecting plan books.[136]

This system of hiring has resulted in some less experienced administrators being hired by teams from larger schools, leading to less senior managers making higher salaries than more experienced principals. That has led to concern among principals that the reforms have not provided an equitable career ladder for them. Moscato says that principals also fear that they will be forced to stay with a school once hired by a team, negating chances for advancement through the managerial hierarchy:

Some of my colleagues are in schools with maybe 300 students, very small schools. Well, I don't know how much you can do. It's good to start out with when you're learning, but one you become established—I would become bored with a school that small and I'd want to move. So the question we've been asking of the previous superintendent and the current one is "Where's the career ladder for administrators?"[137]

To add to the principals' concern, they find that SBP teams look solely to the principal to implement the decisions the entire team has agreed to. According to principals, teacher members of teams are particularly guilty of failing to take responsibility for making sure their constituency group—teachers—is implementing the decision agreed upon by the team.[138] In addition, teachers are apt to look to the principal to do the "dirty work"—for instance, settle disputes between parents, tell teachers who wish to transfer to a building that the team has rejected them.[139] It is clear that the persistence of old patterns of behavior—learned by years of experience with the old pro-efficiency model by all the participants in SBP—is making adoption of new roles and responsibilities for principals, teachers, and parents difficult and trying.

Marc Tucker has said that by decentralizing decision-making, the bureaucracy—so hostile to change—will be bypassed, allowing educational innovation to happen. As we have seen, SBP has been unable to actually shake the control and influence of the managerial bureaucracy. Central office still determines the makeup of final exams. It controls the purse strings of all but a few pilot schools.[140] These devices determine what teachers teach and how resources are to be allocated. However, the bureaucracy has not been alone in hampering innovation. Teams themselves have not supported teachers who have advocated for change. For example, Nancy Sundberg's original proposal for a multiage, multigrade, untracked "cluster" within Douglass Middle School was rejected by the team. The cluster eventually came into being in spite, rather than because, of SBP.[141] Other highly publicized projects attempting to implement the new orthodoxy on efficient education could have occurred without SBP.[142] It appears that SBP has done little to penetrate the classroom, to alter the fundamental interaction between teachers and students. The status quo in teaching methods and opportunities for learning has been left untouched by SBP in the vast majority of classrooms in the district.

Support for SBP has wavered in Rochester. The promised improvements in student achievement have not occurred: test scores are no better, suspensions and dropout rates remain high, the percentage of students taking Regents level courses remains low.[143] With money tight in the district, the financial support necessary for teams to engage in training and to develop and implement improvement plans seems unlikely.[144] Joanne Scully feels that during his short tenure Manuel Rivera did not show a strong commitment to SBP. Even Adam Urbanski seems to be backing off from his endorsement of SBP, saying that the bureaucracy makes the chances for its success slim.[145] Scully sees this lack of strong support from both leaders as presenting a profound danger to the continuation of SBP in the district.

> I think it's coming apart now. It's the first time I think there's a serious threat to either SBP going away or dying of neglect organizationally. I've been sounding that alarm and nobody seems to care.[146]

Having arrived at this conclusion, Joanne Scully left her position in Rochester in 1994 to take a job as assistant superintendent for instruction in the school system of Albany, New York.

Teacher Professionalism

In Nancy Sundberg's mind, teaching can become a profession if three conditions are satisfied: 1) Experienced teachers mentor novices in the vagaries of the craft, 2) teachers engage in continual development of their expertise, and 3) teachers make strides toward reaching educational outcomes that society identifies as important.[147] The Rochester experiment in teacher professionalism has had success in the first two of Sundberg's prerequisites. The reforms have led to little success in Sundberg's third prerequisite—demonstrating that teachers are effectively meeting society's goals for student outcomes. That failure has been the cause of vituperative attacks on the RCSD-RTA plan to professionalize teaching.

The mentor-intern program established by the 1987 reforms have been unanimously deemed "successful" by all constituencies in the RCSD.[148] The peer-remediation program got off to a slow start, but has represented an improvement over the pre-1987 period, when virtually all teachers were rated as above average by their supervisors. Principal Moscato compliments the RTA on working with teachers who are performing poorly by making them realize that they ought to enter the intervention program.[149] The lead teacher idea has been less successful. Deciding who ought to be a lead teacher and what assignments were the "toughest" was more difficult than anticipated.[150] As a result, the lead teachers in the district often do not stay in the classroom, but rather are assigned to duties such as offering remediation to poorly performing teachers.[151] On the whole, however, the Career in Teaching program has made progress in adding the professional development ingredient to the recipe for teacher professionalism. In fact, the contract settled in 1993 expands on the four-level career ladder for teachers.[152]

Teachers themselves are of two minds on the issue of professionalism. It is fair to say that virtually all the Rochester teachers want to be treated like professionals, yet they shy away from taking on the responsibilities professionals typically assume—control of the standards of professional service and accountability for outcomes. In support of professionalism, the Rochester teachers voted to increase their RTA dues to support the Leadership for Reform Institute. The purpose of the institute is to encourage teacher initiative in support of reforms, and to promote group efforts to improve the teaching and learning environment. Urbanski is promoting the idea of "creative insubordination,"of "reforms without permission," so that teachers will take the initiative in changing classroom practices.[153]

Although desiring professional status, many teachers are diffident on the issue of hiring, evaluating, or granting tenure to their colleagues. As historian Wayne Urban points out, the development of a class of supervisors whose job it was to oversee and evaluate teachers' work at the beginning of this century marked the death knell for teacher professionalism.[154]

Mary Toole embodies the contradiction of wanting to be treated as a professional, and yet looking to the school manager to perform the function of evaluating teachers. On the one hand, she bristles at the treatment she receives at the hands of the school administration, the lack of trust shown, the demeaning orders given:

What we do to the children—and I guess this is what is wrong with the system—administrators do to us . . . witness Manny Rivera saying, "You have to have a note (for a day's absence) . . . we punish the whole class because two kids act up in the lunchroom. . . . Reverse that. We teachers should be able to work together cooperatively and then go off and take an idea . . . a theme . . . launch it and go from there. . . . The administrator should say, "I trust my teachers enough to know that they are teaching all areas through this. I don't need to come into their classroom and say, 'Did you get ready to teach the fifth grade writing test?' or 'You have to go to an in-service workshop next Wednesday'. " . . . So trust us enough to make the right decision for our students and do the right thing.[155]

While advocating for professionalism, she simultaneously recoils from the idea that teachers should police their own ranks. She says although she knows who is not pulling their weight, she does not want to be the one to go to those teachers and tell them as much. Fearing she would come off as a shrew to her colleagues, she would rather let the principal do it.[156] The problem of course is, historically, neither the principal nor anyone else has done serious evaluation of teachers' work. If teachers—who best know what it takes to teach well—refuse the responsibility of doing so now, there is little hope they will be granted the type of professional autonomy they say they want.

The issue that the public has grabbed onto and refuses to let go of is that of teacher accountability for student outcomes. The large raises for teachers in the 1987 contract were tied to a promise of better results by Adam Urbanski.[157] The community has not forgotten that promise. And now, all of the problems of the district are being laid at the teacher's door. Catherine Spoto says this is due to using collective bargaining as the vehicle for reform, and adds that laying blame on the teachers "is not fair."[158] However, in the minds of most Rochester residents, many of whom are poor or working class, the 1987 contract translated to a lot of money for teachers. The public is still angry about that settlement, and has fought hard against raises for teachers in two subsequent rounds of negotiation.[159] Accountability was and continues to be the issue: teachers should receive higher salaries if and when they produce the promised improvements in student performance. Despite the fact that Rochester teachers' salaries were ranked ninth in Monroe County in 1993, as opposed to being fifth in 1982, parents are angry that teachers expect a pay raise when students continue to do so poorly. A key provision of the contract settled in late 1993 stated that every third year a teacher's pay increase will be tied to a performance appraisal done by parents, students, and colleagues—a token acknowledgment of the idea of teacher accountability.

The local paper is filled with letters to the editor from outraged parents who oppose granting teachers any raises. The following letter was given the "Golden Pen Award" by the newspaper's editorial staff in 1993:

> All city teachers who have their eyes open know that many, many families in Rochester are in financial crisis. The idea that a raise for well-paid teachers should be given priority over the needs of the children of these struggling families is ridiculous. Children need smaller classes, pre-school programs, all-day kindergartens, social workers in the schools, books . . . the last thing our kids need is a better contract for the teachers. . . . This is a plea to the union—if you care about our children and the city that employs you, stop talking about pay raises. Start talking about how to make our children feel successful in school.[160]

This typifies one of the more civil expressions of dissent against the proposal to grant teachers a wage increase.

An opinion article by columnist Bob Lounsberry puts it more bluntly:

> City school teachers have about as much popular support as Tom Arnold . . . Rochester residents want to see young people able to make a living, not teachers able to make a boat payment . . . Urbanski and his union ought to realize that before they embarrass themselves any more.[161]

In the spring of 1994 the Rochester school system faced a budget shortfall of nearly four million dollars. Superintendent Rivera proposed cutting 316 district employees, increasing class sizes, and dropping football from the sports program. Heated budget hearings drew hundreds of people to voice their condemnation of, or support for, various expenditures. Rivera blamed his predecessor, Peter McWalters, for leaving big deficits behind when he moved on to Rhode Island. The board president, Archie Curry, dropped a bombshell during a city council meeting when he admitted that the school board had not been able to afford any of the teachers' contracts it had approved since 1987.

Letters to the editor of the local paper continued the stream of criticism for Rochester's teachers, blaming their "insatiable appetite" for higher salaries for the budget crisis. Adam Urbanski countered that teachers' salaries accounted for only 35 percent of the total budget. He pointed out that the median teacher salary in the RCSD ranked 123rd—not first—in New York state.[162] His comments did little to stem the tide of condemnation of RCSD teachers' salaries and the calls for greater teacher accountability.

For their part, teachers resist being blamed for poor student outcomes. Dawn Lunt, a math teacher in Rochester, calls accountability a "blaming exercise." In an article published in the newspaper, she lists some of the reasons why teachers have not been successful in improving student performance:

> They cannot keep up with all the problems they are faced with every day: classes with students who fall asleep, refuse to do the work, disrupt the education of others, fight and carry concealed weapons, come unprepared, lose their books, pull fire alarms, set fires, skip class—the list is endless. . . . The parents of the community are frustrated. Understand that the teachers are equally frustrated.[163]

Mary Toole agrees, saying that many teachers are very depressed because of the community's great expectations for what teachers can do for the children of Rochester:

> The expectations for schools are just so high. We feed them breakfast now. We feed them lunch. Classroom teachers are their mother and father, their social worker, their counselor. We . . . teach them values.[164]

She adds that she "cannot see the light at the end of the tunnel" on this central issue of what Rochester teachers are expected to do for the very needy youngsters in their classes. If the granting of professional status is made contingent on Rochester's teachers single-handedly turning around the lives of children who face the serious problems associated with poverty in this nation, the prospects for the professionalization of teaching are bleak, indeed.

Type of Education

On the national scene, education in the mid-1990s is much as it has been during most of the century. Few of the child-centered reforms first proposed by the early educational progressives have been implemented. For most school managers, teachers, parents, and children, the early pro-efficiency model persists.[165] Lessons continue to be driven by state regulations and standardized tests rather than by the needs and interests of the children in a teacher's class.[166] Efforts to end tracking often meet with resistance from those parents whose children are in the most academically demanding track, regardless of the effect this segregation has on less academically successful students.[167] Despite its ambitious attempt to institute school-based planning and create conditions in which teacher professionalism might flourish, despite its plan to encourage pedagogical reforms, the RCSD duplicates the national record on education reform.

Thomas Gillett of the RTA admits that little has changed in the classroom for most students. He estimates that perhaps 5 percent of Rochester teachers have implemented some changes in how instruction takes place in their classrooms. Part of this, he feels, is due to teachers, particularly older teachers, resisting changes in longstanding practices.[168] Nancy Sundberg attributes part of the persistence of old teaching methods to the mandated use of standardized tests: "In general, we're told we can use whatever textbooks we want—or we don't have to use them, but we just have to be prepared for whatever tests. . . . I think that holds tremendous power."[169]

Given the public's demand for "results"—higher test scores—most teachers opt for concentrating on what counts—that is to say, what is quantifiable. They continue to attempt to engage their students in the drill and practice that may lead to better test results for some students, but to little long-term learning or active engagement for any of their charges. Parents, for their part, often dislike "experimental ideas" about how their children ought to be educated. They prefer the familiar to the unknown, and want their children to have the same experience of going to school that they had twenty, thirty, or forty years earlier.

Much of the educational progressives' agenda for education has been adopted by Rochester's leaders in business and education: child-centered, hands-on, project oriented education aimed at developing children's ability to think analytically and solve real-life problems. Yet this vision of education is not yet shared by the vast majority of the participants in the RCSD reform endeavor. If it is ever to be supported, a massive campaign—similar to that being mounted nationally by the Business Roundtable and the Conference Board—will have to occur to create a change in the hearts and minds of parents, teachers, and administrators in Rochester. Education is a very personal affair. To change it, basic beliefs and assumptions about the nature of childhood, the proper role of adults in the learning process, the potential of all students to grow intellectually may have to be altered. That's a tall order and one unlikely to occur unless people see a reason for such a fundamental shift in basic convictions. Add to this significant barrier to change a budget crisis threatening jobs and popular sports programs— and the generosity of spirit and resources necessary to fuel the difficult, complicated process of reform can easily evaporate. The contentious budget process in the spring of 1994 made it clear that when schools are forced to choose between having cleaners and funding modest salary increases for teachers, there can be no winners.

Conclusions

> With significant fanfare, the great Rochester School Reform Movement
> was launched in 1987, and was quickly heralded through the nation.
> Now, after five years, the schools have precious little to show for it.
> Promises haven't materialized and the patience school officials appealed
> for has worn bare. The community is exasperated. There is a compelling
> need to repair the damage, but what we witness instead is a dispiriting
> spectacle of bickering and fingerpointing. Not what can be done, but who
> can be blamed.[170]

By 1993 the editors of the *Rochester Democrat and Chronicle* felt there was
more than enough blame to go around for the "abysmal nose-dive in performance since reform started." The editors pointed to disillusioned teachers, in-
flexible school managers, political posturing board members, and neglectful
parents as all "to blame" for the poor outcomes of this much lauded experiment
in reform. They ran a political cartoon that suggested this amounted to a form
of child abuse. (See figure 7.1.) While the editors granted that the RCSD serves
some of "the poorest, most problem-beset students in the country," they demanded—and rightfully so—that these children have the opportunity to have a
successful school experience. If little else in their lives is as it ought to be, at
least school should be a place where they can be safe and thrive. The editorial
ended with the command, "Let's start again."[171]

A year later, there was little evidence that the editors' call for a new beginning had been heeded by anyone, including the editors themselves. Throughout
its coverage of Manuel Rivera's resignation and the budget crisis, the *Rochester
Democrat and Chronicle* sarcastically referred to the 1987 plan for radical school
change as Rochester's nationally touted "reform" movement. Declining test scores,
high dropout rates, and tight budgets had given reform a bad name. With the rate
of violent assaults against teachers up 66 percent in one year, layoffs of school
personnel in the offing, and the second superintendent in less than three years
to tender his resignation, the editorial board's impatience is not surprising. While
the newspaper's editors chastised all the participants in the district—the teachers' union, city hall, administrators, the students—it saved the lion's share of its
criticism for the school board. It called for citizens to "take back the schools"
by abolishing the elected board and putting the superintendent under the direction of the city council.[172]

Clearly, the new pro-efficiency model for reform—decentralized decision-
making via Total Quality Management, teacher professionalism, and child-centered

Figure 7.1. Political cartoon by Mitchell, "Child Abuse, City School Style." Source: *Rochester Democrat and Chronicle,* March 21, 1993. Reprinted with permission of the *Rochester Democrat and Chronicle.*

education—has never really been implemented in the RCSD. The theoretical framework for reform was all laid out in 1987 by a rather courageous cast of characters; people who were willing to take the risk to be among the first in the nation to attempt to implement a formidable agenda for school reform. What has happened—or not happened—to prevent this blueprint for change from being played out in the Rochester schools?

Barriers to restructuring put up by school managers fearful of loss of authority, power, and employment created an immediate threat to the possibility of making decentralized decision-making a reality. Thomas Gillett puts the problem metaphorically: "If you're the lead dog your view is much better than any of the others, so when someone suggests that we rearrange, the lead dog is not going to like it much."[173] The managers of the RCSD—ensconced in their "lead" position by the old management model—have fought hard to hold on to that which serves their interests best. The ambiguous position in which school principals have been placed—overseeing the implementation of top-down directives while facilitating broad based participation in decision-making—has done nothing to further the principle of decentralized operations.

The goal of teacher professionalism has, to some degree at least, been torpedoed by teachers themselves: teachers who would rather foist difficult problems on their principals than deal with them collaboratively, who put roadblocks in front of fellow teachers attempting to change classroom practice, and who blame parents beset by problems rather than deal with the possibilities inherent in their children. Despite their genuine desire for professional respect and autonomy, teachers will not become professionals unless and until they stop looking to management to "take care of things" and start looking within themselves for answers to troublesome questions. The vitality of the old pro-efficiency model is evident in the reaction of all of the participants to the sweeping changes proposed by the 1987 reform agenda.

Certainly, most of the participants in the Rochester experiment have clung to what they have known rather than take the risk of assuming new roles or new responsibilities, try new teaching methods, or experiment with inventive materials. Yet the failure to implement the proposed changes is due only in part to inertia and resistance to change. Much of what the teachers say is true. It is impossible to engage a child in any type of project when that child falls asleep at his desk because he has gotten little or no sleep the night before. This happens—and not infrequently—due to the chaotic family life many children in Rochester experience. It is difficult to teach children who often do not make it to class because of sickness, fear of the trip to school, or an indifferent attitude toward education on the part of their parents. The problems the teachers cite are real. They are symptomatic of dilemmas that do not originate within the bounds of the schoolhouse gate. Yet, the community is saying, "We want good results— regardless."[174] And if the school system does not show up well on the bottom line, the system—or in the Rochester example, a segment of the system, the teaching force—is vilified.

Past RCSD board president, Catherine Spoto, finds this unjustified:

(This is typical of) the historic role that public schools have played in this country: they're either going to save the world, or they're scapegoats for the community's problems. . . . So if race is a problem, you don't deal with it by housing, you deal with it by desegregating the schools. . . . What I'm fighting against is this: it is very easy to compartmentalize these problems. If you make them all school problems (she wipes her hands) then we don't have to deal with them. People think, "If only the school would deal with the problem of violence then we wouldn't have these other problems. If only the school would educate kids, then poverty would be solved." I know the circumstances of the kids in our schools . . . and I know how often the school is the only stable institution in the child's life, and that it is often through the intervention of the school that kids are saved. People don't want to hear this. They think they are excuses.[175]

She insists, however, that they are not excuses. They make up the tough reality the RCSD is facing. She adds that the schools alone cannot deliver what the community wants. The school is but a part of the greater community. And if the community wants children to have a better school experience, the whole agenda on children and families must be addressed:

That is the fundamental direction that education and schools have to move in because what is so significant is that education reform is not just about changing schools. It's going to require a profound political and social change as well. Until we're ready to come to grips with that, we're going nowhere.[176]

Perhaps of all the lessons education reformers can learn from the Rochester experience, that one is the most difficult, albeit the most essential.

8

The Choices We Face

In the last few years, discussions of education and education reform have been marked by a dreary instrumentality about jobs. The dread vision of "competition in the global economy" has replaced the terror of the Red Menace as a scare tactic to keep Americans in line. . . . There are other reasons for becoming educated, of course. For many, learning can be fun in itself. Educated people live longer, richer lives and may even enjoy life more. These nonutilitarian outcomes of education have virtually disappeared from discourse about education in recent years.[1]

The spark that ignited the current education reform movement was fear; fear that the Japanese and German economies would overtake ours in the race to be the preeminent economic power in the world. The "economic imperative," as it has come to be called, has been accepted whole cloth by policymakers, economic gurus, and educators. Our nation's presumed competitive disadvantage in the global marketplace has been blamed less on changing technology, the restructuring of industries, or poor management of American firms, and more on the way we educate our children. Since A *Nation at Risk* was published more than a decade ago, education has been the prime suspect in America's alleged economic decline. In a defensive move, educational leaders across the country have promised to remake our education system into something more modern and high performance than the bureaucratic, hierarchical school organization that seemed to be the answer to international economic competition nearly a hundred years ago.

The current discussion on school reform is not new. It is a replay of a debate on the purposes and methods of educating the nation's youngsters that took place during that earlier period of reform. The choices offered to policymakers at the turn of the twentieth century have again been offered to our current leaders. They can resolve to educate youngsters primarily to become useful employees in the economy. Or, alternatively, they can resolve to meet a moral commitment to develop each individual child's talents and intellect. Policymakers can choose to institutionalize corporate organizational structures and management principles in the schools, or to encourage the development of organizational models that are uniquely suited to the exigencies of teaching and learning. Despite the passage of nearly one hundred years, the choice will be made between the same two visions: education as a tool for economic supremacy or a moral obligation owed the young.

Education as an Economic Tool

American society places great value on efficiency, wealth accumulation, practicality, and productivity. Business embodies much of what is esteemed in our nation. Business is powerful, not only because it is highly valued, but because it can use its influence and vast economic resources in attempts to sway both the public and the legislatures to its way of thinking on any given issue. Children, on the other hand, are relatively powerless in our society. They are at the mercy of adults to give them experiences that will be in their best interest. As historian Raymond Callahan demonstrated so deftly, educators are another extremely vulnerable group. Dependent on public funding, much as children are dependent on the largesse of the adults in their lives, educators must be careful to please powerful groups in society. The most powerful group that educators must please is that which represents the interests of business.

In the twentieth century's ongoing debate about the purposes of education, business interests have prevailed. Education has and continues to be seen as a production function that starts with little children and, over a twelve- or thirteen-year process of manufacture, molds them into desired educational products. Schools today are reminded continually that they need to shape children into what Kodak now refers to as "the competitive employee." Schools that are highly productive fulfill that purpose efficiently, with a minimum of waste. School "productivity" is assessed by use of quantitative measures—for example, standardized test scores, frequency of retention, graduation rates. Such aggregated data are regarded as representing objective, value-free truth. Yet this narrow, mechanistic view of education fails to capture the intangibles in the education process—the human interactions, the particular needs and interests of youngsters, the inner transformation and gratification that learning can offer people of any age.

Throughout the twentieth century, business has been certain that schools would become more productive places if "universal" management principles developed in industry were utilized by school managers. Management theories that have evolved to meet the demands of new technologies or product markets have been presented as being applicable in the schoolhouse. Corporate forms of organization, roles, and responsibilities, and "manufacturing" processes have been proposed for use in education. Thus, eighty years ago Franklin Bobbitt campaigned for adoption of Frederick Taylor's scientific management principles in classrooms and school district offices alike. In the 1960s, when teachers engaged in crippling strikes in order to become coequal partners with school management in terms of deciding how education would proceed, industrial relations experts crafted legislation that would allow teachers to bargain collectively—like factory workers—over their wages, hours, and conditions of employment. Today business consultants aim to transform schools into "high performance organizations" by use of "total quality management." Adoption of this latest management theory will, it is promised, lead to greater school productivity as we approach the new millennium.

Over the last one hundred years the pro-efficiency advocates have consistently defined the problems with the existing schools as well as the solution to those problems in terms of how efficiently schools are readying children for the requirements of the work place. They have used remarkably similar techniques to move their agenda along: funding surveys to uncover waste and inefficiencies in the schools, shaping public opinion on education by use of the media and public relations, utilizing philanthropy to sponsor either research or projects in education that further the preferred type of management or pedagogy, serving on school boards, and lobbying legislatures to change schools in keeping with the pro-efficiency vision of education of a given period. These techniques have proven productive.

There are a number of reasons I believe we ought to reject the business community's current attempt to re-create the nation's schools to meet its perceived needs. In solely instrumental terms, this latest attack on the schools and call for their reform is based on fear and anxiety generated by unproven arguments about the causal link between education and our nation's economic health and the economic security of our young people.

1) *The economic imperative argument:* Since the beginning of the century, the business community has put forth the theory that the educational treatment given youngsters is directly linked to the nation's economic success. And throughout the century, that theory has been accepted as objective truth by the vast majority of our nation's policymakers. However, many contemporary economists find that the linkage between a nation's economic health and the education of its youngsters is not as clear as it is purported to be.

Roland Strum, the author of a recent RAND study, finds that while a nation's educational attainment is a contributor to its economic performance, how precisely that contribution is made is not clear. There are other factors that are more strongly linked with a nation's economic health—for example, its rate of saving and investment. Stanford's Henry Levin, an educator as well as an economist, found in his research on workers' cooperatives that economic productivity has more to do with work place organization than on the educational level of workers. Paul Krugman, a specialist in international trade and finance at MIT, also questions the validity of linking education with the nation's economic health. He points out that education and training confer benefits on individual students and workers by increasing their earning power. He argues that it is not education and training, however, that lead to national productivity. A nation's consumption of goods produced by its workers—not goods consumed by other countries—determines its economic productivity. He characterizes as naive the economic strategy of investing in "human capital" via education and training. He adds, "What sounds like a futuristic, forward-looking, intellectual basis for economic strategy is basically a set of deeply misleading, simplistic ideas."[2]

Larry Cuban, a critic of the economic imperative argument, has reached the following conclusion: "the myth of better schools as the engine for a leaner, stronger economy was a scam from the very beginning." Cuban makes the point that schools neither influence governmental monetary or fiscal policies, nor create high wage jobs—factors that all greatly contribute to economic health. He calls the economic imperative a "concocted deception about the causal connection between better schools and a healthier economy . . . a swindle" that "diminishes public confidence in schools."[3]

2) *The declining health of the American economy:* There is little substantive proof that the United States is in an economic tailspin relative to its chief international competitors. The United States outstrips both Japan and Germany in labor productivity, economic growth, and share of world merchandising imports. In 1994 and 1995 the World Economic Forum bestowed the title of "most competitive economy" on the United States—beating third-place Japan and sixth-place Germany by all economic indicators. The RAND study cited above found little evidence of the alleged "deindustrialization" or drop in labor productivity that might warrant "dramatic and instantaneous changes in education and training" in this country. Our economy already is, in the words of *Newsweek* writer Bill Powell, "a lean, mean, high-tech production machine."[4] It is the existing and much maligned education system that educated the work force that contributed to this success.

3) *The promise of a "knowledge based" economy:* Although in favor of investing in education and training for the benefits they confer on individuals,

Susannah Berryman of the World Bank describes the promise of a resulting high wage, high skills economy, as wishful thinking. She points out that many young people do not have the skills or the inclination to become highly skilled "knowledge" workers. The new pro-efficiency reformers' effort to set ever higher academic standards mocks and discourages those children—and there are many—who find academic study agonizing for a host of reasons.

Henry Levin finds it absurd to create tougher standards when so many children find it difficult to reach the existing, less rigorous ones. He wonders if the ruling elite—despite their rhetoric to the contrary—has decided that the children from disadvantaged backgrounds do not matter. And, as Berryman astutely suggests, even if all children could be trained to become highly skilled workers, there is no guarantee that the economy could provide them with jobs.[5]

4) *The link between education and personal economic security:* Berryman's point leads to the final flaw in the new pro-efficiency coalition's argument. They warn that without a rigorous education, today's youngsters will not be able to get and hold jobs that will allow them to enjoy a standard of living comparable to that achieved by their parents. They point to uncontested data that show lifetime earnings of college graduates outstripping those of high school graduates. Young people today, they warn, had better learn to "think for a living," or their future, and our nation's future, is doomed. This admonition is powerful enough to spur hundreds of thousands of parents and their children to incur tremendous debts in order to finance higher education. The expectation is that if education credentials are earned, the economy will provide good jobs that require a college or graduate level education. However, our new higher education graduates are confronted by a harsh reality. Despite having prepared themselves for an economy that values serious education—*that* economy does not currently exist—nor do the job opportunities implied, but curiously never promised by the new pro-efficiency reformers.

In fact, we have large numbers of college graduates and Ph.D.s who are unable to find employment for which their education has prepared them. In 1996, one half the 1.2 million college graduates were unemployed three months after graduation. Employment analysts predict a 25 percent unemployment rate for these college graduates a full year after having donned their caps and gowns. Many of those who do gain employment, find themselves in retail and clerical jobs that were competently performed by high school graduates a generation ago. Obtaining an advanced degree does not improve employment prospects as much as one would expect from listening to the economic imperative proponents: 29 percent of 1994 engineering Ph.D.s had no job commitments at the time of their graduation. As *Newsweek* puts it, new Ph.D.s "have unemployment rates like tailors at a nudist colony."

The problem extends beyond the newly educated. Unemployment among chemists is at a twenty-year high due primarily to cutbacks in jobs in industry. The jobless rate for physicists is on the rise, despite their education and training, which certainly readies them to "think for a living." The economy in the first half of the 1990s was in a "jobless recovery," where business worked "smarter" with fewer employees. By one measure, only 4 percent of the new jobs created during that period required higher education. Despite all the rhetoric to the contrary, there is certainly no evidence that good jobs go unfilled because of a lack of educated or skilled applicants.[6]

Why has the business sector and government promoted the idea that schools are directly linked to our nation's economic survival? Critics of the economic imperative argument suggest different possible answers—ranging from conspiracy to an attempt to deflect attention from other problems. Gerald Bracey, an early critic of the current reform movement, attributes the most cunning motives to the business community's push for education reform. Business, he reasons, wants more people well educated to have a better and deeper pool of potential job applicants from which to pick. He projects a scenario where the number of good jobs will decrease due to automation, while the number of well-educated applicants will increase as a result of increased rigor in the schools. He comments, "Not a bad deal for the businessman."[7] The many retail and clerical jobs now filled by recent college graduates lends credibility to this argument. Bracey is joined in his belief in the conspiratorial nature of the current reform movement by David Berliner, an educational psychologist at the University of Arizona. Berliner argues that the entire educational crisis has been manufactured by conservative business leaders, politicians, and the press in order to weaken the public schools and, perhaps, eventually lead to their demise.[8]

On the other hand, Larry Cuban sees no conspiracy; just business and political leaders capitalizing on the political appeal of simplistic solutions for intractable problems.

> Business leaders, national and state policy makers, and practitioners saw the obvious political appeal of harnessing schools to building a stronger economy and dreamed that such concerted efforts to improve schools would indeed improve the economy. The media amplified the delusion. What occurred was a widespread, self-inflicted, but politically useful deception anchored in deep confusion over the many purposes public schools serve in a democracy.[9]

He adds that it was much easier for business and political leaders to blame the schools for economic problems than to accept harsher public judgments about inept governmental and corporate policies, or to appear helpless in the face of intransigent economic cycles. My own opinion lies closer to Cuban's rationale, although the business community's long-held view of education as a mechanism for the preparation of the national work force makes Bracey's point difficult to dismiss. Couple that with business's strong support for privatization of public school management and school choice—that is, publicly funded vouchers for use in private and religious schools—and it seems fair to say, at the very least, that the motivating factors driving the new pro-efficiency reforms are many-layered and complex.

There seems to be little reason to support the business agenda for education reform. Taken on its own utilitarian terms, the validity of its economic rationale is seriously in question. Morally, it whittles the purpose of schooling down to an almost sinister notion of making good little workers for future employment. Yet it is indeed paradoxical that the current incarnation of the pro-efficiency coalition has embraced many compelling ideas on schooling proposed nearly one hundred years ago by educational progressives such as John Dewey, Ella Flagg Young, and Jesse Newlon.

These new pro-efficiency reformers share the progressives' desire to have graduates who can reason and solve difficult problems. They view the factory model of efficient education created by the early pro-efficiency reformers—and prevalent throughout most of this century—as being incapable of producing these newly desired results. They propose to replace it with many principles of school organization and pedagogy proposed by the progressives at the turn of the century: decentralization of curriculum decisions to the school site, the empowerment of teachers so they may create appropriate pedagogical programs and strategies, and custom-tailored education for individual children. These ideas are attractive to many who reject the bureaucratic model of education for reasons wholly unconnected to the economic imperative argument.

Clearly, there are important differences between the proposals of the educational progressives and those of the new pro-efficiency reformers. While these contemporary reformers call for decentralization of decision-making on the *means* of educating youngsters, they stand by the long-standing pro-efficiency belief that only top management can and should set the goals for the school organization. While they recognize the importance of the teacher in creating a generation of critical thinkers, the teacher is still the subordinate of the school manager, now referred to alternatively as a "coach," a "facilitator," or an "educational leader." And while they are demanding that children be taught to think critically and analyze difficult problems, they stop short of the educational progressives' call for the creation of a citizenry that thinks critically about—and often challenges—society's political or economic status quo.

Probably the most fundamental difference between the new pro-efficiency reformers and the educational progressives is the stated motivation behind their recommendations. For the educational progressives, education was a moral enterprise conferring intangible benefits on the nation's young people. Its purpose was to expand their outlook on life, cultivate their inborn talents, always treating their individuality with respect. As such, their support for child-oriented education was impervious to educational fads or pressure from interest groups. For the new pro-efficiency reformers, however, education is first and foremost an economic tool rather than a moral imperative. And, adhering to the ideology of managerial rights and prerogatives, it is up to the elite cadre of top school management to decide—with the advice and backing of the nation's business leaders—how that tool may best be utilized to serve the needs of the economy. Today, top management has decided much of the educational progressives' proposals are useful. When a new economic imperative is envisioned, the usefulness of the progressive agenda may diminish. Should that occur, school management's support for child-centered education will likely be withdrawn.

The educational progressives called for democratically run schools because they were convinced that including all the participants—parents, teachers, students, managers—in educational decision-making was required in a democratic society. They were adamant that democracy could not exist outside the schoolhouse gates if it did not thrive inside. It was not for purposes of efficiency, in the narrow sense of the word, but for purposes of ethics and democratic principles that the progressives advocated for shared decision-making in education. Democratic establishment of both the ends and means of education would not be quick, easy, or without conflict. Yet it might be ultimately "efficient" in that it would result in all of those participants working cooperatively toward goals they established together. The shared decision-making proposed by the vast majority of today's pro-efficiency reformers—allowing teachers at the school site to devise the nuts and bolts of the educational program—is but a distantly related cousin to the vision of democratic school governance promoted by the educational progressives. Concerned solely with promoting efficient outcomes by allowing teachers to find the best way to meet pre-determined organizational goals, it keeps intact a hierarchy of decision-making that makes genuine democracy in the schools impossible.

It is ironic that it is the hard-nosed business community that seeks to enact much of the hundred-year old progressive agenda. And, despite its flaws and the motivation behind it, some educators committed to making a school a better place for children have embraced the new pro-efficiency agenda for school change. As Rochester school board member Catherine Spoto has commented, business no longer wants the schools to merely train youngsters. Business now sees the mission of education as producing people "who can think creatively, work cooperatively, deal with complex problems, (and) . . . ambiguity."[10] The new pro-efficiency reformers state that they want *all* children to be educated in this way—not only the children of the elite classes in society. They profess a desire to have *all* children become thinkers, problem-solvers, and contributors to decisions that will make American firms successful competitors in the world economy. This represents a radical departure from the early pro-efficiency reformers' oft-stated assumption that large numbers of children from poor and working-class families would never go beyond the rudiments of the three Rs. To the degree that this agenda seeks to help children from all segments of society to develop their talents, it ought to be given vigorous support. The problem is that this single goal is so ambitious as to be unattainable unless schooling is taken as but a part of an entire program to improve the lives of children.

Putting Children First

Educators and school board members did not create a society that seems indifferent to poverty and the relative neglect of its youth. We need fresh thinking—among both liberals and conservatives—on ways to make a more just and caring community that supports family life.[11]

The recommendations that I will propose in what follows are in keeping with these thoughts expressed by University of Pennsylvania professor Richard Gibboney. We need fresh thinking, indeed, on the lives the children in our country are living. Our children today seem to be treated as a societal afterthought; too little attention, too few resources, too much emphasis on adult needs at the expense of meeting the needs of children. While we pay lip service to the importance of children as future citizens and our most valuable resource, the facts contradict the rhetoric. For the first time in the century, children today are living in conditions that are worse than those experienced by the preceding generation. If one looks at the realities presented by our nation's policies on families and children, by the legal rights children have, by the status given people who spend their lives working with children—be they homemakers or day-care workers—it is abundantly clear that children are not recognized or valued as a national treasure.

In this chapter I make recommendations that aim to turn things around for children. I ask adults from every point on the political spectrum, and private and public sectors of our economy, to commit to "putting children first." I believe that children's interests must be placed in an "inner sanctum" where they are protected from the hard scrabble business of politics and the combat over societal resources. Their needs must be taken care of *first*—then let the battles among adults proceed as normal. I ask that business leaders, school boards and managers, and teachers and their unions, make this commitment to children come alive by giving something up—be it time, profits, power, or personal glory. Only then may our children have a chance to grow into capable and thoughtful individuals who will be able to make contributions to our communities and our democracy, as well as to our economy.

Over the last twenty years I have taught hundreds of young children from a wide variety of social, economic, racial, and ethnic backgrounds. I realized early on in my career that a child's life outside school affects the likelihood that the child will thrive in the classroom. In my experience the clearest example of this principle was a boy who had been a cheerful, confident first-grader who led his class both in math and reading achievement. When he arrived in my second-grade class in September, his appearance and demeanor had changed so much that I hardly recognized him. He had circles under his eyes. His expression was blank. His clothes were disheveled. When it came time to work, he would tell me that his stomach ached or that he was too tired to even think of a topic to write about. As the term progressed his attendance became spotty. He was often late to school, arriving alone in a cab because he had missed the bus. In one year this boy's scores dropped from 99th percentile to around 50th percentile in every subtest of the Stanford Achievement Test.

What had caused this gruesome transformation of a formerly happy, successful child? During the summer between first and second grade, the boy's parents decided to divorce. His mother announced plans to move 300 miles away to pursue graduate studies. Fearful of losing his son, the father began a custody battle for the boy. The child's greatest fear was that he would be called to testify in court and made to tell the judge which parent he preferred. The thought of having to reject one of the two parents he loved sent him into an anxiety-filled depression. Unable to concentrate, sleep well, or play, he regressed in nearly every way.

The happy ending to this story is that the child's parents had the presence of mind and the resources to get counseling both for their son and for themselves. With the help of a mediator, they were eventually able to put the needs of their child ahead of their own. A relatively amicable divorce was worked out. The child ultimately pulled out of his depression and regained much of his former enthusiasm for living and learning. As he did so, his school achievement improved markedly.

I relate this story because it puts a human face on the statistics that show our youngsters are having a very difficult time growing up. It also demonstrates that resources can make a vast difference in helping parents and children cope with the paralyzing personal problems they may face. As I tried to teach this boy the concept of multiplication, it struck me how irrelevant multiplication must have seemed to him during his year of personal crisis. For many children, their entire childhood is spent in crisis. The fact is that troubled, hungry, abused, neglected, sick, or absent children are unlikely to develop the sophisticated skills employers say they want. Yet with the exception of supporting early childhood education for children of the poor, the new pro-efficiency reformers have, to date, paid scant attention to the desperation many children experience throughout their childhoods.

It is noteworthy that the Business Roundtable withdrew its original proposal for improved social and health services for children from its nine-point agenda for education reform—despite the fact that nearly one-fourth of our children now live below the poverty line.[12] The problems our children face are so immense that the Pew Charitable Trusts abandoned a multimillion dollar effort to overhaul how states provide services to children, citing the impossibility of meeting its goals.[13] A Carnegie Foundation task force has warned of a pattern of social neglect verging on a crisis that dims the prospects of a "staggering number of children."[14] The nation's teachers can corroborate this task force's conclusion.

School alone cannot repair the damage to children's lives. If children have problems in school—poor performance or disruptive behavior—those problems often do not originate in the school. The children of the poor have always found it difficult to excel in the school setting. Organizational and pedagogical reform can do little to correct the root causes of the problems these children face. When school is over—even if that school is an example of the finest pedagogy—these children often return to streets filled with violence and drugs. They must go home to substandard dwellings. They likely have to care for themselves because no adult is willing or able to care for them. Their childhoods are not filled with hopes for a bright future, but with the desire only to survive the present. These are not children apt to complete their homework, commit to long-term school projects, or become engaged in cooperative learning groups. Their experience has prepared them to deal only with today, to fend for oneself, and to trust no one.

The experiment in reform going on in Rochester exemplifies the problem well. Seventy percent of the students in Rochester live in poverty. Nearly half of the children entering the school system are born to teenage or single mothers. Many of these children are exposed to addictive drugs before they are born. In New York state, the streets of Rochester are second only to New York City's in terms of violence. It is no wonder that when the children of Rochester come to school, many of them are ill-equipped to succeed in math and reading, and are prone to falling asleep in class or having violent outbursts that result in their suspension. One is dismayed but not surprised that these children sometimes come to school carrying concealed weapons.[15]

The Rochester school district did not create these problems. Yet the reform experiment proposed to get "good results" regardless of what students had to cope with in the way of violence, drugs, poverty, poor medical care, or parental neglect. In a very real sense, the new pro-efficiency reformers' call for a focus on "outcomes" represents an abandonment of the promise of equity of inputs that originated with Lyndon Johnson's Great Society in the 1960s. It is an illusion that despite how children spend their childhoods, they can attain the same skills, understandings, and competencies. It is little wonder that test scores in Rochester have not gone up since the beginning of their experiment in reform in 1987. The experiment is doomed unless the depth of problems the city's children are facing is both acknowledged and addressed.

Children are educated about the world and their place in it by their family, their neighborhood, television programming and advertising, the Internet, the movies, their parents' employers, as well as their schools. As an educator, I care a great deal about the education given youngsters by the people, the media, and the agencies in their lives. I want for every child what I want for my own: a rich, stable family life, a safe and engaging community to grow in, responsible media, schooling that will provide experiences that are interesting, challenging, and supportive of individual interests and talents. I think if we stop thinking about children in the abstract—and start thinking of them as we think of youngsters in our own family—the debate on school reform will be altered dramatically. We need to ask one question of all policy pundits : "Is the reform you propose good enough for *your own child*?"—be it apprenticeships in industry for high school students or the takeover of the local school by a for-profit corporation.

All too often in the discussion about the instrumental use of the schools for one purpose or another, we forget we are talking about real children; individual kids who deserve our full attention and our commitment to making their childhoods memorable for all the right reasons. If we are to attempt reform of schools at all, the question that should direct our efforts ought to be: "How can we create schools that help caring, knowledgeable adults provide children with the environment they need to become all they can be?" After all, isn't that what we want for our own children? Don't we have an ethical responsibility to provide that for all children? "What the best and wisest parent wants for his own child, that must the community want for all of its children." John Dewey said those words in 1899. Nearly one hundred years later, they remain the beacon that should direct all our efforts.

How Business Can Help

Given my rejection of the business community's attempt to remake our educational system for its own purposes, What role do I think this powerful force in
American society ought to play in the nurturing and educating of our children?
A common saying going around education circles of late is the African proverb,
"It takes a whole village to raise a child." Business is a part of our American
village and it has a legitimate role to play in the lives of young people. Directing
the education system to meet its needs is just not one of them. However, recommitting itself to the ideal of offering every child a free, accessible public education is the first step it can make in assuming its rightful place in our American
village. At its best, public education is a force that enriches the lives of all
children who spring from our diverse American community.

This ideal of public education, so often forgotten in the current debate on
schooling, is one that deserves the unconditional support of our business leaders.
The second critical step for business to take in order to help guarantee better
outcomes for children is to acknowledge the truth in Catherine Spoto's statement: "education reform is not just about changing schools. It is going to require
a profound political and social change as well."[16] Business leaders need to step
back and take a hard look at the rather unpleasant picture of childhood today.
If they are genuine in their concern for the twenty-first-century work force, they
will have to work to improve that picture by acting as staunch advocates for
children and their families—even if it compromises the corporate "bottom line"
in the short run.

Corporations employ countless lobbyists to represent their interests in our
nation's legislatures. They are generally very successful in their work—often to
the detriment of children and their families. I suggest, however, that this blind
advocacy of business interests, regardless of its effect on children, must come
to an end. Whether it be for legislation on family and medical leave or the
current proposal to merge the Department of Education with the Department of
Labor, the business community has got to begin considering the effects on
children and their families when they lobby legislators in an attempt to influence
legislation. Of course, this has rarely—if ever—been done.

Lobbyists represent business interests and aim to sway legislators in ways
that are of direct benefit to business. This use of business lobbyists on behalf of
children, however, can be thought of as a long-term investment in the development of labor pools for the future—representing the corporate interest twenty
years hence. Or, alternatively, business executives can justify it as responsible
corporate citizenry—protecting the interests of otherwise powerless children. As

depicted in the *Wall Street Journal* cartoon, business can "get a piece of the action" by this return to morality. (See figure 8.1)[17] Either as a tool for long-term corporate health, or as a moral obligation, this use of the business community's political muscle on behalf of our children would lead to genuine, measurable improvements in the well-being of our children. Never before would the interests of children be championed by so powerful a political force.

An example of how this could work can be demonstrated by the issue of welfare reform. With the passage of federal welfare reform and the consequent

Pepper . . . and Salt

THE WALL STREET JOURNAL

"Let's make sure that if there's a return to morality, we get a piece of the action."

Figure 8.1. Cartoon, "Pepper . . . and Salt." Source: *Wall Street Journal,* July 24, 1996. Reprinted with permission of Cartoon Features Syndicate.

demise of the Aid to Families with Dependent Children (AFDC) in 1996, individual states became responsible for designing their own welfare systems. The business community can be—and needs to be—a champion of children and their needs in every state house across the nation as states go about the work of refashioning their commitment to the poor.

As Democratic Congressman Robert Matsui posed the problem, giving states the responsibility for welfare programs and allocation of resources forces "children to compete with services like fire and police protection. It doesn't take a genius to figure out where state and local government priorities will be."[18] Matsui and many other opponents of the legislation fear that childhood poverty rates will skyrocket as a result of this revolution in our nation's approach to dealing with the poor. Benefits will be cut off to healthy adults who do not work. The effect of this on children may be disasterous. Will the jobs taken by former welfare recipients offer health insurance for their children who used to be covered by Medicaid? Will there be affordable child care for these workers who previously stayed at home with their children? Will food stamps be available to workers who may earn no more than minimum wage? The likely answer to all of these questions is no. With no minimum standards for health care, child care, and nutritional supports for children of parents who formerly received AFDC, one can reasonably fear for the future of many of our nation's children.

If business leaders are honestly concerned about the children of our country, they must admit that genuine welfare reform—breaking the cycle of welfare dependence that exists in some families—will cost money. Getting people ready for the world of work, matching them up with jobs, providing for child care while this all happens, will not be cheap. It would indicate a genuine commitment to education—in the broadest sense of the word—if the Business Roundtable joined forces with the Children's Defense Fund and formed a coalition that worked in every state protecting children against the dangers inherent in the end of "welfare as we know it." In addition, this powerful coalition could lobby to amend the 1996 federal legislation in order to institute minimum standards for benefits that would go directly to children—medical, nutritional, or childcare vouchers—thus preventing the nightmare that may result if states outbid each other in reducing benefits to families with children. By becoming a public advocate for children, business will heighten the likelihood that the future American work force will be as industrious and productive as those of nations such as Japan and Germany; countries that have many supports for families and very low rates of childhood poverty.[19]

The business community's protection of children in the legislative arena would be a critical piece of the puzzle of improving children's lives. The most constructive and influential role business can play in the lives of children, however, is that of a good employer to the primary educators of children—their mothers and fathers. It is an interesting fact that while 70 percent of Rochester's children are African-American or Hispanic, the city's corporate giants have a very small minority work force. Xerox has the highest proportion of minority employees—with less than 15 percent.[20] The tangible and intangible rewards that spring from a good job are beyond the grasp of the unemployed and underemployed. Decent compensation for work performed goes a long way to making family life possible. The truth of this needs no explanation.

The distressing reality is that unemployment among young minority males in our cities consistently remains in the double digits. The troubling wage gap between white males and women and minorities is stubbornly resistant to reduction. Women head many households and yet earn 72 cents for every dollar earned by men. Median earnings for African-American and Hispanic workers lag those of white workers. With corporate profits at record highs and real average earnings for all workers lower than those of twenty years ago, companies who bemoan the condition of our youth need to rethink their hiring and compensation policies to see what contribution they have made to the lack of well-being of our young today.

Job security is another key to family strength. In today's economic culture, however, secure employment is something that few corporate employees at any level in the organization can count on. The successful firm is one that maximizes profits and improves the value of its stock by cutting jobs of long-time employees. Job losses have affected higher earners as well as those with modest earnings. In 1994 managers and supervisors accounted for a third of corporate jobs eliminated. The *Wall Street Journal* refers to the new work place as "brutal," where the only way to survive is to out-hustle the hungriest young co-worker.[21] This corporate downsizing has caused tremendous losses—both economic and psychological to thousands of American families. The anxiety and insecurity that parents feel cannot be easily hidden from children. I will never forget one of my students, a charming and intelligent eight-year old, telling me that his dad "used to be a researcher but now is the janitor in our church for six dollars an hour." That parent's loss was also his son's loss, in financial as well as emotional terms.

The immediate damage caused by this stress may, I fear, may be followed by a long lasting sense of hopelessness as children learn that education, loyalty to one's employer, and hard work are no guarantee of a good job. If business wants to help educate youngsters about the value of education, job commitment, and hard work, it needs to demonstrate that those things are valued by the firms that employ their parents. Employers' dual loyalty to employees as well as to their stockholders would go a long way to create the conditions needed for youngsters to grow up healthy and hopeful.

Business can support families by creating good, secure jobs and then helping employees balance job and family responsibilities so they may do both well. As anyone who has tried it can testify, child rearing is nothing if not a labor intensive enterprise. Children require a lot of their parents' time and care if they are to thrive. Similarly, jobs, by definition, require time and energy. Working parents need flexibility in their work schedules so that they can meet both the needs of their children and the requirements of their job. A sick child, a school conference, a family emergency are realities that face every working parent. Employers who view requests for accommodation to family life as an indication that employees are "soft" or "not career oriented" cause real damage to children because they make it hard for their parents to meet their needs. The mindset that "employees' personal problems are their own" is an anachronism. For business leaders to be good employers, they have to help parents in concrete ways.

The following list is by no means inclusive, but it points to a direction that firms must move if they are truly concerned about the fate of our nation's youngsters:

1. Provide flextime, allowing parents to meet both their job and family responsibilities.

2. Allow for voluntary job sharing, so two employees with responsibility for children can share one job, thus continuing to grow professionally while caring for their families.

3. Provide on-site, high quality, affordable day care for preschool children.

4. Provide extended child care leaves for up to twelve months at the time of the birth or adoption of a child.

5. Reduce the frequency of transfers that require relocation for employees with children.

These five recommendations alone would make a powerful contribution to the lives of children. Given the record profits our corporations have posted in the 1990s, it is a contribution that the business community can comfortably make.

Business can furnish direct help to our children's schooling in a number of ways. The mentoring and tutoring provided for individual youngsters by employees of firms such as Wegmans Supermarkets and Kodak is an example of one way for business to help children firsthand. The training provided by Xerox and Kodak for Rochester's school-based decision-making teams, lauded by the participants, is an example of another offering the business community can make to schools. Through its efforts at implementing the principles of TQM, business apparently has learned to teach people of varied backgrounds how to work together as they grapple with difficult problems. This type of valuable training can be provided for members of school councils by firms that have become expert in the intricacies of group decision-making.

Finally, to the degree that business now supports serious learning for all children, it ought to lend its resources to getting out the message to the American public that this type of education is both appropriate and valuable; that it is not some experimental fad, but an idea that bodes well for our children and our society.

As Richard Gibboney has asked, "How can schools be better than the society of which they are a part? They can't, and we keep forgetting that."[22] To the extent that business can significantly enrich our society by recommitting to the ideal of a free, public education for every child, by supporting legislation that helps working families and children, by offering good and secure employment to parents, by lending a helping hand to school children and their schools—to that extend they will be helping to ensure a good education, in the broadest sense of the word, for our nation's youngsters.

Education Reform for Our Children

Schooling ought to be seen as one very important aspect of a comprehensive national policy of putting the needs of our children first. Because children spend so much of their lives in schools, we need to begin to reconstruct our educational system to serve their needs. That will not come easily or quickly. But we can initiate an effort to realize Dewey's vision of making children the center of gravity around which all the programs, organizational structures, and adult roles in education revolve. In keeping with his recommendation for school organization, every decision aimed at reconstructing our educational system must be weighed in terms of its effect, either positive or negative, on children. Using children's needs as the primary criterion upon which all other decisions are made, will itself signify a genuine revolution in education.

If children's needs ought to represent the primary principle of an education reform agenda, a recognition of the crazy quilt nature of American society ought to be the second. Recent efforts at developing desired outcomes for our educational system have run into tremendous opposition by people representing every position on the political continuum. Each faction fears that "official knowledge" will obliterate both their values and the opportunity to affect the education of the children in their community. There are many people who approve of the education provided by their local schools. There are others who cannot abide it for many, and sometimes contradictory, reasons. Education presents children with a constructed picture of the world. Different people make different pictures—and so they should. We need schools that allow diversity to exist, that are comfortable places for parents to send their children each day, that are not held up as the only correct way to educate children about the world.

With these two guiding principles in mind—meeting children's needs and respecting diversity in schooling—I will discuss some ideas that promise to help improve educational opportunities for youngsters in our country.

Teacher Education

"As is the teacher, so is the school." Because I am convinced of the truth of this nineteenth-century adage, and because of the projection of 200,000 new teacher hires a year as we reach the millennium, new teacher recruitment and education have to be at the hub of any effort to rethink schooling for our nation's children. As George Counts wrote so long ago, we are looking for men and women of "intelligence, spirit, capacity for leadership, and devotion to the popular welfare" to join the ranks of the teaching profession. As a working teacher I can say without equivocation that the work of a teacher is at once fascinating, satisfying, and exhausting. Of the many jobs I have held, no other has required so much of me in so many ways—and so relentlessly—as the job of teacher. The responsibility is enormous and, when things go as hoped for, the gratification is equally grand. If we aspire to prepare new candidates for the teaching profession in accordance with the guiding principles of child-oriented education for a diverse society, we need—at last—to follow Counts's recommendations and cut out of whole cloth the new profile of the professional teacher: smart, inventive, knowledgeable, and a fearless advocate for children.

The fundamental characteristics of a good prospective teacher are: 1) a strong and basic desire to use his or her considerable talents to help children learn about their world, and 2) an a priori empathy for children and their experience. In other words, the prospective teacher needs to be generous of spirit, resourceful, and intuitively "connected" to children. It has been my experience that without these characteristics, all the education and training in the world will not help a person become a good teacher; with them, others can help the individual develop the repertoire of skills and the knowledge that characterize a fine educator.

All teachers require a strong knowledge base on which to help children learn about the world. I am continually amazed by the demanding, thought-provoking questions asked by young students. Teachers need to be educated in a broad and general way in order to have a sense of how they can help their students begin to find answers to their questions. A rigorous undergraduate education represents a floor beneath which new teachers should not fall in terms of their knowledge of what is known about the world. The undergraduate education major has no place in the education of educators. In its stead ought to be an academic major chosen on the basis of the prospective teacher's interests and curiosity. Whether it be mathematics or the psychology of human development, a rigorous study of an academic discipline will provide a grounding in how one can systematically learn about a subject or area of interest.

A rigorous minor concentration in education might consist of five or six courses aimed at having prospective teachers think critically about what teaching and learning in the United States is all about. Sample course offerings might be as follows:

1. Why educate children? A study of the multiple and competing purposes of education. Helpful would be a research project on why the student is in college.

2. The history of education: A critical examination of how we got what we have in terms of our existing educational system.

3. The politics of education: How competing values and interests influence our school systems; how power is distributed; the ongoing battle to control the schools.

4. How children grow: The amazing process of physical, psychological, social, and cognitive development of youngsters. This course would likely span a full year.

5. The state of childhood in America: The conditions affecting children in the nation today.

Any prospective teacher who finds these courses irrelevant and impractical should be advised to reconsider the decision to become a teacher. What is generally seen as the "practical" aspects of teaching are so controlled by the forces studied in these proposed courses that to be ignorant of them would bode poorly for anyone hoping to make teaching a lifetime profession. Ongoing work with children in and out of schools by the undergraduate prospective teacher—as a tutor, Big Brother/Sister, classroom helper—would provide firsthand experience far more practical than the standard "methods" courses that are as useless as they are omnipresent in the typical teacher preparation program.

I suggest that a Masters Degree leading to professional certification would be based, almost entirely, on a full-year classroom internship. During this internship the teacher-in-training would co-teach a class or set of classes with an experienced, highly regarded master teacher. The job of teacher is a demanding one, and the internship will demonstrate one sound way of going about doing it. The goals of the internship are:

1. To demonstrate at the outset how much there is to learn in order to teach well—the dimensions of the job.

2. To realize how unique and complex children are and how carefully a teacher needs to teach the child, monitor growth, communicate with parents.

3. To get a basic grasp of the curricular goals for the children, as well as the pacing, tools, and direction of teaching that will help the children achieve those goals.

4. To learn one type of classroom organization—a model of monitoring children's growth, using time effectively, communicating with parents.

5. To understand how the school organization works—how to make it work for the students, when to enlist help of colleagues or the teachers' union.

In conjunction with this internship, academic course work could concentrate on learning at least two different approaches to the teaching of reading, writing, math, and other subject areas. The guiding principle of these courses should be that no single approach will ever work for all children. Therefore, a new teacher needs to begin the development of a repertoire of techniques, approaches, and teaching styles in order to meet children's academic needs. Once on the job, the new teacher will add to his or her personal repertoire in terms of ideas about and methods of teaching. Yet every newly minted teacher will, at the end of the internship year, have some well-earned confidence that he or she is ready to take on the many responsibilities of a new teaching position. With the ongoing support of mentors—from either their graduate school or their school community—for the first three years of their teaching career, these teachers will breathe new life into existing schools in sufficient numbers that, collectively, they may have a genuine influence on a system that has been strongly resistant to change.

The Bureaucratic Central School—
Americans Top Choice for Their Children

The bureaucratic, centralized school organization is one model for educating children. It currently characterizes virtually all public school systems in our country. Having taught in three such systems, I can recite their flaws chapter and verse. All too many decisions are made to increase the ease with which the bureaucracy's gears can turn. Concerns are typically addressed by adding another specialist, another office, another layer of supervision, rather than analyzing the cause of the problem or rethinking "standard operating procedure." Managers continue to hold onto power even when it can be clearly shown that by so doing they reduce both the efficiency and the effectiveness of their organizations. Too often teachers operate with a mindset of resignation and subservience to management's edicts rather than with a spirit of creativity and innovation in the service of children. Many parents, long shut out of the closed, bureaucratic school system, have little interest in what happens each day in their children's classrooms.

Adam Urbanski said at the start of Rochester's reform effort, "all these theories and highfalutin' ideas don't mean anything unless it can be demonstrated that they can be translated into local, practical realities." As of this writing, it appears the translation of reform theory into practice has not been possible in most of Rochester's traditional school organization. Perhaps 5 to 10 percent of the district's children are experiencing education in accordance with the agenda proposed in 1987. Rochester's experience demonstrates that centralized school systems functioning in accordance with the principles of bureaucratic, hierarchical control are highly resistant to a revolution in education. Contrary to Peter McWalters' vision, it does not appear possible to turn around a big, bureaucratic school system. By and large, it functions perpetually on its own internal logic. However, it is important to remember that it is not a logic that is seen to be faulty by everyone either within or outside the system. As some analysts have noted, Americans want education reform only to the degree that it allows the bureaucratic system to operate more efficiently and economically.

Despite its flaws, the bureaucratic school system is what is known and accepted by the majority of citizens in this country. Early pro-efficiency reformer Ellwood Cubberley would be pleased to know that it has become an American institution, an institution that has shaped most native-born citizens for more than four generations. Although the frustration arising from my experience in the system made me once hope for its total elimination, I no longer see that as either feasible or wise. It is an institution that most parents want perpetuated. It is important to note that 70 percent of parents polled by Public Agenda in 1995 rated their local public school as either "good" or "excellent." Data from numerous studies all point to the same conclusion: the public values safety, order, and basic skills; it is suspicious of most educational innovations. These facts must be acknowledged by all who seek to change American education.

It is essential that parents support their children's school experience. I have learned through my career that trying to work with a child whose parent does not believe in the methods or philosophy being used in the classroom is difficult for all concerned. Most importantly, it is particularly hard on the youngster. The child is caught in the middle between important adults who do not agree on what is right or appropriate. The situation puts the child into a state of confusion at best—and of divided allegiances at worst. Despite the public relations effort in support of the new pro-efficiency agenda, most parents do not want to enroll their child in what they see as a fad or an experiment. They want the type of education they had. They ought to have that option. This form of education should be supported by public funds. But it should not be the only educational model that should have the benefit of public support.

There are those that are unhappy with the schools that exist. There are teachers who are frustrated in their efforts to deal with individual children in a system that sees only the aggregate. There are parents who feel that their children are not getting a good education or a fair shake in a system aimed at norms and averages rather than their son or daughter. There are students who hate to go to school each day. There are many people currently involved in the bureaucratic system who are eager for other options in education. It is for and with this minority that educational change will occur. It is interesting that Rochester's few successes in educational change did not come about because of the 1987 reform agenda. In Catherine Spoto's opinion, they are the result of a group of dedicated teachers and families committed to a vision of education and willing to work together to make that vision a reality.[23] It is this model of education—one that harkens back to the agenda of the educational progressives—that deserves the same level of public support as that provided to the bureaucratic model of education.

Islands of Reform and the Charter School Alternative

Within some existing school systems there are what statisticians like to call "outliers"—those rare occurrences that fall outside the normal range of experience. These outliers are sometimes referred to as "alternative" schools from the legacy of the sixties, or "schools within schools" in keeping with the contemporary reform agenda. They present children and their parents with options for educational choice within their existing school district. Generally, the district officials have agreed to look the other way and let these isolated efforts in progressive education proceed unimpeded. They are usually small islands of reform, staffed by highly committed teachers, attended by fiercely loyal children, and praised by very satisfied parents. However, efforts to create such schools generally are met with great resistance by all levels within the school district organization.

The following is an account of a recent attempt to establish such an island of reform—a school within a school.[24] A group of highly regarded, energetic, and original classroom teachers worked for several months creating a proposal for an elementary school that would strive to build a heterogeneous school community based on the best elements of the current reform agenda. They planned an integrated, thematic curricula around the needs of their students. They proposed new, flexible uses of the existing school day and school space. They hoped to offer projects based on curricular themes that would be open to all children regardless of their traditional grade levels. They had devised novel ways of dealing with what is typically called "remediation" and "acceleration" of students. They proposed authentic assessment of the children's progress, as well as the traditional norm-based standardized testing. Open to all children in the school district, students already in the school building would have first choice for slots in the new school community. If too many applied, admission would be determined by lottery.

The teachers met several times with their building principal to go over their proposal and, at first, were given reason to believe that their administrator was supportive of their project. However, their optimism was short-lived. Some of their teaching colleagues in the school building were concerned that they might have to change grade levels or rooms if this "school within a school" was to become a reality. The principal was concerned about the effect of the new school on the rest of the building, specifically that other classes in the school building might compare poorly with those in the "school within a school." Despite support from their union, and the teachers' offer to address existing concerns—including encouraging other teachers within the school building to develop their own "school within a school"—the administrator's apprehensions remained. In a letter to the entire staff, the principal wrote:

> The principal of a school has the responsibility for the well-being of the entire school. Sometimes being a "strong leader" may require a principal to squelch an innovative idea that is proposed by a valued portion of the staff. I am prepared to do that if necessary.

Squelching is precisely what was done. The principal vetoed the plan for the new school community. The teachers were devastated. Their enthusiasm and spirits—so high when working on the proposal—plummeted. They lacked the will to openly defy their principal and go to the next layer of administration in an appeal. The result of their months-long effort: their creation was stillborn.

As this single account illustrates, islands of reform carved from within a school district can be hard to get approved. The desire for standardization and uniformity is so great in most districts that any proposed deviation from the norm is viewed with apprehension and suspicion. The overriding mindset I personally have encountered whenever a new idea of any type is proposed is that "it can't be done." The rationales are many; the answer always the same. The prospects for proliferation of reform-minded education by means of semiautonomous schools within schools, while not nil, are compromised by this reality.

More hopeful is the fairly new concept of the charter school. The charter school idea represents a more viable opportunity for groups of like-minded educators and community members to develop school organizations that meet the varying needs of their students. Pioneered in Minnesota in 1991, the charter school idea was implemented on a very limited scale in twenty-five states by the fall of 1996. Many other states are considering charter school legislation. The states that have already passed laws allowing charters vary in a number of ways, but they all permit educators and others the leeway to design and operate small, publicly funded schools organized around a particular vision of education. Depending on the wording of the charter legislation, they are freed from some or all school board oversight, state education rules, regulations, and routines. They are responsible, however, for meeting certain goals for student outcomes set by the state. They must attract parents and students to their school based on a shared philosophy of education. Public funding for the schools is dependent upon student enrollment—the dollars follow the students.[25]

I am intrigued by the charter school concept because it appears to offer the opportunity to put into practice the two principles I feel should guide reform— education focused on the child, and acknowledgment of the need for educational diversity. In addition, charters schools provide the possibility—clearly missing in our existing system—of one what might call "the excitement factor"—teachers, parents, and students letting the creative juices flow in the effort to design from the ground up an educational setting they believe in. Those teachers, parents, and students who want an alternative to a system that is unresponsive to their needs—or those who seek the challenge and revitalization provided by the grassroots creation of a new school based on a shared set of assumptions—are presented with a genuine opportunity by the charter concept.

Although not for everyone, some portion of the public school community will take advantage of the chance to create a school with others who share their vision of "good education." For new teachers, educated in accordance with my recommendations, the opportunity offered by a charter school would be most attractive because it will provide the circumstances in which they can practice their flexible, child-oriented, reflective teaching.

Charters promise to end the remarkable sameness in public education. Our educational system has been substantially unchanged for generations. It serves some children well and they thrive in it. Other children do a good job of enduring it; others do less well. Some children are crushed by it. But for the desire by some to make it easier to control schools in accordance with Ellwood Cubberley's vision of "student manufacture," there is no a priori reason for schools to be so very much alike. Children are different is a host of ways. The public schools should serve them as they are. Instead of imposing on everyone a common way of thinking about education, let us allow people with a shared way of thinking to come together. Rather than argue whether "back to basics" is better than "higher order thinking skills," let parents and teachers decide what philosophy of education suits them. The fundamental questions of education— such as whether cooperation is better than competition in the classroom—are not going to be settled unequivocally by research. They are questions that are answered by belief systems. Let us stop trying to pretend otherwise. Let there be a variety of answers to the questions of how children can learn to be literate, to use math as a tool for solving problems, to learn about themselves, their country, and their world. Let the answers be designed in a manner such that every child has the opportunity to thrive. Allow public schools to be idiosyncratic. As Central Park East founder Deborah Meier puts it, let us create a public "system of exceptions" that reflect their constituents' ideas but adhere to a common set of principles and keep a vigilant eye on the quality of teaching and learning.[26] Charter schools may be able to do just that.

Perhaps the most attractive feature of the charter concept is the possibility of creating small schools that are communities for parents, children, and teachers. The benefits of school-family ties are well documented by many studies. Collaboration between parents and teachers leads to better attendance, higher test scores, more positive attitudes, higher graduation rates, and college attendance. In fact, the best predictor of school success is now thought to be parental encouragement of learning and involvement in school life—rather than the socioeconomic status of the family.[27] The charter concept is predicated on the idea of parents and teachers coming together to form and run a community school around a common educational theme and philosophy. Unlike the bureaucratic school, which provides no legitimate role for parents within the school organization, the charter cannot exist without active parental support.

Creating a school community has always been seen as an ideal by educational progressives. For practitioners in traditional public schools, "community" has been seen as something to strive for perhaps, but far from obligatory—something comparable to "school spirit." However, the woeful lack of community in our country's towns and cities is alarming for those who see the truth in the saying "It takes a whole village to raise a child." This lack of a sense of community is problematic for the well-being of youngsters from all socio-economic groups. Given the vast number of children who are living and growing under stressful circumstances, it is now imperative that we create some safe, consistent, fair, and interesting school communities of which they may become a part. For those children who are lucky enough to have been born or adopted into stable and resourceful families, belonging to a community and being part of a supportive group can help them develop the social skills and social consciousness that all too many of them lack. A school community can affirm all children's successes and disapprove of or help them recover from their mistakes. The anonymity that characterizes most public schools today prevents them from carrying out this critical role.

I do not expect charters to be cheaper than traditional education, but I do expect that they will use our education funding in a manner that will benefit children more directly. I am always amazed at the small portion of total education funding that actually gets to the classroom. For example, a Coopers and Lybrand analysis of the New York City school budget showed that the typical student received only 29 percent of the system's per pupil expenditure.[28] If the center of gravity of charter schools is children, then the money for the schools needs to go into direct services to and materials for children.

A rule of thumb in the new charter schools might be that if a person is employed by the school and does not work with children in some way—every day—then the rationale for that person's position must be held up to the highest scrutiny. There need to be a very few positions that are supportive of the school's mission, but in so indirect a manner that their occupants do not interact with children. The operative word is "few," for everyone from the bus mechanic to the school secretary has much to teach children. I predict an enriched environment for teaching and learning if charter schools spend money in accordance with this idea.

To summarize then, charter schools hold out the exciting opportunity for parents, teachers, and students to create small, idiosyncratic, community schools that use existing funding to directly affect the education of their students. This is the theory behind the schools that has attracted so many people from all points on the political spectrum. As of this writing, more than half the state legislatures in the nation have considered enabling legislation for charter schools. There is reason to believe that the charter concept will find acceptance in this country. It is supported by groups representing both the political left and right. Rob Melnick, policy analyst at Arizona State University, has referred to charters as "a mom and apple pie thing." He has said the charter concept "has the flavor of all these good principles of innovation, but it doesn't have the emotional charge of vouchers or site-based management."[29] As Peter Dow has demonstrated in his work on alternative education in the sixties, educational programs that cannot leap the hurdle of political acceptability are doomed.[30] The fact that the charter concept is politically palatable makes it an avenue of education reform that holds promise.

Why then, some months before his death in 1995, did Ernest Boyer—a strong advocate for small, community schools that are as committed to developing children's characters as they are a coherent educational plan—voice opposition to the charter school movement? His concern: that it would undermine the larger civic and social purposes of education, that children not in charters would be left behind to languish, that the public's commitment to them would not be fulfilled.[31] The assumption underlying that worry is that only more advantaged parents and children will seek out charters, leaving poor children and minority children behind. The predicted phenomenon is referred to as "cream skimming." Boyer's troubling concern can, at least for the present, be relieved by the fact that many—if not most—of the current charter schools enroll children who have had a difficult time being successful in existing schools. Many charter schools are in inner cities. In 1995 Massachusetts' fourteen charter schools had a minority enrollment of 48 percent. Early reports indicate that these schools do indeed have greater parental involvement, parental satisfaction and innovation, than traditional public schools, a promising sign for charters and their students.[32] To date, then, the feared "leaving behind" of disadvantaged students while more advantaged students enjoy the benefits of charters schools' has not materialized.

A more worrisome point, however, is the motivating factors driving many charter supporters. The most vocal advocacy comes from factions that aim to use charters for purposes other than the obvious one of providing youngsters with options for schooling within the public sphere. In fact, among the strongest supporters of charters are those elements in our country who aim to weaken, if not dismantle, our system of public education. The editors of the *Wall Street Journal*—strong advocates of school vouchers—laud charters as "business start-ups" that can "unite Republicans of varying stripes" in the wake of the national push for government devolution.[33]

Under the umbrella of choice, Republican governor Tom Ridge of Pennsylvania has proposed charter legislation as well as the takeover of public schools by for-profit corporations, and state vouchers for use by parents in private and parochial schools. With this proposal he joins forces with Wisconsin governor Tommy Thompson, a long-time and staunch promoter of public funding for private and religious school vouchers, privatization of public school management, and charter schools.[34] For anyone who is committed to the ideal of a publicly funded public education with accessibility for all comers—it is disturbing that those who do not share that commitment endorse the proliferation of charter schools.

Add to this the following statement by charter proponent Ted Kolderie of the University of Minnesota's Center for Policy Studies, and the concern deepens. Although Kolderie's statement implies a commitment to the continued existence of "mainline" school districts, his interest in charter schools is purely ancillary:

> Too often those asking, "What's happening?" (with charter laws' effects) look only at the schools created and the students enrolled: the first-order effects of a law. There are also second-order effects: changes/responses in the mainline system when laws are enacted and schools are created. An evaluation needs to look for these. . . . Despite what the words seem to imply, "charter schools" is not basically about the schools. For the teachers who found them and the students who enroll in them, true, it is the schools that are important. But for others, from the beginning, "charter schools" has been about system-reform . . . a way for the state to cause the district system to improve. *The schools are instrumental.* [emphasis added][35]

Once again, policymakers and policy pundits aim to use schools for some "second-order effects," albeit in Kolderie's case, to improve public schools generally. For them the charter schools are a tool for promoting adults' agendas of one sort or another.

Thus, I state my support for the charter concept with more than a little trepidation. I believe that charter schools deserve the public's attention and financial backing. Clearly, my reasons are wholly different from those who wish to use charters as a means of realizing some goal distant from the learning opportunities offered charter school students. I can only hope that with vigilance about the motives of some of the charter movement's most vocal supporters, and with luck, the "unintended consequence" of charter legislation will be to provide a rich variety of free, accessible educational alternatives for children within the public domain.[36]

I acknowledge that I look forward to two secondary benefits that may result from charters. First, in cases where the enabling legislation opens charters to all state residents, charter schools hold out the hope of undoing the economic and racial segregation that characterizes so many of our existing schools. Under this most liberal type of the charter legislation, all parents—not only those who have the resources to provide transportation and pay tuition to neighboring districts—are free to send their children to public schools other than those closest to their homes. This may mitigate the segregation caused by enrolling children in schools solely on the basis of their place of residence.

Second, I also suspect that the insidious gender stratification that characterizes the nation's schools will not be replicated in the charter school model. By allowing parents and teachers to form and govern schools, women will have the opportunity to be educational leaders in ways that the overwhelmingly male bureaucratic school management has precluded. I expect that the principalship in many charter schools will revert to the head teacher or principal teacher concept. And, just as the majority of principal teachers in the early part of the century were female, I predict that many of the charters' head teachers will be women. Rather than being a stepping stone to central office administration and higher compensation, the role of principal teacher will be the high point of a career devoted to children and their learning. This educational leader will be an integral member of the school community, chosen by that community and paid on the same scale as colleagues; a first among equals. Unlike the situation we saw in Rochester, where principals had to divide their allegiance between their school and central office, the principal teacher will be answerable to no one but the charter school's teachers, parents, and students. A secondary benefit perhaps, but one that I expect will also serve children.

A New Role for Teacher Unions

Lately teacher unions and school reform are rarely mentioned in the same breath except to note how unions are the enemies of school improvement. Equally rare is mention of an identity of interests between teachers and our children—or the belief that teacher unions protect children's interests. During the last few years I have noted a sea change in the attitudes toward teacher unions expressed by citizens, the media, and policy experts alike. As a student of teacher union history, I am not surprised. Teacher unions have always enjoyed as much acceptance and been offered as much latitude in regard to issues subject to negotiation as private sector unions. The only difference is that teacher unions lag their private sector equivalents in terms of time. Granted legitimacy in the post–World War II era—albeit begrudgingly—private sector unions saw their public esteem plummet during the 1980s as the fortunes of firms like General Motors and Ford fell. Poor product design and illogical work organization were often considered less important to the American automakers' decline than were their contracts with the United Auto Workers. As seems to fit the pattern, public sector teacher unions are currently "catching up" with private sector unions—now in terms of being held in low regard. Today teacher unions are seen as being largely responsible for the problems in our public schools.

Hoping to score points in the presidential campaign of 1996, Republican Bob Dole blasted the teacher unions, blaming them for "running our schools into the ground." Advocates of school vouchers and privatization cite the unions as the reason public schools need to be abandoned. The *Wall Street Journal* cites the teachers' unions as "the biggest impediment to making public schools better," and proposes changes in labor law to limit their influence.[37] In keeping with this idea, Pennsylvania and Michigan, formerly two very strong pro-labor states, have altered their collective bargaining laws to restrict bargaining rights for teachers. Teacher unions have become a target for a generalized dissatisfaction with the commonweal. The public is tired of paying taxes, and although less than half of school taxes go to teachers' salaries, teachers are seen as the prime villain in the heavy tax burden shouldered by property owners.

Unions are neither selfless martyrs for children's welfare nor selfish demons destroying our schools. What is paradoxical about this attack on the unions is that they are precisely what society allowed them to become in the 1960s. Legislators never empowered them to work for school improvement—only for the wages, hours, and working conditions of their members. While unions have developed powerful lobbies in state legislatures across the country, influencing lawmaking on educational issues to a remarkable degree, they have considerably less power and influence within the schools themselves. In her 1984 study of teacher unions, Harvard professor Susan Moore Johnson found that collective bargaining's effects on the operation of schools were less extensive, formal, and fixed than they were generally thought to be. School sites in her study were remarkably autonomous in interpreting and administering the teachers' contract. Teachers were often ambivalent about unionism. In schools with collegial working relations between the principal and the teaching staff, commitment and allegiance to the principal was greater than it was to the union.[38] My experience corresponds with the picture of unionism in the schools presented by Moore's research. Despite the stated goal in the sixties of becoming co-leaders with management, unions rarely have any part in substantive discussions on or decisions about the content and character of educational services. To many teachers the union seems irrelevant to their daily work with children. Union leaders privately acknowledge—and bemoan—their limited power and influence within the day to day operation of the schools.

Also ironic is the public's reaction to unions like the Rochester Teachers Association, which attempt to be in the vanguard of reform. When unions take the chance to attempt an alteration of business as usual—including policing their own ranks and influencing educational practice—they are held wholly responsible when expectations for improvement are not met. As shown in Rochester, the children's problems were blamed on the teachers. The teacher union president, Adam Urbanski, was depicted in the local press as being akin to a public enemy. If efforts at reform fail, the union is cited as the primary suspect by those looking for easy answers. If nothing else, however, the Rochester experiment clearly taught us that there is no single "villain" and there are no easy answers when attempts to change schools prove futile.

Union leaders are clearly aware of what appears to be a campaign to damage their organizations' image, reduce their collective bargaining rights, and constrict their power and influence on both the national and state levels. The American Federation of Teachers and the National Education Association are now on the defensive, albeit with different strategies. The once cautious NEA is touting reform—including support for charter schools that are staffed with certified teachers. It has pledged help to members who wish to open charters in six states. It promises to stay for the long haul and help assess the charters' performance in terms of improving student learning. The AFT, stung by its losses in Rochester and elsewhere, has gone on a back to basics crusade for orderly schools and high academic standards called the Lessons for Life campaign. Noting public opinion polls that cite these as the most desired school characteristics, the AFT hopes to counteract its negative public image by supporting what Americans seem to want from their schools.[39]

It is only through unions that teachers have any legal standing in the existing school organization. Without unions individual teachers are powerless in the face of an unwieldy bureaucratic machine. Unions inject a small degree of work place democracy into an otherwise autocratic system. They also provide teachers with a voice—on the local, state, or national levels—to express the concerns of their profession. These are legitimate roles that need to be played. But I feel the future of teacher unions is now in question. It is doubtful that current public relations efforts will significantly improve unions' public image. If they are to remain a force in public education, they will have to transform themselves into far different organizations than they are today. For unions to survive and provide a recognized voice for their members in the hostile climate of this current era, they will have to concentrate on becoming the organ through which professional teachers work to improve school experiences for children. In a return to their early twentieth-century roots and the agenda of the 1960s, unions have to demonstrate a bona fide identity of interests between teachers and their students.

One way for unions to illustrate their commitment to making things better for children is to tackle the serious problem in the way education is funded and monies distributed to children. They need to loudly and persistently champion the cause of equity in education funding for all children within a state. Just as I have recommended that the business community put its political lobby to work to protect children's welfare, I ask the two teacher unions to jointly use their well-oiled political lobbying machines in a vigorous campaign to replace the property tax as a major source of funding for education. These taxes provide approximately half of all education funding. Use of the local property tax base as the determinant of how much can be spent on education has led to vast disparities from district to district. For example, in Illinois the range in annual school district spending in 1994 was $2,400 to $8,300 per child. Teacher pay and benefits vary from district to district according to the localities' ability to pay. Wealthy districts can attract and retain the most qualified and experienced teachers far more easily than can poor ones. Wealthy districts can provide better facilities, more extensive materials, and smaller classes than can their poorer counterparts.

Disparities such as these have led to a wave of lawsuits challenging finance systems in nearly half of the states.[40] Rather than stand on the sideline in these lawsuits, unions should file amicus curie briefs supporting equity in education funding. Proposals to fund education via a statewide income tax rather than through local property taxes are being seriously considered in many states. The state union organizations should pull out all the stops and lobby to get bills passed that do just that. If implemented, this method of financing education would make possible equal funding for every child within a state.

In addition, teachers in schools all across a state could be paid on the same pay scale—charter and traditional schools alike. Compensation packages would be funded directly from state coffers rather than from those of localities, eliminating the huge disparities in pay and benefits that currently exist between teachers working in poor regions and teachers working in wealthy areas. State teacher unions could adapt their role to this new system of education funding and represent teachers in negotiations with the state over salaries and benefits.[41] On the issue of basic fairness and equity in education funding, teacher unions would take the high road, acting as an advocate for children while representing their members' interests.

One way for unions to prove they are not guilty as charged on the issue of impeding innovation is for them to embrace and nourish teacher-led experiments in reform. In this regard, the NEA has begun to show interest in the possibilities charter schools present. At first an outspoken opponent of the concept for fear that teachers would lose hard won benefits and working conditions, it found itself marked by politicians and the media as the enemy of school improvement. After realizing it did not have the power to stop charter legislation from passing in many newly-Republican led legislatures, it decided to lend its support to charters that employed certified teachers. And so it should. The charter school concept decentralizes school governance, making teachers partners with parents and students in the determination of issues vital to school operation. It gives teachers the professional self-determination they have long sought but have never achieved. Charter schools can provide for teachers what unions have been unable to accomplish. By supporting teachers who wish to join charter schools, and by giving them financial support to help them work out the kinks in their new organizations, the NEA can demonstrate that it promotes professionalism in teaching and efforts to create new educational opportunities for children.

With the exception of improved equity in funding and the improvements that may spring from it, I do not foresee the possibility of massive pedagogical or organizational changes within the existing school systems across the nation. I expect local support for traditional local schools to continue and traditional education to carry on as it has for so long—with periodic minor adjustments in response to outside pressure for change, and the occasional outlier of alternative education. If teachers' salaries are to be bargained at the state level as I propose, what role will the teacher unions play in the public schools of tomorrow? Local unions representing teachers in the traditional bureaucratic school systems will likely function as they have since the 1960s—negotiating work rules, using the local collective bargaining agreement to process grievances on contested managerial actions against teachers. However, in the charter school the union's role can be quite different. It may be the role for unions envisioned so many years ago by Margaret Haley: the professional organization through which teachers work to hire, mentor, evaluate, and—if necessary—dismiss their colleagues.

The teachers' union can be the organ through which the collective voice of professional educators in any given charter school may speak. In addition, once freed from having only the narrowly proscribed role of protecting teachers' interests against management, the national and state teacher union organizations can devote much of their attention to educational questions—developing programs that support teaching and learning. Rather than be the limited, rule-oriented economic organizations they have sometimes been, unions may have the chance to move further toward the goal of fostering innovative practice in our public schools.

Closing Thoughts

I have come a long way from the questions that started my investigation. I have satisfied my personal curiosity about seemingly contradictory events and trends in my classroom, my school, and my district. Along the way, on my search for answers, I found myself continually confronted by new questions. My investigation took me to areas of study that I would never had imagined at the outset of the journey. While this was fascinating from a researcher's point of view, it was distressing from a teacher's vantage point. The complexity of the problems uncovered—problems facing children and public education—could have led me to throw up my hands in defeat. Yet my daily work with youngsters has enabled me to maintain a sense of hope. So many of my students have suffered so many losses, and yet they enter my class each day with a smile and a wave or a hug for their teacher. They are eager for whatever the day will bring. How can I do less than my best to bring them a good day? How can we, as a society, do less than our best for them everyday? The simple answer is—we cannot.

It is this determination to have us do our best by our youngsters that drives my proposals for improving children's "education," as liberally defined. The recommendations I have outlined—creating national and corporate policies that serve to make children and families a priority; restructuring teacher training for a cadre of professional teaching candidates; revising school governance laws to support charter schools that deliver child-centered, individualized education; eliminating disparities in education funding; reshaping the role of teacher unions—are all aimed at helping us, as a society, do our best by our children. They are not the delusions of an impossible optimist, however. They are recommendations that are rooted in both my experience in the schools and the germs of trends that are already making themselves felt in education and politics on the national level. I am encouraged by the Family and Medical Leave Act; optimistic that it represents a first step in our nation's recognition of and adaptation to the changing needs of American families. The public backlash at the Republican-led effort to reduce support for school lunches in order to reduce the 1996 federal budget deficit illustrated that most Americans do not want the budget balanced on the backs of children. I am hopeful this sentiment will provide an important lesson for legislators as states begin to fashion welfare programs for the twenty-first century.

The public, the media, and many politicians have begun to attack corporate downsizing policies that maximize profits and compensation packages for top management at the expense of employees' jobs. Some forward-looking firms have begun to incorporate one or more of my ideas for accommodating the needs of working parents. Teacher colleges are currently revising their programs to counter the scathing criticism by analysts of teacher preparation. Enabling legislation for charter schools has been passed in many states; hundreds of small charters are up and running across the country. State legislatures are tackling the thorny question of school funding. And, if teacher unions are smart, they will begin to follow their best inclinations and operate proactively—as the champions of equity in education funding for children and as the leaders in professional innovation for teachers.

In terms of improving schooling for children—if history is any guide—it is unlikely that any change in our education systems will happen without the approval and active support of business. Business executives remain strong supporters of school reform experiments that are much in keeping with the progressive agenda of so many years ago. They have succeeded in nudging—if not revolutionizing—bureaucratic schools toward adoption of some progressive ideas. Business has lent strong support to the charter concept through philanthropy aimed at promoting these "entrepreneurial" endeavors. I expect the business community to continue to be one of the strongest advocates of the charter concept as it is debated in state legislatures across the nation in upcoming years. Business leaders may also answer my call to become protectors of children, as they come to recognize that it is in their firms' long-term interest to pay attention to the lives our children are living—as well as the schools they are attending. By lending support to public policies that help children grow up in safe, healthy, and secure environments, business will ultimately become a beneficiary, albeit a secondary one, of the nationwide effort to put our children and their needs at the head of our national political agenda. A generation nurtured physically, emotionally, and educationally will be a generation ready to enrich and strengthen all facets of our society with its many skills and talents.

Thus, my optimism persists. I thank the many young children I have had the privilege of working with for so many years for nourishing my sense of hope. Generally, my students cross the threshold of my classroom in early September as unknown entities. It is both my job and my joy to discover what is unique about each of these youngsters. They can be artistic, cerebral, funny, serious, emotional, phlegmatic, athletic, musical—and these human characteristics are combined in what can only be called a singular way for every individual child. Each one of my students has something at which they excel. The challenge I face is to find that talent and develop it in every way I can, using it as an entry port through which they may gain the basic skills and knowledge they will need to learn about and contribute to their world. By its very nature, a teacher's challenge is rooted in hope.

I wish I could say that the school systems I have worked in have served as my helper in meeting that challenge. With a few gratifying exceptions, they have not. On the contrary, the systems' rules and regulations, their routines and mandates, have often seemed impervious to any effort to respect each child's individuality. Whether it be processing an order for special instructional materials, providing adequate transportation for a child living far from a bus stop, or accommodating an unusual learning style without labeling the child "handicapped," the systems I have worked in—systems that remain remarkably in keeping with Ellwood Cubberley's eighty-year old design—have been a disappointment. On the other hand, when I read the hundred year old writings on teaching and learning by John Dewey, I find an affirmation of what my experience with youngsters has been. When I think about Ella Flagg Young's concept of school governance shared by teachers, parents, staff, and students, I see a governance system that offers much greater possibilities for enhancing the educational experience of youngsters than the one I have worked under for the better part of two decades. When I compare Jesse Newlon's writings on a curriculum generated cooperatively by teachers to suit the needs of their students, I think it far preferable to the "one size fits all" mandates I am forced to obey regardless of the interests, talents, or needs of my students. Given my experience in teaching youngsters, I have concluded that the best opportunity for providing them a rigorous, public education offered by committed, professional teachers in a supportive school community is now represented by the islands of reform offered by experiments such as the "school within a school" and by independent charter schools.

As we approach the twenty-first century, a design for reform crafted nearly one hundred years ago by educators who put the needs of the child the center of their plan today offers us a blueprint for reform. With some luck—and the support of the business community—it is a blueprint we may finally decide to follow because it promises to make our companies more efficient and our economy more competitive as we approach the dawn of a new millennium.

NOTES

Introduction

1. The National Commission on Excellence in Education, *A Nation at Risk,* Cambridge, Mass.: USA Research, 1984.

2. Larry Cuban, *The Managerial Imperative and the Practice of Leadership in the Schools,* Albany: State University of New York Press, 1988.

Chapter 1

1. Jesse Newlon, *Educational Administration as Social Policy,* New York: Charles Scribner's Sons, 1934, p. 231.

2. Joan K. Smith, *Ella Flagg Young: Portrait of a Leader,* Ames, Iowa: Educational Studies Press, 1976, pp. 40–42.

3. David Tyack, Thomas James, and Aaron Benavot, *Law and the Shaping of Public Education,* Madison: University of Wisconsin Press, 1987, p. 112; David Tyack, *The One Best System; A History of Urban Education,* Cambridge: Harvard University Press, 1974, p. 105.

4. Samuel Haber, *The Quest for Honor and Authority in the American Professions, 1750–1900,* Chicago: University of Chicago Press, 1991, pp. 196–97.

5. Louis Galambos, *The Public Image of Big Business in America, 1880–1940,* Baltimore: Johns Hopkins University Press, 1975, pp. 6–10, 18.

6. Newlon, *Educational Administration,* pp. 18–19.

7. Merle Curti, *The Social Ideas of American Educators,* Patterson, N. J., Littlefield, Adams and Co., 1961, p. 99.

8. Raymond Callahan, *Education and the Cult of Efficiency: A Study of the Social Forces that Have Shaped the Administration of the Public Schools,* Chicago:

University of Chicago Press, 1962, p. 12. The theme of German competition and the need to fashion our schools after the German system was a common one during the period 1900 to 1920. See also Leonard Ayres, *Laggards in Our Schools: A Study of Retardation and Elimination in City School Systems*, New York: Russell Sage Foundation, 1907, pp. 123, 185; Lawrence Cremin, *The Transformation of the Schools: Progressivism in American Education, 1876–1957*, New York: Alfred A. Knopf, 1962, p. 38.

9. Grace Strachan, *Equal Pay for Equal Work: The Story of the Struggle Being Made by the Women Teachers of the City of New York*, New York: B. F. Buck and Company, 1910, p. 223.

10. Thomas Cochran, *Business in American Life: A History*, New York: McGraw-Hill, 1972, pp. 92–93.

11. Tyack, *One Best System*, pp. 74–75.

12. Cochran, *Business*, p. 94.

13. Newlon, *Educational Administration*, p. 10.

14. George Counts, *The Social Foundations of Education*, New York: Charles Scribner's Sons, 1934, pp. 260, 533.

15. Ibid., p. 260.

16. William Graham Sumner, *Folkways: A Study of the Sociological Importance of Usages, Manners, Customs, Mores, and Morals*, Boston: Ginn, 1906, pp. 628–29.

17. Larry Cuban, *How Teachers Taught: Constancy and Change in American Classrooms, 1890–1980*, New York: Longman, 1984, p. 25.

18. Ellwood Cubberley, *The History of Education*, Boston: Houghton Mifflin, 1920, p. 699.

19. Tyack, *One Best System*, pp. 33–36.

20. Cremin, *Transformation*, pp. 21–22.

21. David Tyack and Elizabeth Hansot, *Managers of Virtue: Public School Leadership in America, 1820–1980*, New York: Basic Books, 1982, pp. 260–61; Charles Spain, *The Platoon School*, New York: MacMillan, 1924, pp. v, 82; Counts, *Foundations*, pp. 535–36. George Counts's thesis in *The Social Foundations of Education* is that at the center of every educational program or philosophy is a selection of certain values. Accordingly, each educational philosophy rejects other competing values.

22. Tyack and Hansot, *Managers*, p. 13; Newlon, *Administration*, p. 38; Cochran, *Business*, pp. 88–89; John Dewey, *The Educational Situation*, Chicago: University of Chicago Press, 1902, p. 19.

23. Samuel Haber, *Efficiency and Uplift: Scientific Management in the Progressive Era, 1890–1920*, Chicago: University of Chicago, 1964, p. ix.

24. Ibid., pp. ix–x.

25. Barbara Berman, "Business Efficiency, American Schooling, and the Public School Superintendency," *History of Education Quarterly,* Fall 1983, pp. 304–5.

26. Cochran, *Business,* p. 138.

27. Counts, *Foundations,* pp. 72–73.

28. William Bagley, *Classroom Management: Its Principles and Techniques,* New York: MacMillan, 1912, p. 261.

29. Louis Galambos, *The Public Image of Big Business in America, 1880–1940,* Baltimore: Johns Hopkins University Press, 1975, p. 102; Edward DeAntoni, "Coming of Age in the Industrial State," Cornell University, Ph.D. dissertation, 1971, p. 184; Haber, *Efficiency,* pp. 84–95.

30. Callahan, *Education,* p. 5.

31. Ellwood Cubberley, *Public School Administration,* Boston: Houghton Mifflin, 1916, p. 326.

32. Haber, *Efficiency,* p. 74.

33. Counts, *Foundations,* pp. 6–11.

34. Haber, *Quest,* p. 195.

35. Ibid., p. 295; Haber, *Efficiency,* pp. 9–10.

36. Haber, *Efficiency,* pp. xi, 29, 173.

37. Tyack and Hansot, *Managers,* p. 203.

38. Haber, *Quest,* p. 198.

39. Tyack, *One Best System,* p. 129.

40. Andrew Draper, *Adaptation of the Schools to Industry and Efficiency,* Albany: New York State Education Department, 1908, pp. 6–9.

41. Tyack and Hansot, *Managers,* pp. 6–8; Haber, *Efficiency,* pp. 114–16.

42. Counts, *Foundations,* pp. 110–11.

43. Corrine Lathrop Gilb, *Hidden Hierarchies,* New York: Harper and Row, 1966, pp. 46–48. Professions at the turn of the century were dominated by WASP men. Women were typically shut out of membership in professional associations, forcing them to form their own organizations, which had little or no power.

44. Haber, *Quest,* pp. 332–35.

45. John Almack and Albert Lang, *Problems of the Teaching Profession,* Boston: Houghton Mifflin, 1925, p. 124.

46. Sandra Acker, ed., *Teachers, Gender and Careers,* New York: Falmer Press, 1989, p. 1.

47. Cochran, *Business,* pp. 5–6, 88–91.

48. Curti, *Social Ideas,* p. 13.

49. Cochran, *Business,* pp. 131–32.

50. Ibid., pp. 197, 139.

51. Alfred Chandler Jr., *The Invisible Hand,* Cambridge: Harvard University Press, 1977, pp. 1–4.

52. Ibid., pp. 8, 240–41.

53. Ibid., pp. 6–8.

54. Cochran, *Business,* pp. 160–61.

55. Chandler, *Visible Hand,* pp. 8, 273, 241, 244, 267–68.

56. Ibid., pp. 10, 491–92.

57. Ibid., pp. 241, 249.

58. Haber, *Efficiency,* p. 23.

59. Ibid., pp. 24–25; Chandler, *Visible Hand,* pp. 273–77.

60. Newlon, *Administration,* p. 20.

61. Robert Lynd and Helen Merrell Lynd, *Middletown,* New York: Harcourt, Brace and Co., 1929, pp. 79, 52.

62. Tyack and Hansot, *Managers,* p. 110.

63. A common example of an economic externality is the smoke belching from industrial smokestacks, a by-product of production. The smoke pollutes the environment, results in respiratory problems for people living nearby, causes acid rain, etc. The costs of this by-product are not part of the corporation's internal cost analysis, however. The costs of this by-product of private enterprise are borne by society—i.e., are external to the firm.

64. Cochran, *Business,* chapter 20, pp. 5–6. Cochran asserts that the growing complexity of laws and regulations increased business influence in politics, because firms specifically interested in an issue were likely to know more and be better represented by lobbyists than the typical dispersed opposition.

65. Galambos, *Public Image,* pp. 256, 261. Galambos tracked public opinion of big business from 1880 to 1940. He concluded that by 1940 even farmers and labor had greatly improved opinions of business, although they had been among its most vocal opponents at the close of the nineteenth century.

66. Cochran, *Business,* pp. 151–52. Corporations spent tremendous amounts on advertising (4% of the national income in 1910) in an effort to stimulate good will toward its operations.

67. Newlon, *Administration,* p. 37.

68. Lynd and Lynd, *Middletown,* p. 73.

69. Curti, *Social Ideas,* pp. 82, 85.

70. Ibid., pp. 197, 341–43.

71. Ibid., p. 77.

72. Tyack, *One Best System,* pp. 109–10. Tyack writes: "During the nineteenth century no group in the United States had a greater faith in the equalizing power of schooling or a clearer understanding of the democratic promise of education than did black American."

73. Curti, *Social Ideas,* p. 199.

Chapter 2

1. Ellwood Cubberley, *Public School Administration,* p. 338.

2. Tyack and Hansot, *Managers of Virtue,* p. 110.

3. Cochran, *Business in American Life,* p. 278.

4. Robert Reid, ed., *Battleground,* Urbana: University of Illinois Press, 1982, p. 86. Haley was the co-founder of the Chicago Teachers Federation at the turn of the century, an organization that opposed the emulation of business methods in the schools. She wrote her memoirs in the 1930s.

5. Curti, *The Social Ideas of American Educators,* p. 230; Katz, *Reconstructing American Education,* p. 71; Counts, *The Social Foundations of Education,* p. 562.

6. Tyack, *One Best System,* pp. 129–30, 131–35.

7. Tyack, Thomas, and Benevot, *Law and the Shaping of Public Education,* pp. 109–10. For a detailed description of the development of the profession of school management, see Raymond Callahan, *Education and the Cult of Efficiency.* Callahan writes the field of educational administration was legitimized by institutions such as Columbia and Harvard, which developed numerous graduate-level courses in school management by the 1920s.

8. Tyack, *One Best,* p. 191; Tyack et al., *Law,* p. 113.

9. Callahan, *Education,* pp. 112–13, 115, 117. Some famous examples of such expert efficiency studies were those conducted by Ellwood Cubberley in Portland, Oregon, and Franklin Bobbit Denver.

10. Tyack, *One Best*, pp. 192–93.

11. Callahan, *Education*, p. 116.

12. Tyack, *One Best*, pp. 132–33.

13. Ibid., pp. 134–35, 138–39. It was common for university presidents to become superintendents, and vice versa, in the newly centralized big city districts.

14. Tyack et al., *Law*, pp. 113–14.

15. The formal name of this 248-page report was "The Report of the Educational Commissioner of the City of Chicago." It was based on research done on big city school systems around the country.

16. Samuel Haber, *The Quest for Authority and Honor in the American Professions, 1750–1900*, Chicago: University of Chicago Press, 1991, pp. 285–86.

17. Reid, *Battleground*, pp. xix, xx, xxii, 35–36, 94, 115. In addition to recommending extraordinary power for the man placed in the position of superintendent of schools, the report also suggested that schools pay male teachers more than female teachers in order to attract more highly educated men with numerous career options. Another unrelated recommendation was that the Chicago school system extend land leases to corporations and newspapers for ninety-nine years without reevaluation. The bill met strong opposition from one of the few teachers' unions of the time, the Chicago Teachers Federation.

18. Cubberley, *Administration*, p. 84.

19. Wayne Urban, *Why Teachers Organized*, Detroit: Wayne State University Press, pp. 26–27.

20. Cubberley, *Administration*, p. 92, note 1.

21. Tyack, *One Best*, pp. 136–43.

22. Cubberley, *Administration*, p. 130.

23. Tyack, *One Best*, 128.

24. Tyack and Hansot, *Managers*, pp. 6, 107–8, 157.

25. Cubberley, *Administration*, pp. 104–5.

26. Neil Chamberlain, *Union Challenge to Management Control*, New York: Harper Bros., 1948, pp. 13–15.

27. Tyack, *One Best*, pp. 128–29. The way to please these powerful constituents was to support low cost, practical training of youngsters—i.e., vocational education—and citizenship training for immigrant children.

28. Chamberlain, *Challenge,* pp. 49–50, 60, 65. Chamberlain noted that business managers were often sons of businessmen—they were born into their societal position. Only 10% of business managers from 1928 to 1932 had fathers who were workers. In contrast, 56.7% of these managers were sons of businessmen. Chamberlain wrote that management's opposition to sharing authority with those beneath them in the organization's hierarchical structure was due, at least in part, to the personal philosophy of these members of the managerial class. School managers also saw themselves as part of an elite class. See Cubberley, *Administration,* pp. 132–56.

29. Tyack, *One Best,* p. 130. Draper made this comment in 1893. The leaders he referred to came from Cleveland's business elite, of which Draper was a part.

30. Cited in Nancy Hoffman, *Woman's "True" Profession: Voices from the History of Teaching,* Old Westbury, N.Y.: Feminist Press, McGraw Hill, 1981, p. 230. See also Adele Shaw, "The True Character of the New York City Public Schools," *The World's Work,* Vol. 7, No. 2, December 1903, pp. 4204–21.

31. Samuel Haber, *Efficiency and Uplift,* pp. 19, 24.

32. Katz, *Reconstructing,* pp. 67–71.

33. Alfred Chandler Jr., *The Visible Hand,* p. 273.

34. William Bagley, *Classroom Management: Its Principles and Techniques,* New York: MacMillan, 1912, pp. 262, 265–66.

35. Ellwood Cubberley, *The History of Education,* p. 808. What Cubberley neglected to point out was that this functional specialization took power and control away from craftsmen and women, who had the knowledge to create the entire item.

36. Cubberley, *Administration,* pp. 171, 300; *History,* pp. 817–18.

37. Cubberley, *Administration,* pp. 424, 274, 377, 379.

38. Callahan, *Education,* p. 62. James P. Munroe, an industrialist-educator and president of the National Society for the Promotion of Industrial Education, wrote in 1912 that "educational engineers' should make a thorough study of "the demands of society in general and of industry in particular upon boys and girls," and at the lowest cost possible develop the "means and methods of instruction and development."

39. Callahan, *Education,* p. 129.

40. Spain, *Platoon,* pp. 21–22.

41. Ibid., p. 24.

42. Tyack, *One Best,* p. 250.

43. Spain, *Platoon,* p. 25.

44. Franklin Bobbitt, *Elementary School Journal XII*, cited in Callahan, *Education*, pp. 54–55.

45. Cremin, *The Transformation of the School*, pp. 114–15.

46. Edward Thorndike, "The Nature, Purposes, and General Methods of Measurements of Educational Products" in *Seventeenth Yearbook*, Bloomington, Ill.: National Society for the Study of Education, 1918, p. 16.

47. Callahan, *Education*, pp. 247–48.

48. Robert and Helen Merrell Lynd, *Middletown*, p. 52. The Lynds found that the workers in Middletown were closely directed by managers or owners. Their work was monotonous and needed "to be strained through a pecuniary sieve before it assumes vital meaning."

49. Cited in Curti, *Social Ideas*, p. 203.

50. Tyack, *One Best*, 73.

51. Cremin, *Transformation*, pp. 34–37.

52. Cubberley, *Changing Conceptions of Education*, Boston: Houghton Mifflin, 1909, pp. 56–57.

53. Tyack, *One Best*, pp. 188–91, 264–67. The old guard of the NEA was considered the aristocracy of educators—university presidents, large city school superintendents, and notable education professors such as Cubberley; Cremin, *Transformation*, pp. 34, 37, 51. See also, Andrew Draper, *The Adaptation of the Schools to Industry and Efficiency*, Albany: New York State Department of Education, 1908.

54. Tyack, *One Best*, p. 189; Cochran, *Business*, p. 161. As a rule, business used philanthropy to support endeavors that preserved social stability or improved the performance of workers. Support for institutions such as the YMCA was provided for the former reason, vocational education for the latter.

55. Cited in Callahan, *Education*, p. 13.

56. William Maxwell, "On a Certain Arrogance in Educational Theorists," *Educational Review*, February 1914, pp. 175–76.

57. Callahan, *Education*, p. 14.

58. Bagley, *Management*, pp. 14, 2, 18. Bagley made it clear at the outset that the problem of classroom management was primarily one of economy—deciding in what manner "the working unit of the school plant" should operate in order to reap the biggest dividends. He wrote: "Classroom management may be looked upon as a 'business' problem."

59. Ibid., pp. 262–63.

60. Ibid., pp. 263–64.

61. Ibid., pp. 3–4.

62. Ibid., p. 9.

63. George Counts, *The Social Foundations of Education,* New York: Charles Scribner's Sons, 1934, pp. 274–75, 556–57. Writing over twenty years later, George Counts commented that most teacher training was distinguished by the acquisition of method separated from content of thought, and obedience by the child to the teacher, and the teacher to her supervisor. It was a case of form over substance, with the effort to make teachers meticulous with respect to small matters, and mindful of the wishes of the most powerful and respectable forces in the community.

64. John Almack and Albert Lang, *Problems of the Teaching Profession,* Boston: Houghton and Mifflin, 1925, p. vi. Cubberley wrote the introduction to this book.

65. Ibid., p. 71. The authors of this 1925 book weakly suggest that a teacher caught between her professional judgment and her employer's direct order might try appealing to a local commission on professional ethics, if one existed. This type of commission had no force of law.

66. Marion Dogherty, *'Scusa Me Teacher,* Francistown, N.H.: Marshall Jones, 1943.

67. Robert and Helen Merrell Lynd, *Middletown in Transition,* New York: Harcourt, Brace and Co., 1937, p. 206.

68. Reid, *Battleground,* pp. 132–33. In fact, Haley's allegations were shortly found to be accurate, and hundreds of thousands of dollars in back taxes were collected from Chicago-based corporations such as Pullman and Otis Elevator. Harris was the U. S. commissioner of education, as well as former superintendent of schools in St. Louis.

69. Patricia Schmuck, *Women Educators,* pp. 1, viii.

70. Urban, *Teachers,* pp. 30–32, 155.

71. Hoffman, *Profession,* pp. 238–41. In 1920, 55% of elementary principals were women. The proportion of females dropped throughout the century, with only 18% of elementary principalships being held by women in 1978. See also Schmuck, *Women,* pp. 85–86.

72. Alison Prentice and Marjorie Theobald, eds., *Women Who Taught,* Toronto: University of Toronto Press, 1991, pp. 4–5.

73. Tyack and Hansot, *Managers,* p. 182.

74. Prentice and Theobald, *Women,* pp. 4–5.

75. Tyack, *One Best,* p. 45.

76. Ernest C. Moore, *Fifty Years of American Education: 1867–1917*, pp. 60–61.

77. Tyack, *One Best*, p. 265.

78. Counts, *Foundations*, p. 536.

79. Kathleen Casey and Michael Apple, "Gender and the Conditions of Teachers' Work" in Sandra Acker, ed., *Teachers, Gender, and Careers*, New York: Falmer Press, 1989, p. 176.

80. Tyack, et al., *Law*, p. 123; Tyack and Hansot, *Managers*, pp. 205–7; Tyack, *One Best*, p. 104.

81. Tyack, *One Best*, pp. 126, 129.

82. Cited in Curti, *Social Ideas*, p. 203.

Chapter 3

1. Robert Reid, *Battleground*, pp. 286, 25.

2. Tyack and Hansot, *Managers*, p. 202. See also Callahan, *Education*, p. 120.

3. Barbara Berman, "Business Efficiency," pp. 308–9. See also Wayne Urban, *Why Teachers Organized*, p. 32. Many of the superintendents and education professors of the pro-efficiency coalition had no teaching experience.

4. Berman, "Efficiency," p. 309.

5. Tyack, *One Best System*, p. 196.

6. Ella Flagg Young, "Isolation in the School," Chicago: Ph.D. dissertation, University of Chicago, 1900, p. 16. Young became the first female superintendent of an urban district when she as appointed the head of the Chicago school system in 1910. Prior to that, she had many years of experience in the classroom and in teaching future teachers, as well as in school management.

7. John Dewey, *The School and Society*, p. 35.

8. Ibid., pp. 31–34.

9. William Kilpatrick, *Education for a Changing Civilization*, pp. 60–67. Kilpatrick felt that given the rapid changes in society over the previous hundred years, adults had no right to fasten their conclusions on their children.

10. Young, "Isolation," p. 19.

11. Ibid., p. 43.

12. William Bagley, *Management*, p. 35.

13. Counts, *Social Foundations,* pp. 11, 53.

14. Young, "Isolation," pp. 32–36.

15. Dewey, *School,* pp. 12–13.

16. Young, "Isolation," pp. 4, 19.

17. Ibid., p. 20.

18. Dewey, *School,* p. 22.

19. Cited in Cremin, *Transformation,* p. 63. Interestingly, Cremin commented that Addams's idea could be seen as "romanticism." Thirty years after his comment and over eighty years after Addams originally proposed the idea, autonomous work terms are employed by modern management in many parts of the industrialized world.

20. Young, "Isolation," p. 41.

21. Kilpatrick, *Education,* p. 27.

22. Cited in Reid, *Battleground,* pp. 174–75.

23. Young, "Isolation," p. 54.

24. Kilpatrick, *Education,* pp. 75-77. Kilpatrick said: "Modern educational theory tells us that we do not learn what we do not practice. If we would learn democracy, we must then practice it." This idea actually was expressed twenty years earlier by William T. Harris, former U.S. commissioner of education and advocate of the pro-efficiency model of reform. Harris, however, used the idea to further the notion that obedience should be demanded of children in school. He observed that the child "simply gets used to established order and expects it and obeys it as a habit." Cited in Jesse Newlon, *Educational Administration,* p. 536.

25. Dewey, *School,* pp. 15–16.

26. Ibid., pp. 27–28.

27. Richard Altenbaugh, ed., *The Teacher's Voice,* pp. 170, 30.

28. Young, "Isolation," p. 16.

29. Edward DeAntoni, "Coming of Age in the Industrial State," Cornell University, pp. 95–97.

30. Urban, *Teachers,* pp. 30–31. The high value placed on teaching experience led the educational progressives to challenge the empowerment of pro-efficiency superintendents, many of whom had never taught.

31. Joan Smith, *Ella Flagg Young,* pp. 14, 19.

32. Dewey, *School,* pp. 111–12.

33. Cremin, *Transformation*, pp. 131–32.

34. Smith, *Young*, p. 51. Ella Flagg Young was one of the first educators to suggest using literature in this interdisciplinary approach to learning. This is a cornerstone of the current movement to reform education.

35. Young, "Isolation," pp. 17–18.

36. Dewey, *School*, p. 39.

37. Ibid., pp. 17, 22.

38. Newlon, *Administration*, p. 248.

39. Young, "Isolation," pp. 16–17.

40. Counts, *Foundations*, pp. 540–56.

41. Samuel Haber, *Quest*, pp. x, 201. At the turn of the century the average urban teacher's salary was $650 a year, less than almost every blue-collar or clerical occupation. By 1911, a time when few persons attended high school, the average years of schooling for teachers was thirteen and rising sharply due to increased requirements for state licensing. See also Grace Strachan, *Equal Pay for Equal Work*, pp. 138–39; Tyack, *One Best*, p. 258.

42. Haber, *Quest*, pp. xiii, 195, 198.

43. Cited in Callahan, *Education*, p. 203. This quote was taken from a speech made by Jesse Newlon at the NEA convention in 1925. Newlon was president of the NEA at the time of this address.

44. Dewey, *School*, p. 64. Dewey insisted that the teacher had to be a master of both content and methodology. He advocated for a type of teacher training that prepared new teachers in both areas of expertise. See also Cremin, *Transformation*, p. 138.

45. Cuban, *Teachers*, pp. 254–55. Cuban writes that the child-centered education proposed by the educational progressives required a tremendous amount of energy and expertise on the part of the teacher; far more than did the mechanistic model of education proposed by the pro-efficiency reformers. Cuban quips: "Monitoring what children are doing, what skills they need to work on, and resolving unexpected problems as they arise demands the teacher's additional investment in radar equipment, if not an intensive management course."

46. Smith, *Young*, pp. 38–39.

47. Counts, *Foundations*, pp. 555–56.

48. Ibid., pp. 556–58.

49. Ibid., pp. 558–59. Counts suggested that the best way for teachers to secure these conditions was to organize and present their case "forcefully, intelligently, and persuasively before the public."

50. Reid, *Battleground*, pp. 280–81.

51. Smith, *Young*, pp. 16, 27, 42, 71, 102, 148, 158, 224. Her successor at the Chicago Normal School, William Owen, paid tribute to Young saying: "Had she been a man, she would have held a foremost position in world affairs. She could have directed a great corporation, managed a railroad, served as governor of a state, or commanded an army. She was a born leader with an equipment that challenged comparison."

52. Ibid., p. 36.

53. Dewey, *School*, pp. 72–76.

54. Smith, *Young*, pp. 51, 55.

55. Young, "Isolation," pp. 12–13.

56. Newlon, *Administration*, pp. 201, 200. Newlon held a variety of administrative posts before becoming superintendent of Denver schools in the 1920s.

57. Ibid., p. 200. Acting on his belief, he instituted a system of shared decision-making between the school managers and teachers of Denver, which thrived during the 1920s.

58. Cited in Reid, *Battleground*, p. 89. First published in the *Elementary School Teacher*, 4 (December 1903).

59. Cited in Cuban, *Teachers*, pp. 71–72.

60. Newlon, *Administration*, pp. 200–201. Margaret Haley, too, supported the idea of school councils as an essential facet of the professionalization of teaching. Her vision of these councils was even more expansive than Newlon's. In her mind councils would do more than determine the goals of instruction and the curriculum to realize these goals; they would set forth and enforce the standards of admission to the teaching profession as well as discharge from it. Teachers, not boards of education, would be the judge of fitness or unfitness of colleagues. Teachers would be leaders in the educational system. Teachers would be free to voice and exercise their professional opinion and action. Finally, school councils would develop a code of ethics by which professional teachers would live and work. Academic freedom would be the pivotal principle around which all ethical questions would turn. See Reid, *Battleground*, pp. 274–75.

61. Dewey, *The Educational Situation*, p. 18. Dewey felt that without this unified vision of the aims of education, schools would continue to be at the mercy of pressure from powerful community leaders to teach the latest fad.

62. Young, "Isolation," p. 36.

63. Tyack, *One Best*, p. 130. According to Andrew Draper, superintendent of Cleveland schools in the 1890s, three lawyers and a businessman pushed through the Ohio legislature the bill centralizing control of education in that city; Tyack, *Law*, pp. 6–7, 15, 114–15.

64. Draper, *Adaptation*, pp. 8–9.

65. DeAntoni, "Coming," p. 154.

66. Lynd and Lynd, *Middletown*, pp. 190–96.

67. Ibid., pp. 196–98.

68. Cochran, *Business*, pp. 174, 273. See also Lynd and Lynd, *Middletown*, p. 194.

69. Almack and Lang, *Problems*, pp. 320–21. For a detailed discussion of the effort to Americanize immigrant children, see Tyack, *One Best*, pp. 229–55.

70. Lynd and Lynd, *Middletown*, pp. 196–97.

71. Cuban, *Teachers*, pp. 102–3.

72. Ibid., p. 103.

73. Ibid., pp. 259, 113. Cuban quoted from Dewey's 1952 assessment of progressivism's influence on the schools.

74. Dewey, *The Educational Situation*, pp. 22–23.

Chapter 4

1. Tyack and Hansot, *Managers*, p. 223.

2. Ibid., p. 224.

3. Tyack, *One Best*, p. 276. For a discussion of how *Brown v. Board of Education* affected existing school systems, see Marilyn Gittell, *Participants and Participation*, New York: Praeger, 1967, pp. 40–45; Robert Bendiner, *The Politics of Schools*, pp. 43–82.

4. Neal Gross and Ann Trask, *The Sex Factor and the Management of Schools*, p. 8. See also Donald Myers, *Teacher Power*, pp. 45–46.

5. Myron Lieberman, *Education as a Profession*, pp. 248–50. In 1910, 5.1% of physicians were female; 6.1% of physicians were female in 1950. The percentage of lawyers who were women rose from 0.5% in 1910 to 2.5% in 1950. Harvard Law School did not begin admitting women until 1950.

6. Louis Galambos, *The Public Image of Big Business in America*, p. 267. See also Thomas Cochran, *Business*, p. 338.

7. Peter Dow, *Schoolhouse Politics*, pp. 1–3, 10–12.

8. *Life*, March 24, 1958, pp. 25, 37, cited in Cochran, *Business*, p. 283.

9. Cochran, *Business*, p. 282.

10. Jonathan Kozol, *Death at an Early Age;* James S. Coleman et al., *Equality of Educational Opportunity.*

11. *Fortune,* October 1958, cited in Callahan, *Education,* p. 256.

12. Cited in Cochran, *Business,* p. 282.

13. Cubberley, *Public School Administration; Education Week,* March 3, 1993, p. 3. Consolidation of districts, strongly recommended by Cubberley, continued through this period. In 1942 there were 108,579 districts nationwide; in 1952 there were 67,355; in 1972 only 15,781 remained.

14. Larry Cuban, *How Teachers Taught,* p. 196.

15. Cubberley, *Administration,* p. 125, note 1; p. 100; Bendiner, *Politics,* pp. 9–14, 182; Patrick Carlton and Harold Goodman, eds., *The Collective Dilemma,* p. 57.

16. Bendiner, *Politics,* p. 40.

17. Tyack and Hansot, *Managers,* pp. 222–23.

18. Myers, *Teacher Power,* p. 117. The task of filling a vacancy in the superintendent's office was, and continues to be, both time-consuming and expensive; Gittell, *Participants,* p. 55; Harmon Zeigler, *The Political Life of American Teachers,* p. 130.

19. William Boyd, "The Public, the Professionals, and Educational Policy-Making," *Teachers College Record,* Vol. 77, 1976, pp. 539–77; Tyack and Hansot, *Managers,* p. 223.

20. Neal Gross, *Who Runs Our Schools?* pp. 45–47.

21. Patricia Schmuck, ed., *Women Educators,* pp. 85–88. In 1922 there were 31 female superintendents in the nation. In 1932 there were 25 states that did not have a single female superintendent heading a school district. By 1977 there were only 93 female superintendents nationwide, representing less than 1% of the nation's more than 15,000 districts.

22. Gross and Trask, *Sex Factor,* pp. 217–27, 45–50.

23. Cited in Tyack and Hansot, *Managers,* p. 222; U.S. Commission on Civil Rights, *Racial Isolation in the Public Schools,* Washington, D.C.: Government Publishing Office, 1967. See also Tyack, *One Best,* pp. 281–82; Kenneth Clark, *Dark Ghetto,* p. 131.

24. Gittell, *Participants,* p. vi, 11–13.

25. Myers, *Teacher Power,* p. 78.

26. Ronald Corwin, "Professional Persons in Public Organizations," in *Readings in Collective Negotiations in Public Education,* Stanley Elam et al., eds., p. 64.

27. E. Wright Bakke, "Teachers, School Boards and the Employment Relationship," in *Employer-Employee Relations in the Public Schools,* Robert E. Doherty, ed., pp. 41–59.

28. Marjorie Murphy, *Blackboard Unions,* p. 220. There was, however, a 94% increase in the number of male school teachers between 1954 and 1964. In 1951, 78.7% of teachers were female; Myers, *Teacher Power,* p. 39.

29. Zeigler, *Life,* p. 2; Lieberman, *Education,* pp. 57–58, 87–115; Gittell, *Participants,* p. 30; Myers, *Teacher Power.* pp. 8–9.

30. Ronald Corwin, "The Anatomy of Militant Professionalism," in Carlton and Goodman, eds., *The Collective Dilemma,* pp. 237–48. See also Myers, *Teacher Power,* pp. 16–17.

31. Edward Shils and C. Taylor Whittier, *Teachers, Administrators and Collective Bargaining,* p. 161.

32. Callahan, *Education,* p. 255; *New York Times,* April 15, 1962, p. E9.

33. Myers, *Teacher Power,* pp. 44–45, 49–50; Gittel, *Participants,* p. 36.

34. Ronald Corwin, "Professional Persons in Public Organizations," in Elam, *Readings,* pp. 47–67.

35. George Taylor, "The Public Interest in Collective Negotiations in Education," in Elam, *Readings,* pp. 11–23. Taylor authored the New York law that guaranteed teachers and other public employees collective bargaining rights.

36. Cubberley, *Administration,* pp. 276–77.

37. Albert Shanker, "The Future of Teacher Involvement in Decision Making," in Carlton and Goodman, *Dilemma,* pp. 76–83.

38. Zeigler, *Life,* pp. 125, 130; Lieberman, *Education,* p. 235. Lieberman's analysis of teacher conformity, done some ten years earlier, was corroborated by Ziegler's work. See also Cuban, *Teachers,* p. 167.

39. Myers, *Teacher Power,* pp. 32, 35. The author feels that schools did not become as highly rationalized as industry only because little scientific research on the technology of teaching was done.

40. Ibid., p. 83; Zeigler, *Life,* 28–29.

41. Lieberman, *Education,* p. 410; Shanker, *Future,* p. 83. Educational research continued to show, as it did earlier in the century, that class size was unrelated to achievement of students as measured by standardized tests. See Myers, *Teacher Power,* p. 134.

42. Cuban, *Teachers,* p. 167.

43. Ibid., p. 167. As a student in New York City schools during the 1950s and 1960s, I only now understand the origin of the weekly ritual of clearing my desk of all its contents except textbooks.

44. Ibid., p. 148.

45. Shanker, "Future of Decision Making," in Carlton and Goodman, *Dilemma,* p. 79.

46. Murphy, *Blackboard,* pp. 217–18. Tyack, *One Best,* p. 287.

47. Murphy, *Blackboard,* pp. 175–84, 222; Lieberman, *Education,* pp. 299–301. After World War I many districts forced teachers to sign "yellow dog" contracts in exchange for their jobs. Courts upheld the legality of these contracts, which required teachers to sever their union ties, citing the inability of adjudicators to second-guess school board judgments on how teachers' union might affect the public welfare.

48. Murphy, *Blackboard,* pp. 1, 6, 19, 32–34, 216, 222.

49. Shanker, "Future of Decision Making," in Carlton and Goodman, *Dilemma,* p. 77.

50. Ibid., pp. 77–78.

51. Ibid., p. 77; Doherty, "Factories versus the Schools," in Carlton and Goodman, *Dilemma,* p. 222; Myers, *Teachers Power,* p. 1.

52. Charles Kerchner and Douglas Mitchell, *The Changing Idea of a Teachers' Union,* pp. 33–34.

53. Carlton and Goodman, *Dilemma,* pp. 1, 58; Corwin, in Carlton and Goodman, *Dilemma,* pp. 240–41; Richard Altenbaugh, ed., *The Teacher's Voice,* pp. 167–69.

54. Joseph A. Alutto and James Belasco, "A Typology for Participation in Organizational Decision Making," in *The Employment of Teachers,* Donald Gerwin, ed., pp. 311–24.

55. "Collective Bargaining and the Professional Employee," 69 *Columbia Law Review,* 2, February 1969, pp. 277–98.

56. Tyack, *One Best,* p. 285; Carlton and Goodman, *Dilemma,* p. 25; Corwin, in Carlton and Goodman, *Dilemma,* p. 238; Murphy, *Blackboard,* pp. 212–16.

57. Harold Goodwin and Gerald Thompson, "Teacher Militancy and Countervailing Power," in Carlton and Goodman, *Dilemma,* pp. 72–80; Myers, *Teacher Power,* p. 96.

58. The sixties provided fertile ground for experiments in alternative education. For an excellent discussion on the rise and fall of alternative education from 1965 to 1975, see Cuban, *Teachers,* pp. 148–200; see also Bendiner, *Politics,* pp. 165–213; Dow, *Schoolhouse.*

59. Charles Perry and Wesley Wildman, *The Impact of Negotiations on Public Education*, pp. 14–15; Myers, *Teacher Power*, p. 4; Corwin, in Carlton and Goodman, *Dilemma*, p. 239.

60. Albert Shanker, "The Development of Collective Bargaining in Education— A Union Point of View," *Critical Issues in Education*, pp. 25–29.

61. Tyack, *One Best*, p. 288.

62. Joseph Shedd and Samuel Bacharach, *Tangled Hierarchies*, p. 181; Murphy, *Blackboard*, p. 1.

63. Shanker, "Future of Decision Making," in Carlton and Goodman, *Dilemma*, p. 78.

64. Ibid., p. 78; Tyack, *One Best*, p. 82; Lieberman, *Education*, pp. 87–90; Myers, *Teacher Power*, p. 14.

65. Quote by Myron Lieberman and Michael Moskow, cited in Kerchner and Mitchell, *Idea*, p. 109.

66. T. M. Stinnett, Jack Kleinmann, and Martha Ware, *Professional Negotiation in Public Education*, pp. 154–55.

67. Lieberman, *Education*, p. vii. See also Corinne Gilb, *Hidden Hierarchies*, p. 105.

68. Murphy, *Blackboard*. Murphy's book describes the histories of the AFT and the NEA from the time of the pro-efficiency reforms through 1980. See also Myers, *Teacher Power*, p. 96. The rivalry between the two associations is often cited as a contributory factor in the rise of teacher militancy during this period.

69. Stinnett et al., *Negotiation*, pp. 3–7.

70. Kerchner and Mitchell, *Idea*, p. 109.

71. George Taylor, 1966. Cited in Myers, *Teacher Power*, p. 73.

72. Amitai Etzioni, ed., *The Semi-Professions and Their Organization*.

73. Lieberman, *Education*, p. 247.

74. Myers, *Teacher Power*, p. 8.

75. Murphy, *Blackboard*, p. 250.

76. Lorraine McDonnell and Anthony Pascal, *Organized Teachers in American Schools*, p. 52.

77. Corwin in Carlton and Goodman, *Dilemma*, p. 246. Teachers asserted that they would free themselves from the control/conformity mentality with which they had long operated, albeit by necessity, to develop innovative solutions to difficult problems.

78. Shanker, "Future of Decision Making," in Carlton and Goodman, *Dilemma*, p. 80. See also Robert Doherty and Walter Oberer, *Teachers, School Boards, and Collective Bargaining*, pp. 91–92.

79. Lieberman, "Power and Policy," in Elam, *Readings*, pp. 37–46.

80. Shanker, "Future," in Carlton and Goodman, *Dilemma*, p. 83.

81. *Third National Workshop on Professional Rights and Responsibilities*, National Education Association, pp. 14–15. The recognition of the gulf between school managers and teachers inherent in a union approach was what the NEA objected to most vigorously.

82. Ibid., p. 36. Stinnett et al., *Negotiations*, pp. 2–3.

83. Tyack, *One Best*, p. 287.

84. Murphy, *Blackboard*, p. 100.

85. American Association of School Administrators, *Roles, Responsibilities, Relationships of the School Board, Superintendent, and Staff*, pp. 12–13; idem, "School Administrators View Professional Negotiations," in Elam, *Readings*, pp. 203–18.

86. American Association of School Administrators, in Elam, *Readings*, p. 216.

87. Stinnett et al., *Negotiation*, pp. 113–17.

88. Ibid., p. 103.

89. Murphy, *Blackboard*, p. 226.

90. Stinnett et al., *Negotiation*, p. 154.

91. *First National Workshop on Professional Rights and Responsibilities*, NEA, p. 21; Murphy, *Blackboard*, p. 228.

92. *Second National Workshop on Professional Rights and Responsibilities*, NEA, p. 12.

93. Murphy, *Blackboard*, pp. 227–28. The AFT asserted that supervisors and teachers could not be represented by the same organization; that their interests were not only different but of an adversarial nature. In this respect they were faithful to the early roots of the organization. See also Gilb, *Hierarchies*, p. 167.

94. Shils and Whittier, *Teachers*, p. 148.

95. Ibid., pp. 148–49.

96. Bendiner, *Politics*, pp. 105–6.

97. Cited in Myers, *Teacher Power*, p. 3.

98. Gilb, *Hierarchies*, pp. 153–55.

99. Etzioni, *Semi-Professionals*, p. vi. Etzioni said that although teachers aspired to professional status, they did not deserve it and would never get it. He supported his conclusion with his model of professionalism, which was characterized by considerable autonomy, freedom from external control by managers and lay boards, independent practice, more than five years of training, and male practitioners. Because teachers did not fit this model, Etzioni was certain that teaching would forever remain what he called a "semi-profession."

100. Milton Derber, *The American Idea of Industrial Democracy*, pp. 496–97. At the end of the tumultuous sixties, Derber commented that it was not clear whether the AFT would succeed in its quest for democratic school governance; Tyack, *One Best*, pp. 288–89.

101. American Association of School Administrators, *Roles, Responsibilities, Relationships*, pp. 12–13.

102. Shanker, Wollman Lectures, "Development," p. 25. Shanker recalled that the superintendent of New York City schools, Dr. Theobald, refused to bargain with the UFT in 1960 because "I do not bargain with members of my own family." See also Bendiner, *Politics*, pp. 96–97.

103. Altenbaugh, *Politics*, p. 160.

104. Carlton and Goodman, *Dilemma*, p. 165; Lieberman, "Implications of the Coming NEA-AFT Merger," in Carlton and Goodman, *Dilemma*, pp. 44–56. Lieberman explains how NEA was convinced to compete with the AFT on the AFT's terms by a New York City management law firm, Kaye, Scholer, Fierman, Hays, and Handler. Lieberman says the lawyers' advice saved the NEA from catastrophe by guiding it toward collective bargaining. "Ironically, corporation lawyers succeeded in convincing NEA leadership (correctly it appears) that NEA had to cease rejecting collective negotiations and demonstrate its determination to negotiate better agreements for teachers than those negotiated by the AFT."

105. Paul Prascow et al., *Scope of Bargaining in the Public Sector*, pp. 29–35.

106. Howell Harris, *The Right to Manage*, p. 97.

107. Neil Chamberlain, *Union Challenge to Management Control*, pp. 20–27, 13–16.

108. Harris, *Right*, p. 97.

109. Joan Parker Weitzman, "Scope of Bargaining in Public Education," pp. 8–16.

110. Fred Landis, *The Impact of the Taylor Law*, p. 24.

111. Bendiner, *Politics*, pp. 108–9. Tenured school managers could be removed from their jobs if their position was eliminated or if they were found guilty of specific offenses in a legal proceeding. Source: Hal Byer, NEA-NY, phone conversation, March 22, 1993.

112. Shils and Whittier, *Teachers*, 595, 505, 361–62.

113. Bernard Donovan, "Speaking for Management," in Elam, *Readings*, p. 289.

114. Gene Geisert, "The Effect of Collective Bargaining on Curriculum," *Government Union Review*, Vol. 4, No. 1, 1980, p. 39.

115. Cited in Chamberlain, *Union*, p. 65, note 18.

116. Harris, *Right*, p. 99.

117. Ibid., pp. 100–101. See also James Atleson, *Values and Assumptions*, p. 8.

118. Thomas Kochan, Harry Katz, and Robert McKersie, *Transformation of Industrial Relations*, pp. 12, 56–59; Chamberlain, *Union*, p. 3; Harris, *Right*, pp. 10, 101, 105. After World War II they mounted an offensive campaign to change both public policy on labor and public opinion on unions; Donald Cullen and Marica Greenbaum, *Management Rights and Collective Bargaining*, p. 9.

119. Harold Webb, "The National School Boards Association," in Elam, *Readings*, pp. 196–202. This was a reprint of a 1965 speech made by Mr. Webb.

120. *New York Times*, April 12, 1962; Bendiner, *Politics*, pp. 96–99. See also Murphy, *Blackboard*, p. 218. Murphy writes that the 1961 NYC teachers' strike "was treated by the newspapers as something catastrophic."

121. Kochan et al., *Transformation*, pp. 22–23.

122. Cullen and Greenbaum, *Management*, pp. 19–31; Chamberlain, *Union*, p. 50.

123. Karl Klare, "Labor Law as Ideology," *Industrial Relations Law Journal*, No. 3, 1981, pp. 450–82.

124. Kochan et al., *Transformation*, pp. 27–29, 89.

125. Derber, *American*, p. 496; Harris, *Right*, p. 74.

126. Atleson, *Values*, pp. 95–97. These rare exceptions involved a narrowly defined concept of health and safety, i.e., employees could refuse to work if there was "ascertainable, objective evidence" that "an abnormally dangerous condition for work" existed. *Gateway Coal Co. v. United Mine Workers*, 94 S. Ct. (1974), at 640–41.

127. Atleson, *Values*, pp. 112–31.

128. Katherine Van Wezel Stone, "Post-War Paradigm in American Labor Law," 90 *Yale Law Journal*, No. 7, June 1981, pp. 1511–80.

129. Derber, *American*, pp. 495–97; Atleson, *Values*, p. 177; Kochan et al., *Transformation*, p. 27; Harris, *Right*, p. 103.

130. Atleson, *Values*, p. 180.

131. Murphy, *Blackboard*, p. 219.

132. The Taylor Law, *New York State Public Employment Relations Board*, Albany: PERB, 1987, pp. 1–2.

133. Murphy, *Blackboard*, p. 219.

134. Kerchner and Mitchell, *Idea*, pp. 206–11.

135. John P. Pisapia, "What's Negotiable in Public Education," *Government Union Review*, Vol. 1, No. 3, Summer 1980, pp. 26–27; Denise Gelberg, "Scope of Bargaining for Teachers: The Issue of Textbook Selection," unpublished paper, 1989, pp. 3–5.

136. Charles Young, "The Superintendent of Schools," in Carlton and Goodman, *Dilemma*, pp. 102–12.

137. Weitzman, "Scope," p. 292.

138. Ida Klaus, "The Emerging Relationship," an address made at the Conference on Public Employment and Collective Bargaining, University of Chicago, February 5, 1965, cited in Shils and Whittier, *Teachers*, pp. 548–49.

139. John Metzler, "The Role of Management," in Carlton and Goodman, *Dilemma*, pp. 85–91.

140. Kerchner and Mitchell, *Idea*, pp. 14–15, 138–39.

141. *Ridgefield Park Education Association v. Ridgefield Park Board of Education*, 78 NJ 144 (1978). The New Jersey Public Employee Relations Commission subsequently relied on this case, ruling that boards needed "unfettered discretion" in such areas as curriculum, course content, and textbooks.

142. Shanker, Wollman Lectures, "Development," pp. 27–28.

143. Don Vial, *The Scope of Bargaining Controversy*.

144. Derek Bok and John Dunlop, *Labor and the American Community*, p. 327.

145. Harry Edwards, "The Emerging Duty to Bargain," pp. 885–934. Edwards later became a federal court judge on the First Circuit Court of Appeals.

146. Perry and Wildman, *Impact*, pp. 167–68.

147. Sam Bacharach and Joseph Shedd, "Power and Employment," in *The Politics of Reforming School Administration*, Jane Hannaway, ed., p. 153.

148. Gelberg, "Scope," pp. 5–7. Although states vary somewhat in their judicial interpretation of what constitutes a working condition, they uniformly use the test of whether bargaining over the issue would compromise management's policy-making authority.

149. Jim Bowles, "Defining the Scope of Bargaining for Teacher Negotiations," *Labor Law Journal*, Vol. 29, No. 10. October 1978, pp. 649–65.

150. Kochan, et al., *Transformation,* pp. 178–82.

151. Metzler, "Role," p. 92.

152. Irving Sabghir, *The Scope of Bargaining,* pp. 60–62. See also Geisert, "Effect," pp. 39–40.

153. McDonnell and Pascal, *Organized,* p. 77.

154. Comment made in 1968 by Jack Frymier. Cited in Myers, *Teacher Power,* p. 89.

155. Michael Finch and Trevor Nagel, "Collective Bargaining," *Wisconsin Law Review,* Vol. 1984, No. 6, pp. 1573–1670. See also Gelberg, "Scope." In this study of cases involving the issue of teacher bargaining over textbook selection, not one jurisdiction deemed textbook selection a mandatory subject of bargaining.

156. Murphy, *Blackboard,* pp. 220, 209. By 1986, 77% of all teachers were covered by a collective bargaining contract. See also David Lipsky and Sharon Conley "Incentive Pay and Collective Bargaining in Public Education," paper presented at the American Educational Research Association, San Francisco, 1986, p. 5; Myers, *Teacher Power,* pp. 160, 43–45.

157. Myers, *Teacher Power,* p. 92. This comment was made by Alan Rosenthal who undertook a study of power distribution within five large school systems after teachers organized in the 1960s.

158. Kerchner and Mitchell, *Idea,* p. 15; Murphy, *Blackboard,* p. 6.

159. Tyack and Hansot, *Managers,* p. 239. Susan Moore Johnson, *Teacher Unions,* p. 176.

160. Tyack and Hansot, *Managers,* p. 239.

161. Metzler, "Role," p. 87; Bacharach and Shedd, "Power," p. 178.

162. Murphy, *Blackboard,* p. 209.

163. Sam Bacharach, Scott Bauer, and Joe Shedd, *The Learning Workplace,* p. 4; McDonnell and Pascal, *Teachers Unions,* pp. vi–x.

164. Bacharach and Shedd, "Power," pp. 3–4; Tom Gillett, chief negotiator for the Rochester Teachers' Association, interview by author in Rochester, N. Y., on March 11, 1993.

165. Myron Lieberman, "The Impact of Collective Negotiations," in Elam, *Readings,* pp. 229–33.

166. Larry Cuban, *The Managerial Imperative,* p. 4.

167. Myers, *Teacher Power,* p. 8.

168. Taylor, in Elam, *Readings,* p. 17.

169. Altenbaugh, *Politics,* p. 170.

170. Kerchner and Mitchell, *Idea,* pp 234–35. The authors feel that good teaching has nothing to do with the industrial model of work organization; therefore, the use of a model of collective bargaining that worked for industrial unions was wholly inadequate in education.

171. Myers, *Teacher Power,* p. 75.

172. Bacharach and Shedd, "Power," p. 177.

173. Robert Doherty, "Labor Relations," in Carlton and Goodman, *Dilemma,* pp. 218–28.

174. Bacharach and Shedd, "Power," p. 176.

175. *Fibreboard Corporation v. National Labor Relations Board,* 379 U. S. 203 (1964). In this Supreme Court case, Justice Potter Stewart ruled that employers need not bargain over decisions that go to the "core of entrepreneurial control." State adjudicators also relied heavily on *National Labor Relations Board v. Wooster Division of Borg-Warner Corp.* 356 U. S. 342 (1958), which divided issues into mandatory, permissive, or prohibited subjects of bargaining. See *Journal of Law and Education,* Vol. 13, No. 4, October 1984, pp. 477–507.

176. Bowles, "Defining," p. 650.

177. Galambos, *Image,* 267.

178. Sandra Acker, ed., *Teachers, Gender and Careers,* p. 1; Kathleen Casey and Michael Apple, "Gender and the Conditions of Teachers' Work," in Acker, *Teachers,* pp. 171–86.

179. Murphy, *Blackboard,* p. 6.

180. Dow, *Schoolhouse.* Dow presents a powerful case study of how one effort to implement child-centered education was undermined by "politics in the schoolhouse."

Chapter 5

1. National Commission on Excellence in Education, *A Nation at Risk,* Cambridge, Mass.: USA Research, 1984, p. 5.

2. Ibid.

3. William J. Bennett, "Is Our Culture in Decline?," *Education Week,* April 7, 1993, p. 32. The eight cultural indicators are: average daily television viewing, SAT scores, percentage of illegitimate births, children with single mothers, children on wel-

fare, teen suicide rates, violent crime rates, and median prison sentences. Bennett's definition of the purpose of education is in keeping with that of educational progressives such as Ella Flagg Young. It is a definition that has not been generally used by conservative politicians or business leaders.

4. *Teacher Magazine,* October 1994, p. 11.

5. "Teacher Survey Cites Students' Lack of Readiness," *Education Week,* September 23, 1992, p. 11. 77% of teachers who worked with predominately poor youngsters said a significant proportion of their students were not ready to do grade-level work, versus 23% of teachers who worked with few children from the lowest socio-economic group. See also *The Condition of Teaching: A State Analysis,* Princeton, N. J., Carnegie Foundation for the Advancement of Teaching, 1988. In this study 89% of the teachers cited abused and neglected children as a problem in their school. These data jibe with my experience and that of my teaching colleagues.

6. "Dressing for Danger," *Education Week,* September 19, 1990, p. 3. The developer of the vest, former New York City policeman Stephen D'Andrilli, commented that the need for protective clothing for children "is a terrible reflection of the collapse of law and order in our society."

7. *Condition of Teaching;* "Protecting Yourself: What the Law Allows," *NEA Today,* February 1993, p. 20; "Growing Up Scared: How Our Kids Are Being Robbed of Their Childhood," *Newsweek,* January 10, 1994 (cover story).

8. "Report Calls for New Actions to Redress Inequalities Cited by Kerner Commission," *Education Week,* March 10, 1990, p. 8.

9. Daniel Weinberg, *Current Population Reports, June 1996,* Washington: U. S. Census Bureau, 1996.

10. "The Shrinking Middle Class," *Education Week,* March 4, 1992, p. 3. Those in the highest income brackets rose from 10.9% to 14.7% during the same period.

11. *Education Week,* September 29, 1993, p. 3. Data collected by the United Nations in 1991 show that the United States, with a childhood poverty rate of 22.3%, compares poorly to the former West Germany, which had a rate of 8.4%. The data on the United States are corroborated by the Children's Defense Fund's report, *The State of America's Children 1992; Education Week,* October 19, 1994, p. 4. The U. S. childhood poverty rate in 1993 inched up 0.4% to 22.7%.

12. Valerie Polakow, *Lives on the Edge;* Daniel Patrick Moynihan, *Family and Nation,* pp. 89–92.

13. "Tracking Hampers Minorities' Access to Math, Science Careers, Study Finds," *Education Week,* September 26, 1990, p. 8. The study, "Multiplying Inequalities: The Effects of Race, Social Class, and Tracking on Opportunities to Learn Mathematics and Science," was conducted by the RAND Corporation.

14. *Digest of Education Statistics, 1990,* Washington: United States Department of Education, 1991, p. 112.

15. U. S. Department of Commerce, *115th Statistical Abstract of the U. S., 1995,* Lanham, Md.: Bernam Press, 1995; *Digest of Educational Statistics, 1992,* Washington: U.S. Department of Education, 1993, p. 391. In 1989, women with five years of education beyond high school earned 60 cents to every dollar earned by men with comparable educational attainment, an increase of only 4 cents since 1972.

16. Ann Morrison, *Breaking the Glass Ceiling;* Terri A. Scandura, *Breaking the Glass Ceiling in the 1990's.*

17. Cynthia Taeuber, *Statistical Handbook on Women in America,* Oryx Press, 1991, p. 335. This represents a 4,700% increase. From 1964 to 1985 there was a 216% increase in the number of men graduating from law school.

18. *Syracuse Herald American,* October 9, 1994, p. D1. President Clinton, however, is naming women to the federal judiciary at a record rate. See also Paula Ries and Anne J. Stone, eds., *The American Woman, 1992–93,* p. 410. There is some improvement from the 1970s when, for example, only 2% of all judges in the southern district and circuit courts were female. See *Equal Employment Opportunity Practices in the Federal Judiciary,* Washington: GPO, 1981, p. 137.

19. Patricia Schmuck, ed., *Women Educators,* pp. 1, 11.

20. *Equal Opportunity for Women: Regents Policy Papers and Action Plan for the 1990s,* Albany: State Education Department, 1993, p. 5.

21. *Digest 1990,* pp. 238, 94, 77. In 1987–1988, 4,002 masters degrees in educational administration were awarded to men, while 5,583 were awarded to women. The Ph.D., fast becoming a requirement for the position of school superintendent, is earned by roughly equal numbers of men and women. In 1987–1988, 684 men earned a Ph.D. in educational administration; 621 women did so in that year. Nationally, only 24.5% of school principals were women, the vast majority of female principals working in elementary schools. In 1987–1988, 68.8% of the nation's public school teachers were women.

22. *Teacher Magazine,* May 1992, pp. 48–49.

23. *Education Week,* January 10, 1990, p. 3.

24. *Education Week,* January 15, 1992, p. 2. Women teachers in New York state filed a class action suit charging that the pension system's practices are discriminatory.

25. "More Girls are Playing Sports, but Fewer Women are Coaching Them," *Teacher Magazine,* October 1992, pp. 12–13.

26. *How Schools Shortchange Girls,* Washington, D.C.: American Association of University Women, 1992; Myra Sadker and David Sadker, *Failing at Success,* New York: Charles Scribner's Sons, 1994.

27. The case involved a student who was verbally harassed by her teacher over the course of a year. She alleged that she was forced to have sex with the teacher a number of times. Associate Justice Byron White, writing for the majority, cited *Meritor Savings Bank v. Vinson*, 106 S. Ct. 2399 (1985), a case of sexual harassment of a female employee by a supervisor in the private sector. His ruling permitted the student to sue for damages. *Education Week*, December 11, 1991, pp. 1, 15, and March 4, 1992, pp. 1, 24.

28. *Digest, 1990*, pp. 91–92; *Digest of Educational Statistics*, 1995, Washington, U. S. Department of Education, 1995, p. 92.

29. "Where Principals Come From," *Education Week*, March 17, 1993, p. 7.

30. *Digest, 1990*, p. 104.

31. "Armed with Research, Georgia Legislator Takes Aim at Plans for Consolidation," *Education Week*, November 20, 1991, p. 23. The legislator, Representative Charles Thomas, cited an article by William Fowler Jr. and Herbert Walberg in the journal *Education Evaluation and Policy Analysis* (Summer 1990). The authors published the findings of their study, which indicated that larger schools correlated with poorer student outcomes as measured by test scores, retentions, suspensions, employment, and college attendance.

32. *Education Week*, March 3, 1993, p. 3.

33. Shedd and Bacharach, *Tangled Hierarchies*, p. 2.

34. *Digest, 1990*, p. 83. In constant 1989 dollars, the 1972 average annual salary of teachers was $29,344. In 1980 the average salary was $25,256. In 1989 the average salary rose to $30,497, about a 4% increase over the 1972 figure.

35. The following beginning salaries for 1992 college graduates were estimated by the Northwestern University Lingquist Report and NEA: teaching—$22,000; business administration, $27,700; chemistry, $30,900; and engineering, $34,700. *NEA Today*, March 1993, p. 32.

36. *Digest, 1990*, p. 83.

37. *Education Week*, April 1, 1992, p. 6. A 1990 Carnegie Foundation study found that 96% of teachers spend their own money for materials. This finding was corroborated by a New York State United Teachers study, which found that New York teachers spend approximately $62 million annually for basic supplies such as toilet paper, food for children's lunches, pencils, books, used clothing, art and theater supplies. The average individual outlay was $333 a year, with amounts ranging from zero to $2,500 annually.

38. "Many Minority Teachers Plan to Quit, Poll Finds," *New York Times*, October 5, 1988; "Many New Teachers in Louisiana are Throwing in the Towel," *Education Week*, November 10, 1994, p. 10.

39. Lee Friedman and Stephen Sugarman, "School Sorting and Disclosure," *Journal of Law and Education*, p. 53–89.

40. David Schimmel and Louis Fischer, *Parents, Schools and the Law*, pp. 134–42.

41. Michael Finch and Trevor Nagel, "Collective Bargaining," pp. 1573–1670.

42. Linda McNeil, *Contradictions of Control*, pp. 8–16.

43. *Digest, 1990*, p. 108; *Digest, 1995*, p. 111.

44. *Digest, 1995*, p. 44, *Digest, 1990*, p. 113.

45. *Education Week*, February 5, 1992, p. 9; Thomas Cochran, *Business in American Life*, p. 282.

46. Task Force in Education as a Profession, *A Nation Prepared*, 1986, p. 19. 85% of mothers surveyed were either satisfied or very satisfied with their children's academic performance; Theodore Sizer, *Horace's School*, p. 11.

47. *Digest, 1990*, p. 95. For example, in a survey begun in 1965, secondary school principals have consistently rated basic skill acquisition the number one purpose of school. Appreciation for and experience with the fine arts has been rated lowest among the possible purposes of education; *Teacher Magazine*, January 1996, pp. 18–19. A 1995 study conducted by Public Agenda showed that the public highly valued basic skills, order, and safety in the schools.

48. Sizer, *Horace's School*, p. 127.

49. Larry Cuban, *How Teachers Taught*, p. 209; Dow, *Schoolhouse*, pp. 5–7.

50. "Study Finds U. S. Schools Lag in Learning Attitudes," *Education Week*, April 7, 1993, p. 16. An author of the study, Donald Chalker, concluded that American schools are organized to deliver what most Americans want, and that is not serious, rigorous learning. See also "Well Off Schools Ponder Barriers to Reform," *Education Week*, February 2, 1994, pp. 1, 7.

51. Secretary of education Richard Riley, in *NEA Today*, March 1993, p. 6.

52. Thomas Timar and David Kirp, *Managing Educational Excellence*, pp. ix, 4.

53. *Digest, 1990*, p. 80; *GERR*, vol. 26, September 1988, pp. 1319–20. Boyer wrote, "We are beginning to discover that outside regulation has its limits. Education is a human enterprise with teachers and students interacting with each other. There is just so much that can be accomplished by directives from above."

54. Arthur Wise, "Professional Teaching," in *Schooling for Tomorrow*, Thomas Sergiovanni and John Moore, eds., pp. 301–10.

55. Robert Reich, "Education and the Next Economy," in *Education Reform*, Samuel Bacharach, ed., 1990.

56. Marc Tucker. Address made at "Building on Collective Bargaining," a conference on education reform jointly sponsored by the Public Employee Relations Board and

the New York State School of Industrial and Labor Relations, October 25, 1988, Rochester, N. Y.

57. *A Nation Prepared*, p. 13.

58. "Preparing Your Child for the 21st Century," *McCall's Magazine*, September 1989, pp. 41–49. The article quotes Robert Reich as well as the Bureau of Labor Statistics to make the case that the changing work place requires a radical change in the type of education we offer children.

59. Peter Drucker, "How Schools Must Change," *Psychology Today*, May 1989, pp. 18–20.

60. Arthur Wirth, *Education and Work*.

61. *A Nation Prepared*, p. 15.

62. "Vision of Schooling in the 'Information Age' Sought," *Education Week*, November 24, 1993, p. 5; "The Last Mile," *Education Week*, March 2, 1994, pp. 31–34.

63. "Americans Give Schools Low Marks on Job Preparation, Poll Asserts," *Education Week*, September 12, 1990, p. 2.

64. "First State-Level Assessment Finds Wide Variation," *Education Week*, June 12, 1991, pp. 1, 23.

65. "Panel Blueprint Seeks to Relate School to Work," *Education Week*, April 15, 1992, pp. 1, 10.

66. "Lacking Good Results, Corporations Rethink Aid to Public Schools," *Wall Street Journal*, June 27, 1989, pp. A1, A8.

67. David Osborne and Ted Gaebler, *Reinventing Government*, p. 16.

68. Milo Hillegas, *The Elements*, p. 5.

69. Preston Townley, president and CEO of the Conference Board (1991). Barbara Peters and Jim Peters, eds., *Total Quality Management*, New York: Conference Board, 1991, p. 5.

70. Ibid., pp. 10–11.

71. Other current, albeit less popular, management models share the concept of managers as leaders who must pursue efficient production through inclusion of subordinates in decision-making. See Robert Blake and Jane Mouton, *Managerial Grid III*, Houston: Gulf Publishing Co., 1985.

72. Peters and Peters, *Management*, pp. 7, 10, 11.

73. Ibid., p. 10.

74. Ibid., p. 11.

75. Andy Banks and Jack Metzger, *Participating in Management*, pp. 2–5. Many in the labor movement are suspicious of this new version of industrial relations, fearing that management is using participation and cooperation to gain productivity and quality improvements without relinquishing any real control over the goals and processes of the organization. One long-time observer of labor-management relations asks, "Isn't a boss by any other name still a boss?"

76. Peters and Peters, *Management*, p. 11.

77. Frederick Taylor, *The Principles*, p. 13.

78. Peters and Peters, *Management*, p. 7.

79. Sergiovanni and Moore, *Schooling for Tomorrow*, p. 5; Blake and Mouton, *Grid*, p. 13.

80. Corporations such as IBM, Sears, General Motors—and its Saturn subsidiary—have all received much media coverage for their efforts to decentralize decision-making. For an example of such coverage in the popular media, see "The Fall of the Dinosaurs," *Newsweek*, November 23, 1992, p. 47.

81. *Newsweek*, November 30, 1992, pp. 62, 63.

82. Phillip Schlechty, *Schools for the 21st Century*, p. xvi. Employee involvement has not occurred because business leaders have agreed to the premises of industrial democracy. Rather, it is motivated by the idea that employees who have knowledge must be in a position to apply what they know for purposes of efficiency. Genuine work place democracy is predicated on the assumption that workers have the *right* to participate in decisions that affect their lives.

83. Peters and Peters, *Management*, p. 12.

84. Kathryn Troy, *Employee Buy-in to Total Quality*, p. 11.

85. Ibid., p. 14. In companies that say they are very much satisfied with progress toward involving employees in TQM, the level of support for TQM varies greatly by level in the organization. 87% of top management, 37% of middle management, and 25% of first-line supervisors say they are extremely well satisfied with involving employees in the TQM process.

86. Peters and Peters, *Management*, p. 11.

87. Troy, *Employees*, p. 14. In fact, "buy in" by middle and front-line managers has been weak. This has been viewed as a major obstacle to implementation of the new management model.

88. "A Touching Presidency: Bill Clinton is a Boss for the New Age," *Newsweek*, February 22, 1993, p. 44.

89. Osborne and Gaebler, *Government*, p. xvii.

90. Ibid., p. 181.

91. Ibid., pp. 106–7.

92. Jerome Rosow and Robert Zager, *Allies in Educational Reform*, pp. 13–14, 52–57.

93. David Kearns and Denis Doyle, *Winning the Brain Race.*

94. Ibid., p. 3.

95. Kearns and Doyle, *Winning*, p. 8.

96. Ibid., pp. 4–5.

97. Ibid., pp. 10, 20, 46–49, 39. It is noteworthy that Kearns's redefinition of management's role is similar to that proposed by teacher unions in the sixties. He proposes that principals and teachers cooperatively manage schools, i.e., profit and loss centers. Together they should act as suppliers who create a specialized curriculum aimed at attracting customers (parents).

98. Drucker, "Schools," pp. 18–20; Marc Tucker, "Creating an 'Entrepreneurial' School System," *Education Week,* June 21, 1989, pp. 36, 26; Richard Sagor, "The False Premises of Strategic Planning," *Education Week,* April 1, 1992, p. 28; Chris Shy, "Strategic Planning or the 'Titanic Solution,' " *Education Week,* April 29, 1992; p. 29; Steven Frankel, "There Are Better Ways to Cut Costs," *Education Week,* March 17, 1993, pp. 36, 27; "Thefts in Detroit Spur Inventory Control Efforts," *Education Week,* March 30, 1994, pp. 1, 10; Dale Mann, "Bankrolling Educational Entrepreneurs," *Education Week,* December 5, 1990, pp. 32, 23.

99. Schlechty, *Schools.* Schlechty's work was funded by Matsushita and Bell South. He is a former sociology professor at the University of North Carolina. He now heads the Center for Leadership in School Reform in Louisville, Kentucky.

100. Ibid., p. xvi.

101. Ibid., pp. 14–15

102. Ibid., p. 36.

103. Ibid., pp. 44, 49–50. Although Schlechty advocates participatory management, acknowledging that good ideas come from people at all levels of the school organization, he feels that top school managers should lead a school district. As he puts it, "one's ideas do not . . . necessarily deteriorate as one moves up the hierarchy."

104. Ibid., p. 52. Schlechty points out that similarities between shared decision-making and democratic school governance are merely coincidental.

105. Ibid. pp. 56, 95, 59, 111–14.

106. Raymond Callahan, *Education and the Cult of Efficiency.*

107. The advertisement shown in Figure 5.1 comes from the March 2, 1994 (p. 54) issue of *Education Week.* Figures 5.2 and 5.3 appeared in the May 19, 1993 (p. 17) and February 16, 1994 (p. 39) issues of *Education Week.*

108. William Glasser, M.D., *The Quality School: Managing Students Without Coercion,* 1992; idem, *The Quality School Teacher: A Companion Volume to the Quality School,* 1993; Leo Bradley, Ed.D., *Total Quality Management for Schools,* 1993.

109. *NEA Today,* April 1993, p. 7. The Tupelo district has used corporate grants to bring TQM into the schools; William Berkson, "Mastery Learning and 'Total Quality,'" *Education Week,* March 24, 1993, p. 46. Johnson City, New York, has been cited as one of the best working examples of TQM in the education setting.

110. "Schools Getting Swept Up in Current of Business's 'Quality' Movement," *Education Week,* March 11, 1993, pp. 1, 25–27; Lewis Rhodes, "Is There a Standard for Meeting Standards?", *Education Week,* April 6, 1994, pp. 33–40.

111. "Business Officials Extol 'Principal for a Day' Program," *Education Week,* March 17, 1993, pp. 6–7.

112. "Workforce Skills Hamper Productivity, Manufacturers Say," *Education Week,* December 11, 1991, p. 5.

112. "Fed Up with Tinkering, Reformers Now Touting 'Systemic Approach,'" *Education Week,* September 9, 1992, pp. 1, 30. The nine-point agenda on school restructuring fits hand-in-glove with omnibus school reform bills introduced into Congress in 1992. The bills, S2 and HR 4323, encouraged "systemic change in our schools" according to the Business Roundtable; Joseph Gorman, "Harsh Reality at Graduation Season," *Education Week,* June 21, 1995, pp. 60, 51. Mr. Gorman is CEO of TRW Inc. Until 1995 he was chairman of the Roundtable's Education Task Force, a group committed to the state-by-state transformation of the nation's schools.

114. "Business Roundtable Assessing State Progress on Reforms," *Education Week,* November 20, 1991, p. 22. For example, in the state of Iowa the director of operations for the Iowa Business and Education Roundtable logged 26,000 miles speaking to civic, business, and education groups in an effort to convince them of the need for, as well as the efficacy of, the roundtable's nine-point agenda. See also "Signing the Public Up," *Education Week,* April 7, 1993, pp. 9–14. In Flint, Michigan, the Flint Roundtable combined with the local newspaper and the Charles Stewart Mott Foundation to wage a public relations campaign on school reform.

115. "Arizona Leaders Issue School-Reform Plan," *Education Week,* November 14, 1990, p. 22.

116. "LEARN Begins Community Meetings on its Proposal to Improve Schools," *Los Angeles Times*, February 17, 1993, p. B3; "LEARN Launches Publicity Campaign," *Los Angeles Times*, February 19, 1993, p. B4; "Amid Uncertainty, Los Angeles Board Approves Reform Plan," *Education Week*, March 24, 1993, p. 5; "Reform Plan Runs Up against a Divided Union," *Education Week*, June 9, 1993, pp. 1, 19, 20.

117. Centre for Educational Research and Innovation, *Schools and Business: A New Partnership*, Paris: Organization for Economic Cooperation and Development, 1992, p. 7.

118. Schlechty, *Schools*, p. 14.

119. Ibid., p. 14.

120. *Education Week*, April 7, 1993, p. 11.

121. "Board to Oversee School-Business Clearinghouse," *Education Week*, June 20, 1990, p. 8; National Advisory Council on Vocational Education, *A Nation at Work: Education and the Private Sector*, Washington, D.C.: National Alliance of Business, 1984.

122. *Education: The Next Battleground for Corporate Survival, An Urgent Message from Twenty-One Harvard Business School Students*, Washington, D.C.: National Alliance of Business, 1990, p. vii.

123. *Education Week*, January 20, 1991, p. 15. These partnerships exist in small as well as large districts. Such a partnership exists in the small county in upstate New York where I teach. *Business + Education = Partnering for Employable Youth* is a flyer outlining several types of school-business partnerships in the county.

124. Rosow and Zager, *Allies*, p. 159; *Education Week*, April 7, 1993, p. 19.

125. "Corporations Back Up Their Calls for Reform by Lending Their Expertise to Schools," *Education Week*, November 14, 1990, pp. 10–11. See also *Education Week*, April 7, 1993, pp. 12, 19; *Education Week*, March 11, 1992, pp. 1, 25–27.

126. *Education Week*, October 18, 1989, pp. 11–12.

127. *Education Week*, March 17, 1993, pp. 6–7. Corporate managers found that there were many similarities between the school and the industrial work place.

128. "Bridging the Gap," *Education Week*, January 26, 1994, pp. 20–26.

129. "On the Career Track," *Education Week*, February 23, 1994, pp. 28–31.

130. "Despite Recession's Impact, Tampa High on School-to-Work Link," *Education Week*, February 26, 1992, pp. 1, 16–17.

131. "Putting Theory into Practice," *Education Week*, March 23, 1994, pp. 25–27. This article was part of the series "Learning to Earn," underwritten by the John D. and Catherine T. MacArthur Foundation; "Leading Business Executives Create Council to Promote School-to-Work Programs," *Education Week*, December 14, 1994, p. 19.

132. "Nearly 700 Teams Submit School-Design Overhauls," *Education Week*, March 11, 1992, pp. 1, 22. This competition was funded by the New American Schools Development Corporation, a private group of 226 business partners, 140 colleges, and 136 think tanks; "Five 'Next Century' Projects Get Final RJR Grant," *Education Week*, April 28, 1993, p. 8.

133. "Consortium to Scrutinize Productivity of Education," *Education Week*, April 1, 1992, p. 12. This consortium is funded by the Ball Foundation, a philanthropy of Geo. Ball, Inc., a garden and agriculture firm.

134. "A Matter of Choice: Minnesota Puts 'Charter Schools' Idea to Test," *Education Week*, November 25, 1992, pp. 1, 10–11.

135. *Education Week*, November 11, 1992, p. 6.

136. "Basic Training," *Education Week*, March 24, 1993, p. 17.

137. "Annenberg Gift Prompts Praise and Questions," *Education Week*, January 12, 1994, pp. 1, 12, 13; "Annenberg Gift May Focus on Four Urban Areas," *Education Week*, June 8, 1994, pp. 1, 14.

138. "Whittle Unveils Team to Design New Schools," *Education Week*, March 4, 1992, pp. 1, 13; "Massachusetts Officials Endorse Idea of Whittle Run Schools," *Education Week*, October 20, 1993, p. 16; "Edison Project Applies to Run 5 Charter Schools," *Education Week*, February 23, 1994, p. 10; "Milwaukee Eyes Edison Project to Run Some District Schools," *Education Week*, March 16, 1994, p. 4.

139. "Disney Holds Up School as Model for Next Century," *Education Week*, June 22, 1994, pp. 1, 16. Disney had given serious consideration to investing as much as $500 million in Whittle's Edison Project in 1993. It also considered hiring EAI to run this new school before deciding to manage the school itself.

140. "For-Profit Firm Hired to Manage Schools in Duluth," *Education Week*, March 18, 1992, pp. 1, 18; "Dade County School is Marketing Tool for Company Seeking Profit in the Public Sector," *Education Week*, April 14, 1993, pp. 1, 12–13; "EAI Reaches Tentative Accord to Run Michigan District," *Education Week*, January 19, 1994, p. 3; "Education, Inc.," *Education Week*, December 15, 1993, p. 34.

141. "Signing Up the Public: The Community at Large Must Help Pull the Lever for Change," *Education Week*, April 7, 1993, pp. 9–14.

142. "Former E.D. Official, Xerox Chief Kearns to Head NASDC," *Education Week*, June 16, 1993, p. 5; "Former IBM Executive Appointed to NASDC President," *Education Week*, December 15, 1993, p. 4.

143. *Education Week*, October 20, 1993, p. 44.

144. *A School is a Workplace*, New York: New York State Industrial Cooperation Council, 1989. In this report, parallels are drawn between the school and the industrial

work place. Collaborative decision-making and labor-management cooperation are touted as industrial models that ought to be adopted by schools.

145. Centre for Educational Research and Innovation, *Schools and Business*, p. 14.

146. National Education Association, *Site-Based Decisionmaking: the 1990 NEA Census of Local Associations*, Washington, D.C.: NEA, 1991, pp. 2, 8, 18. Over 52% of districts reported state-level support of site-based decision-making, with 46% reporting financial incentives tied to decentralization. An example of state-level support of decentralization is New York State Education Commissioner's Regulation 100.11, which mandated every district to develop a decentralization plan by February 1994.

147. "Quality-Management Movement Spurs Interest in New Awards for Education," *Education Week*, March 18, 1993, p. 8. Interestingly, W. Edwards Deming, developer of the TQM process, called these awards "misguided" because they focus solely on results rather than on the principles of quality management; *Education Week*, December 8, 1993, p. 5.

148. Commission on Achieving Necessary Skills, *What Work Requires of Schools: A SCANS Report for America 2000*, Washington, D.C.: U. S. Dept. of Labor, 1991, p. 1. McLaughlin left the Department of Labor post to head the New American Schools Development Corporation in 1991, an organization formed at the request of the Bush administration.

149. Ibid., pp. 2–6.

150. Ibid., p. 12.

151. "President Signs School-to-Work Transition Law," *Education Week*, May 1994, pp. 1, 21.

152. "Human Capital Touted in Clinton Economic Agenda," *Education Week*, June 22, 1994, pp. 1, 24, 25.

153. *Teacher Magazine*, May 1993, p. 44. A Harris poll of new graduates of education schools was taken in 1990. The same questions were asked of them after completing their first and second years of teaching. As new graduates, only 28% felt their students' personal problems would interfere with school success. This figure rose to 47% after one year of teaching and 50% after two years of teaching.

Chapter Six

1. Michael Kirst, an education professor at Stanford, has said in regard to decentralization, "The assumption is, you let off input regulations, and 1,000 flowers will bloom." *Education Week*, March 17, 1993, p. 13.

2. A clarification in terminology: the *early* pro-efficiency reformers refers to the coalition formed around the turn of the century to institute centralized, bureaucratic management in education and introduce the principles of scientific management into the teaching-learning process. The *new* pro-efficiency reformers are working today to rid

schools of both bureaucracy and vestiges of scientific management, replacing them with TQM, and much of the educational progressives' recommendations from the turn of the century.

3. Many education reformers have written on how the bureaucratic school structure cannot deliver this newly popular concept of education. See Theodore Sizer, *Horace's Compromise*. Larry Cuban, *How Teachers Taught;* idem, *The Managerial Imperative*. Philip Schlechty, *Schools for the Twenty-First Century*.

4. Linda McNeil, *Contradictions in Control*.

5. Theodore Sizer, *Horace's School: Redesigning the American High School*.

6. Samuel Bacharach and Joseph Shedd, "Power and Empowerment," in *The Politics of Reforming School Administration*, p. 149.

7. Among the many corporations and foundations that provide funding for Sizer's work in school reform are Citibank, Aetna Life and Casualty Foundation, Exxon Education Foundation, RJR Nabisco Foundation, the Xerox Foundation, the William Randolph Hearst Foundation, the Rockefeller Brothers Fund, and the Annenberg Foundation.

8. Sizer, *Horace's Compromise*, p. 211.

9. Ibid., pp. 212–13.

10. Schlechty, *Schools*, pp. 51–52. Schlechty prefers to discuss teacher participation in decision-making less on ethical terms and more in terms of getting better results from schools. Schlechty writes, "Indeed, it seems likely that one of the reasons why those who control our schools distrust the idea of teacher empowerment . . . is that the arguments for participatory leadership have too often been framed in terms of truth, beauty, and justice rather than in terms of organizational effectiveness."

11. Gary Philips Speech given in Racine, Wisconsin, broadcast on the Wingspread Series on Issues in Education, WRVO, Oswego, New York, April 11, 1993.

12. Joanne Yatvin, "Let More Teachers 'Reinvent the Wheel,'" *Education Week*, September 19, 1990, p. 25.

13. Ella Flagg Young, *Isolation in the School*, p. 4.

14. Sizer, *Horace's School*, p. xi.

15. "Dewey Disciple: A Conversation With the Most Ardent Backer of Active Learning," *Wall Street Journal*, September 11, 1992, p. B4. Sizer, in fact, sees himself as a disciple of John Dewey's theory of education.

16. John Dewey, *The Educational Situation*, p. 30.

17. John Dewey, *The School and Society*, p. 35. Accordingly, the educational program would vary from school to school and from year to year, depending on the children involved.

18. Susan Rosenholtz, "Effective Schools," pp. 352–87.

19. Task Force on Teaching as a Profession, *A Nation Prepared: Teachers for the 21st Century*, Carnegie Forum on Education and the Economy, 1986, p. 25.

20. Kenneth Sirotnik, "The School as the Center of Change," in *Schooling for Tomorrow: Directing Reforms to Issues that Count*, Thomas Sergiovanni and John Moore, eds., Boston: Allyn and Bacon, 1989, pp. 89–113. Sirotnik writes that knowledge "is always situated in a human context of beliefs, values and interests." Through rational discourse he expects that teachers will tease out—resurrect from the individual and collective subconscious—tacit beliefs and values in their own knowledge and the knowledge of others.

21. Sizer, *Horace's Compromise*, pp. 87–88. Sizer feels that the state may encourage a person who wants to be employable, but compulsion is out of the question. The decision to learn skills that will be applicable in the work place is one the student and his or her family must be free to make.

22. Sizer, *Horace's School*, pp. 186–87.

23. Ibid., pp. 172–73, 179–80. Schools would be in charge of their own budgets, curriculum design, work rules for teachers, rules of behavior for students, etc.

24. Schlechty, *Schools*, p. 51.

25. Jerome Rosow and Robert Zager, *Allies in Reform*, pp. 6–7. As the authors see it, managers are those who bear responsibility for running the school system and the authority to decide how education is to be conducted. Teachers have the power to make it happen.

26. Schlechty, *Schools*, p. 81.

27. Ibid., p. 149.

28. Philips, op. cit. (see note 11).

29. Peter Drucker, "How Schools Must Change," pp. 18–20.

30. Marc Tucker Speech given at the conference, "Building on Collective Bargaining," sponsored by the Public Employee Relations Board and the New York State School of Industrial and Labor Relations. Rochester, New York, October 25, 1988.

31. Joseph Murphy, *Restructuring Schools*, p. 24.

32. Ibid., p. 26.

33. J. T. Murphy, "The Paradox of Decentralizing Schools: Lessons from Business, Government, and the Catholic Church," *Phi Delta Kappan*, June 1989, pp. 808–12.

34. Mark Maier, "A Feminist Lens: Contrasting Gendered Organizational Practice," Working paper, 1992.

35. " 'Outstanding' Teachers Say They Want Leading Role in Restructuring Efforts." *Education Week*, June 29, 1990, p. 8; 96% of the teachers surveyed in this Gallup poll said they welcomed more involvement in curricular, budget, and scheduling decisions.

36. Murphy, *Restructuring*, pp. 29–33.

37. Young, *Isolation*, pp. 21–22.

38. Murphy, *Restructuring*, p. 45. An extension of this idea is that the school should become a community center that provides a variety of services for both adults and children.

39. Rosow and Zager, *Allies*, pp. 12, 20–28; Robert Doherty and David Lipsky, "The Education Reform Movement and the Realities of Collective Bargaining," Proceedings of the 41st Annual Meeting, Industrial Relations Research Association, 1988, pp. 52–58; Thomas Kochan, Harry Katz, and Robert McKersie, *The Transformation of American Industrial Relations*, pp. 176–205.

40. NEA Research, *Site-Based Decision-Making: The NEA 1990 Census of Local Associations*, Washington, D.C.: NEA, 1991, pp. 10–11. School management unilaterally initiated SBDM in 44% of the local districts that had embarked on decentralization via SBDM. The local teachers' union worked with the school management in 30% of the districts with SBDM projects. Yet only 19% of districts with such projects codified the agreement in the collective bargaining agreement. In 50% of the districts no agreement of any kind—e.g., an informal verbal agreement or a letter of agreement—existed between school management and the teachers' union.

41. Ibid., p. 14. Only 25% of the districts surveyed had the union appoint teacher representatives to SBDM projects; Sizer, *Horace's School*, pp. 193–95. Sizer calls this type of unilateral implementation of SBDM "sadly ironic" and a reaffirmation of the idea that central office management knows best in all matters. He warns that this will inevitably lead teachers at the school site to an "ugly cynicism and reinforcement of their belief that central office leaders (are) hypocrites."

42. "New York City Schools Take First Steps Toward Management at the School Site," *Education Week*, May 9, 1990, p. 5; "Despite Fiscal Crunch, New York City To Raise Teachers' Pay by 5.5%," *Education Week*, October 10, 1990, p. 6. "Remembering 1988," *Education Week*, January 11, 1989, pp. 2–3; "How School-Based Management is Faring in Miami," *Education Week*, June 12, 1991, p. 26; Rosow and Zager, *Allies*, chapter 9 on Cincinnati; "L.A. Board Adopts Guidelines on School-Based Management," *Education Week*, April 4, 1990, p. 5; "Uneasy Alliance Marks Launch of L.A. Plan," *Education Week*, April 11, 1990, pp. 1, 10; "Amid Uncertainty, Los Angeles Board Approves Reform Plan," *Education Week*, March 24, 1993, p. 5.

43. Joseph Shedd, "Participation Through Bargaining: Collective Bargaining, School Reform, and the Management of School Systems," in *Education Reform: Making Sense of It All*, Samuel Bacharach, ed., Boston; Allyn and Bacon, 1990, pp. 92–102; Charles

Kerchner and Douglas Mitchell, *Changing Idea of a Teachers' Union*, New York: Falmer Press, 1988; Susan Moore Johnson. "Pursuing Professional Reform in Cincinnati," *Phi Delta Kappan*, June 1988, pp. 746–51.

44. Shedd, "Participation," p. 100.

45. *A Nation Prepared*, p. 95.

46. "Basic Training," *Education Week*, March 24, 1993, pp. 14–15.

47. Sizer, *Horace's Compromise*, p. 150; John Board. "Great Teachers are not Solo Performers," *Education Week*, April 29, 1992, p. 28.

48. Carnegie Foundation for the Advancement of Teaching, "Teacher Involvement in Decision-Making: A State by State Profile." Summary published in *GERR*, Vol. 29, pp. 1319–20, September 1988.

49. *A Nation Prepared*, p. 2.

50. George Counts, *The Social Foundations of Education*, New York: Charles Scribners' Sons, 1934, pp. 555–56.

51. *A Nation Prepared*, p. 81. White education majors' mean combined SAT scores were 932. The mean combined scores for black education majors was 715.

52. Rita Kramer, "Reciting the Sins of a 'Professional Education Industry,'" *Education Week*, October 23, 1991, p. 36. Kramer has also written *Ed School Follies*.

53. *A Nation Prepared*, p. 25.

54. Richard Schwab, "Reforming Teacher Education: Lessons Learned from a Five Year Program," in Bacharach, *Education Reform*, pp. 325–40.

55. Michael Sedlak, "Reforming Teacher Education," *Teachers College Record*, Spring 1987, pp. 314–25. This article summarizes the findings of the Holmes Group Report on overhauling teacher education.

56. Albert Shanker, "The Conditions of Teaching: Flexibility and Authority in the Classroom," in Bacharach, *Education Reform*, p. 357.

57. New York State Industrial Cooperation Council, *A School is a Workplace*, New York, 1989, p. 3.

58. Barnett Berry, Christine McCormick, and Tom Buxton, "Recruiting the Next Generation of Teachers," *American Educator*, Spring 1989, pp. 38–44.

59. Shanker, "Conditions," p. 360.

60. Recall that teacher unions in the 1960s sought to free teachers from these duties. Although collective bargaining put a limit on how many of these duties a teacher would have to perform, it did not lead to their elimination.

61. *A Nation Prepared*, pp. 57–62; "Time and Space," *Education Week*, March 3, 1993, pp. 13–19. Educators such as John Goodlad have recommended that teachers be hired on a year-round basis in order to provide the necessary time for professional planning and development.

62, "Basic Training," *Education Week*, p. 15.

63. Ibid., pp. 15–16.

64. Sirotnik, "School," pp. 93–100.

65. "Ohio Lawmakers Sanction Teacher Peer-Reviews as Fair," *Education Week*, March 7, 1990, p. 14.

66. "Hammond, Ind., Teachers and District Agree to Unprecedented 12 Year Pact," *Education Week*, March 7, 1990, p. 10.

67. "Dade County Will Solicit Ideas Nationwide for Design, Structuring of 49 New Schools," *Education Week*, June 7, 1989, pp. 1, 21.

68. Paul Hill, Arthur Wise, and Leslie Shapiro, *Educational Progress*.

69. NEA, *Preliminary Report of the 1990–91 Resolutions Committee*, Washington, D.C.: NEA, 1991, p. 47.

70. "Futrell Hints NEA Will Give Local More Support in Risky Reform Efforts," *Education Week*, February 8, 1989, pp. 1, 20; "NEA State Coordinators Launch Search for 'Learning Laboratories,'" *Education Week*, February 15, 1989, p. 6; "In 'Second Wave' of NEA Research Project, a Handful of Schools Apply Lessons Learned," *Education Week*, June 12, 1991, pp. 6–7. The "first wave" of reforms did not produce the changes NEA had hoped for because of the lack of broad community support.

71. "NEA Creates Center to Promote School Renewal Efforts," *Education Week*, February 28, 1990, p. 5.

72. Sizer, *Horace's School*, p. 5.

73. William Bagley, *Classroom Management*, p. 16.

74. "Balanced" sections in a given elementary grade are often created by dint of distribution of children by gender, race, and reading scores. Rarely considered is whether a particular child would work best with a particular teacher.

75. Sizer, *Horace's School*, p. 35.

76. "New York Chief Outlines Plan for 'Results' System," *Education Week*, May 30, 1990, pp. 1, 16; "Taking Account: States Move from 'Inputs' to 'Outcomes' in Effort to Regulate Schools," *Education Week*, March 17, 1993, pp. 9–13.

77. "Panel Blueprint Seeks to Relate School to Work," *Education Week*, April 15, 1992, pp. 1, 10.

78. "Taking Account," *Education Week*, pp. 11, 12. An opponent of the Pennsylvania state outcomes, which included "tolerance" and "cooperation," said, "We believe the purpose of public schools is to teach academics. Period"; "With Students' Aid, Clinton Signs Goals 2000," *Education Week*, April 6, 1994, pp. 1, 21; "The Threat to Freedom in Goals 2000," *Education Week*, April 6, 1994, pp. 52, 40.

79. Sizer, *Horace's Compromise*, pp. 89, 135–37.

80. Murphy, *Restructuring*, pp. 50–63.

81. "Budget Cutters, School Reformers Taking Aim at Gifted Education," *Education Week*, March 18, 1992, pp. 1, 14, 15. Cooperative learning aims to eliminate the academic and psychological damage done to children consigned to lower ability groups.

82. "The Group Classroom: Why Team Learning May Finally Be Catching On," *Newsweek*, May 10, 1993, p. 73; Dewey, *School*, p. 13.

83. "Vocational Ed Students Benefit from Academics," *Teacher Magazine*, February 7, 1993, p. 7.

84. *A Nation Prepared*, p. 61.

85. "Time and Space: Reformers Explore New Frontiers to Escape the Confines of 'Cells and Bells,'" *Education Week*, March 3, 1993, pp. 13–19.

86. "Personal Best," *Teacher Magazine*, October 1992, pp. 30–34. This article describes an alternative school in Modesto, Calif., that works as a school community; Sizer, *Horace's School*, pp. 197, 208, 189; Sizer, *Horace's Compromise*, pp. 121–23. The values Sizer recommends as the basis for school communities are decency, fairness, generosity, and tolerance; "Right and Wrong: Teaching Values Makes A Comeback," *Wall Street Journal*, September 11, 1992, p. B6; "National Commitment to Parent Role in Schools Sought," *Education Week*, April 15, 1992, pp. 1, 11.

87. Standardized tests also had the purpose of insuring that teachers followed the mandated curriculum—i.e., they were a control device used by management to insure that teachers did not stray far afield from what school or state authorities directed.

88. "The Trouble With Tests, Part Two," *Newsweek*, October 26, 1992, p. 58.

89. Ross Brewer, "Can Performance Assessment Survive Success?" *Education Week*, April 15, 1992, p. 28.

90. "Large 'Faculty Meeting' Ushers in Pioneering Assessment in Vermont," *Education Week*, October 10, 1990, pp. 1, 18; Sizer, *Horace's School*, pp. 159–62.

91. Cuban, *How Teachers Taught*, p. 221.

92. The Alternative Community School in Ithaca, New York, was established in the 1970s. It was tolerated for years by school officials as a place for teachers, parents, and students considered to be on the fringe of the community. In the early 1990s it was

singled out as one of 13 schools in the state embodying the principles of the New York State Regents' reform agenda, the New Compact for Learning. It was one of the first 200 schools in the nation accepted into the Coalition of Essential Schools headed by Theodore Sizer. The school is cited by local school board members—including a retired bank president—as the ideal for other schools in the district to fashion themselves after.

93. Murphy, *Restructuring*, p. 92.

94. There are rare exceptions to this rule. In Kentucky the state legislature created parent-teacher councils at every school to take over much of the power wielded by local school boards. For a discussion of Kentucky's reform effort, see "Trailing in Education For Years, Kentucky Tries Radical Reforms," *Wall Street Journal*, January 5, 1993, pp. A1, A6; "Off and Running," *Education Week*, April 21, 1993, pp. 4–11. For a discussion of the 1988 law that empowered parents to run school councils in Chicago, see the following editions of *Education Week:* January 10, 1990, p. 3; December 5, 1990, p. 11; November 20, 1991, p. 8; April 8, 1992, p. 4. For articles updating Chicago's experience with reform, see 'Strong Democracy Yields Improvements in Chicago Reforms,' July 14, 1993, pp. 1, 13; "Council Votes Spur New Round of Questions in Chicago," November 3, 1993, pp. 1, 14, 15. See also "Good Intentions," *Teacher Magazine*, March 1993, pp. 28–32.

95. For example, the scope of bargaining in education has not been expanded to included teachers' professional concerns. Education reform initiatives are not mandatory subjects of bargaining. Thus, school employers can implement a host of reform initiatives unilaterally. Teachers can only force bargaining on the impact of those initiatives on their wages, hours, and conditions of employment.

96. "Redefine Role, Duties of School Boards To Focus on Policy, Report Advocates," *Education Week*, April 8, 1992, pp. 1, 14.

97. For an example of criticism in this vein, see "In the Press," *Education Week*, September 12, 1990, p. 27. The article summarizes an issue of *The Washington Monthly* devoted to appraising school management.

98. Nailene Wiest, "When the Job Candidate Can't Count," *Education Week*, March 18, 1992, p. 27.

99. Nathan Glazer, "Do We Need Big-City School Superintendents?" *Education Week*, March 18, 1992, p. 36.

100. Ibid.

101. Jack Kaufhold, "An Ex-Superintendent on Why He Quit," *Education Week*, March 18, 1992, p. 26.

102. National School Boards Association, *Communicating Change*, p. 25.

103. Schlechty, *Schools*, p. xvi.

104. Tucker, see note 30, above.

105. "School Restructuring Efforts Forcing Principals to Redefine Their Roles," *Education Week*, November 1, 1989, pp. 1, 12.

106. Albert Shanker, "Shared Decision Making: Why Managers Are Scared," *American Teacher*, May 1990, p. 5.

107. "Amid Uncertainty, Los Angeles Board Approves Reform Plan," *Education Week*, March 24, 1993, p. 5.

108. Lewis Rhodes, "Is There a Standard for Meeting Standards?" *Education Week*, April 6, 1994, pp. 33, 40. Rhodes was the associate director of the American Association of School Administrators in 1994.

109. "Fernandez Management Views Concerns of Principals," *Education Week*, October 11, 1989, p. 5.

110. Yatvin, *Education Week*, p. 25; Sizer, *Horace's School*, p. 61. Sizer agrees with Yatvin's appraisal. He adds that school boards "believe that only they know what the people really need."

111. Marc Tucker, "Creating an 'Entrepreneurial' School System" *Education Week*, June 21, 1989, pp. 36, 26. Other functions managers often reserve for themselves are the assessment of results and the structuring of rewards for good performance.

112. "Personal Best," *Teacher Magazine*, p. 34. For the full citation, see note 86, above.

113. "Scrap School Boards? What Would Replace Them?" *Education Week*, December 11, 1991, p. 28. Letter to the editor by Thomas Shannon, executive director of the National School Boards Association; Thomas Shannon. *Local Control of the Public Schools and Education Reform*, Alexandria, VA.: National School Boards Association, 1990.

114. "Communicating Change," p. i. For the full citation, see note 102, above.

115. Sizer, *Horace's School*, p. 61; "Chicago School Board's Restructuring Plan Rejected," *Education Week*, April 8, 1992, p. 4. The Chicago Board of Education was declared incapable of decentralizing decision-making to individual schools by an oversight panel charged by the governor and the mayor with assessing the board's efforts at reform.

116. "Denver Schools, Board in 'Power Struggle' Over Testing Policy," *Education Week*, March 4, 1992, p. 5.

117. "RJR Nabisco Lays $30 Million Bet on 'Bottom Up' Reform Strategy," *Education Week*, June 10, 1992, pp. 1, 11–12. Some individual schools that have received grant money have found themselves entangled in the web of district rules and regulations that have hamstrung their reform efforts.

118. Merle Marsh, "12 Difficulties Encountered When Attempting to Start a Revolution in Education," *Education Week*, November 25, 1992, p. 20.

119. Murphy, *Restructuring*, p. 94.

120. "Effort to Cut Back D.C.'s Bureaucracy Proves Nettlesome," *Education Week*, November 20, 1991, pp. 1, 18–19.

121. "Self Promotion," *Teacher Magazine*, February 1993, p. 6. The network is a consortium of the National Association of Secondary School Principals and its 43 state affiliates.

122. Ted Elsberg, "Restructuring Raises Doubts and Questions," paid advertisement in *Education Week*, January 10, 1990, p. 11.

123. Ted Elsberg, "Restructuring: No Help for Students," paid advertisement in *Education Week*, March 7, 1990, p. 7.

124. "School Restructuring," *Education Week*, p. 12.

125. Dewey, *School*, pp. 45, 37.

126. Young, *Isolation*, p. 12.

127. Jesse Newlon, *Educational Administration as Social Policy*, pp. 170–202. This idea that leadership can be exercised by people at all levels of the organization is very popular today. See Cuban, *The Management Imperative*, pp. 179–217.

128. Newlon, *Educational Administration*, pp. 231–45.

Chapter Seven

1. Catherine Spoto, president of the RCSD School Board, interview by the author, tape recording, Rochester, New York, April 1, 1993; Courtenay Slater and George Hall, eds., *1993 County and City Extra: Annual Metro, City and County Data Book*, Latham, Md.: Bernan Press, 1993. Rochester is situated in Monroe County. According to the 1990 census, the county has 271,944 households. The median income for county households is $35,337.

2. In Monroe County as a whole, 7.7% of the families live below the poverty line.

3. Adam Urbanski, "Real Change is Real Hard: Lessons Learned in Rochester," *Education Week*, October 23, 1991, p. 29.

4. *Rochester Report: Focus on the Family and Early Childhood Education*, a publication of the RCSD which began in the late 1980s.

5. "After Two Tough Years in Rochester, School Reformers Look to the Future," *Education Week*, October 18, 1989, pp. 1, 10–12.

6. Adam Urbanski. Address at the conference, "Building on Collective Bargaining," sponsored by the New York State School of Industrial and Labor Relations and the New York State Public Employee Relations Board, Rochester, New York, October 25, 1988.

7. Blake Rodman, "Friendship and Trust: Unusual Keys to Radical Pact," *Education Week*, Volume 7, number 4, September 30, 1987, pp. 1, 20–21.

8. Adam Urbanski, "Real Change is Real Hard: Lessons Learned in Rochester," *Stanford Law and Policy Review*, Winter 1992–93, pp. 123–34. Over 400 assaults against staff members are reported each year in Rochester; Salter and Hall, *County*. The violence in the schools mirrors the high incidence of violence in the greater community.

9. Peter McWalters. Address at conference, "Building." McWalters was superintendent of the RCSD at the time; Slater and Hall, *County*. While 70% of the children in the RCSD are African-American or Hispanic, 84.1% of the county population is white, reflecting the abandonment of the city for the suburbs by whites.

10. Edwin Bridges, *The Incompetent Teacher: Managerial Responses*, Washington, D.C.: Salmer, 1992 (revised edition).

11. Nancy Sundberg, interview by author, tape recording. Rochester, New York, April 1, 1993. Sundberg's disturbing findings are consistent with national figures for students labeled as having "a handicapping condition."

12. *Superintendent's Assessment and Proposed Mission*, adopted by the Board of Education, December 19, 1985.

13. Urbanski, "Real Change," *Education Week,* p. 29. There are two articles by Urbanski by the same title—one published in *Education Week,* one in *Stanford Law and Policy Review* (see chapter 7, notes 3 and 8, above).

14. McWalters, "Building." See also "Friendship," *Education Week,* p. 20. After returning from the Peace Corps in 1970, McWalters began his teaching career in the RCSD. He taught for a time in the district's alternative junior high school. He then was recruited for a job in the central office, which centered on the district's magnet schools project. Throughout his tenure in this job he kept his teacher status, going out on strike in 1980 with other members of the RTA. In the early 1980s he was chosen to head the district's budget office. When appointed superintendent he had never held the position of principal, coordinator, or director—typical stepping stones to the superintendency. This unusual career path would become significant in his effort to implement school change.

15. Urbanski, "Building."

16. "Friendship," *Education Week*, p. 1.

17. Task Force on Teaching as a Profession, *A Nation Prepared: Teachers for the 21st Century*, Washington, D.C.: Carnegie Forum on Education and the Economy, 1986.

18. Ibid., p. 2.

19. Urbanski, "Real Change," *Education Week*, p. 29.

20. Joanne Scully, interview by author, tape recording, Rochester, New York, April 8, 1993. At the time of this interview Ms. Scully was still the only central office administrator who had been hired from outside the district. Scully's duties centered on implementing site-based decision-making in the Rochester schools.

21. "All children can learn" became the centerpiece of the district's mission.

22. "Friendship," *Education Week*, p. 20.

23. Scully interview.

24. Thomas Gillett, interview by author, tape recording, Rochester, New York, March 11, 1993.

25. Scully interview.

26. Albert Shanker, "Building." In the 1980s Shanker argued that once they had developed a mature relationship, a strong union, and a strong school management could disregard the industrial model of bargaining and its associated narrow scope of bargaining. In this mature relationship, bargaining would be as Shanker had originally envisioned it—a forum for dealing with educational issues not only "wages, hours, and conditions of employment."

27. Spoto interview.

28. This was often referred to later as their "agreement to agree"—they agreed in principle to school-based planning, but would agree on the specifics of how it might operate in Rochester at a later date.

29. "After Two," *Education Week*, p. 10.

30. "Friendship," *Education Week*, p. 20.

31. Thomas Gillett and Kim Halkett, *Performance Appraisal Redesign for Teachers—A Report on Initial Efforts*, RCSD, 1989, p. 3.

32. "Friendship," *Education Week*, p. 21. Generous financial support from both the county and state government allowed the district to fund average raises of 40% over the three-year term of the agreement. The lion's share of the money came from the state legislature, which, according to McWalters, saw the money as an investment in the "production function" of schooling—the teacher being the key human resource involved in education. McWalter, "Building."

33. Spoto interview.

34. A peer assistance program already established by the district, whereby new teachers received mentors, was quickly incorporated into the "Career in Teaching" initiative.

35. "Friendship," *Education Week*, p. 20.

36. *A Nation Prepared*, p. 95.

37. Urbanski made the comment in August 1987 before the board ratified the three-year agreement. *Rochester Democrat and Chronicle*, March 31, 1993, p. 1A.

38. "Friendship," *Education Week*, p. 20.

39. Although Urbanski and McWalters were not specific about how student outcomes would be measured, it was assumed by both the public and the media that scores on standardized tests would reflect the improvements promised by their reform initiative.

40. In the 1960s teachers first won the right to transfer by seniority. This was seen as protection against school managers who punished teachers by transferring them to less desirable schools. With transfers theoretically out of the hands of school managers, teachers could give up seniority as the prime criterion used for transfer decisions.

41. McWalters, "Building." McWalters was frank about the fact that society was only now interested in having minority students succeed because the economic well-being of the nation depended upon it. While personally motivated by a desire for equity, McWalters said the economic imperative gave Rochester the opportunity to enter into this experiment aimed at breaking the link between race, poverty, and school achievement.

42. Adam Urbanski. "Restructuring Schools for Greater Choice: The Rochester Initiative" in *Education Reform: Making Sense of It All*, Samuel Bacharach, ed., Boston: Allyn and Bacon, 1990, pp. 298–308.

43. Gillett and Halkett, *Performance*, pp. 8–9.

44. Urbanski, "Real Change," Stanford, p. 127.

45. Urbanski, "Restructuring," p. 301.

46. "After Two," *Education Week*, p. 10.

47. Scully interview.

48. Ibid.

49. "After Two," *Education Week*, p. 1.

50. Richard Stear, president of the administrators' union in RCSD, interview by author, tape recording, Rochester, New York, April 1, 1993.

51. Spoto interview.

52. Gillett interview.

53. Rochester Business Educational Alliance, *Monroe County Educational Outcomes/Standards Project*, 1993, p. 1.

54. "Corporations Back Up Their Calls for Reform By Lending Their Expertise to Schools," *Education Week*, November 14, 1990, pp. 10–11.

55. Ibid., p. 10.

56. John Foley, interview by author, Rochester, New York, March 12, 1993. Foley cited this as an explanation for why many people he has worked with in schools fail to see the need for change.

57. "Rochester Site of Research Center," *Education Week*, January 13, 1988, p. 25. Besides directing the center, Tucker was appointed a professor in the education department at the University of Rochester as well as a policy analyst within the RCSD.

58. Ibid. In 1993 the chairman of the National Center's board of trustees was John Sculley, former CEO of Apple Computer. Former North Carolina governor, James Hunt, was the vice-chair. Hillary Rodman Clinton, Louis Harris, Ira Magaziner, David Rockefeller Jr., and former Kodak CEO, Kay Whitmore, were among the members of the board of trustees.

59. Ibid.

60. Scully interview.

61. "Corporations," *Education Week*, p. 10. John Foley, a Xerox employee for 27 years, subsequently left the company to work directly for the National Center.

62. Rochester City School District, *Teamwork*, Volume 1, Number 1, p. 6. The National Center provided training to members of the district in the principles of TQM on a continuous basis.

63. "After Two," *Education Week*, p. 12. The poll was part of the "Expectations Project" run by the National Center, a program to draw the community into the RCSD's mission. Kodak gave $200,000 and Gannett contributed $50,000 to fund the project.

64. *Rochester Business*, pp. 1, 3 (see note 53, above).

65. *Profile of Tomorrow's High School Graduate and Competitive Employee*. This profile was developed jointly between Eastman Kodak and the Greece district, a Rochester suburb, as part of the Monroe County project.

66. Catherine Spoto says that GOMS was jointly developed by the school board and area businesses. Spoto interview.

67. Scully interview.

68. *Guidelines for School-Based Planning, 1988–1989*, Rochester City School District, p. 7.

69. Foley interview.

70. Scully interview. Scully said that McWalters never realized that he could not operate in keeping with TQM because he had his own style, which did not fit squarely in any particular management theory.

71. "Corporations," *Education Week*, p. 10.

72. Foley interview. Foley suggests that there are three kinds of decisions, all of which are appropriate under different circumstances: 1) autocratic decisions, which are made when the manager has all the necessary information, 2) consultation, which occurs when the manager needs information before he or she can make the decision, and 3) consensus, which assumes everyone joins in making the decision and the manager agrees to live with the group's determination.

73. In keeping with TQM principles, the National Center gives surveys to its customers, in this case—the training participants—to assess how well they are meeting their customers' expectations; Volume 1, Number 1, *Teamwork*, p. 5. A majority of SBP team members who have participated in this training rate the experience as either "good" or "excellent."

74. Board president Spoto calls the Kodak's facilitators invaluable in "helping teams become effective decision-making groups around the education agenda." Spoto interview.

75. "After Two," *Education Week*, pp. 11–12. Marvin Jackson, a Kodak engineering technician, says he can bring important expertise to his child's school team. "Teachers don't know what industry wants. To bridge that gap, they need someone in industry."

76. Gillett interview. Rochester City School District, *Teamwork*, Volume 2, number 1, p. 5; *Making Things Happen*, pp. 18, 22.

77. Spoto interview.

78. *Rochester Report*, p. 4.

79. "Corporations," *Education Week*, p. 11.

80. Gillett interview.

81. Spoto interview. As attacks on the district's leadership have grown since the implementation of the reform initiative, Spoto says, "The only constituency in the entire community where we have any base of support is business."

82. Peter McWalters. Address at the Chatauqua Institute, aired on WSKG-FM, Binghamton, New York, April 12, 1989.

83. Gillett interview. McWalters and the RTA communicated freely. Gillett commented, "If there was a problem and he [McWalters] needed the cooperation and support of the teachers, he'd pick up the phone . . ." and call the union leadership.

84. Scully interview. Teachers were given training early on by personnel from the National Center, the RTA, and the AFT. Principals were not included in the early rounds of training.

85. Spoto interview.

86. Gillett interview.

87. Gillett interview.

88. "Friendship," *Education Week*, p. 21. The great rise in teachers' salaries implemented by the 1987 contract also was cause for concern by school managers, although this was not part of the lawsuit. Richard Stear worried that "an administration that rewards teachers will not reward administrators equally."

89. "School-Restructuring Efforts Forcing Principals to Redefine Their Roles," *Education Week*, November 1, 1989, pp. 1, 12.

90. Urbanski, "Real Change," *Education Week*, p. 29.

91. Stear interview. Stear believes that evaluation and instructional leadership are uniquely administrative functions. He feels that McWalters seriously eroded the structures of administration and supervision—to the ultimate detriment of the system and the children in Rochester.

92. Stear interview.

93. Charles Moscato, principal of Elementary School 35, interview by the author, tape recording, Rochester, New York, April 8, 1993. This opinion was also expressed by principals as a group in a district publication. Principals cited, "the need for the District to share information in a timely fashion to all audiences at the same time," *Teamwork*, Volume 2, number 1, p. 3.

94. *Education Week*, March 8, 1989, p. 12.

95. Stear interview.

96. "After Two," *Education Week*, pp. 10, 11. After two years Stear concluded that the reforms were "more form than substance."

97. Stear interview.

98. Stear interview.

99. Moscato interview. At the time of the interview Moscato was president of the Rochester Elementary Leadership Council, a professional association made up of principals, vice-principals, and special education coordinators in RCSD elementary schools.

100. Sundberg interview.

101. Moscato interview.

102. Stear interview. Stear's position harkens back to one voiced by Bernard Donovan, superintendent of the New York city schools in the 1960s, when teachers challenged managerial authority.

103. Scully interview. If an assistant superintendent did not support the idea of school-based planning, he would veto the school improvement plans devised by school planning teams. See also Urbanski, "Real Change," *Stanford*, p. 128.

104. "Cut Administrators, Rochester Teachers Urge Board," *Education Week*, January 22, 1992, p. 4.

105. Career in Teaching Program. Intervention Handbook. Rochester City School District, 1989, pp. 1–2. The program originally allowed only the principal or some other "appropriate supervisor" to recommend a teacher to the program. More recently, school-based planning teams were given the power to recommend a teacher to the program. Teachers also gained the right to seek remediation voluntarily. In 1991–92, 100 teachers chose to get help in improving their teaching, *Rochester Democrat and Chronicle*, March 9, 1993, pp. 1A, 5A.

106. In the superintendent's statement of district goals, *Making Things Happen*, two of the three stated goals relate to TQM. Goal one is supporting "continuous improvement in our schools." Goal three is creating "a high performance organization" through the implementation of Total Quality Management. November, 1992, pp. 4, 24.

107. Scully interview. Deets and Foley discontinued their practice of running central office meetings aimed at modeling the principles of TQM.

108. Stear interview.

109. Moscato interview.

110. "Regan Lashes Cost to Run City Schools: Calls Administration Here State's Most Wasteful," *Rochester Democrat and Chronicle*, April 1, 1993, p. 1A; "School Chief Rips State Report: Rivera Faults Methods, Data," *Rochester Democrat and Chronicle*, April 2, 1993, pp. 1B, 2B. Regan's study charged that RCSD spent 200% of what he estimated ought to be spent on school administration. Other Rochester area school districts were between 100–146% of that estimate.

111. Gillett interview. As an example, Gillett cites the appointment of the former district supervisor for reading to a position charged with implementing TQM in the schools.

112. Scully interview. Another characteristic of the old pro-efficiency model of school management is gender segregation, with males having control over females in the system. Rivera has been accused of this brand of sexism by women administrators because of his seeming hesitation to include women administrators in the power loop.

113. "A Bumpy First Year for Rivera," *Rochester Democrat and Chronicle*, March 18, 1993, pp. 1A, 10A. Catherine Spoto, president of the board who appointed Rivera,

refused the local newspaper's request that she give Rivera a grade for his performance. "We're not giving grades," she said. "This is a pass-fail. He passed."

114. "Rocky Relationship Between Rivera, Union Chief," *Rochester Democrat and Chronicle*, March 18, 1993, p. 10A. The "Adam-Peter show" referred to the frequent national appearances the two men made to discuss education reform in Rochester. They also often announced decisions together locally. McWalters was criticized by some members of the community for making Urbanski a "co-superintendent."

115. "Teacher Absences Prompt Request for Doctor's Notes," *Rochester Democrat and Chronicle*, April 6, 1993, pp. 1A, 5A; "New Sick-Day Policy Among Strictest in State," *Rochester Democrat and Chronicle*, April 7, 1993, pp. 1A, 12A. Among the four upstate New York urban districts, Rochester followed Buffalo and Albany in average annual teacher absences: Buffalo—13 days, Albany—8 days, Rochester—7 days, Syracuse—5 days.

116. "Rochester, New York Contract Links Accountability, Resources," *Education Week*, December 15, 1993, p. 3. The pact stipulated that teachers take part in more comprehensive evaluations by colleagues, parents, and students.

117. *Rochester Democrat and Chronicle*, June 7, 1994, pp. 1, 10A.

118. Scully interview.

119. Scully interview. A waiver process whereby schools could be released from board policies was established so that the board could decide the issue on a case-by-case basis. A similar process involving the RTA was established for waivers from the teachers' contract.

120. Volume 1, number 1, *Teamwork*, p. 1.

121. Mary Toole, teacher at School 35, interview by the author, Rochester, New York, April 8, 1993. Toole, a veteran with nearly thirty years of teaching experience, says she felt that SBP was "the answer." She and her colleagues got to choose their principal when SBP was first institutionalized. She felt like she was treated like a professional for the first time in her career.

122. Scully interview.

123. Scully interview. Although a believer in the model of power-sharing at the building level among the principal, teachers, other school personnel, and parents, Scully accepts the managerial hierarchy, the chain of command, and school board prerogatives.

124. Spoto interview. Catherine Spoto cites the lack of follow-up to the initial training as an error made by the board. To be fair, intensive and continuing training for the 15 to 20 members of teams from 50 schools would be a massive undertaking, and one that few districts could commit to financially. Some of the more successful SBP teams have received further training by Kodak executives as a part of their 21st Century Learning Challenge.

125. Spoto interview.

126. Scully interview.

127. *Students First*, Rochester City School District, February/March 1993, p. 5. By reassigning the entire teaching staff, every classroom now has two full-time teachers. Class size has remained at 28–30 students. The point of this plan is to provide extra attention for individual students. Interestingly, this idea is a very old one. Its original name is the Oswego Plan, and it was popular before the pro-efficiency reforms were instituted in the first decades of the century.

128. Volume 2, number 1, *Teamwork*, p. 4.

129. Sundberg interview.

130. Sundberg interview.

131. Scully interview. In Scully's words, "You won't believe some of the stuff that has happened in shared decision-making."

132. Volume 2, number 1, *Teamwork*, p. 2. In this newsletter on SBP, DeBruyn, a Xerox field engineer, suggests that teachers and parents share accountability for student success. The Home-Based Guidance Program, which aimed to develop a partnership between parents and teachers, never got off the ground due to resistance from teachers.

133. *Guidelines*, p. 5 (see note 68, above).

134. In fact, principals in the RCSD do indeed "take the fall" for schools that do not perform well. The principals of Marshall High School and Elementary School No. 9 were held personally responsible for their schools' problems in 1993. See "Marshall Leader Under Fire," *Rochester Democrat and Chronicle*, April 8, 1993, pp. 1A, 5A; Scully interview.

135. Toole interview. Toole gave the example of the principal's proposal to cut six minutes of cleaning from each classroom so that the custodian would have more time to clean "high-profile" areas. The teachers on the SBP team polled the school's teachers, who voted the proposal down. The teachers then got a note from the principal that the custodian would no longer vacuum the rugs teachers had brought to school for their classrooms; Sundberg interview. Sundberg notes that this type of retaliation—getting back if your proposal is not supported—is common, and engaged in by all constituencies.

136. Moscato interview.

137. Moscato interview.

138. Spoto interview.

139. Scully interview.

140. Moscato interview. Moscato said that by 1993 more schools were supposed to control their own budgets. He added, "I have a feeling it is years away."

141. "After Two," *Education Week*, p. 10; Spoto interview. Sundberg interview.

142. Spoto interview. Spoto comments, "Flower City or the Children's School . . . those things did not come about because of SBP. They came about because a group of dedicated teachers wanted them to come about."

143. "School Reform Gets Low Marks," *Rochester Democrat and Chronicle*, March 31, 1993, pp. 1A, 5A.

144. Urbanski, "Real Change," *Stanford*, p. 128. When the budget deficit materialized in 1991, funds allocated to support team plans were cut.

145. Spoto interview. The AFT on the national level appears to be backing away from site-based decision-making as a vehicle for reform, as well.

146. Scully interview.

147. Sundberg interview.

148. Spoto interview. Spoto says, "Our mentor-intern program is one of our clear successes"; Moscato interview. Moscato has come to support this program. He feels interns trust mentors more than they do principals. He says mentors also have more time than principals to help the interns. He calls mentoring "a legitimate role."

149. Moscato interview.

150. "After Two," *Education Week*, p. 11; Toole interview. Toole was angered by a rejection of her application to become a lead teacher. She cited union cronyism as key to understanding who got appointed to the coveted positions.

151. Spoto interview. Spoto says, "One of the concerns of the Board has been that the lead teachers primarily have not become lead teachers in the sense of staying with the kids but have become lead teachers to do other things."

152. "Rochester, New York," *Education Week*, p. 3.

153. Urbanski, "Real Change," *Stanford*, p. 131; "Column One," *Education Week*, June 10, 1992, p. 6.

154. Wayne Urban, *Why Teachers Organized*, p. 155. Urban writes about the roots of authoritarian teacher-manager relations in the early 20th century: "Perhaps the key change in establishing the new supervision took place when elementary principals stopped teaching and became full-time administrators. At that point the principal was no longer the 'principal teacher' but had become a sort of mini-superintendent who rated her underlings."

155. Toole interview. Toole says, "Here's the central office administrator telling the principals what to do, who then tell the teachers what to do, who then tell the students what to do . . . No one trusts anyone to think for themselves." Toole's theory of how the relations between school managers and school teachers affect the way teachers and stu-

dents interact is corroborated by Linda McNeil in her book, *Contradictions of Control*, New York: Routledge and Kegan Paul, 1986; Theodore Sizer, *Horace's School*, pp. 122–25. Toole's analysis of how a lack of trust drives personal interactions in schools is identical to that presented by Sizer.

156. Toole interview. Toole feels that she would need to be given training in order to evaluate a colleague in a professional manner. The latest collective bargaining agreement, in fact, allows for some degree of peer evaluation. As a postscript, Toole wrote to me in 1996 after having participated in both peer evaluation and summative self-evaluation as prescribed by the 1993 RTA contract. Her reluctance to participate in both diminished after the experience. In fact, she found working with her colleagues in this way to be exciting and energizing.

157. The 1987–90 contract raised teachers' salaries an average of 40%. In 1992–93, the average teacher in Rochester earned $46,000, had eighteen years of experience and a masters degree.

158. Spoto interview.

159. "Proposed Pay Hike Decried," *Rochester Democrat and Chronicle*, March 10, 1993, p. 1B; "School Board Votes Down RTA Contract," *Rochester Democrat and Chronicle*, March 13, 1993, pp. 1B, 2B. For a running commentary on the protracted 1990–91 negotiations for a successor agreement to the 1987 contract, see the following issues of *Education Week:* September 26, 1990; October 3, 1990; October 10, 1990; January 23, 1991; January 30, 1991; February 6, 1991; April 24, 1991; May 1, 1991.

160. Letter to the editor by Sheila Driscoll, a lawyer and parent of two children in the RCSD, *Rochester Democrat and Chronicle*, April 11, 1993, p. 15A.

161. Bob Lounsberry, "Here's A Lecture for the Teachers," *Rochester Democrat and Chronicle*, March 19, 1993, p. 1B. Tom Arnold is the former husband of television star Roseanne Barr. His television show was canceled after only a few episodes during the winter of 1993.

162. *Rochester Democrat and Chronicle*, May 4, 1994, p. 1B; May 9, 1994, pp. 1, 4B; June 9, 1994, pp. 9A, 1B; May 3, 1994, p. 9A.

163. Dawn Lunt, "Accountability: A Blaming Exercise," *Rochester Democrat and Chronicle*, April 13, 1993, p. 11A.

164. Toole interview.

165. "Study Finds Formidable Barriers to Promising Reform Strategies," *Education Week*, April 26, 1995, p. 8; "Fed Up With Tinkering, Reformers Now Touting 'Systemic' Approach," *Education Week*, September 9, 1992, pp. 1, 30.

166. "Math-Teachers' Survey Finds a Schism Between Practice, Reformers' Vision," *Education Week*, April 1, 1992, p. 10.

167. "Effort to End Tracking Sparks Uproar in Virginia District," *Education Week*, April 7, 1993, p. 15.

168. Gillett interview.

169. Sundberg interview.

170. "Sniping and Squabbling Won't Fix the Schools." Editorial in *Rochester Democrat and Chronicle*, March 21, 1993, p. 14A.

171. Ibid.

172. *Rochester Democrat and Chronicle*. Editorials in the following issues: June 8, 1994, p. 10A; June 17, 1994, p. 14A; May 15, 1994, p. 12A.

173. Gillett interview.

174. Gillet and Halkett. Appendix A. In defining a good teacher for the Career in Teaching program, teachers wrote paragraphs to capture the essence of teacher professionalism. The consultant from the National Center, Sonia Hernandez, had a much briefer definition: "The good teacher does what needs to be done so that students learn what needs to be learned."

175. Spoto interview.

176. Spoto interview.

Chapter Eight

1. Gerald Bracey, "What If Education Broke Out All Over?" *Education Week*, March 30, 1994, pp. 44, 33.

2. "Human Capital Touted in Clinton Economic Agenda," *Education Week*, June 22, 1994, pp. 1, 14, 25; Roland Sturm, *How Do Education and Training Affect a Country's Economic Performance?* Santa Monica: Rand Corporation, 1994; "Full Speed Ahead," *Teacher Magazine*, November 1994, pp. 44–49.

3. Larry Cuban, "The Great School Scam," *Education Week*, June 15, 1994, p. 44; for other critiques of the economic imperative argument, see Bracey, "Education"; Iris Rotberg, "Separate and Unequal," *Education Week*, March 9, 1994, p. 44. Rotberg points out that economic problems in the 1980s were caused by business practices such as poor organization of the work place, not our educational system, which, in her opinion, remains unequaled in the world in terms of high school graduation rates, enrollment in advance placement courses, college attendance, and productivity in basic and applied research.

4. Sturm, *Education;* Bill Powell, "Keep Your Profits," *Newsweek*, November 6, 1995, p. 98.

5. "Human Capital," *Education Week;* "Full Speed Ahead," *Teacher Magazine*, p. 46.

6. "1996 Grads Aren't in High Demand," *The Ithaca Journal*, May 29, 1996, p. 3A; The National Research Council, *Highlights from the 1994 Survey of Earned Doctorates*, p. 2; "No Ph.D.'s Need Apply," *Newsweek*, December 5, 1994, pp. 63–64.

7. Bracey, *Education Week.*

8. David Berliner and Bruce Biddle, *The Manufactured Crisis: Myth, Fraud, and the Attack on America's Public Schools*, Reading, Mass.: Addison-Wesley, 1995.

9. Cuban, *Education Week*, tape recording.

10. Catherine Spoto, interview by the author, tape recording, Rochester, New York, April 1, 1993.

11. Richard Gibboney, *The Stone Trumpet: A Story of Practical School Reform, 1960–1990*, Albany: State University of New York Press, 1994, p. 3.

12. The poverty line in 1994 was an annual income of $14,400 for a family of four.

13. "Pew Abandons Its Ambitious 10 Year 'Children's Initiative,'" *Education Week*, April 6, 1994, p. 9.

14. "Carnegie Corporation Presses Early Childhood Policies," *Education Week*, April 13, 1994, pp. 1, 13.

15. In September 1995 a middle-school student was stabbed to death by another student as she got off her school bus. The two girls were engaged in an ongoing argument over a boyfriend. The mother of the slain youngster instituted a lawsuit against the school district, citing negligence in the district's handling the alleged assailant.

16. Spoto interview.

17. "Pepper . . . and Salt," political cartoon, *Wall Street Journal*, July 24, 1996.

18. "With Welfare Transformed, Some Are Optimistic, Others Fearful," *New York Times*, (American Online) August 4, 1996.

19. The United States lags behind many of its fiercest economic competitors in having national policies that support families, e.g., pregnancy and child-bearing leave, universal access to health care.

20. "Elusive Equality: Minority Hiring Lags," *Rochester Democrat and Chronicle*, February 21, 1993, pp. 1, 6A. Only 9% of all Rochester area employees are African American.

21. "Their Careers: Count on Nothing and Work Like a Demon," *Wall Street Journal*, October 31, 1995, pp. B1, B10.

22. "Is the Education Crisis a Fraud?" *Teacher Magazine*, November 1995, p. 28–33.

23. Spoto cites the much lauded Flower City School, the Children's School, and the Head First middle-school project.

24. I was asked by the teachers who shared their experience with me that I not identify their school district or use their names.

25. "Charter Schools Idea Gaining Converts," *Education Week*, July 14, 1993, p. 18; "Varied Laws Raise a Question: What is a Charter School?" *Education Week*, January 19, 1994, p. 14; "Heritage Survey Finds Growth in Charter Schools," *Education Week*, June 15, 1994, p. 13; "Twelve States Join Move to Pass Charter Laws," *Education Week*, May 10, 1995, pp. 1, 15; "Charting the Charters," *Teacher Magazine*, January 1997, pp. 12–15.

26. "Strange Bedfellows Strive to Scale Down Schools," *Education Week*, March 22, 1995, p. 41. From a cursory inspection of the mission statements of the charter schools already approved, it appears that the educational visions that drive their founders' work with youngsters are many and varied, from holistic "integrated, theme and project-based" education, to "practical experience in business and entrepreneurial skills" in "an innovative and caring environment that promotes academic excellence." The former mission statement comes from the Central Academy charter school in Ann Arbor, Michigan; the latter from Walter French Academy of Business and Technology in Lansing, Michigan.

27. "Report Documents Benefits of School-Family Ties," *Education Week*, June 22, 1994, p. 5.

28. "Less Than Half of NYC Budget is Spent on the Classroom," *Education Week*, October 12, 1994, p. 9. The system had an eight billion dollar budget for its student population of approximately one million. The report said that the system spent about $4,280 per regular classroom student, and that only $2,300 of that made it into the classroom. For special education students, only $11,000 of the $16,900 allocated to each student made it into the classroom.

29. "Charter Schools," *Education Week*.

30. Peter Dow, *Politics in the Schoolhouse*, Cambridge: Harvard University Press, 1991.

31. Ann Bradley, "The Importance of Being Ernest," *Education Week*, May 24, 1995, pp. 24–29.

32. "Charters' Impact on Parental Involvement Studied," *Education Week*, June 14, 1995, p. 8; "Debunking Myths: Charter School Study Rebuffs Critics," (Worcester) *Sunday Telegram*, July 21, 1996, p. C2.

33. "Now, the Schools," *Wall Street Journal*, December 5, 1994, p. A14.

34. "Pennsylvania's Ridge Takes Point Position for G.O.P. Governors," *Education Week*, June 7, 1995, pp. 1, 14, 15.

35. Ted Kolderie, "The Charter Idea: Update and Prospects, Fall '95," From America Online, keyword, "Charter."

36. To help ensure that this hope is not in vain, and that charters are faithful to the principles of child-oriented and diverse education, I propose the following as a guide to charter school legislation. Charter schools must have:

1. a safe physical plant;

2. a cadre of teachers who meet newly revised, rigorous standards for professional teaching;

3. a strong showing of parental support or partnership;

4. a plan for meeting statewide goals, which incorporates a child-oriented pedagogical philosophy;

5. a set of school-specific goals as well as a plan to meet those goals;

6. a well-defined democratic governance plan, which describes how the members of the school community—parents, teachers, staff, and older students—will elect their leader (s) and reach decisions;

7. a budget that demonstrates funding will go to services, programs, equipment, and facilities that will directly benefit the children;

8. a school population reflective of the socio-economic and racial composition of the school-age population in the county or metropolitan area. Schools that fail to meet this requirement will need to demonstrate a good faith effort to recruit children from all socio-economic and ethnic groups. For purposes of equity, publicly funded transportation should be provided for all students to and from the charter school of their choice. (A fairly good example of this is the North Carolina law that stipulates that the charter must provide transportation to a child who resides anywhere within the district in which the charter is located. It may also provide transportation for children who live beyond the district's boundaries.);

9. a demonstration of compliance with all statutes concerning civil and constitutional rights, e.g., nondiscriminatory hiring practices, a wall of separation between religion and the publicly funded school, etc.

To secure and maintain accreditation from the state, all of the above requirements should be met by a charter school. According to research on existing charters, start-up money–funding for a year's planning time and extra costs associated with the first year of operation–needs to follow approval of the plan. Oversight and support—conducted perhaps by a redesigned state department of education—should be required so that every charter school can and does meet these fundamental requirements. The statewide goals ought to be as basic as possible. The goals outlined by Theodore Sizer would be acceptable to most Americans: basic reading and math skills, an understanding of the theory and operation of our democratic governance system, and an appreciation of the values of decency, generosity, fairness, and tolerance. Amitai Etzioni, a proponent of rebuilding American communities, adds teaching control of impulses and sympathy as two goals about which citizens would agree. Schools can vary in their individual goals, emphasizing, for example, the literary arts, science, multiculturalism, practical arts, technology, or music and art. Every teacher, parent, and student who is part of a particular charter school should be there by choice, finding its educational program and organization in keeping with their personal preferences and interests.

Accountability and assessment are two buzz words of the current pro-efficiency agenda. To be legitimate recipients of public funding, charter schools need to be accountable for meeting both the statewide and schoolwide goals. Statewide achievement tests of basic skills should be taken by all children in publicly funded schools to demonstrate proficiency in literacy and math, as well as an understanding of our system of governance. Charter schools can assess accomplishment of their individual goals in a variety of ways. The "authentic assessment" so popular in the current education reform movement, e.g., portfolios, would be one way of measuring children's progress toward meeting schoolwide goals. Parents should have the freedom to leave a school if it does not meet the goals set by the state, the school, as well as the personal goals they set for their child.

37. Bob Dole made a speech on the state of education on July 17, 1996. He chose Milwaukee as the site for the speech, a city where school vouchers have been instituted on a limited basis; "The Unions' Schools," *Wall Street Journal*, October 11, 1995, p. A14.

38. Susan Moore Johnson, *Teacher Unions in the Schools*, Philadelphia: Temple University Press, 1984.

39. "Trading Places," *Teacher Magazine*, March 1996 pp. 14, 15.

40. "Lawmakers Weigh Plans to Ditch Property Taxes," *Education Week*, March 2, 1994, pp. 1, 18; Rotberg, *Education Week*, (see note 3, above).

41. One can foresee the need for cost of living adjustments by region, similar to those used by Medicare. The COLAs—based on housing costs, utilities, etc.—could be part of the negotiations process.

SELECTED BIBLIOGRAPHY

Ackner, Sandra, ed. *Teachers, Gender and Careers.* New York: Falmer Press, 1989.

Almack, John, and Lang, Abert. *Problems of the Teaching Profession.* Boston: Houghton Mifflin Co., 1925.

Altenbaugh, Richard. *The Teacher's Voice: A Social History of Teaching in Twentieth Century America.* London: Falmer Press, 1992.

Alutto, Joseph A., and James Belasco. "A typology for Participation in Organizational Decision Making," in *The Employment of Teachers,* Donald Gerwin, ed. Berkeley: McCutchan Publishing, 1974.

American Association of School Administrators. *Roles, Responsibilites, Relationships of the School Board,* Superintendent, and Staff. Washington, D.C.: NEA, 1963.

Anderson, Earl. *The Teacher's Contract and Other Legal Phases of Teacher Status.* New York: Teachers College, Columbia University, 1927.

Antin, Mary. *The Promised Land.* Boston: Houghton Mifflin, 1912.

Atleson, James. *Values and Assumptions in American Labor Law.* Amherst: University of Massachusetts Press, 1983.

Ayres, Leonard. *Laggards in Our Schools: A Study of Retardation and Elimination in City School Systems.* New York: Russell Sage Foundation, 1907.

Bacharach, Samuel, ed. *Education Reform: Making Sense of It All.* Boston: Allyn and Bacon, 1990.

Bacharach, Sam, and Scott Bauer, and Joe Shedd. *The Learning Workplace: Conditions and Resources of Teaching.* Ithaca, N.Y.: Organizational Analysis and Practice, 1986.

Bacharach, Samuel, and Joseph Shedd. "Power and Empowerment," in *The Politics of Reforming School Administration,* Jane Hannaway, ed. New York: Falmer Press, 1989.

Bagley, William. *Classroom Management: It's Principles and Techniques.* New York: MacMillan Co., 1912.

Bakke, E. Wight. "Teachers, School Boards and the Employment Relationship," in *Employer-Employee Relations in the Public Schools,* Robert E. Doherty, ed. Ithaca: New York State School of Industrial and Labor Relations, 1967.

Banks, Andy, and Jack Metzgar. *Participating in Management: Union Organizing on a New Terrain.* Chicago: Midwest Center for Labor Research, 1989.

Beale, Howard. *Are American Teachers Free? An Analysis of Restraints upon the Freedom of Teaching in American Schools.* New York: Charles Scribner's Sons, 1936.

Bendiner, Robert. *The Politics of Schools: A Crisis in Self-Government.* New York: Harper and Row, 1969.

Berman, Barbara. "Business Efficiency, American Schooling, and the Pubic School Superintendency: A Reconsideration of the Callahan Thesis." *History of Education Quarterly.* Fall 1983.

Blake, Robert, and Jane Mouton. *Managerial Grid III.* Houston: Gulf Publishing Co., 1985.

Bobbitt, Franklin. *The Supervision of City Schools: Some General Principles of Management Applied to the Problems of City School Systems.* Twelfth Yearbook of the National Society for the Study of Education, Part I. Bloomington, Ill., 1913.

———. "The Elimination of Waste in Education." *Elementary School Journal,* XII, p. 260.

Bok, Derek, and John Dunlop. *Labor and the American Community.* New York: Simon and Shuster, 1970.

Bowles, Jim. "Defining the Scope of Bargaining for Teachers Negotiations: A Study of Judicial Approaches." *Labor Law Journal.* Vol. 29, No. 10, October 1978, pp. 649–65.

Boyd, William. "The Public, the Professionals, and Educational Policy-Making: Who Governs?" *Teachers College Record.* Vol. 77, 1976.

Bridges, Edwin. *The Incompetent Teacher: Managerial Responses.* Washington, D.C.: Salmer, 1992. (revised edition).

Callahan, Raymond. *Education and the Cult of Efficiency: A Study of the Social Forces that Have Shaped the Administration of the Public Schools.* Chicago: University of Chicago Press, 1962.

Carlton, Patrick, and Harold Goodman, eds. *The Collective Dilemma: Negotiations in Education.* New York: Charles Jones Publishing Co., 1969.

Carnegie Foundation for the Advancement of Teaching. *Teacher Involvement in Decision-Making: A State by State Profile.*

Centre for Educational Research. *Schools and Business; A New Partnership.* Paris: Organization for Economic Cooperation and Development, 1992.

Chamberlain, Neil. *Union Challenge to Management Control.* New York: Harper and Brothers, 1948.

Chandler, Alfred, Jr. *The Visible Hand: The Managerial Revolution in American Business.* Cambridge: Harvard University Press, 1977.

Clark, Kenneth. *Dark Ghetto.* New York: Harper and Row, 1965.

Cochran, Thomas. *Business in American Life: A History.* New York: McGraw-Hill, 1972.

Coleman, James S., et al. *Equality of Educational Opportunity.* Washington: Government Printing Office, 1966.

"Collective Bargaining and the Professional Employee." 69 *Columbia Law Review,* 2, February 1969, pp. 277–98.

Commission on Achieving Necessary Skills. *What Work Requires of Schools: A SCANS Report for America 2000.* Washington, D.C.: U. S. Dept. of Labor, 1991.

Conant, James Bryant. *Slums and Suburbs: A Commentary on Schools in Metropolitan Areas.* New York: McGraw-Hill, 1961.

Counts, George. *The Social Composition of Boards of Education.* Chicago: University of Chicago Press, 1927.

———. *The Social Foundations of Education.* New York: Charles Scribner's Sons, 1934.

Cremin, Lawrence. *The Transformation of the School: Progressivism in American Education, 1876–1957.* New York: Alfred A. Knopf, 1962.

Cuban, Larry. *How Teachers Taught: Constancy and Change in American Classrooms, 1890–1980.* New York: Longman, 1984.

———. *The Managerial Imperative and the Practice of Leadership in Schools.* Albany: State University of New York Press, 1988.

Cubberley, Ellwood. *Changing Conceptions of Education.* Boston: Houghton Mifflin, 1909.

———. *Public School Administration: A Statement of the Fundamental Principles Underlying the Organization and Administration of Public Administration.* Boston: Houghton Mifflin, 1916.

———. *The History of Education: Educational Practice and Progress Considered as a Phase of the Development and Spread of Western Civilization.* Boston: Houghton Mifflin, 1920.

Curti, Merle. *The Social Ideas of American Educators.* Patterson, N. J.: Littlefield, Adams and Co., 1961.

DeAntoni, Edward. "Coming of Age in the Industrial State—The Ideology and Implementation of Rural School Reform 1893–1925: New York State as a Case Study." Cornell University: Ph.D dissertation, 1971.

Dewey. John. *The Educational Situation.* Chicago: University of Chicago Press, 1902.

———. *The School and Society.* Chicago: University of Chicago Press, 1900.

DiMaggio, Paul J., and Walter W. Powell. "The Iron Cage Revisited: Institutional Isomorphism and Collective Rationality in Organizational Field." *American Sociological Review,* Vol. 48, pp. 147–60.

Doherty, Marian. *'Scusa Me Teacher.* Francestown, New Hampshire: Marshall Jones, 1943.

Doherty, Robert, and Walter Oberer. *Teachers, School Boards, and Collective Bargaining: A Changing of the Guard.* Ithaca: New York State School of Industrial and Labor Relations, 1967.

Dow, Peter. *Schoolhouse Politics: Lessons from the Sputnik Era.* Cambridge: Harvard University Press, 1991.

Draper, Andrew. *The Adaptation of the Schools to Industry and Efficiency.* Albany: New York State Department of Education, 1908.

Drucker, Peter. "How Schools Must Change." *Psychology Today.* May, 1989, pp. 18–20.

Edelman, Lauren. "Legal Environments and Organizational Governance: The Expansion of Due Process in the American Workplace." *American Journal of Sociology,* Vol. 95, Number 6, May 1990, pp. 1401–40.

Education: The Next Battleground for Corporate Survival, An Urgent Message from Twenty-One Harvard Business School Students. Washington, D.C.: National Alliance of Business, 1990.

Edwards, Harry. "The Emerging Duty to Bargain in the Public Sector." *Michigan Law Review,* Vol. 71, No. 5, April 1973, pp. 885–934.

Edwards, Newton. *The Courts and the Public Schools.* Chicago: University of Chicago Press, 1933.

Elam, Stanley et al., eds. *Readings in Collective Negotiations in Public Education.* Chicago: Rand McNally, 1967.

Equal Opportunity Practices in the Federal Judiciary. Washington: GPO, 1981.

Equal Opportunity for Women: Regents Policy Paper and Action Plan for the 1990's. Albany: State Education Department, 1993.

Etzioni, Amitai, ed. *The Semi-Professing and Their Organization: Teachers, Nurses, Social Workers.* New York: Free Press, 1969.

Finch, Michael, and Trevor Nagel. "Collective Bargaining in the Public Schools: Reassessing Labor Policy in an Era of School Reform." *Wisconsin Law Review,* Vol. 1984, No. 6, pp. 1573–1670.

First National Workshop on Professional Rights and Responsibilities. Washington, D.C.: National Education Association, 1962.

Flanders, J. K. *Legislative Control of the Elementary Curriculum.* New York: Bureau of Publications, Teachers College, Columbia University, 1925.

Friedman, Lee, and Stephen Sugarman. "School Sorting and Disclosure: Disclosure to Families as a School Reform Strategy." *Journal of Law and Education,* Vol. 17, No. 1, Winter 1988, pp. 53–89.

Galambos, Louis. *The Public Image of Big Business in America, 1880–1940: A Quantitative Study in Social Change.* Baltimore: Johns Hopkins University Press, 1975.

Geisert, Gener. "The Effect of Collective Bargaining on Curriculum." *Government Union Review,* Vol. 4, No. 1, 1980.

Gilb, Corinne Lathrop. *Hidden Hierarchies: The Professions and Government.* New York: Harper and Row, 1966.

Gittell, Marilyn. *Participants and Participation: A Study of School Policy in New York City.* New York: Frederick Paeger, 1967.

Gross, Neal. *Who Runs Our Schools?* New York: John Wiley and Sons, 1976.

Gross, Neal, and Ann Trask. *The Sex Factor and the Management of Schools.* New York: John Wiley and Sons, 1976.

Haber, Samuel. *Efficiency and Uplift: Scientific Management in the Progressive Era, 1890–1920.* Chicago: University of Chicago Press, 1964.

———. *The Quest for Honor and Authority in the American Professions, 1750–1900.* Chicago: University of Chicago Press, 1992.

Harris, Howell. *The Right to Manage: Industrial Relations Policies of American Business in the 1940's.* Madison: University of Wisconsin Press, 1982.

Hill, Paul, Arthur Wise, and Leslie Shapiro. *Educational Progress: Cities Mobilize to Improve Their Schools.* Santa Monica: RAND Corporation, 1989.

Hillegas, Milo. *The Elements of Classroom Supervision.* Chicago: Laidlaw, 1931.

Hoffman, Nancy. *Woman's "True" Profession: Voices from the History of Teaching.* Old Westbury, N. Y.: Feminist Press, McGraw Hill, 1981.

How Schools Shortchange Girls. Washington, D.C.: American Association of University Women, 1992.

Johnson, Susan Moore. *Teacher Unions in Schools.* Philadelphia: Temple University Press, 1984.

Katz, Michael. *Reconstructing American Education.* Cambridge: Harvard University Press, 1987.

Kearns, David, and Denis Doyle. *Winning the Brain Race: A Bold Plan to Make Our Schools Competitive.* San Francisco: Institute for Contemporary Studies, 1988.

Kerchner, Charles, and Douglas Mitchell. *The Changing Idea of a Teachers' Union.* New York: Falmer Press, 1988.

Kilpatrick, William. *Education for a Changing Civilization; Three Lectures Delivered at Rutgers University, 1926.* New York: American Book Co., 1894.

King, Robert. *School Interests and Duties.* New York: American Book Co., 1894.

Klare, Karl. "Labor Law as Ideology: Toward a Historiography of Collective Bargaining Law." *Industrial Relations Law Journal,* No. 3, 1981.

Kochan, Thomas, Harry Kantz, and Robert McKersie. *The Transforming of American Industrial Relations.* New York: Basic Books, 1986.

Kozol, Jonathan. *Death at an Early Age: The Destruction of the Hearts and Minds of Negro Children in the Boston Public Schools.* Boston: Houghton Mifflin, 1967.

Kramer, Rita. *Ed School Follies: The Miseducation of America's Teachers.* New York: Free Press, Macmillan, 1991.

Landis, Fred. *The Impact of the Taylor Law on the Operation of the Public Schools: A School Board Point of View.* New York State Commission on the Quality, Cost, and Financing of Elementary and Secondary Education, 1971.

Lieberman, Myron. *Education as a Profession.* Englewood Cliffs, N. J.: Prentice-Hall, 1956.

Lipsky, David, and Sharon Conley. "Incentive Pay and Collective Bargaining in Public Education." Paper presented at the American Educational Research Association, San Francisco, 1986.

Lynd, Robert, and Helen Merrell Lynd. *Middletown.* New York: Harcourt, Brace and Co., 1929.

———. *Middletown in Transition: A Study in Cultural Conflicts.* New York: Harcourt, Brace and Co., 1937.

Maxwell, William. "On a Certain Arrogance in Educational Theorists." *Educational Review,* February 1914, pp. 175–76.

McDonnell, Lorraine, and Anthony Pascal. *Organized Teachers in American Schools.* Santa Monica: Rand Corporation, 1979.

————. *Teacher Unions and Educational Reform.* Santa Monica: Rand Corporation, 1988.

McNeil, Linda. *Contradictions of Control: School Structure and School Knowledge.* New York: Routledge and Kegan Paul, 1986.

Moore, Ernest C. *Fifty Years of American Education: 1867–1917.* Boston: Ginn, 1918.

Morrison, Ann. *Breaking the Glass Ceiling: Can Women Reach the Top of America's Largest Corporations?* Reading, Mass.: Addison-Wesley, 1992.

Moynihan, Daniel Patrick. *Family and Nation: The Godkin Lectures, Harvard University.* San Diego: Harcourt Brace Jovanovich, 1982.

Murphy, J. T. "The Paradox of Decentralizing Schools: Lessons from Business, Government, and the Catholic Church." *Phi Delta Kappan,* June 1989.

Murphy, Joseph. *Restructuring Schools: Capturing and Assessing the Phenomena.* New York: Teachers College Press, 1991.

Murphy, Marjorie. *Blackboard Unions: The AFT and the NEA, 1900–1980.* Ithaca: Cornell University Press, 1990.

Myers, Donald. *Teacher Power—Professionalization and Collective Bargaining.* Lexington, Mass.: D. C. Health, 1973.

The National Commission on Excellence in Education. *A Nation at Risk.* Cambridge: USA Research, 1984.

National Education Association. *Site-Based Decisionmaking: The 1990 NEA Census of Local Associations.* Washington, D.C.: NEA, 1991.

National Labor Relations Board v. Wooster Division of Borg-Warner Corp. 356 U. S. 342 (1958).

National School Boards Association. *Communicating Change: Working Toward Educational Excellence Through New and Better School District Communication.* 1988.

New York State Industrial Cooperation Council. *A School Is a Workplace.* New York, 1989.

Newlon, Jesse. *Educational Administration as Social Policy.* New York: Charles Scribner's Sons, 1934.

Nutt, Hubert Wilbur. *The Supervision of Instruction.* Boston: Houghton Mifflin, 1920.

Osborne, David, and Ted Gaebler. *Reinventing Government: How the Entrepreneurial Spirit is Transforming the Public Sector.* Reading, Mass.: Addison-Wesley, 1992.

Perry, Charles, and Wesley Wildman. *The Impact of Negotiations on Public Education.* Worthington, Ohio: Charles A. Jones Publishing, 1970.

Peters, Barbara, and Jim Peters, eds. *Total Quality Management.* New York: The Conference Board, 1991.

Philbrick, John. *City School Systems in the United States.* U. S. Bureau of Education, Circular of Information no. 1. Washington, D.C.: GPO, 1885.

Pois, Joseph. *The School Board Crisis.* Chicago: Educational Methods, 1964.

Polakow, Valerie. *Lives on the Edge: Single Mothers and Their Children.* Chicago: University of Chicago Press, 1993.

Prascow, Paul, et al. *Scope of Bargaining in the Public Sector: Concepts and Problems*. Washington: United States Department of Labor, 1972.

Prentice, Alison, and Marjorie Theobald, eds. *Women Who Taught: Perspectives on the History of Women and Teaching*. Toronto: University of Toronto Press, 1991.

Professional Administration for America's Schools. *1960 Yearbook of the American Association of School Administrators*. Washington, D.C.: NEA, 1961.

Reid, Robert, ed. *Battleground: The Autobiography of Margaret A. Haley*. Urbana: University of Illinois Press, 1982.

Reutter, E. Edmund, Jr. *Law of Public Education*. Mineola, New York: Foundation Press, 1985.

Ridgefield Park Education Association v. Ridgefield Park Board of Education 78 NJ 144 (1978).

Ries, Paula, and Anne J. Stone, eds. *The American Woman, 1992–93: A Status Report*. New York: Norton, 1992.

Rosenholtz, Susan. "Effective Schools: Interpreting the Evidence." *American Journal of Education*, May 1985, pp. 352–87.

Roscow, Jerome, and Robert Zager, eds. *Allies in Reform: How Teachers, Unions, and Administrators Can Join Forces for Better Schools*. San Francisco: Jossey-Bass, 1989.

Sabghir, Irving. *The Scope of Bargaining in Public Sector Collective Bargaining*. Albany: Public Employment Relations Board, 1970.

Scandura, Terri A. *Breaking the Glass Ceiling in the 1990's*. Washington: United States Department of Labor, Women's Bureau, 1992.

Scharf, Lois. *To Work and To Wed: Female Employment, Feminism and the Great Depression*. Westport, Conn.: Press, 1980.

Schimmel, David, and Louis Fischer. *Parents, Schools and the Law*. Columbia, Md.: National Committee for Citizens in Education, 1987.

Schlechty, Phillip. *Schools for the 21st Century: Leadership Imperatives for Educational Reform*. San Francisco: Jossey-Bass, 1990.

Schmuck, Patricia, ed. *Women Educators: Employees of Schools in Western Countries*. Albany: State University of New York Press, 1987.

Second National Workshop on Professional Rights and Responsibilities. Washington, D.C.: National Education Association, 1963.

Sedlak, Michael. "Reforming Teacher Education." *Teachers College Record*, Spring 1987, pp. 314–25.

Sergiovanni, Thomas, and John Moore, eds. *Schooling for Tomorrow: Directing Reforms to Issues that Count*. Boston: Allyn and Bacon, 1989.

Shanker, Albert. "The Development of Collective Bargaining in Education—A Union Point of View," in *Critical Issues in Education: The Morton Wollman Distinguished Lectures, 1969–1970*. New York: Bernard Baruch College, 1970.

Shaw, Adele. "The True Character of the New York City Public Schools." *The World's Work*, Vol. 7, No. 2, December 1903.

Shedd, Joseph, and Samuel Bacharach. *Tangled Hierarchies: Teachers as Professionals and the Management of Schools.* San Francisco: Jossey-Bass, 1991.

Shils, Edward, and C. Taylor Whittier. *Teachers, Administrators and Collective Bargaining.* New York: Thomas Crowell Co., 1968.

Sizer, Theodore. *Horace's Compromise: The Dilemma of the American High School.* Boston: Houghton-Mifflin, 1985.

———. *Horace's School: Redesigning the American High School.* Boston: Houghton-Mifflin, 1992.

Slater, Courtenay, and George Hall, eds. *1993 County and City Extra: Annual Metro, City and County Data Book,* Latham, Md.: Bernard Press, 1993.

Smith, Joan K. *Ella Flagg Young: Portrait of a Leader.* Ames, Iowa: Educational Studies Press, 1976.

Spain, Charles. *The Platoon School.* New York: MacMillan, 1924.

Stinnet, T. M., Jack Kleinmann, and Martha Ware. *Professional Negotiation in Public Education.* New York: MacMillan, 1966.

Stone, Katherine van Wezel. "Post-War Paradigm in American Labor Law." 90 *Yale Law Journal,* No. 7, June 1981, pp. 1511–80.

Strachan, Grace. *Equal Pay for Equal Work: The Story of the Struggle for Justice Being Made by the Women Teachers of the City of New York.* New York: B. F. Buck and Co., 1910.

Sumner, William Graham. *Folkways: A Study of the Sociological Importance of Usages, Manners, Customs, Mores, and Morals.* Boston: Ginn, 1906.

Taeuber, Cynthia. *Statistical Handbook on Women in America.* Oryx Press, 1991.

Task Force as Teaching as a Profession. *A Nation Prepared: Teachers for the 21st Century.* Carnegie Forum on Education and the Economy, 1986.

Taylor, Frederick. *The Princples of Scientific Management.* New York: Harper and Brothers, 1915.

The Taylor Law. Albany: New York State Public Employment Relations Board, 1987.

Third National Workshop on Professional Rights and Responsibilities. Washington, D.C.: National Education Association, 1964.

Thorndike, Edward. "The Nature, Purposes, and General Methods of Measurements of Educational Products," in the *Seventeenth Yearbook.* Bloomington, Ill.: National Society for the Stufy of Education, 1918.

Timar, Thomas, and David Kirp. *Managing Educational Excellence.* New York: Falmer Press, 1988.

Troy, Kathryn. *Employee Buy-In to Total Quality: A Corporate Progress Report.* New York: Conference Board, 1991.

Tweedie, Jack. "Parental Rights and Accountability in Public Education: Special Education and Choice of School," in *Yale Law and Policy Review,* Vol. 7, No. 2, 1989.

Tyack, David. *The One Best System: A History of American Urban Education.* Cambridge: Harvard University Press, 1974.

Tyack, David, and Elisabeth Hansot. *Managers of Virtue: Public School Leadership in America, 1820–1980.* New York: Basic Books, 1982.

Tyack, David, Thomas James Thomas, and Aaron Benavot. *Law and he Shaping of Public Education.* Madison: University of Wisconsin Press, 1987.

Urban, Wayne. *Why Teachers Organized.* Detroit: Wayne State University Press, 1982.

Urbanski, Adam. "Real Change is Real Hard: Lessons Learned in Rochester." *Stanford Law and Policy Review,* Winter 1992–93.

Vial, Don. *The Scope of Bargaining Controversy: Substantive Issues v. Procedural Hangups.* Sacramento: California Public Employee Relations, No. 15, November 1972.

Waller, Willard. *The Sociology of Teaching.* New York: Wiley, 1965.

Weitzman, Joan Parker. "Scope of Bargaining in Public Education and the Issue of Class Size: The Study of a Concept and Its Application." Cornell University: Ph.D dissertation, 1974.

Wirth, Arthur. *Education and Work for the Year 2000: Choices We Face.* San Francisco: Jossey-Bass, 1992.

Young, Ella Flagg. *Isolation in the School.* Chicago: University of Chicago Press, 1900.

Zeigler, Harmon. *The Political Life of American Teachers.* Englewood Cliffs, N. J.: Prentice-Hall, 1967.

INDEX

317